D0487707

Taxes, Expenditures, and the Economic Base

Roy W. Bahl
Alan K. Campbell
David Greytak

Published in cooperation with the
Maxwell School of Citizenship
and Public Affairs
Syracuse University

The Praeger Special Studies program—
utilizing the most modern and efficient book
production techniques and a selective
worldwide distribution network—makes
available to the academic, government, and
business communities significant, timely
research in U.S. and international economic, social, and political development.

Taxes, Expenditures, and the Economic Base
Case Study of New York City

PRAEGER SPECIAL STUDIES IN U.S. ECONOMIC, SOCIAL, AND POLITICAL ISSUES

Praeger Publishers New York Washington London

Library of Congress Cataloging in Publication Data

Bahl, Roy W
    Taxes, expenditures, and the economic base.

    (Praeger special studies in U.S. economic, social,
and political issues)
    Includes bibliographical references.
    1. New York (City)—Economic conditions.   2. Taxa-
tion—New York (City).   3. New York (City)—Appropriations and expenditures.   I. Campbell, Alan K., joint
author.   II. Greytak, David, joint author.   III. Title.
HC108.N7B25   336.747'1   74-1742
ISBN 0-275-08810-3

PRAEGER PUBLISHERS
111 Fourth Avenue, New York, N.Y. 10003, U.S.A.
5, Cromwell Place, London SW7 2JL, England

Published in the United States of America in 1974
by Praeger Publishers, Inc.

Printed in the United States of America

DIRECTORS AND RESEARCH STAFF,
MAXWELL RESEARCH PROJECT ON THE
PUBLIC FINANCES OF NEW YORK CITY

Project Directors

Dr. Roy W. Bahl

Professor of Economics and Director, Metropolitan Studies Program, The Maxwell School of Citizenship and Public Affairs, Syracuse University, Syracuse, New York

Dr. Alan K. Campbell

Dean, the Maxwell School of Citizenship and Public Affairs and Professor of Political Science and Public Administration, Syracuse University, Syracuse, New York

Dr. David Greytak

Associate Professor of Economics and Associate Director, Metropolitan Studies Program, The Maxwell School of Citizenship and Public Affairs, Syracuse University, Syracuse, New York

Research Staff

Dr. David Bjornstad

Acting Director, Urban Research Section, Oak Ridge National Laboratory, Oak Ridge, Tennessee

Dr. Richard Gustely

Assistant Professor of Environmental and Urban Systems, Virginia Polytechnic Institute, Blacksburg, Virginia

Dr. Bernard Jump

Associate Professor of Economics, Hollins College, Roanoke, Virginia

Dr. Astrid Merget

Assistant Professor of Political Science, Barnard College, Columbia University, New York, New York

Dr. Donald Phares

Assistant Professor of Economics, University of Missouri-St. Louis, St. Louis, Missouri

Dr. Robert Wolfson   Professor of Economics, The Maxwell School of Citizenship and Public Affairs

Mr. Richard Bowen   Department of Economics, The Maxwell School

Ms. Deborah Chollet   Department of Economics, The Maxwell School

Mr. Robert Dinkelmeyer   Department of Economics, The Maxwell School

Mr. John Mallen   Committee for Economic Development, New York, New York

Ms. Elaine Morley   Social Science Department, The Maxwell School

Mr. Walter Vogt   Department of Economics, The Maxwell School

CONTENTS

LIST OF TABLES, CHART, AND FIGURE

xi

xvi

Taxes, Expenditures, and the Economic Base

CHANGES IN THE STRUCTURE
OF THE NEW YORK CITY
ECONOMY

While the total population of New York City remained approximately constant over the 1960-70 decade, there were significant
changes in the composition of that population as well as in the composition of the city's employment, income, and land use. Since a basic
theme of this research is that such compositional changes are ultimately translated into tax revenue and expenditure demand effects,
they have important implications for an evaluation of the longer-term
fiscal health of the city government. Accordingly, the objective in
this chapter is to examine the available data to determine the extent
to which such changes have taken place.

A complete and very detailed analysis of changes in the city's
economic and population base—desirable though it may be—is clearly
beyond the scope of this study. Rather, the emphasis will be on those
quantifiable facets of economic, demographic, and social change that
have a particular relevance to the city fisc. First, we will deal with
both the long-term and the more recent changes in the level and
composition of city employment, which are having a significant effect
on the tax base of the city. Next, we will discuss reported changes
in the level and interpersonal distribution of personal income, and
with the level and sectoral distribution of earnings. Such changes
affect the fisc on both the expenditure side—by inducing changed service
level demands—and the revenue side—by directly affecting the size
of at least the earnings and sales tax bases. Then we will examine
compositional changes in the population of the city over the 1960-70
decade, in the belief that city government expenditures (through workload changes) are affected by changes in the composition of population.
The final section is concerned with land-use changes—a crucial element in an analysis of the continuing viability of the property tax,
the city government's single most important tax source.

CHANGES IN EMPLOYMENT

The purpose of this section is to examine changes in the level and composition of employment in New York City. The detail in the presentation is particularly labored because of the importance of the employment indicator in gauging changes in economic activity and because employment is used as the primary link between tax revenue change and economic activity change.

The long-term 1960-70 trends and then the more recent changes (1969-72) in the composition of employment are considered. Employment changes over the 1960-70 period are examined in some detail, thus developing a profile of long-term change in the structure of city employment. This 10-year period was chosen because of conformity with Census years—other data used in this study are drawn from the Census—and because comparable employment data are available for these years. There have been substantial changes in the level of employment in New York City since 1970, and these are given special attention in a later part of this section. The more recent trends are given separate attention because these data are not strictly comparable with the 1960 and 1970 statistics and because it is not clear whether these changes are a short-term phenomenon or the beginning of a long-term decline.

In the 1960s, total employment in New York City rose by 6 percent, a net increase of some 212,000 jobs.* (See Table 1.1.) This change in total employment may be viewed as the combination of nearly 450,000 new jobs created in industries undergoing employment increase and the loss of almost half again that many in industries undergoing employment decline. This rate of job turnover, about 15 percent for the decade, leaves considerable room for a changing composition of employment (as well as of population and income) in the city.

With regard to secular trends in employment, the sectors of growth and decline in New York City generally correspond to those of the nation, with the principal difference between the city and the remainder of the nation being one of magnitude—that is if an industry experienced slow growth or decline nationwide, it tended to experience slower growth or more rapid decline in New York City.† As a

---

*It should be emphasized that the data in this section relate to employment of all persons working in New York City regardless of their residence. "Employment" is defined as the full-time work of one person for a year. The terms "jobs" and "positions" are used synonymously.

†Throughout this discussion, employment is ascribed to categories identified as "industrial sectors." These industries are general categories drawn from detailed industrial classifications in

TABLE 1.1

Employment in New York City by Public and Private
Sector, 1960 and 1970
(employment figures in thousands)

	Employment 1960	Employment 1970	Employment Change 1960-70	Percent Change 1960-70	Percent of Total N.Y.C. Employment 1960	Percent of Total N.Y.C. Employment 1970
Private sector	3,126.7	3,184.1	57.4	1.84	88.5	84.9
Public sector	408.2	562.8	154.6	37.87	11.5	15.0
Total*	3,534.9	3,746.9	212.0	5.99	100.0	100.0

*Columns may not add to total due to rounding.

Sources: New York State Department of Labor, Division of Employment, Research and Statistics Office, Employment Statistics, Vol. 6 (Albany, N.Y.: N.Y.S. Department of Labor, September 1970); Employment Review, Vols. 24 and 25 (Albany, N.Y.: N.Y.S. Department of Labor, May 1971 and February 1972).

consequence of differential rates of growth and decline among industries, the composition of the city's economic base differed substantially in 1970 from what it has been in 1960. Similarly, the wide
variation in the rates of growth and decline among the various elements
of the city's population resulted in (or were a result of) a major re-
structuring of the city's residential population composition.

Trends in Government Employment

Perhaps the most often-cited element of change in the economy
of the city is the rapid growth of government sector employment.
Indeed, for every four new jobs added to the New York economy between
1960 and 1970, three were provided by the public sector. This differs
from the national pattern of employment increase, which shows an
increase of one public sector job for every five-employee increase
in the private sector.[1] The comparable statistic for the 11 largest
metropolitan central cities (including New York City) is a 1.39 increase
in public sector jobs for every one private sector job increase.[2] As
the percentage increase in government employment has been greater
in New York City, and the percentage increase in private employment
lower than in either the nation or the 11 largest central cities, the
relatively heavy increase in public over private sector employment
in New York City departs substantially from the norm.

As a result of the relatively large increase in the number of
public employees, the private sector's share of the city's total employment fell from 88.5 percent in 1960 to about 85 percent in 1970, while
the public sector share rose from 11.5 percent to 15 percent (See
Table 1.2). It should be emphasized that the public sector increase
was supported entirely by employment gains in state and local government agencies, i.e., state and local government employment not only
offset a loss in federal jobs, but expanded sufficiently to account for
a net addition of 154,700 positions. The turnover of personnel involved
in government employment in New York City can be illustrated by

---

the Standard Industrial Classification (SIC) Manual, which is published
by the Office of Management and Budget, Executive Office of the
President. Thus, the discussion will center on 21 general categories
of manufacturing industries, on 13 nonmanufacturing industries, and
on government, which is subdivided into 5 subsectors (federal government, state general government, state education, local general government, and local education). For convenience of discussion, all of these
are sometimes collapsed into two shorthand terms: public sector
and private sector.

TABLE 1.2

Public Sector Employment in New York City by Government
Level and General Function, 1960 and 1970
(employment figures in thousands)

	Employment 1960	Employment 1970	Employment Change 1960-70	Percent Change 1960-70	Percent of Total Public Sector Employment 1960	Percent of Total Public Sector Employment 1970	Percent of Total New York City Employment 1960	Percent of Total New York City Employment 1970
Federal	116.4	107.5	-8.9	-7.65	28.5	19.1	3.3	2.9
State	23.6	40.9	17.3	73.31	5.8	7.3	0.7	1.1
Education	1.5	3.4	1.9	126.66	0.4	0.6		0.1
Other	22.7	37.0	14.3	62.99	5.6	6.6	0.6	1.0
Local	268.2	414.5	146.3	54.55	65.7	73.6	7.6	11.1
Education	79.5	153.8	74.3	93.45	19.5	27.3	2.2	4.1
Other	188.7	259.8	71.1	37.67	46.2	46.2	5.3	6.9
Total government*	408.2	562.8	154.6	37.87	100.0	100.0	11.5	15.0

*Columns may not add to total due to rounding.

Sources: New York State Department of Labor, Division of Employment, Research and Statistics Office, Employment Statistics, Vol. 6 (Albany, N.Y.: N.Y.S. Department of Labor, September 1970); Employment Review, Vols. 24 and 25 (Albany, N.Y.: N.Y.S. Department of Labor, May 1971 and February 1972).

5

the fact that the sum of employment increases and employment declines (all declines were in the federal government sector) amounted to approximately 172,500 positions—4.6 percent of total employment in the city in 1970.

During the decade, a decline in federal employment of almost 9 percent lowered the federal sector share of total city employment from 3.3 percent in 1960 to only 2.9 percent in 1970. State government employment, which represented 0.7 percent of all New York City employment in 1960, increased more than 73 percent (or by 17,300 positions) to represent 1.1 percent of the city's total work force in 1970. However, during the same period, local government showed an even more significant increase (nearly 55 percent in the 1960s), from a level of 268,200 jobs in 1960 to 414,500 in 1970. The growing dominance of city government employment within the government sector is clear— 89.4 percent of the total increase in government employment in New York City between 1960 and 1970 was in the local government sector. As a result of these differential rates of employment growth among levels of government, by 1970, 15 out of every 100 persons working in New York City were employed by the public sector and, of these, 11 were in local government, three in federal government, and one in state government employment.

Finally, it ought to be noted that the rate of public versus private sector employment increase during the 1960s is less a new trend than an acceleration of relative public sector employment growth in the preceding decade.

Although employment figures are not strictly comparable because of different data sources and means of categorizing industries, the general employment trends identified by Emanuel Tobier for the years 1952 through 1960 support the findings reported here. In those years, Tobier shows public (governmental) employment as having increased at a rate six times greater than that by which private sector industries grew. Private sector employment grew by 0.04 percent. Public employment grew by 25 percent. Further, governmental employment accounted for nearly one-third (28.33 percent) of the total employment increase of approximately 6,000 positions.[3]

Trends in Private Sector Employment

Despite the quickened pace of public employment growth in New York City, the private sector remains the primary employer. In absolute figures, the leadership of the private sector as an employer clearly emerges: By 1970, more than 3.7 million persons were employed in New York City, and, although the numbers of public sector employees had grown to 15 percent of that total (some 562,800 positions), private sector industries still supported nearly 85 percent of total employment (almost 3.2 million workers).

Two general conclusions may be drawn from the private sector data. The first is that employment in the private sector in New York City is dynamic—the number of jobs gained and lost in the decade (528,000) almost equaled the total amount of public sector jobs in 1970. Second, the underlying pattern of private sector employment change during the decade is one of a "shifting-out" between manufacturing and nonmanufacturing—that is, there is a clear shift of the employment balance away from manufacturing and into nonmanufacturing activities. The nonmanufacturing sector made the major contribution to the net increase in employment that the private sector experienced between 1960 and 1970—it gained four employees for every three that the manufacturing industries lost.

Nonmanufacturing Industries

The nonmanufacturing sector was clearly the major private sector employer during the 1960-70 decade. As the data in Table 1.3 indicate, the net shift away from manufacturing toward nonmanufacturing activity was approximately 6 percent of total private sector employment. Thus, manufacturing, which in 1960 provided more than 30 percent of the private sector's employment, provided less than 25 percent of its in 1970. Nonmanufacturing gained, rising from less than 70 percent to almost 76 percent in 1970.

TABLE 1.3

Employment in Manufacturing and Nonmanufacturing
Industries in New York City as Percentage of
Total Private Sector Employment, 1960 and 1970

Employment	1960	1970
Total private sector employment	100	100
Manufacturing	30.2	24.1
Nonmanufacturing	69.8	75.9

Sources: New York State Department of Labor, Division of Employment, Research and Statistics Office, Employment Statistics, Vol. 6 (Albany, N.Y.: N.Y.S. Department of Labor, September 1970); Employment Review, Vols. 24 and 25 (Albany, N.Y.: N.Y.S. Department of Labor, May 1971 and February 1972).

7

The total change in nonmanufacturing employment—the combination of its gain and losses—was nearly 50 percent larger than the net increase of 232,700 positions. Employment decreases totaling 57,300 jobs were registered by six nonmanufacturing industries, with construction employment sustaining the most severe decline. The remaining seven nonmanufacturing industries compiled a combined employment growth of 290,000 positions (See Table 1.4).

Employment in nonmanufacturing industries increased most dramatically for the service industries, which, in the aggregate, recorded an increase 176,000 positions, or 30 percent. (For a listing of the employment sectors contained in the services category, see Table 1.5.) Within the services category, the major employment additions occurred in miscellaneous services (particularly miscellaneous business services), medical and health services, and educational services* (See Table 1.5). Moreover, while in terms of percentage changes, other employment sectors such as finance and communications experienced equally large increases, of the three major employment sectors in 1960 (services, wholesale trade, and retail trade), only services increased its percentage share of employment, and wholesale trade actually declined in absolute employment. The picture is clearly one of an increasing reliance on the service sector by the local employment base. This pattern of increasing concentration in the industry mix is also described in the cumulative employment distribution shown in Table 1.6. Together, the five leading industries (service, retail, wholesale, finances, and transportation) accounted for 52.3 percent of the city's total employment in 1970, whereas, 10 years earlier, the same five industries accounted for 48.6 percent of the total work force.

The employment shifts described in Tables 1.4-1.6 in terms of changes in the percent of total employment in any given sector are all represented by changes of only a few percentage points. While such a shift seems small, it should be noted that, for example, a 3 percent employment increase represents the addition of some 112,400 employees to the city's work force. The implications of such an increment are considerable.

———————————

*Included within the miscellaneous services category are advertising, credit and collection agencies, services furnished for direct mailing, blueprinting, stenographic and duplicating services, cleaning and other services to buildings, news syndicates, and private employment agencies. Included within the miscellaneous services category are engineering and architectural services, nonprofit educational and scientific research agencies, accounting, auditing and bookkeeping services, and establishments offering other services such as those involving artists, lecturers, and writers and counseling.

8

TABLE 1.4

Private Nonmanufacturing Employment in New York City
by Industry, 1960 and 1970
(employment figures in thousands)

	Employment 1960	Employment 1970	Employment Change 1960-70	Percent Change 1960-70	Percent of Total New York City Employment 1960	Percent of Total New York City Employment 1970
Forestry and fisheries	1.6	2.5	0.9	56.25	0.05	0.07
Mining	1.9	1.9	0.0	0.00	0.05	0.05
Construction	125.3	110.1	-15.2	-12.13	3.54	2.94
Transportation	219.1	204.7	-14.4	-6.57	6.19	5.47
Communication	71.8	94.5	22.7	31.62	2.03	2.52
Public utilities	27.2	25.5	-1.7	-6.25	0.77	0.68
Wholesale trade	314.7	302.0	-12.7	-4.04	8.89	8.07
Retail trade	430.1	433.5	3.4	0.79	12.16	11.58
Finance	149.6	236.6	87.0	58.16	4.23	6.32
Insurance	123.6	119.8	-3.8	-3.07	3.49	3.20
Real estate	112.7	103.2	-9.5	-8.43	3.19	2.76
Services	605.7	781.7	176.0	29.06	17.12	20.88
Total nonmanufacturing employment*	2,183.30	2,416.00	232.70	10.65	61.77	64.47

*Columns may not add to total because of rounding.

Sources: New York State Department of Labor, Division of Employment, Research and Statistics Office, Employment Statistics, Vol. 6 (Albany, N.Y.: N.Y.S. Department of Labor, September 1970); Employment Review, Vols. 24 and 25 (Albany, N.Y.: N.Y.S. Department of Labor, May 1971 and February 1972).

TABLE 1.5

Employment in Service Industries in New York City, 1960 and 1970
(employment figures in thousands)

	Employment		Employment Change	Percent Change	Percent of Total Nonagricultural Employment	
	1960	1970	1960-70	1960-70	1960	1970
Hotels and lodging places	42.0	35.5	-6.5	-15.47	1.2	0.9
Personal services	62.7	82.8	-9.9	-15.78	1.8	1.4
Miscellaneous business services	135.0	202.3	67.3	49.85	3.8	5.4
Automobile repair, services, and garages	15.2	19.1	3.9	25.65	0.5	0.5
Miscellaneous repair services	10.1	9.8	-0.3	-2.97	0.2	0.3
Motion pictures	22.0	25.2	3.2	14.54	0.6	0.7
Amusement and recreation services	21.5	25.2	2.3	10.69	0.6	0.6
Medical and health services	97.1	145.7	48.6	50.05	2.7	3.9
Legal services	22.2	28.9	6.7	30.18	0.6	0.8
Educational services	51.5	79.4	27.9	54.17	1.5	2.1
Museums, botanical, and zoological gardens	2.2	3.9	1.7	77.27	0.1	0.1
Nonprofit membership organizations	78.8	95.0	16.2	20.55	2.2	2.5
Miscellaneous services	41.9	62.2	20.3	48.44	1.2	1.7
Total service employment	605.9	783.6	177.7	29.32	17.1	20.9

Note: The data in this table are based on unrevised annual averages and, therefore, do not correspond exactly to the data contained in other tables.

Sources: New York State Department of Labor, Division of Employment, Research and Statistics Office, Employment Statistics, Vol. 6 (Albany, N.Y.: N.Y.S. Department of Labor, September 1970); Employment Review, Vol. 24 (Albany, N.Y.: N.Y.S. Department of Labor, May 1971).

TABLE 1.6

Nonmanufacturing Industries in New York City
as Employers, 1960 and 1970

Industry by Rank Order	1960			Industry by Rank Order	1970		
	Rank	Percent of City Employment	Cumulative Percent of Total City Employment		Rank	Percent of City Employment	Cumulative Percent of Total City Employment
Service	1	17.12	17.12	Service	1	20.88	20.88
Retail trade	2	12.16	29.28	Retail trade	2	11.58	32.46
Wholesale trade	3	8.89	38.17	Wholesale trade	3	8.07	40.53
Transportation	4	6.19	44.36	Finances	4	6.32	46.85
Finances	5	4.23	48.59	Transportation	5	5.47	52.32
Construction	6	3.54	52.13	Insurance	6	3.20	55.52
Insurance	7	3.49	55.62	Construction	7	2.94	58.46
Real estate	8	3.19	58.81	Real estate	8	2.76	61.22
Communications	9	2.03	60.84	Communications	9	2.52	63.74
Public utilities	10	0.77	61.61	Public utilities	10	0.68	64.42
Mining	11.5	0.05	61.66	Forestry and fisheries	11	0.07	64.49
Forestry and fisheries	11.5	0.05	61.71	Mining	12	0.05	64.54

Sources: New York State Department of Labor, Division of Employment, Research and Statistics Office, Employment Statistics, Vol. 6 (Albany, N.Y.: N.Y.S. Department of Labor, September 1970); Employment Review, Vols. 24 and 25 (Albany, N.Y.: N.Y.S. Department of Labor, May 1971 and February 1972).

In summary, it can be said that, although large changes occurred in the composition of employment within the private nonmanufacturing sector, it is important to note (1) that the private nonmanufacturing industries that were leading private sector employers in 1960 maintained this status in 1970 and (2) that, despite large employment declines in individual industries, all 12 nonmanufacturing industries taken together supported more of the city's work force in 1970 than in 1960. In 1960, the 12 private sector, nonmanufacturing industries accommodated 61.8 percent of all persons working in New York City, and in 1970, they accounted for 64.5 percent of total city employment.

Manufacturing Industries

When manufacturing industries are viewed as contributors to total employment in the years between 1960 and 1970, the emergent theme is one of diminishing importance. In 1970, the manufacturing industries provided 180,600 fewer jobs than they supplied in 1960—a decline of about 19 percent (See Table 1.7). This decline is not dominated by any one sector but is widely spread over all manufacturing activities.

Among the 21 industries listed in Table 1.7, only two registered any growth over the decade. However, neither of these "growth sectors"—tobacco and rubber-plastics—represents a significant portion of city employment: The tobacco industry employment is only 0.1 percent and rubber-plastics employment 0.2 percent of the total work force.

Employment in the 19 "declining" industries ranges from the greatest absolute job loss of 63,500 in the apparel industry to a loss of 800 in the lumber and wood products industry. However, in percentage terms, the employment declines were large in nearly every case—the smallest percentage decline in employment in any industry was 5 percent. For the apparel industry—long an important component of the city's economic base—the effect was a decline of nearly 24 percent from its 1960 employment level. For the tiny lumber and wood products industry, the decline from a 1960 work force of 6,000 to 5,200 in 1970 spelled a 13.3 percent decrease. Least severe of all employment losses was the 5 percent decrease experienced by the printing and publishing group—a traditionally strong New York City activity.

The pattern is less severe for those industries that experienced very large percentage decreases. With the exception of food processers, those manufacturers that sustained the greatest losses—measured as a percentage of their respective 1960 employment levels—contributed little to total city employment in 1960. For example, the ordnance industry, which declined by 78 percent over the decade,

TABLE 1.7

Manufacturing Employment in New York City by Major Industry: 1960 and 1970
(employment figures in thousands)

| | Employment | | Employment Change | Percent Change | Percent of Total New York City Employment | |
	1960	1970	1960-70	1960-70	1960	1970
Ordnance	4.2	0.9	-3.3	-78.57	0.1	—
Lumber and wood products	6.0	5.2	-0.8	-13.33	0.2	0.1
Furniture and fixtures	17.7	16.3	-1.4	-7.90	0.5	0.4
Stone, clay, glass products	11.3	7.6	-3.7	-32.74	0.3	0.2
Primary metal industries	13.4	12.4	-1.0	-7.46	0.4	0.3
Fabricated metal products	44.4	34.8	-9.6	-21.62	1.3	0.9
Nonelectrical machinery	35.2	25.9	-9.3	-26.42	1.0	0.7
Electrical equipment	60.3	45.4	-14.9	-24.70	1.7	1.2
Transportation equipment	11.7	8.7	-3.0	-25.64	0.3	0.2
Instruments and related products	24.2	20.4	-3.8	-15.70	0.7	0.5
Food and related products	81.6	56.6	-25.0	-30.63	2.3	1.5
Tobacco products	2.7	2.9	0.2	7.40	0.1	0.1
Textile mill products	36.1	32.2	-3.9	-10.80	1.0	0.9
Apparel and other textile products	267.4	203.9	-63.5	-23.74	7.6	5.4
Paper and allied products	30.2	23.9	-6.3	-20.86	0.9	0.6
Printing and publishing	127.2	120.8	-6.4	-5.03	3.6	3.2
Chemicals and allied products	45.9	40.3	-5.6	-12.20	1.3	1.1
Petroleum and coal products	9.9	7.7	-2.2	-22.32	0.3	0.2
Rubber and miscellaneous plastics products	10.5	10.6	0.1	0.95	0.3	0.3
Leather and leather products	31.6	26.7	-4.9	-15.50	0.9	0.7
Miscellaneous manufacturing	75.1	62.9	-12.2	-16.24	2.1	1.7
Total manufacturing employment*	946.8	766.2	-180.6	19.07	26.8	20.4

*Columns may not add to total due to rounding.

Sources: New York State Department of Labor, Division of Employment, Research and Statistics Office, Employment Statistics, Vol. 6 (Albany, N.Y.: N.Y.S. Department of Labor, September 1970); Employment Review, Vols. 24 and 25 (Albany, N.Y.: N.Y.S. Department of Labor, May 1971 and February 1972).

dropped from a 0.1 percent share of total employment (approximately 4,200 employees) in 1960 to a share of less than 0.1 percent in 1970. A similar observation may be made for the stone, clay, and glass product industry, nonelectrical manufacturing, and the manufacture of transportation equipment. The manufacture of food and related products—mostly packers and processers—unlike the above industries, sustained both a dramatic percentage drop in employment between 1960 and 1970 and represented a relatively significant portion of the city's work force. The food industry lost nearly 31 percent of its 1960 work force, dropping nearly 25,000 employees between 1960 and 1970.

In addition to the continued historic decline in the importance of manufacturing, the 1950s witnessed the continuation of another historic trend in New York City, that of increasing specialization within the manufacturing sector. In 1960, only 9 of the 21 manufacturing industries represented 1 percent or more of the city's total employment, but, in 1970, only six represented a share of 1 percent or more of city employment: apparel and other related textiles (5.4 percent), printing and publishing (3.2 percent), miscellaneous manufacturing (1.7 percent), food and related products (1.5 percent), electrical equipment (1.2 percent), and chemicals and allied products (1.1 percent). Therefore, in manufacturing, as in nonmanufacturing, the trend is toward less diversity in the industry mix.

The Nature of Manufacturing Employment

The decade of the 1960s was not only one in which substantial changes in the level and sectoral composition of manufacturing employment occurred but one in which the type of activities within manufacturing underwent considerable change.

Within the manufacturing industries, this changing composition of activities is reflected in changes in the relative proportion of production and nonproduction employment.* As can be seen in Table 1.8, the proportion of total manufacturing employees engaged in nonproduction activities increased from 28.1 percent in 1960 to 34.2 percent

---

*Production workers include all production and related workers (up through the working foreman level) engaged in fabricating, processing, assembling, inspection, receiving, storage, handling, packing, warehousing, shipping, maintenance, repair, janitorial, and watchman services, product development, auxiliary production for plants own use, record-keeping, and other services closely associated with these production operations. Nonproduction includes all other employees, who are primarily administrative and managerial.

TABLE 1.8

Production and Nonproduction Employment as
Percentage of Manufacturing and Total Employment
in New York City, 1960 and 1970

	As Percent of New York City Manufacturing Employment		As Percent of Total New York City Employment	
	1960	1970	1960	1970
Manufacturing total	100	100	26.7	20.5
Nonproduction	28.1	34.2	7.2	6.7
Production	71.9	65.8	19.5	13.8

Sources: Derived from "Production Workers in Manufacturing, New York City, 1960-1971" (unpublished table, New York State Department of Labor); New York State Department of Labor, Division of Employment, Research and Statistics Office, Employment Statistics, Vol. 6 (Albany, N.Y.: N.Y.S. Department of Labor, September 1970); and Employment Review, Vols. 24 and 25 (Albany, N.Y.: N.Y.S. Department of Labor, May 1971 and February 1972).

in 1970. Moreover, an increase in nonproduction as a proportion of total employment occurred in all but two of the smaller manufacturing industries—that is, ordnance and accessories, and lumber and wood products (See Table 1.9). In eight of the other 19 manufacturing industries, the increase in the proportion of nonproduction employees resulted from both an increase in the number of nonproduction employees and a decrease in the number of production employees. In the remaining 11 industries, the relative increase in the proportion of nonproduction employment resulted from a decrease in production employment which exceeded the decrease in nonproduction employment. Thus, nonproduction employment emerges as the single element of employment growth in the manufacturing industries. For the nation as a whole, the relative proportions of production and nonproduction employment have remained almost constant, 75 percent for production and 25 percent for nonproduction. Thus, New York City differs from the national norm on two counts. First, the proportion of nonmanufacturing workers engaged in production activities has been consistently below the national average, and second, the ratio of production (nonproduction) to total manufacturing employees has been declining

TABLE 1.9

Nonproduction Manufacturing Employees as Percent
of Total Employment in New York City by
Industry, 1960 and 1970

	1960	1970
Ordnance	44.7	38.6
Lumber and wood products	23.3	21.9
Furniture and fixtures	20.1	21.4
Stone, clay, glass products	25.6	30.6
Primary metal industries	29.7	55.5
Fabricated metal products	21.6	27.4
Nonelectrical machinery	37.9	46.0
Electrical equipment	32.6	41.0
Transportation equipment	31.8	40.3
Instruments and related products	29.3	31.8
Food and related products	38.0	45.9
Tobacco products	100.0	100.0
Textile mill products	18.6	21.4
Apparel and other textile products	13.3	15.8
Paper and allied products	29.4	30.9
Printing and publishing	44.8	55.2
Chemicals and allied products	55.6	65.7
Petroleum and coal products	94.6	100.0
Rubber and miscellaneous plastics products	15.7	28.1
Leather and leather products	12.2	16.0
Miscellaneous manufacturing	16.6	20.6
Total manufacturing employment	28.1	34.2

Source: Derived from "Production Workers in Manufacturing,
New York City, 1960-1971" (unpublished table, New York State Department of Labor).

(increasing), while, for the nation as a whole, production and nonproduction components of manufacturing employment have remained stable.

However, this increase in the proportion of employment engaged in nonproduction activities was, in absolute terms, more than offset by the decline in manufacturing production employees—hence the overall decline in manufacturing employment. Moreover, nonproduction manufacturing employment grew at a slower rate than total city employment; hence, its share of total employment declined from 7.2 percent in 1960 to 6.7 percent in 1970. The decline experienced in manufacturing production employment was more than 11 times greater than that for nonproduction employment—that is, production worker employment dropped nearly 5.7 percent, from nearly 19.5 percent of all city employment in 1960 to less than 14 percent in 1970. These changes in proportionate shares of total employment are shown in Table 1.8.

Headquarters Firms

New York City has been and continues to be the nation's major business headquarters city. However, during the late 1960s, much concern was voiced about the apparent erosion of New York City's primacy as a location for firms' headquarters. In 1960, 131 of the major industrial firms had headquarters in New York City (See Chart 1.1).[4] Of these firms, 27 had moved out of New York City by 1971, and the movement of 8 of these was due to mergers. Sixteen firms had merged with other firms located in New York City, while 9 were no longer classified among the top 500 firms. In 1971, therefore, the number of major industrial firms headquartered in New York City stood at 116. Of this number, 101 were located in the city before 1960, while 15 has established their location in the city since 1960. Thus, between 1960 and 1971, New York City incurred a net loss of 12 major industrial firm headquarters due to relocation.

Of slightly smaller firms (the second 500 largest), New York City provided the headquarters for 79 in 1969, the first year of which data are available. By 1971, this number had increased to 82.[5] This fact, coupled with the fact that 27 of the top 500 firms that had headquarters in New York City in 1971 were growing firms (not included among the top 500 in 1960), may indicate a continued vitality of New York City as a location for headquarters of expanding firms.

More Recent Trends

In the foregoing analysis, the secular trend in the New York City employment structure was described through a comparison of

17

CHART 1.1

Fortune Top 500 Industrial Firms with Headquarters in New York City, 1960 and 1970

Status in 1971 of Firms Headquartered in New York City in 1960

Firms headquartered in New York City in 1960	131
Firms still on 500 in 1971—located in New York City	79
Firms still on 500 in 1971—moved out of New York City	19
Firms not on 500 because of merger—New York City headquarters	16
Firms not on 500 because of merger—headquarters outside New York City	8
Firms not on 500 because of slow sales growth in New York City	8
Firms not on 500 because of reclassification in New York City	1

Status in 1960 for Firms Headquartered in New York City in 1971

Firms headquartered in New York City in 1971	116
Firms on the 500 in 1960—located in New York City in 1960	79
Firms on the 500 in 1960—moved to New York City since 1960	10
Firms not on the 500 in 1960—located in New York City in 1960	22
Firms not on the 500 in 1960—moved to New York City	5

Source: Karen Gerard, "Headquarters Firms in New York Fortune Directory—1971" (unpublished paper, Chase Manhattan Bank, July 1972, mimeographed).

the distribution of employment in 1960 and 1970. The years 1960 and 1970 were selected in order to obtain temporal comparability with measures of change in the social and demographic characteristics of the population, as provided by the decennial Census. In addition, at the time of this writing, 1970 was the latest year for which revised, rather than preliminary, employment data were available. For an analysis of employment in 1971 and 1972, those data that are available consist of preliminary estimates of nonagriculture employment. Still, in spite of the limitations inherent in the use of preliminary estimates, these are the only data available for an examination of the most recent employment changes. Because of what seem to be dramatic changes in employment structure and level in these two years, those data are presented here.

An examination of the employment trends for which comparable data are available highlights a reversal, commencing in 1969, in the earlier pattern of employment change among industries. In 1969, total nonagriculture employment reached a peak of 3,797,300 jobs (See Table 1.10). In the following three years, there was a substantial job loss of 251,800, and by the end of 1972, total employment had fallen to 3,545,500, a level just slightly above that of 1967. In the public sector, state and local government continued to decline. Between 1971 and 1972, however, government employment declined by 6,300 jobs. In manufacturing, total employment continued to decline, with a particularly large job loss occurring in the apparel, printing, and miscellaneous manufacturing industries. In total, manufacturing employment declined by 141,700 jobs between 1969 and 1972.

Even in the private nonmanufacturing sector, employment declined between 1969 and 1971. In fact, only four of the private nonmanufacturing sectors experienced employment growth between 1969-71. To some extent, the job loss in transportation and public utilities may be attributed to work stoppage due to labor disputes. In communications, insurance, and real estate, employment gains between 1969 and 1971 were slight; however, preliminary estimates indicate that, in 1972, employment fell below its 1969 level. In general, the fall in private sector employment marks a reversal of the previous long-term growth trend. Nowhere is the reversal of a previous trend more pronounced than in the services industry, which declined from a high of 784,200 employees in 1970 to 752,700 in 1972. As was indicated earlier, it has been the miscellaneous business, health, and educational services and nonprofit organizations that have been the major contributors to the growth of service employment. While the available data do not permit a detailed examination of the components of change within the service industry between 1971 and 1972, it seems probable that, given the general decline in business activities, the major loss of service employment occurred in the area of business service. However, this is speculation.

19

TABLE 1.10

Estimated Annual Average Employment and Percent Change in New York City by Industry, 1969-72
(employment figures in thousands)

	1969	1970	1971	1972	Employment Change 1969-71	Percent Change 1969-71	Employment Change 1971-72	Percent Change 1971-72	Percent Change 1969-72
Government	547.0	562.9	569.0	562.7	22.0	4.0	6.3	1.1	2.9
Federal	105.5	107.5	103.1	N.A.	- 2.4	- 2.3	N.A.	N.A.	N.A.
State	38.2	40.9	43.2	N.A.	5.0	13.1	N.A.	N.A.	N.A.
Local	403.3	414.5	422.8	N.A.	19.5	4.8	N.A.	N.A.	N.A.
Mining	2.0	1.9	1.7	N.A.	- 0.3	-15.0	N.A.	N.A.	N.A.
Construction	104.5	110.1	112.8	100.3	8.3	7.9	12.5	11.1	4.0
Transportation	212.3	203.4	187.5		- 24.8	-11.7			
Communication	86.1	94.5	86.2	297.3	0.1	0.1	- 1.3	- 0.4	- 8.2
Public utilities	25.5	25.5	24.9		0.6	-2.4			
Wholesale trade	308.8	302.0	287.0	698.9	- 21.8	- 7.1	-10.0	- 1.4	- 6.7
Retail trade	440.3	433.5	421.9		- 18.4	- 4.2			
Finance[a]	251.6	244.4	239.9		- 11.7	- 4.7			
Insurance[b]	119.3	119.8	116.7	447.9	2.6	2.2	- 4.7	- 1.0	- 3.8
Real estate	94.8	95.4	96.0		1.2	1.3			
Services	779.4	784.2	764.6	752.7	- 14.8	- 1.9	-11.9	- 1.6	- 3.4
Manufacturing	825.8	766.2	705.0	684.1	-120.8	-14.6	-20.9	-2.9	-17.2
Total Nonagriculture	3,797.4	3,743.8	3,613.4	3,545.5d	-184.0	- 4.8	-67.9	- 1.9	- 6.6

N.A. = not available.

aIncludes banking, security and commodity brokers, credit agencies, and holding and investing companies.
bIncludes insurance carriers, agents, and brokers.
cIncludes real estate and combinations with insurance.
dIncludes mining not elsewhere classified.

Sources: New York State Department of Labor, Division of Employment, Research and Statistics Office, Employment Review, Vols. 24 and 25 (Albany, N.Y.: N.Y.S. Department of Labor, February 1971 and February 1972); "Jobs in City down Third Year in a Row," New York Times, March 1, 1973; unpublished preliminary estimates provided by the Middle Atlantic Regional Office, Bureau of Labor Statistics, U.S. Department of Labor.

Thus, while it appears that the trends charted for the manufacturing and government sectors during the 1960s have continued, at least through 1971, the pattern of growth in total employment, in government employment, and in the services particularly has been reversed. Simply stated, expansion in the growing industries after 1970 has not been sufficient to offset the employment loss in the declining industries.

It should be noted that the fall in total employment experienced in New York City since 1970 has been accompanied by similar but less dramatic changes in New York State and in the greater metropolitan area.[6] However, unlike New York City, the fall in total employment in suburban New York and in northeastern New Jersey can be attributed primarily to a loss of manufacturing and construction jobs since, in addition to government, private nonmanufacturing employment in these areas increased between 1970 and 1971,[7] in contrast to New York City's loss.

CHANGES IN INCOME AND EARNINGS

Two aspects of changes in the level and composition of income (earnings) are important in the context of this research. One is the changing level of the city's income within the region—that is, within the Standard Metropolitan Statistical Area (SMSA). (The New York SMSA, as defined by the Bureau of the census, includes the Bronx, Kings, Queens, New York, Richmond, Nassau, Rockland, Suffolk, and Westchester Counties but does not include counties in New Jersey and Connecticut.) The other is the change in the composition of income as among sources. These are the subjects of this section, and they are considered in the context of work-place location—that is, where income is earned. A third matter of importance—the changing interpersonal distribution of income by place of residence—is covered in the next section.

Income Trends: City Versus SMSA

Total personal income earned in New York City in 1959 accounted for approximately 79 percent of the total personal income of the New York SMSA (See Table 1.11). Personal income in New York City increased at an annual rate of less than 4 percent during the 1960s; however, the city's share of total personal income earned in the SMSA declined slightly. (For a comparison of resident income received in the city and in the SMSA, see the section on population composition changes below.)

21

TABLE 1.11

Total and Per-Employee Personal Income in New
York City and New York SMSA, 1959, 1962, and 1965-70

	New York City		New York City SMSA		New York City as Percent of New York SMSA	
Year	Total Personal Income	Per-Employee Personal Income	Total Personal Income	Per-Employee Personal Income	Total Personal Income	Per-Employee Personal Income
1959	$29,098,000	$ 6,450	$32,171,000	$ 6,670	79.0	96.8
1962	32,204,000	7,340	37,161,000	7,490	78.5	98.0
1965	36,024,000	8,620	43,303,000	8,580	78.6	100.5
1966	37,314,000	9,150	46,211,000	9,040	78.5	101.5
1967	38,405,000	9,610	50,154,000	9,670	76.6	99.4
1968	40,400,000	10,400	54,968,000	10,410	76.6	99.9
1969	41,295,000	10,980	59,310,000	10,970	76.4	100.1
1970	41,650,000	11,880	63,599,000	11,800	76.2	100.7
Percent change 1959-70	43.14	84.18	97.69	76.91		

Sources: "Earnings by Broad Industrial Sector" and "Earnings as a Percent of Personal Income" (unpublished tables, Regional Economics Information System, Bureau of Economic Analysis, U.S. Department of Commerce).

22

A different picture emerges if personal income is allocated on a per employee basis in the city and the SMSA. A slower rate of employment growth in the city, relative to that of the suburbs, has more than offset the faster SMSA income growth rate and has enabled the city to maintain an approximate parity with the SMSA in per employee income.

The Sources of Income and Earnings in New York City

The principal source of New York City personal income is the earnings of employed individuals. (Earnings consist of total wage and salary disbursement and proprietor's and other labor income. Personal income equals the sum of earnings, transfer payments, and property income minus personal contributions for social security.) In 1959, total earnings amounted to nearly $21 billion, of which about 90 percent represents private nonfarm earnings* (See Table 1.12). However, the nonearnings components of income—transfers and property income—increased more rapidly than earnings over the 1959-70 period, and, as a result, the proportion of personal income attributable to earnings declined from 82.6 to about 76 percent in 1970. This experience reflects the nationwide trend of an increased proportion of personal income attributable to property and transfer income.

The contributions of the major employment sectors to the growth in aggregate earnings, show that the largest percentage increases in earnings occurred in government (150 percent), services (116 percent), finance, insurance and real estate (102 percent), and the "other" category (132 percent) (See Table 1.13). By far, the lowest rate of increase in aggregate earning occurred in manufacturing (36.24 percent). It should be noted, however, that the manufacturing increase, although relatively small, occurred at a time when total manufacturing employment declined. In two other sectors—wholesale and retail trade (52.5 percent) and construction (53 percent)—there were relatively small increases in total earnings, while employment did not increase. (Total earnings declined in only one sector, farming, by 11.4 percent.)

The government sector's share of total earnings generated in the city increased from 9.68 percent in 1959 to 13.65 percent in 1970, while the private sector share declined from 90.31 percent in 1959 to 86.35 percent in 1970. (As a result of the decline of earnings in the farm sector, its share of total earnings declined to less than 0.01

*Farm earnings, which accounted for 1 percent of personal income in 1959, declined throughout the decade, and since 1967 no farm earnings have been recorded in New York City.

23

TABLE 1.12

Total Earnings and Private Nonfarm Earnings
in New York City, 1959, 1962, and 1965-70

Year	Total Earnings (thousands of dollars)	Private Non-farm Earnings (thousands of dollars)	Total Earnings as Percent of Personal Income	Private NonFarm Earnings as Percent of Personal Income
1959	20,972	18,940	82.56	74.56
1962	23,739	21,280	81.36	72.94
1965	26,975	23,979	79.24	70.44
1966	28,736	25,436	79.23	70.13
1967	30,002	26,399	78.12	68.74
1968	32,710	28,600	77.70	67.94
1969	35,226	30,751	77.69	67.82
1970	37,201	32,122	76.80	66.31
Percent Change 1959-70	77.38	69.60		

Sources: "Earnings by Broad Industrial Sector" and "Earnings as a Percent of Personal Income" (unpublished tables, Regional Economics Information System, Bureau of Economic Analysis, U.S. Department of Commerce).

TABLE 1.13

Percent Change in Total Earnings and Proportion of Total
Earnings by Industry in New York City, 1959 and 1970 and
Proportion of Total Employment by Industry, 1960 and 1970

	Percent Change 1959–70	Proportion of Total Earnings 1959	Proportion of Total Earnings 1970	Proportion of Total Employment 1960	Proportion of Total Employment 1970
Farm	-11.44	0.01		0.04	0.06
Nonfarm	77.39	99.99	100.00	99.96	99.94
Government	150.11	9.68	13.65	11.54	15.01
Federal	156.59	3.42	3.21	3.29	2.86
State and local	195.46	6.26	10.43	8.25	12.14
Private Nonfarm	69.96	90.31	86.35	88.42	84.92
Manufacturing	36.24	25.99	19.99	26.77	20.43
Mining	88.23	0.09	0.10	0.05	0.05
Construction	53.12	4.55	3.93	3.54	2.93
Transportation, communication and public utilities	84.57	10.16	10.57	8.99	8.66
Wholesale and retail trade	52.55	21.56	18.57	21.06	19.61
Finance, insurance, and real estate	102.09	11.22	12.72	10.91	12.25
Services	116.60	16.62	20.29	17.02	20.89
Other	132.85	0.09	0.12	0.05	0.06
Total	77.38	100.00	100.00	100.00	100.00

Source: U.S. Department of Commerce, Bureau of Labor Statistics, Survey of Current Business (Washington, D.C.: U.S. Government Printing Office, May 1972).

percent.) The increase in state and local government earnings, whose share of total earnings rose from 6.26 percent in 1960 to 10.43 percent in 1970, not only accounted for the total increase in the government share but also compensated for a slight decline in the federal government sector's share of total earnings in New York City.

It is interesting to note that even with such a dramatic shift in the shares of employment and earnings to the public sector, there remains a considerable inequality between the earnings of the public and private sectors. For example, in 1960, the public sector accounted for 11 percent of employment, but only 9.68 percent of earnings, whereas in 1970, it accounted for 15 percent of employment and 13.65 percent of earnings. The often discussed "catch-up" effect in public versus private earnings is not evidenced by these statistics.

In the private sector, changes in the shares of three industries in total earnings stand out. The shares of manufacturing and wholesale and retail trade declined, while that of the services increased. Generally, the changes in earnings shares viewed here correspond, at least in direction, to the changes that occurred in total employment. Among all the industrial categories examined, the greatest change occurred in manufacturing, where the share of earnings declined from 25.9 percent in 1959 to 19.9 percent in 1970. The increase in the service sector's share of total earnings from 16.62 percent to 20.29 percent parallels its employment growth and underscores its importance as a source of New York City generated income. In fact, in 1970 the service sector was the largest single source of earnings.

In terms of the categories of major growth (services) and major decline (manufacturing) in the private sector, 1970 earnings per employee are relatively low. However, per employee earnings in the most rapidly growing sector, government ($10,456), and in the finance, insurance, and real estate (FIRE) industry ($10,220), also a source of growth in the private sector, are moderately high, (See Table 1.14). The revenue implications suggested by such a pattern, at least for personal taxation, are clear. For example, the "trading" of a manufacturing worker for a service worker costs, on average, $972 in annual income tax base, while trading a manufacturing job for a government or finance, insurance, or real estate job would, on the average, add $758 and $522 respectively to the tax base (calculated as the difference in per employee earnings).

Population Composition Changes

Employment and income are directly relevant to the tax revenue side of the fiscal equation, but perhaps more directly relevant to the expenditure side are changes in the level and composition of the city

TABLE 1.14

Earnings per Employee in New York City
by Industry, 1970

Type of Employment	Earnings (dollars)
Farm	9,191
Government*	10,456
Manufacturing	9,698
Mining	18,671
Construction	13,232
Transportation, communication, and public utilities	12,142
Wholesale and retail trade	9,337
Finance, insurance, and real estate	10,220
Services	8,726
Other	10,264

*Average October earnings of full-time equivalent employment multiplied by 12. Earnings figures taken from U.S. Department of Commerce, Bureau of the Census, Local Government Employment in Selected Metropolitan Areas and Large Counties: 1970, Series GE70-No. 3 (Washington, D.C.: U.S. Government Printing Office, 1971).

Sources: "Earnings by Broad Industrial Sector" and "Earnings as a Percent of Total Personal Income" (unpublished tables, Regional Economics Information System, Bureau of Economic Analysis, U.S. Department of Commerce).

population. For example, New York City's population has remained approximately constant over the past decade, yet there has been a substantial increase in city government employment. If government service levels do respond to changes in the needs of the population, then the source of this employment increase is to be found in changes in the composition of the population of the city.

Three general kinds of population characteristics are examined below: general characteristics such as age and sex, economic characteristics such as income distribution, and social characteristics such as educational attainment.

General Population Characteristics

In describing the population composition changes that may affect city government expenditures, four general characteristics of the population are examined: total population size, age distribution, sex, and minority population.

New York City has not experienced significant growth in population since 1960. In the 1960-70 decade, total population increased by 1.5 percent to 7,894,862 (See Table 1.15). On the other hand, the population in the outside central city portion of the New York SMSA increased during the same period by 26 percent.

The under-18 and over-65 age groups require particular packages of public services. Changes in the under-18 age group indicate current and, to some extent, future needs for public school facilities. For lower-income groups, this age distribution suggests the need for funds for programs such as Aid to Families with Dependent Children (ADC), day care centers, and medical support facilities. As indicated in Table 1.15, the under-18 age group in New York City increased by 3 percent between 1960 and 1970, to a total of 2,234,819. With respect to the proportion of population over 65, New York City experienced a 16.5 percent increase. A comparison of the distribution of age groups as between the central city and the outer portion of the SMSA shows a much lower percentage of persons under 18 in New York City than in the rest of the SMSA. Conversely, the city has a larger proportion of persons of 65 years and over.

The changes in age distribution by sex are also indicative of trends in population composition. While the female population within New York City rose by 3 percent between 1960 and 1970, a decrease of 7 percent in the female population in the 40-64 age group occurred. The total male population remained stable and experienced less growth than the female population in all categories except the 19-and-younger. The male population underwent an even larger decline in the 40-64 age group—12 percent as compared to a 7 percent decline for females. By contrast, in the rest of the SMSA, the total female population grew by 27 percent, and the total male population by 26 percent. The largest difference in growth occurred in the 65-and-over category, where the female population increased by 44 percent, compared to 30 percent for the male population (See Table 1.16).

Clearly, minority groups (identified in the Census of Population as "Negro and Other Non-white" population) form a major component of New York's demographic structure.* In total, the minority population

---

*Other nonwhites include American Indians, Orientals, Eskimos, Aleuts, and other nonwhites of foreign descent. Puerto Ricans, another

TABLE 1.15

General Characteristics of Population of New York City and
New York SMSA, 1960 and 1970

	New York City	New York SMSA	Outer SMSA
Total all ages			
1970	7,894,862 (100)a	11,571,899 (100)	3,677,037 (100)
1960	7,781,984 (100)	10,694,633 (100)	2,912,649 (100)
Percent change 1960-70	1.5	8.2	26.4
Minorityb			
1970	1,846,021 (23)	2,082,528 (18)	236,507 (6)
1960	1,141,322 (15)	1,287,878 (15)	146,556 (5)
Percent change 1960-70	61.8	61.7	61.3
Under age 18			
1970	2,234,819 (28)	3,548,177 (31)	1,313,358 (36)
1960	2,164,527 (28)	3,227,368 (30)	1,062,841 (37)
Percent change 1960-70	3.3	10.0	23.6
Age 65 and over			
1970	947,878 (12)	1,256,804 (11)	308,926 (8)
1960	813,827 (11)	1,037,623 (10)	223,796 (8)
Percent change 1960-70	16.5	21.2	38.0

aFigures in parentheses represent population divisions as percentages of total population.
bMinority is used to indicate that population classified by the Bureau of the Census as "Negro and Other," which does not include Puerto Ricans.

Sources: Compiled from U.S. Department of Commerce, Bureau of the Census, Census of Population: 1960, Detailed Characteristics: New York, PC-(1)-D34 and Census of Population: 1970, General Population Characteristics: New York, PC(1)-B34 (Washington, D.C.: U.S. Government Printing Office, 1962 and 1971).

TABLE 1.16

Change in Population Levels in New York City and New York SMSA by Age and Sex, 1960-70

	Female			Male		
	1960	1970	Percent Change	1960	1970	Percent Change
New York City						
Total all ages	4,062,727	4,191,507	3	3,719,257	3,703,355	—
Age 19 and under	1,170,291	1,224,825	5	1,174,445	1,249,247	6
Age 20-39	1,093,111	1,152,434	5	992,775	1,017,723	3
Age 40-64	1,351,624	1,257,313	-7	1,185,911	1,045,442	-12
Age 65 and over	447,701	556,935	24	366,126	390,943	7
New York SMSA						
Total all ages	5,559,699	6,091,326	10	5,134,934	5,480,573	7
Age 19 and under	1,719,535	1,925,229	12	1,739,387	1,974,639	14
Age 20-39	1,496,120	1,621,036	8	1,339,139	1,421,811	6
Age 40-64	1,768,414	1,804,090	2	1,594,415	1,568,290	-2
Age 65 and over	575,630	740,971	29	461,993	515,883	12
Outer SMSA						
Total all ages	1,496,972	1,899,819	27	1,415,677	1,777,218	26
Age 19 and under	549,244	700,404	28	564,942	725,392	28
Age 20-39	403,009	468,602	16	346,364	404,088	17
Age 40-64	416,790	546,777	31	408,504	522,848	28
Age 65 and over	127,929	184,036	44	95,867	124,890	30

Sources: Compiled from U.S. Department of Commerce, Bureau of the Census, Census of Population: 1960, Detailed Characteristics: New York, PC(1)-D34 and Census of Population: 1970, General Population Characteristics: New York, PC(1)-B34 (Washington, D.C.: U.S. Government Printing Office, 1962 and 1971).

30

(not including Puerto Ricans) increased by 62 percent in New York City. Minority groups accounted for 23 percent of the New York City population in 1970, while, in 1960, they accounted for 15 percent. In the outer SMSA, however, minority groups accounted for only 6 percent of the population in 1970, a slight rise from 5 percent in 1960.

The data on the demographic characteristics for New York City and its environs for 1960 and 1970 appear to bear out what has now become the sterotype of at least the older eastern metropolitan areas—that is, a population with heavy concentrations of the young, old, females, and minorities, in the central city. To the extent these concentrations suggest a "high cost" population, the fiscal implications of such change will have important public impact.

Economic Characteristics

Three aspects of change in the economic characteristics of the city population are relevant in terms of fiscal implications: the distribution of income, the amount of poverty, and the level of unemployment. Tax base issues aside, increases in the share of the population that is poor and/or relatively dependent on public services hold the key to understanding one important determinant of city expenditure increase. The focus below, then, is on identification and measurement of changes in the low-income component of the city population.

As a prelude to the discussion of the economic circumstances of New York City's population, certain characteristics should be noted. First, since these are Census data, the reference is to income earned by city residents rather than income earned in the city. Second, Census income does not include imputed items or capital gains and is alleged to underreport nonwage and salary receipts. (Personal income as defined in the Census includes earnings, property income, and transfer payments less personal contributions for social insurance.) Third, these data are reported in current rather than constant dollars; hence all increases are expressed in money rather than real terms.

---

substantial minority group (846,731 in 1970), constituted 9.3 percent of New York City's population. (See "Total Puerto Rican Descent in the City Put at 846,731," New York Times, March 5, 1973.) This figure represents a 34 percent increase over the 1960 Puerto Rican population (629,430), which in that year accounted for 8.17 percent of the total city population. See U.S. Department of Commerce, Bureau of the Census, Census of Population and Housing: 1960, Census Tracts, Final Report PHC(1)-104 (Washington, D.C.: U.S. Government Printing Office, 1962), p. 23.

In the simple terms of change over time, the experience of New York City's residents in terms of income is generally one of improvement as the percentage of families in all income groups below $10,000 either decreased or remained stable between 1959 and 1969. At the same time, the proportion of total families with an income of $10,000 or more increased dramatically, from 19 percent in 1959 to 49 percent in 1969.

However, in relative terms, the residents of New York City did not fare as well as their suburban neighbors. In fact, the average city-suburb income difference has increased—that is, the median level of income in the city was 93 percent of the median level of income in the entire SMSA in 1959 but fell to 89 percent by 1969. The relative changes are about as might be expected—that is, the suburban concentration is greatest in the higher-income brackets and the disparity is increasing. Three-fourths of the outer SMSA families earned over $10,000 in 1969, as compared with about half of New York City families (See Table 1.17).

While one approach to measuring changes in the low-income component is to examine the income distribution, another is to measure directly the proportion of families living in poverty. It is difficult to establish a poverty level of income on a objective basis. The 1970 Census includes a definition of poverty level, which is determined by such factors as family size, sex of family head, and number of children under 18. The computations are made on a national basis and, therefore, do not reflect local cost of living conditions. According to the Census defintion, the average poverty threshold for a nonfarm family of four headed by a male in 1969 was $3,745. In New York City, 12 percent of all families and 27 percent of all unrelated individuals in 1969 had incomes below this poverty level (See Table 1.18). Thus, a total of 15 percent of the city's population was classified as living below the poverty level in 1969. (Clearly, if local cost-of-living variations were allowed, the percentage in New York City would be substantially higher.) However, only 37 percent of the city's poverty families received public assistance. Of the population outside the central city, only 4 percent of families were below the poverty level (See Table 1.19). However, it is interesting to note that 31 percent of unrelated individuals were in this category (a larger percentage than in New York City), resulting in a total of 5 percent of all persons in the outer SMSA with incomes below the poverty level (See Table 1.19).

Other objective indicators of poverty level may also be examined. These include the number of public assistance recipients and the number of female-headed families. Almost 10 percent of all New York City families received some sort of public assistance income, compared to only 3 percent of families in the rest of the SMSA. Almost

32

TABLE 1.17

Families in New York City and New York SMSA by Income Class, 1959 and 1969

	1959			1969		
	New York City	N.Y. SMSA	Outer SMSA	New York City	N.Y. SMSA	Outer SMSA
Total families	2,079,832	2,807,603	727,771	2,058,943	2,970,425	911,482
	(100)*	(100)	(100)	(100)	(100)	(100)
Income class						
Under $1,000	72,853	86,785	13,932	71,385	83,834	12,449
	(4)	(3)	(2)	(4)	(3)	(1)
$ 1,000– 1,999	102,220	119,755	17,535	55,934	67,464	11,530
	(5)	(4)	(2)	(3)	(2)	(1)
$ 2,000– 2,999	141,642	164,383	22,741	91,375	107,174	15,799
	(7)	(6)	(3)	(3)	(4)	(2)
$ 3,000– 3,999	195,681	228,628	32,947	103,277	121,634	18,357
	(9)	(8)	(5)	(4)	(4)	(2)
$ 4,000– 4,999	233,399	283,561	50,162	107,040	126,613	19,573
	(11)	(10)	(7)	(5)	(4)	(2)
$ 5,000– 5,999	272,970	348,769	75,799	123,679	148,115	24,436
	(13)	(12)	(10)	(6)	(5)	(3)
$ 6,000– 6,999	231,879	313,622	81,734	128,236	157,577	29,341
	(11)	(11)	(11)	(6)	(5)	(3)
$ 7,000– 7,999	184,151	260,894	76,743	131,193	168,124	36,931
	(9)	(9)	(11)	(6)	(6)	(4)
$ 8,000– 8,999	148,692	214,635	65,943	132,751	176,177	43,426
	(7)	(8)	(9)	(7)	(6)	(6)
$ 9,000– 9,999	111,832	162,761	50,929	124,027	171,456	47,429
	(5)	(6)	(7)	(6)	(6)	(5)
$10,000–14,999	259,403	398,505	139,102	504,622	773,905	269,283
	(13)	(14)	(19)	(25)	(26)	(30)
$15,000–24,999	89,843	157,430	67,587	361,542	622,508	260,966
	(4)	(6)	(9)	(18)	(21)	(29)
$25,000 and over	35,177	67,875	32,698	123,882	245,844	121,962
	(2)	(2)	(5)	(6)	(8)	(13)
Median income	$6,091	$6,548		$9,682	$10,870	

*Figures in parentheses represent percent of column total in each category.

Sources: Compiled from U.S. Department of Commerce, Bureau of the Census, Census of Population, 1960 and 1970, General Social and Economic Characteristics: New York, PC(1)-C34 (Washington, D.C.: U.S. Government Printing Office, 1962 and 1972).

TABLE 1.18

Distribution of New York City Families and Individuals with Incomes Below Poverty Level, 1969

	Distribution
Poverty-level families	
Total	236,507
Percent of all families	(11.5)
With children under age 18	168,864
Percent of poverty-level families	(71)
With female head	111,469
Percent of all families with female head	(31)
With female head and children under age 18	98,685
Percent of poverty-level families with female head	(89)
Mean income	$1,870
Percent of poverty-level families on public assistance	(37.0)
Poverty-level individuals	
Total	1,164,673
Percent of total population	(14.9)
Age 65 and over as percent of all poverty-level individuals	(17.7)
Unrelated individuals	266.053
Percent of all unrelated individuals	(27.4)

Source: Compiled from U.S. Department of Commerce, Bureau of the Census, Census of Population: 1970, PC(1)-B34, General Population Characteristics: New York (Washington, D.C.; U.S. Government Printing Office, 1971). The figures are taken from the third count of the Census.

8 percent of the city's unrelated individuals received public assistance, compared to 4 percent for the rest of the SMSA (See Table 1.19).

Of particular interest are those female-headed families that composed 17 percent of the total population in New York City in 1970 (See Table 1.20). Of these families 64 percent included children under 18 years of age; 62 percent were white, including Puerto Ricans; and 36 percent were black. (These data refer to blacks alone and do not

TABLE 1.19

Distribution of Families Receiving Public Assistance and with Incomes Below
Poverty Level in New York City and New York SMSA, 1969

	New York City	N.Y. SMSA	Outer SMSA
Total population	7,801,926	11,401,122	3,599,196
Receiving social security	866,013	1,140,112	274,099
Percent of total	(11.1)	(10.0)	(7.0)
With below poverty-level income	1,164,673	1,357,181	192,508
Percent of total	(14.9)	(11.9)	(5.0)
Total families	2,058,943	2,970,425	911,482
Receiving public assistance	198,697	225,272	26,575
Percent of total	(9.7)	(7.6)	(2.9)
With below poverty-level income	236,507	274,687	38,180
Percent of total	(11.4)	(9.2)	(4.0)
With female head	354,735	429,004	74,269
With below-poverty level income	111,469	125,595	14,126
Percent of total	(31.0)	(29.0)	(19.0)
With children under Age 18	98,685	110,502	11,817
Percent of total	(89.0)	(88.0)	(84.0)
Total unrelated individuals	969,898	1,158,009	181,111
Receiving public assistance	75,839	83,738	7,899
Percent of total	(7. 8)	(7.2)	(4.3)
With below poverty-level income	266,053	321,610	55,557
Percent of total	(27.4)	(27.8)	(31.0)

Source: Compiled from U.S. Department of Commerce, Bureau of the Census, Census of Population: 1970, General Social
and Economic Characteristics: New York, PC(1)-C34 (Washington, D.C.: U.S. Government Printing Office, 1972).

TABLE 1.20

Distribution of Families in New York City, 1970

	Distribution
Total families	2,043,765
With own children under age 18	995,501
Percent of total	(49)
With husband and wife	1,573,387
Percent of total	(77)
Total families with female head	353,692
Percent of total families	(17)
With own children under age 18	227,854
Percent of families with female head	(64)
White families	220,319
Percent of families with female head	(62)
With own children under age 18	98,165
Percent of white families with female head	(45)
Negro families	127,225
Percent of families with female head	(36)
With own children under age 18	88,117
Percent of Negro families with female head	(69)

Source: Compiled from U.S. Department of Commerce, Bureau of the Census, Census of Population: 1970, General Population Characteristics: New York, PC(1)-B34 (Washington, D.C.: U.S. Government Printing Office, 1971).

include other minorities.) Forty-five percent of the white families and 69 percent of the Negro families had children under 18. These families, with a mean income of $6,891, consistently receive incomes that are lower than the $11,639 mean income for all families (See Table 1.21). In addition to having generally lower incomes, 31 percent of female-headed families had incomes below the poverty line (See Table 1.18).

Finally, in 1970, 4 percent of the city's male civilian labor force was unemployed, compared to 5 percent in 1960 (See Table 1.22). Unemployment was higher in the female civilian labor force in both years, though in 1970 the gap between the male and female unemployment rates was larger. Outside the central city, the rate of unemployment was generally less, though the male-female differentials are similar.

Social Characteristics

Two other factors that are measurable and that can add to an understanding of the changing structure of the city's population are educational attainment and housing characteristics. To the extent public service demands are a function of education levels, the former may give some notion of this determinant of city government expenditure increases. Housing characteristics, on the other hand, are a potential indicator of needs for increased service levels, and another proxy measure for poverty.

Both New York City and the outer SMSA displayed greater educational attainment in 1970 than in 1960. There was a decrease in the number of non-high school graduates and an increase in all other categories of educational attainment. However, as fully 52 percent of the city's population failed to complete high school, compared to 38 percent in the rest of the SMSA, the outer SMSA obviously houses a more educated population than does the city. Moreover, only 8 percent of the city's population completed four or more years of college, while 22 percent of the population of the rest of the SMSA reached this level (See Table 1.23).

In housing, as in education, the 1960s was a decade of improvement. Thus, while total population in New York City increased by 1.5 percent, total housing units in the city increased by 6 percent between 1960 and 1970. However, at the same time, there was a 31 percent housing unit increase in the rest of the SMSA. The major portion of housing units in the outer SMSA—71 percent in 1970—was owner-occupied, compared to a 74 percent portion in the city that was renter-occupied. The majority of housing in the outer SMSA consists of

TABLE 1.21

Mean Incomes of New York City Families, 1969

	Distribution
Total families	2,058,943
Mean income	$ 11,639
Families with female head	354,735
Mean income	$ 6,891

Source: Compiled from U.S. Department of Commerce, Bureau of the Census, Census of Population: 1970, General Social and Economic Characteristics: New York, PC(1)-C34 (Washington, D.C.: U.S. Government Printing Office, 1972).

TABLE 1.22

General Unemployment Characteristics in New York City
and New York SMSA by Sex, 1960 and 1970

Civilian Labor Force	1960			1970		
	New York City	N.Y. SMSA	Outer SMSA	New York City	N.Y. SMSA	Outer SMSA
Total male	2,212,355	2,972,806	760,481	1,985,001	2,926,708	941,707
Unemployed	109,832	130,523	20,691	78,381	102,578	24,147
Percent of total	(5)	(4)	(3)	(4)	(4)	(3)
Total female	1,275,886	1,613,430	337,544	1,361,782	1,890,667	528,885
unemployed	70,192	83,073	12,881	63,499	82,951	19,452
Percent of total	(6)	(5)	(4)	(5)	(4)	(4)

Sources: Compiled from U.S. Department of Commerce, Bureau of the Census, Census of Population:
1960, Detailed Characteristics: New York, PC(1)–D34 and Census of Population: 1970, General Social and
Economic Characteristics: New York, PC(1)–C34 (Washington, D.C.: U.S. Government Printing Office,
1962 and 1972).

TABLE 1.23

Educational Attainment of Population in New York City and New York SMSA, 1960 and 1970

	1960			1970		
	New York City	N.Y. SMSA	Outer SMSA	New York City	N.Y. SMSA	Outer SMSA
Total population age 25 and over	4,955,081	6,632,377	1,677,296	4,774,864	6,801,877	2,027,013
Non-high school graduates	2,935,488	3,902,357	966,869	2,502,442	3,276,979	774,537
Percent of total	(60)	(59)	(58)	(52)	(48)	(38)
High school graduates	1,094,941	1,569,943	475,002	1,350,764	2,061,739	710,975
Percent of total	(22)	(24)	(28)	(28)	(30)	(35)
High school +	1,789,439	2,730,020	940,581	2,136,653	3,524,898	1,388,245
Percent of total	(36)	(41)	(56)	(45)	(52)	(69)
1-3 years of college	351,996	527,561	175,565	382,761	618,598	235,837
Percent of total	(7)	(8)	(11)	(8)	(9)	(12)
4 + years of college	342,502	632,516	290,014	403,128	844,561	441,433
Percent of total	(7)	(10)	(17)	(8)	(12)	(22)

Sources: Compiled from U.S. Department of Commerce, Bureau of the Census, Census of Population: 1960, Detailed Characteristics: New York PC(1)-D34 and Census of Population: 1970, General Social and Economic Characteristics: New York, PC(1)-C34 (Washington, D.C.: U.S. Government Printing Office, 1962, and 1972).

TABLE 1.24

General Housing Characteristics in New York City and New York SMSA, 1960 and 1970

	1960			1970		
	New York City	N.Y. SMSA	Outer SMSA	New York City	N.Y. SMSA	Outer SMSA
Total housing units	2,758,116	3,642,624	884,508	2,917,699	3,991,157	1,073,458
Owner-occupied	577,873	1,166,770	588,897	669,349	1,427,445	758,096
Percent of total	(21)	(32)	(67)	(23)	(36)	(71)
Renter-occupied	2,076,572	2,285,796	209,224	2,167,523	2,449,058	281,535
Percent of total	(75)	(63)	(24)	(74)	(61)	(26)
Number of units in structure*						
1 Unit	367,511	1,047,136	679,625	341,227	1,099,197	757,970
Percent of total	(13)	(29)	(77)	(12)	(28)	(71)
2 Units	396,196	457,835	61,639	429,762	512,235	82,473
Percent of total	(14)	(13)	(7)	(15)	(13)	(8)
3 and 4 units	242,235	282,356	40,121	222,676	266,020	43,344
Percent of total	(9)	(8)	(5)	(8)	(7)	(4)
5 or more units	1,750,824	1,853,752	102,928	1,842,598	1,994,772	152,174
Percent of total	(64)	(51)	(12)	(63)	(50)	(14)

*Does not add up to "all units" or all occupied units.

Source: Compiled from U.S. Department of Commerce, Bureau of the Census, Census of Housing, 1960, and 1970, General Housing Characteristics: New York, HC(1)–A34 (Washington, D.C.: U.S. Government Printing Office, 1961 and 1971).

TABLE 1.25

Rental Housing Characteristics in New York City and New York SMSA, 1960 and 1970

	1960			1970		
	New York City	N.Y. SMSA	Outer SMSA	New York City	N.Y. SMSA	Outer SMSA
Total renter-occupied units*	2,076,572	2,285,796	209,224	2,167,523	2,449,058	281,535
Gross rent						
$59 or less	572,556	598,179	25,623	112,876	119,456	6,580
Percent of total	(28)	(26)	(12)	(5)	(5)	(2)
$60-79	636,839	678,109	41,270	324,220	336,787	12,567
Percent of total	(31)	(30)	(20)	(15)	(14)	(5)
$80-99	370,809	413,187	42,378	459,499	482,521	23,022
Percent of total	(18)	(18)	(20)	(21)	(20)	(8)
$100-149	336,001	398,860	62,859	698,256	776,739	78,483
Percent of total	(16)	(18)	(30)	(32)	(32)	(28)
$150 or more	121,671	147,078	25,407	539,103	684,777	145,674
Percent of total	(6)	(6)	(12)	(25)	(28)	(52)
No cash rent	40,014	51,378	11,364	31,513	44,064	12,551
Percent of total	(2)	(2)	(5)	(2)	(2)	(5)

*Totals do not add up to total renter-occupied units.

Source: Compiled from U.S. Department of Commerce, Bureau of the Census, Census of Housing, 1960 and 1970, General Housing, Characteristics: New York, HC(1)-A34 (Washington, D.C.: U.S. Government Printing Office, 1961 and 1971).

one-unit structures, while the majority of housing in the city has five or more units (See Table 1.24). However, in New York City, the fact that owner-occupied units increased by 16 percent, while renter-occupied units increased by only 4 percent, implies that the primary beneficiaries of the increased supply of housing have been those whose economic and social circumstances facilitate home ownership—that is, the middle and upper classes. Nonetheless, while housing units costing $100 or more to rent constituted 80 percent of all rental units in the outer SMSA in 1970, only 57 percent of all rental units in New York City rented for $100 or more (See Table 1.25). In fact, in constant dollar terms, the median city rent in 1970 was $89, compared to $86 in 1960. (These figures are expressed in constant dollars: 1967 = 100.)

Another indication of improvement in the housing situation is the fact that housing lacking some or all plumbing facilities decreased substantially within the city over the 1960-70 period. However, it should be noted that, in 1969, 16.3 percent of all New York City households had incomes below the poverty level (See Table 1.26). About 5 percent of these were living in owner-occupied units, with an average value of $24,215. This would seem to indicate a heavy concentration of the aged. The remaining 95 percent of poverty households were

TABLE 1.26

Households with Income Below Poverty Level in
New York City, 1969

	Distribution
Total households with income below poverty level	401,404
Percent of all households	(16.3)
Owner-occupied	17,453
Mean value of unit	$ 24,215
Renter-occupied	383,951
Mean value of rent	$ 101
Percent of households with below poverty-level income lacking some or all plumbing	(4.2)

Source: Compiled from U.S. Department of Commerce, Bureau of the Census, Census of Population: 1970, General Social and Economic Characteristics: New York, PC(1)-C34 (Washington, D.C.: U.S. Government Printing Office, 1972).

renter-occupied, with a mean rent of $101. Over 4 percent of households with incomes below the poverty level lacked some or all plumbing facilities.

These data on population characteristics offer a comparison of central city with outside central city and reinforce the expectations about the city vis-à-vis its suburban areas. New York City, in short, has higher percentages of groups that have been associated with public program needs: the old, the less educated, minorities, and families headed by women.

CHANGES IN PROPERTY VALUES AND LAND USE

Clearly, the quantity of land in New York City cannot change (except be annexation or landfill), but the composition of land uses may change and thus affect the level and growth of land values. An analysis of such changes is carried out in some detail because they reflect the changing employment and population composition of the city and because of their importance for the property tax—a major source of city government tax revenue.

This section is concerned specifically with the changing composition of land use and the changing level of property values in New York City between 1961 and 1971,* in order to describe and analyze these patterns of change. The focus is on the manner in which the market value of property in a land-use class may change because of changes in the overall value (price) of property in that class, and because of net additions to, or subtractions from, the quantity of property (land and improvements) in that class.

The first part of the section is concerned with the changes that have occurred in taxable and nontaxable components of real property and examines, in some detail, the changes that have occurred in the composition of nontaxable property. The second part considers the changing composition of property values by land-use class, by examining changes in the number and average value of parcels in each land-use class, as well as changes in the land and improvement shares of property value. The third part examines changes in the composition of land use and market values among the boroughs. The final part is a summary of the changes in land use and market values that occurred between 1961 and 1971.

---

*All years referred to in this section are fiscal years—that is, 1961 = 1960/61.

The Composition of Real Property

The changes in the composition of real property that occurred in New York City between 1961 and 1971 are presented as differential rates of growth in the value of taxable and nontaxable property.[8] Changes in the composition of nontaxable property relative to ownership will also be considered here.

Property Values*

In 1971, the total assessed value of property in New York City was $36,136,000 (See Table 1.27). Of this total, 65 percent is taxable. This represents a decline from 1961, when 69 percent of assessed real property values was taxable. Thus, over the decade, of every dollar increase in total assessed value, 42 cents were in exempt property and 58 cents in taxable property.

Components of Nontaxable Property

In both 1961 and 1971, the majority of nontaxable property was held by the government sector, with the city itself the largest holder.

TABLE 1.27

Taxable, Nontaxable, and Total Assessed Real Property
Values in New York City, 1961 and 1971

	Assessed Value (in thousands of dollars)		Percent of Total Real Property	
	1961	1971	1961	1971
Taxable property	24,944	$35,329	69.0	65.5
Nontaxable property	11,192	18,642	31.0	34.5
Total real property	36,136	53,971	100.0	100.0

Source: City of New York Tax Commission, Annual Report (New York: Tax Commission, 1961 and 1971).

---

*As there is no satisfactory method of estimating the market value of tax-exempt property, the property values discussed in this section are assessed values.

In 1971, 81 percent of assessed value of nontaxable property was owned by the government sector, with the New York City government holding 45 percent, while, in 1961, the government sector held 84 percent, with the city holding 49 percent. (See Table 1.28).

The assessed value of non-governmentally held nontaxable property increased by 98 percent over the decade.* As a result, it increased from 15.8 percent of the assessed value of total nontaxable property in 1961 to 18.8 percent in 1971. In this group, religious organizations received the largest exemption in 1961 but were surpassed by 1971 by schools and libraries, whose assessed value increased by 254 percent over the decade. In total, exempt property values increased by 66 percent over the decade, outpacing the 41 percent increase in taxable values. This growth in both government and nongovernment property values closely parallels the employment increases in public and private services—particularly education, health and hospitals, and nonprofit organizations.

Changes in the Composition of Taxable Property

Although the city divides taxable real property into three classes—ordinary real estate, real estate of public utilities, and special franchises—the discussion here is primarily concerned with ordinary real estate, with that property further subclassified into 14 categories. Special franchise and public utility property, except for a brief discussion of the total sums involved, are not treated in this analysis. Such properties are combined as a single item in Tax Commission reports, yet the two are so different as to preclude concurrent analytic treatment. In addition, the basic capital structure of public utilities and the treatment of this capital by New York State Tax Law makes any comparison with ordinary real estate property misleading.[9]

Changes in the Total Market Value of Taxable Property

Total market value of taxable property—that is, land and the improvements placed upon it—in New York City increased by 72.8

---

*As of 1971, real property owned by persons 65 years of age or over whose aggregate annual income does not exceed $3,000 is exempt from taxes on real estate to the extent of 50 percent of its assessed value. In 1971, this exemption in total amounted to $49.06 million of assessed valuation. (City of New York Tax Commission, Annual Report: Fiscal 1970-71 New York: City of New York Tax Commission, 1971 .)

TABLE 1.28

Assessed Value of Nontaxable Property in New York City by Ownership, 1961 and 1971[a]

	Assessed Value (millions of dollars)		Percent of Assessed Value of Total Nontaxable Property		Percent Change
	1961	1971	1961	1971	1961-71
Governmental					
New York City	5,506	8,450	49.2	45.4	53.5
Public authorities	1,868	3,012	16.7	16.2	61.2
Public housing[b]	1,211	1,804	10.8	9.7	49.0
Nonpublic housing[c]	182	771	1.6	4.1	323.6
U.S. Government	424	603	3.8	3.2	42.2
New York State	148	395	1.3	2.1	166.9
Foreign governments and United Nations	82	95	0.7	0.5	15.9
Subtotal	9,432	15,133	84.1	81.2	60.3
Nongovernmental					
Religious	569	793	5.1	4.2	39.4
Hospitals and Asylums	387	728	3.5	3.9	88.1
Schools and libraries	262	929	2.3	5.0	254.6
Benevolent organizations	191	210	1.7	1.1	9.9
Cemeteries	122	163	1.1	0.9	33.6
Veterans, clergy, and parsonages	175	374	1.6	2.0	113.7
Exempted railroads	59	309	0.5	1.7	423.7
Subtotal	1,768	3,509	15.8	18.8	98.0
Total	11,192	18,642	100.0	100.0	69.0

[a]Columns may not add to total due to rounding.
[b]Nontaxable public housing in New York City is currently composed of (1) federally aided housing; (2) state-aided housing; (3) city-aided housing; and (4) old federal emergency housing. In 1971, federally aided housing constituted 44 percent of nontaxable public housing.
[c]Nontaxable nonpublic housing in New York City is currently composed of (1) privately owned housing; (2) limited dividend housing; (3) redevelopment housing; and (4) limited profit housing. In 1971, limited profit housing constituted 57 percent of nontaxable private housing.

Source: City of New York Tax Commission, Annual Report (New York: Tax Commission, 1961 and 1971).

percent between 1961 and 1971, from $35.2 billion to $60.8 billion. During this period, the number of taxable parcels remained nearly constant, increasing by only 0.9 percent. Consequently, the market value of the average parcel increased by 71.2 percent, from $43,447 to $74,387 (See Table 1.29).

The market value of land (that is, not including improvements) increased by 69.9 percent and grew at a rate slower than the rate of increase in the total value of property. As a result, the ratio of improvement values (taxable capital) to total value increased from 67

TABLE 1.29

Market Value of Total Taxable Real Property, Ordinary
Real Estate, and Public Utilities and Special Franchises
in New York City, 1961 and 1971

	Taxable Real Property	Ordinary Real Estate	Public Utilities and Special Franchises
Market value (millions of dollars)			
1961	35,218	31,141	4,077
1971	60,844	54,716	6,128
Percent change			
1961-71	72.8	75.7	50.3
Market dollar value per parcel			
1961	43,447	38,864	453,437
1971	74,387	67,604	713,969
Percent change			
1961-71	71.2	74.0	64.0
Ratio of improvements to total			
1961	0.67	0.63	0.94
1971	0.70	0.66	0.97
Percent change			
1961-71	16.7	4.8	3.2

Sources: City of New York Tax Commission, Annual Report (New York: Tax Commission, 1961 and 1971). Market values calculated from unpublished information from the New York State Department of Equalization and Assessment.

percent in 1961 to 70 percent in 1971. Such a phenomenon may result from either the price or the quantity of improvements increasing more rapidly than the price of land, or both.

The value of ordinary real estate property grew by 75.7 percent over the decade, compared to 50.3 percent for the public utility and special franchise group. (As was noted above, because of basic incomparability, the public utility-special franchise category will not be considered beyond this subsection.) As a result of these differential amounts of growth, ordinary real estate increased its share of total market value from 88 percent to 90 percent. In 1971, 97 percent of the market value of the public utility-special franchise group was attributed to improvements; in ordinary real estate, the market value of improvements was 66 percent. In that year, the average value of the ordinary real estate parcel was $67,604; for the public utility-special franchise group, the corresponding figure was $713,969.

Compositional Changes in Ordinary
Real Estate: Market Value*

This differential rate of increase in market values of ordinary real estate suggests that significant changes may have occured in land-use patterns throughout the city, and, therefore, in the proportion that different land uses contribute to the increase in the total value of property. Elevator apartments, office buildings, and two-family and one-family dwellings accounted for 78.8 percent of the $25.7 billion growth in the market value of ordinary real estate throughout the decade (See Table 1.30). Elevator apartments accounted for 24.8 percent of the growth in total property value; office buildings, 20.5 percent; two-family dwellings, 18.4 percent; and one family dwellings, 15.1 percent. Three of these four property uses are classified as residential. Walkup apartments, the only remaining residential category, provided the fifth largest contribution of the growth in the value of property (5.4 percent). None of the other 9 (of the 14) categories of ordinary real estate accounted for more than 3.2 percent of the increase. One category, theaters, declined in absolute value.

With respect to increases in land values, office buildings contributed the largest share, 21 percent, followed by elevator apartments, 20.6 percent, one-family dwellings, 14 percent, and two-family dwellings, 13.5 percent. In the improvement components of total value,

---

*In the remainder of the paper, consideration will be directed toward the ordinary real estate component of total value. Therefore, this amount will be referred to as "total market value" with the understanding that the public utility-special franchise component has been left out.

48

TABLE 1.30

Contribution to Total Land and Improvement Market
Value Increases in New York City by Land-Use Classes of
Ordinary Real Estate, 1961-71
(as percent)

	Total Values	Land Values	Improvement Values
One-family dwelling	15.1	14.0	15.5
Two-family dwelling	18.4	13.5	20.4
Walkup apartment	5.4	6.9	4.7
Elevator apartment	24.8	20.6	26.6
Warehouse	1.3	1.4	1.3
Factory	3.2	3.3	3.1
Garage	0.9	1.7	0.5
Hotel	1.5	1.6	1.4
Theater	0.1	0.0	-0.1
Store building	3.0	5.0	2.2
Loft building	2.2	3.1	1.9
Miscellaneous building	2.9	4.4	2.3
Office building	20.5	21.0	20.2
Vacant land	1.0	3.3	0

Note: Columns may not add to 100 due to rounding.

Sources: City of New York Tax Commission, Annual Report
(New York: Tax Commission, 1961 and 1971). Market values calculated from unpublished information from the New York State Department of Equalization and Assessment.

the largest contribution was made by elevator apartments, 26.6 percent,
followed by two-family dwellings, 20.4 percent, office buildings, 20.2
percent, and one-family dwellings, 15.5 percent. Thus, while the
market values of these four land-use classes have grown rapidly, in
the three residential classes, improvement values have increased
more rapidly than land values. In the fourth class, office buildings,
the increase of land values was slightly greater than that of improvement values. This phenomenon can probably be attributed to the fact
that most of the "absence-of-elevator" apartments are located in the
outer boroughs, where land is relatively less expensive. By contrast,
elevator apartments and office buildings tend to be located on the
relatively expensive land of Manhattan.

49

The contribution to the increase in the market value of property by other land-use classes showed a significant disproportion between land and improvements. Store buildings, for example, accounted for 5 percent of the increase in land values but only 2.2 percent of the increase in improvement values. Garages made up 1.7 percent of the increase in land values but only 0.5 percent of the increase in improvement values. In all nine of these land-use classes, the value of land has risen more rapidly than the value of improvements.

As a consequence of different growth rates over the decade, the share of each land-use class in the total market value of ordinary real estate has also changed. Columns (4) and (5) of Table 1.31 show each land-use class as a percentage of total market value for the years under consideration. Elevator apartments, which contributed the largest single amount to the overall growth in market value, increased its share of total market value from 18.2 percent to 21.1 percent. The proportion of total market value attributable to office buildings increased from 12 percent to 15.7 percent. Detached residences (one- and two-family dwellings) increased from 29.8 percent to 31.4 percent of total market value. At the same time, one-family dwellings' proportion of market value declined by 0.6 percent. The proportion of market value comprised of two-family dwellings increased from 13.3 percent to 15.5 percent, to produce an overall 1.6 percent increase in the proportion of total value accounted for by detached residences.

With regard to growth in market value, shown in Columns (1-3) of Table 1.31, office buildings showed the greatest overall gain, 129 percent over the decade, followed in turn by two-family dwellings, 104 percent; warehouses, 88 percent; factories, 79 percent; and hotels, 70 percent, which all grew more rapidly in value than one-family dwellings, 69 percent. Values of walkup apartments (25 percent), garages, vacant land, and loft buildings (all 33 percent) grew most slowly. The market value of theaters declined by 7 percent.

As a result of the relatively rapid growth in the market value of elevator apartments, office buildings, and two-family dwellings, the proportion of total market value in all other uses, with one exception, declined between 1961 and 1971. In warehouses, the only other class whose share of market value rose, that increase was only 0.1 percent.

Compositional Changes in Ordinary
Real Estate: Number of Parcels and
Average Values per Parcel

From the discussion above, we can gather that the changes in market value are attributable to a combination of changes in the

TABLE 1.31

Market Values and Growth Rates for Ordinary Real Estate
in New York City by Land-Use Class, 1961-71

	Market Value (in millions of dollars)		Percent Change	Percent of Total*	
	1961	1971		1961	1971
One-family dwelling	5,169.4	8,722.2	69	16.5	15.9
Two-family dwelling	4,157.0	8,488.0	104	13.3	15.5
Walkup apartment	5,038.2	6,302.7	25	16.3	11.5
Elevator apartment	5,666.6	11,519.7	103	18.2	21.1
Warehouse	345.3	648.7	88	1.1	1.2
Factory	952.1	1,703.2	79	3.1	3.1
Garage	627.1	833.6	33	2.0	1.5
Hotel	488.6	831.9	70	1.6	1.5
Theater	198.3	184.0	- 7	0.6	0.3
Store building	1,466.8	2,183.4	49	4.7	4.0
Loft building	1,585.8	2,115.0	33	5.1	3.9
Miscellaneous building	994.2	1,679.0	69	3.1	3.1
Office building	3,749.5	8,573.7	129	12.0	15.7
Vacant land	702.4	931.3	33	2.3	1.7

*Columns may not add to 100 due to rounding.

Sources: City of New York Tax Commission, Annual Report (New York: Tax Commission, 1961 and 1971). Market values calculated from unpublished information from the New York State Department of Equalization and Assessment.

numbers of parcels in the city and to increase in the average value of a parcel. What follows is an attempt to partition these separate effects. (It should be noted that definite conclusions should be cautiously drawn when abstracting from changes in parcel numbers, because, in addition to changing uses, parcels are also subdivided and consolidated. In Manhattan, for example, due to consolidation, the number of parcels declined by 7,457 over the decade.)

The percentage change in numbers of parcels, presented in Column (3) of Table 1.32, is difficult to interpret, since "parcels" themselves are nonstandard units, varying over time in size—both within and among land-use classes. Considering the change in the number of parcels in conjunction with the change in average full value per parcel clarifies the manner in which changes in land use affect overall market values.

Consideration of the "average parcel value" somewhat corrects for the effect of changing property usage on total market value. In other words, if, in some land-use class, both the market value and the number of parcels doubled, the average value per parcel would remain constant. If there were reason to believe that the parcels were reasonably constant in size and comparable in price, the doubling of total market value could be attributed to a change in land use (that is, an increase in the quantity of land in this use) and not to increasing values of existing parcels. Because land prices and parcel sizes do vary throughout the city, the following discussion, which is based on this procedure, should be considered only a rough approximation of the time trend.

The first three columns of Table 1.32 show the number and change in parcels by land-use class. The total number of ordinary real estate parcels increased by 7,360 over the decade. However, this table reveals that, in spite of this small net change, nearly 84,000 additional parcels changed land-use class over this same period, bringing the gross number of parcel changes to nearly 91,000. (This figure was arrived at by taking the sum of the absolute value of the difference between Columns [1] and [2] of Table 1.32. It should be noted that less than 84,000 parcels were involved in use change since this method "double-counts" by including both movement out and movement into each class.) Almost one-half of the 91,000 changes were additions to the one- and two-family dwelling categories. Nearly another third are accounted for by a decrease in vacant parcels. In other words, approximately five-sixths of the gross change in parcels may be accounted for by changes in detached dwellings, parcels, and vacant parcels. It seems reasonable to conclude that a large number of the vacant parcels were absorbed into the former category. (Over 55 percent of the 91,000 changes may be accounted for by one- and two-family dwellings and vacant land parcels in Queens and Richmond.)

TABLE 1.32

Number of Parcels and Average Market Values per Parcel for Ordinary
Real Estate in New York City by Land-Use Class, 1961 and 1971

	Number of Parcels		Percent	Average Market Value per Parcel (dollars)		Percent
	1961	1971	Change	1961	1971	Change
One-family dwelling	292,656	309,483	5	17,667	28,190	60
Two-family dwelling	214,528	243,629	14	19,379	34,844	80
Walkup apartment	132,794	128,139	-7	37,966	49,201	30
Elevator apartment	8,647	10,118	17	655,325	1,135,835	74
Warehouse	2,376	2,676	13	145,332	242,414	67
Factory	8,017	8,770	9	118,760	194,207	63
Garage	10,200	8,609	-16	61,480	96,828	57
Hotel	456	427	-6	1,071,491	1,948,244	82
Theater	443	3 34	-25	447,629	550,898	23
Store building	11,556	12,084	5	126,929	180,685	42
Loft building	6,460	4,840	-25	245,479	436,983	78
Miscellaneous building	16,137	15,505	-4	61,609	108,288	76
Office building	1,971	2,332	18	1,902,334	3,676,543	93
Vacant land	94,983	62,415	-34	7,395	14,921	102

Sources: City of New York Tax Commission, Annual Report (New York: Tax Commission, 1961 and 1971). Market values calculated from unpublished information from the New York State Department of Equalization and Assessment.

Because of zoning and locational considerations, it appears unlikely that nonvacant, nonresidential land has been converted to detached dwelling purposes in great amounts. Subdivisions of vacant land for construction of detached dwellings in the outer portions of the boroughs could account for the increase in parcel numbers.

It is significant that, of the seven land-use classes that declined as a proportion of total value, six also incurred a net decrease in number of parcels. Store buildings alone accounted for a decreasing share of total market value as the class accumulated an increasing number of parcels. However, the average store parcel, for example, increased in value by 42 percent, while the value of the average parcel in New York City increased by 70 percent. This implies that the net increase in store properties failed to offset what must have been a small increase in the unit price of such property.

The average market value of vacant land increased at the highest rate: 102 percent. This should not be surprising since, at any given distance from the central portion of the metropolitan area, the quantity of land is fixed. Land buyers who demand access to the central portion of the metropolitan area must bid against one another, thereby increasing the price of land. In fact, buyers might pay "premium" prices for vacant land to avoid the expense of demolition or refurbishment. Ranking second in the highest rate of increase in market value per parcel are office buildings (93 percent), followed by hotels (82 percent), two-family dwellings (80 percent), and loft buildings (78 percent). The smallest increases in per parcel value occurred in walkup apartments (30 percent) and theaters (23 percent).

Theaters serve as the best example of the changing character of land use. The number of theater parcels declined by 25 percent, their total value declined by 7 percent, and the value per parcel increased by 23 percent. It would appear that the lowest-value parcels were drawn into other uses, thereby causing the value of the average parcel to increase. What appears to have been a decrease in the quantity of land apparently has been offset by an increase in the price at which the land remaining in this use is valued.

In the case of loft buildings, the increase in average value per parcel is almost solely attributable to price increases and to the attrition of low-value parcels.* In contrast, the number of parcels

---

*The City Planning Commission reports that only one new loft structure has been constructed in the city since 1930. Decreasing parcels in this case, therefore, mean that the absolute quantity of lofts has decreased. (See New York City Planning Commission, Planning for Jobs, Supplement to Plan for New York City [New York: Planning Commission, March 1971], p. 35.)

occupied by office buildings increased by 18 percent, while average office parcel values increased from $1.9 million to $3.6 million—by 93 percent. This suggests that a sizable portion of the growth in office values and increasing average office parcel values may be attributed to a small number of highly valued structures using small amounts of land very productively. Residential land-use classes evidence a mixed pattern of growth. The highest per-parcel growth, 80 percent, occurred in the two-family dwelling category, but the highest absolute growth occurred in elevator apartments, where per-parcel values increased by 74 percent. The differential in scale in this sector is noteworthy as well. In 1971, the average two-family parcel was valued at $34,884, while the average elevator apartment parcel was valued at more than $1.1 million.

Compositional Changes in Ordinary
Real Estate: Improvements to Total
Value Ratios

The final indicator of market activity is the ratio of value of improvements to total property value (that is, the proportion of total value constituted by improvements). This indicator may change in response to growth or decline in the value of either the land or improvement components of total property values, which in turn respond to both price-level changes and physical-quantity changes. If all else is constant and if the price of land increases, then the value of the improvement ratio will fall. If land values are constant, and the trend is toward increasing dollar amounts of improvements relative to land (as it has been for the city as a whole), then the improvement ratio will increase.

For the city as a whole, improvements accounted for 63.4 percent of total value in 1961 and 66.5 in 1971 (See Table 1.33). It is interesting to note that office buildings and hotels, which are usually associated with high-capital land ratios in New York City, possess a lower improvement ratio than one- and two-family dwellings, which are usually associated with much lower-capital land ratios. This phenomenon results from the price, not the quantity, of land. Most office buildings are in Manhattan, where land prices are highest and improvement ratios, consequently, the lowest in the city.

On the average, values of improvements have increased faster than land values for the loft building group. A similar pattern is shown for hotels and for miscellaneous buildings, where there was a decline in the number of parcels during the period. Theaters and garages show falling improvement ratios over the period. In these two classes of property, the land values increased more rapidly than values of improvements. Factories, for which the 1961 improvement ratio was

55

TABLE 1.33

Value Improvements as Percent of Total Value
for Ordinary Real Estate in New York City by
Land-Use Class, 1961-71

	Value Improvements as Percent of Total Value		Ratio of 1971 to 1961*
	1961	1971	
One-family dwelling	67.8	69.8	1.03
Two-family dwelling	71.1	74.8	1.05
Walkup apartment	69.6	68.3	0.98
Elevator apartment	74.0	74.8	1.01
Warehouse	69.3	69.1	1.00
Factory	72.2	70.9	0.98
Garage	49.7	47.8	0.96
Hotel	56.4	60.7	1.08
Theater	39.0	34.2	0.88
Store building	38.1	42.6	1.12
Loft building	53.5	55.1	1.03
Miscellaneous building	47.9	50.1	1.05
Office building	62.0	66.4	1.07
Vacant land	—	—	—
Total	63.4	66.5	1.05

*Column (3) is the result of dividing Column (2) by Column (1).

Sources: City of New York Tax Commission, Annual Report (New York: Tax Commission, 1961 and 1971). Market values calculated from unpublished information from the New York State Department of Equalization and Assessment.

second only to elevator apartments, also declined slightly over the 10-year period.

Compositional Changes in Ordinary
Real Estate: Borough Patterns

In Manhattan, the number of parcels in each land-use category declined, while average market values per parcel increased, at a rate

exceeding that in the remaining boroughs.* (See Table 1.34.) In
Manhattan, consolidation of parcels—particularly in residential
categories—has been the rule rather than the exception. This trend
contrasts with evidence of an increase in residential parcels and a
rapid decrease in vacant parcels in the other boroughs. Improvements
constitute a smaller share of total values in Manhattan than in the
other boroughs, because of the high unit prices that centrally located
land commands in Manhattan. The improvement ratio for residences
in the outer boroughs in 1961 ranged from a high of 0.84 in the Bronx
to a low of 0.74 in Brooklyn; in Manhattan, the corresponding ratio
was 0.60. Industrial properties display similar measures, with
Brooklyn possessing the highest ratio of 0.75 in 1971, and Manhattan
the lowest at 0.55. A similar relationship among the borough improvement ratios exists in the commercial class. Manhattan had the highest
improvement to total value ratio in 1971 of 0.61 Brooklyn, the second
highest improvement ratio of 0.56, and the Bronx, the lowest, of 0.47.
In addition, when comparing 1961 and 1971 commercial ratios, Manhattan's improvement ratio relative to the other boroughs appears
to be increasing.

In terms of overall land-use patterns, residential use accounts
for a smaller proportion of property value in Manhattan than in any
other borough. Yet, at 39.3 percent of total market value, residential
land use in Manhattan is clearly significant. Outside Manhattan, the
residential proportions of total value in 1971 ranged from 82 percent
in Brooklyn to 76.6 percent in Richmond. In Manhattan, the residential
proportion of total value remained unchanged between 1961 and 1971.
In 1971, the average residential parcel in Manhattan was valued at
$267,893, whereas in the Bronx, which had the second highest average
residential value, the amount was $52,539, a difference that under-
scores the special character of Manhattan.

The nature of the central borough is best illustrated by the
growth in commercial property value; it measured 48.6 percent of
total value in 1971, up from 44.3 percent in 1961. Commercial

---

*In this discussion, the 14 land-use classes of ordinary real
estate have been aggregated into four general land-use classes: industrial, commercial, residential, and vacant land. Industrial use
has been defined to include factories, warehouses, and lofts; residential use has been defined to include one-family dwellings, two-family
dwellings, walkup apartments, and elevator apartments. The remaining nonvacant parcels have been classed as commercial. This aggregation has been made primarily to allow a parsimonious comparison
between boroughs and is intended to be representative of only broad
property value changes.

TABLE 1.34

Market Value as Percent and Change in Parcels for
Property Classes in New York City by Borough,
1961 and 1971

	Percent to Value in Borough 1961	1971	Change Parcels 1961-71	Improvement to Total Value Ratio 1961	1971
Manhattan					
Industrial	15.3	10.8	- 1,864	0.54	0.55
Commercial	44.3	48.6	- 894	0.55	0.61
Residential	39.3	39.3	- 4,995	0.56	0.60
Vacant	1.0	1.0	- 131		
Bronx					
Industrial	4.5	5.4	149	0.72	0.69
Commercial	14.2	13.3	- 208	0.43	0.47
Residential	78.1	79.3	4,549	0.85	0.84
Vacant	3.2	2.2	- 7,176		
Brooklyn					
Industrial	6.7	6.3	493	0.74	0.75
Commercial	13.3	11.0	- 77	0.54	0.56
Residential	79.0	82.0	10,882	0.73	0.74
Vacant	1.0	0.6	- 5,918		
Queens					
Industrial	5.7	7.2	712	0.73	0.71
Commercial	10.3	9.8	82	0.49	0.54
Residential	80.9	81.5	17,805	0.73	0.75
Vacant	3.0	1.5	-11,068		
Richmond					
Industrial	1.7	2.5	81	0.63	0.64
Commercial	11.1	7.7	- 176	0.58	0.54
Residential	70.2	76.6	14,503	0.70	0.77
Vacant	16.9	13.1	- 8,275		

Sources: City of New York Tax Commission, Annual Report
(New York: Tax Commission, 1961 and 1971). Market values calculated from unpublished information from the New York State Department of Equalization and Assessment.

property for any of the outer boroughs accounted for no more than 14 percent of total value in 1971. In each case, commercial property declined as a proportion of total value over the decade. Of the five boroughs, it was in Manhattan that industrial property was found to constitute the largest proportion of total borough value—10.8 percent of all property in 1971, a decline from 15.3 percent in 1961.* Industrial values also declined relatively in Brooklyn but increased in the Bronx, Queens, and Richmond.

With regard to residential land use, Manhattan's property market all but precludes the use of land for detached (one- and two-family) dwellings, which accounted for only 5.4 percent of the total residential value in this borough in 1971 (See Table 1.35). One- and two-family dwellings outside Manhattan ranged from 37.7 percent of total residential value in the Bronx to 93 percent in Richmond. However, the distribution of one- and two-family dwellings varied among boroughs. In the Bronx and Brooklyn, two-family dwellings accounted for substantially larger proportions of total value than did one-family dwellings, whereas in Queens and Richmond the roles were reversed. In Queens, the pattern of residential land-use change favors two-family dwellings, which accounted for the use of more than six times the parcels occupied by one-family dwellings. In Queens, two-family dwellings increased from 24.8 percent to 28.8 percent.

Elevator apartment values have generally increased in all five boroughs. The increase appears to be centered in Manhattan, where this category accounted for 68.1 percent of residential values in 1971, up from 60.3 percent in 1961. Conversely, the value of walkup apartments as a proportion of total residential property value declined in each borough. This decline was matched by a decline in number of parcels in Manhattan and the Bronx.

Residential improvement ratios generally follow the same borough patterns as total market values. The lowest ratio for each land-use class is found in Manhattan. Elevator apartments in all boroughs record the highest improvement ratios. In Manhattan, improvements account for an increasing share of total value for elevator apartments, whereas in the Bronx and Queens, improvements claim a declining share of total value.

_____

*The size of this category in Manhattan is largely a consequence of classifying loft buildings in the industrial category, and the sharp decline is a result of the decline in the number of loft parcels.

TABLE 1.35

Total Value as Percent and Change in Parcels for Residential
Property Classes in New York City by Borough, 1961 and 1971

	Percentage of Residential Value in Borough		Change in Parcels 1961-71	Improvement to Total Value Ratio	
	1961	1971		1961	1971
Manhattan					
One-family	3.6	3.7	- 917	0.39	0.44
Two-family	1.3	1.7	32	0.38	0.42
Walkup apartment	34.8	26.4	-4,596	0.44	0.47
Elevator apartment	60.3	68.1	486	0.64	0.67
Bronx					
One-family	16.3	16.3	597	0.72	0.75
Two-family	17.4	21.4	4,114	0.72	0.78
Walkup Apartment	35.6	26.1	- 402	0.75	0.76
Elevator apartment	30.7	36.1	240	0.83	0.82
Brooklyn					
One-family	19.1	19.8	4,768	0.68	0.69
Two-family	32.6	40.5	6,417	0.70	0.73
Walkup apartment	29.1	19.9	- 354	0.74	0.75
Elevator apartment	19.1	19.7	318	0.82	0.84
Queens					
One-family	47.1	41.7	2,322	0.69	0.70
Two-family	24.8	28.8	14,277	0.73	0.77
Walkup apartment	12.6	9.6	839	0.77	0.75
Elevator apartment	15.5	19.8	403	0.85	0.83
Richmond					
One-family	69.5	66.5	10,057	0.69	0.75
Two-family	25.6	26.5	4,261	0.74	0.80
Walkup apartment	3.6	2.7	161	0.68	0.76
Elevator apartment	1.2	4.6	24	0.84	0.85

Note: Total may not equal 100 due to rounding.

Sources: City of New York Tax Commission, Annual Report (New York: Tax Commission, 1961 and 1971). Market values calculated from unpublished information from the New York State Department of Equalization and Assessment.

TABLE 1.36

Selected Property Classes as Percent of Total Ordinary Real Estate in New York City by Borough, 1961 and 1971

Borough	Total Value 1961	1971	Office Buildings 1961	1971	Elevator Apartments 1961	1971	Detached Residences[a] 1961	1971
Manhattan	37.3	40.8	94.0	96.3	48.8	52.0	2.4	2.0
Bronx	10.6	8.6	1.0	1.0	14.0	11.7	9.4	8.2
Brooklyn	23.5	20.8	2.8	1.9	19.6	16.0	32.1	32.0
Queens	25.4	25.5	1.5	1.6	17.5	19.6	49.4	46.6
Richmond	3.0	4.2	1.0	0.1	0.1	2.8	6.7	9.6
Total[b]	100.0	100.0	100.0	100.0	100.0	100.0	100.0	100.0

[a]Defined as any family dwellings plus two-family dwellings.
[b]Columns may not add to total due to rounding.

Sources: City of New York Tax Commission, Annual Report (New York: Tax Commission, 1961 and 1971); market values calculated from unpublished information from New York State Department of Equalization and Assessment.

61

Summary of Market-Value and Land-Use Change
by Major Use Classes

The principal findings of the foregoing analysis can be briefly summarized: First, the rate of growth in the assessed value of non-taxable property exceeds that for taxable property. Though the city government is the primary holder of nontaxable property, the largest growth in the tax-exempt sector occurred in service-related activities—for examples schools, hospitals, private nonprofit organizations. The pattern of growth observed in assessed values of nontaxable properties generally follows the employment trends discussed above.

The general increase in value of ordinary real estate property over the decade of the 1960s reveals two major trends: (1) a large increase in value accounted for by elevator apartment and office buildings—characterized by a small number of individual parcels in which improvement value makes up a large and increasing share of total property value and (2) a large increase in values accounted for by detached dwellings outside Manhattan. These four property classes together account for 78.8 percent of the growth in market values over the decade.

With respect to interborough variations, only Manhattan and Richmond experienced increases in their proportion of the city's total market value. The Queens share of total market value remained almost constant, while the Bronx and Brooklyn decreased their relative shares. Manhattan is characterized by high, and increasing, concentration of office buildings. In fact, while Manhattan contained 94 percent of the value of office buildings in 1961, its share had increased to 96.3 percent by 1971.* In the Bronx and Queens, the office buildings proportion remained nearly constant, and in Brooklyn and Richmond, it declined. (See Table 1.36.)

In the detached-dwelling-use class, an opposite pattern is apparent. Manhattan possesses an extremely low concentration of detached residential dwellings relative to the rest of the city, while the outer boroughs possess detached dwellings in value amounts generally proportional to one another. In the Bronx, both detached dwellings and the borough's proportion of total value declined. In Brooklyn, the detached residence proportion remained almost constant,

---

*Note that Column (1) of Table 1.36 provides a useful reference to Columns (2), (3), and (4). If the proportion of a single use class (such as office buildings) claimed by one borough is greater (lower) than the borough's proportion of total market value, it may be inferred that the borough holds a high (low) concentration of that use class relative to the city as a whole.

though at a level significantly higher than the borough's share of total value. For Queens, which claimed 46.6 percent of the city's residential value in 1971, the detached residence proportion declined relative to the borough's share of total value. Only Richmond's share of detached residence value increased significantly, paralleling the borough's growth in its share of toal city property value.

A much more varied pattern is evident with regard to elevator apartments. Most of the elevator apartment valuation is situated in Manhattan, which claimed 52 percent in 1971. However, heavier concentrations of elevator apartment values are situated in the outer boroughs than was true for office buildings. Elevator apartments in the Bronx decreased as a proportion of total value but remained greater than the borough's share of total market value. In Brooklyn, elevator apartments also declined as a share of total value, but in Queens and Richmond, the borough proportion increased.

A separate pattern may be noted for each of the three major sources of property value growth. Office buildings are concentrated in Manhattan. The share of growth in total market value for which this class accounts is almost entirely attributable to that borough. The opposite is true for detached dwellings, most of whose values are situated, and most rapidly growing, outside Manhattan. Elevator apartments, unlike the other two classes, have flourished throughout the city. They make the largest single dollar contribution to property value growth in the Bronx, Brooklyn, and Queens, while these apartments accounted for the second largest value increase in Manhattan and Richmond. In Manhattan, office buildings provided the largest increase in the aggregate market value of borough property. In Richmond, single-family dwellings make the largest contribution.

NOTES

1. For the 1962-70 period, see Roy W. Bahl et al., "Intergovernmental and Functional Aspects of Trends in Public Employment in the United States," Public Administration Review, No. 6 (November/December 1972), 815-32.

2. For the 1960-70 period, see Alexander Ganz, "Our Large Cities; New Light on Their Recent Transformation; Elements of a Development Strategy; A Prototype Program for Boston" (Cambridge: Laboratory for Environmental Studies, Massachusetts Institute of Technology, February 1972).

3. See Emanuel Tobier, "Economic Development Strategy for the City," in Agenda for a City: Issues Confronting New York, ed. by Lyle C. Fitch and Annmarie H. Walsh (Beverly Hills, Calif.: Sage Publications, 1970), p. 56.

4. "Major industrial firms" refers here to those firms listed in the Fortune Directory of the 500 largest industrial corporations.

5. Karen Gerard, "Headquarters Firms in New York Fortune Directory—1971" (unpublished paper, Chase Manhattan Bank, July 1972, mimeographed).

6. Council of Economic Advisers, Annual Report (New York: New York State Council of Economic Advisers, 1973).

7. U.S. Department of Labor, Bureau of Labor Statistics, "The Economics of Working and Living in New York City," BLS Regional Report No. 29 (New York: Middle-Atlantic Regional Office, Bureau of Labor Statistics, July 1972).

8. For a complete discussion of definitional characteristics of the New York City property tax base and the sources of the data discussed in this section, see David J. Bjornstad, "The New York City Property Tax Base: Definition, Composition and Measurement" (Internal Working Paper No. 7, Maxwell Research Project on the Public Finances of New York City, Syracuse University, Syracuse, New York, October 1972).

9. For a discussion of legal tax base definitions, see ibid.

2

NEW YORK CITY
TAX REVENUES
AND ECONOMIC BASE

The purpose of this chapter is to establish a linkage between the structure of the New York City tax system and the structure of the economic base of the city. While the revenue forecasting issue is not directly addressed here, the results of this analysis do have important implications for the long-run yield behavior of the present New York City tax system. Specifically, the purpose is to identify and measure the relative contribution of each of the city's industries to its tax base and its tax revenues. However, rather than being an analysis and projection of the trends in tax payments by industries, this chapter focuses on the revenue yield implications of interindustry differences in tax base and tax payments. The specific purpose is an evaluation of the implications for the revenue responses of the city's tax system of changes in composition of the city's economic base.

While there has not been a large body of specific research on this question, it has been the subject of some speculation by observers of the city. For example, in a recent study, it was alleged that "the service revolution has debilitated the city's property tax base."[1] If such a statement portrays reality and if it holds for other local taxes, the long-term growth of New York City's service sector and the corresponding decline in its manufacturing sector may have a negative impact on the secular trend in tax receipts. It should be noted that this is solely an effect of a changing economic structure and is additive to the tax revenue effects of any absolute growth or decline in the city's economy. In light of the service sector growth described above, this issue takes on particular relevance for New York City.

The scope of this analysis is limited both as to taxes considered and as to time period analyzed. The analysis is focused on the four principal forms of local taxation and considers nine specific taxes:

the property tax; the transportation, finance, insurance, and general corporation taxes and the public utilities tax (which together form the business income tax); the resident income and commuter earnings taxes (which together form the personal income tax); and the retail sales tax. The detail in which each of the nine is considered is generally determined by its relative importance in the city's tax system and the nature of the data available. Because of the difficulty of obtaining data that would enable tax base and yield to be related to their industrial source, the detail of the empirical analysis varies among the taxes.

The remainder of this chapter is divided into three parts. The following section attempts to place New York City's tax structure in a national perspective through a comparative analysis of the nation's 10 largest cities and presents a brief overview of historical changes in the New York City revenue structure. Included in this section is a brief analysis of the yield performance of the city's tax system.in recent years. The material in the section entitled "Tax Base and Revenue Implications . . ."—the heart of this chapter—is an analysis of the tax revenue implications of change in the economic base of New York City. To this end, the four parts of that section contain empirical analyses of the relationships between the composition of economic activities and the base and revenues associated with each of the four principal forms of taxation in New York City. The final section presents a summary of the analysis and evaluates the revenue implication of changes in the composition of the New York City economic base.

It should be noted that there are differences in data sources used in this chapter, and, accordingly, there is some lack of conformity in the statistics presented in various parts of the chapter. For example, in order to ensure comparability in the intercity revenue structure comparison, data from the annual Department of Commerce publication Compendium of City Government Finances were used;[2] however, the evaluation of the structure and revenue performance of New York City's tax system is based primarily on data obtained from the New York City Comptroller's Annual Report.[3] There are a number of reasons why the data from these sources may differ. The most likely source of divergence is the manner in which the data are collected. The Bureau of the Census reports data that are compiled from a survey questionnaire, while the Comptroller's Reports contain data collected as part of the corporate bookkeeping and accounting process performed by New York City's government. However, the data reported in both sources are internally uniform and consistent, and, therefore, any analysis based wholly upon either one of these sources is valid.

More important data differences exist in the analysis of specific taxes, which is reported in the section beginning on page 78. In most cases, the data on which the analysis is based were derived from a number of sources including special tabulation of unpublished records of various departments of both the New York State and the New York City governments. The pecularities of these data and the procedures by which they were obtained are noted in the discussion accompanying the analysis of each tax.

INTERCITY COMPARISONS AND HISTORICAL TRENDS

The New York City government is unique in one important respect. It is, by most measures, the largest local government in the nation. Local government size, in this case, may be taken to describe the level of spending or the wide range of public services for which the city has financial responsibility—few, if any, other city governments provide such a broad scope of services. The purpose in this section is to describe the revenue structure of New York City and to analyze its secular performance, taking its unique situation into account.

Historical Revenue Growth in New York City

Total revenues of the New York City government grew at an average annual rate of about 12 percent over the 1961-71* period, but, when only revenues raised from own sources are considered, the annual rate of growth averages 7.8 percent (See Table 2.1). Further, if the period following the major changes in the city's tax structure (1967-71) is examined separately, the growth rates in total revenues and in revenues from own sources are less (10.1 and 6.4 percent, respectively). It is clear that a part of the explanation for this difference is a slower growth in income, since the 1967-71 period does coincide with a nationwide decline in economic activities. (A crude estimate of the income elasticity is presented later in this section.) Whether the causal factors behind this change in revenue growth are

---

*The fiscal year adopted by New York City runs from 1 July- 30 June. Therefore, fiscal 1961 refers to the period 1 July 1960 to 30 June 1961. For all fiscal data in this analysis, except the special tabulations of the general corporation income tax, and the resident personal income tax, the years referred to are fiscal years. These special tabulations and employment data are based on calendar years.

TABLE 2.1

Revenue Trends in New York City, 1961 and 1967-71

Fiscal Year	Total Current Revenues			Current Revenues Raised from Own Sources			
	Amount	Per Employee	Percent of Personal Income	Amount	Per Employee	Percent of Personal Income	Percent of Total Current Revenues
1961	$2,421,696,892	$ 686	N.A.	$1,930,047,982	$ 547	N.A.	79.7
1967	4,497,098,111	1,228	11.79	2,996,843,788	818	8.28	66.6
1968	5,296,128,851	1,423	13.79	3,310,188,408	889	8.64	62.5
1969	6,066,600,898	1,598	14.41	3,499,499,549	921	8.32	57.7
1970	6,705,196,485	1,781	14.78	3,892,796,653	1,034	8.58	58.1
1971	7,466,813,773	2,066	15.41	4,086,485,607	1,119	8.43	54.7
Average annual increase (percent)							
1961-71	11.9	11.7		7.8	7.4		
1967-71	13.5	13.9		8.0	8.1		

N.A.: not available.

Sources: Comptroler of the City of New York, Annual Report (New York: Office of the Comptroller, 1961 and 1967-71; Personal Income data taken from "Personal Income, New York City" (unpublished tables, Bureau of Labor Statistics). (This is the source of city income data only. The data used for each fiscal year are income figures for the calendar year, for example, 1966/67 = 1966); New York State Department of Labor, Division of Employment, Research and Statistics Office, Employment Statistics, Vol. 6 (Albany, N.Y.: N.Y.S. Department of Labor, September 1970); and Employment Review, Vols. 24 and 25 (Albany, N.Y.: N.Y.S. Department of Labor, May 1971 and February 1972).

automatic or discretionary, the conclusion to be drawn is that the rate of growth in revenues from own sources and in state and federal assistance is slowing. In fact, with respect to the former, the percentage of revenues raised from own sources dropped from nearly 80 percent in 1961 to about half of total city government revenues in 1971. Thus, in the most general terms, the picture is one of a slowing in the revenue growth rate and a declining revenue self-sufficiency.

Since these revenue trends underlie the trend in the city government's power to purchase public services, it would seem useful to express them in per capita terms. The percentage increases in total revenues, when coupled with a relatively constant population size, result in rapidly rising per capita revenues. While per capita revenues show the average amount available for spending on behalf of each resident of the city, examination of revenues per dollar of personal income earned and per employee reflects the relationship between revenues and economic activity.* As may be seen in Table 2.1, current revenues as a percent of personal income increased from 12.72 percent in 1967 to 15.41 percent in 1971. While this indicates an increase in the level of the city government's operation relative to the overall city economy, the small increase (approximately 1.8 percent) in the ratio of revenues raised from own sources to personal income (8.28 percent in 1967 and 8.43 percent in 1971) indicates that the growth in own source revenues has proceeded at a rate roughly equivalent to that by which income earned in the city has increased. That is, on average, the city government extracts in taxes an amount roughly equivalent to 8 cents of each dollar of personal income earned.

Since employment, and particularly its distribution among activities and industries, reflects the city growth process, the linkage of tax revenues to employment is another important ingredient in developing the relationship between the changing composition of economic activity in the city and the city's fiscal future. The data in Table 2.1 show that the amount of revenues raised from own sources that may be prorated to the average employee in New York City is over $1,000 and has shown a pattern of secular increase of 7.4 percent since 1961. The implications of this pattern are discussed later in the more appropriate context of the relationship between the composition of economic activity and revenues from individual taxes.

----

*It should be noted that the income earned and employment data discussed in this section relate to those economic activities that are located in New York City. These data differ from the more often cited data on the employment of, and the income earned by, residents. The former were selected for use in this analysis because they relate directly to activities located in the city, while the latter are more closely related to the welfare of residents.

Turning attention to the components of the tax system in New York City, it should be noted that the structure of taxation was greatly changed in the 1960s. The principal modification involved the elimination of the general business tax (gross receipts tax) and the introduction of a series of business income taxes and the resident income and commuter earnings tax.[4] These taxes, along with the property tax, the public utilities tax, and the retail sales tax have, since 1967, accounted for three-quarters of New York City's locally raised revenues. In total, revenues from these taxes increased by 35.5 percent between 1967 and 1971.

The growth in revenues from these taxes can be divided into two components: automatic growth resulting from growth in the tax base (with tax rates held constant), and discretionary growth, which stems from increases in the tax rate (with the tax base held constant). Except in the case of the property tax, there were no major rate increases between 1967 and 1971. In 1972, however, the rates of the resident income, commuter earnings, general corporation, and insurance corporation taxes were changed. Therefore, by dividing the six-year period during which all of these taxes existed into two segments—one in which rates were held constant, and one in which they changed—the approximate size of the automatic and discretionary components of revenue growth can be roughly estimated. (One of the rates imposed by the insurance corporation tax was reduced during the period 1967-71. Therefore, the automatic growth component contains an unestimable negative discretionary effect.) Though the estimation procedure used here is rough, the normative intent is to divide city taxes into those that are income elastic—that is, those whose yield rises automatically at a faster rate than income—and those that are not.

Table 2.2 shows increases in revenues from the nine major taxes and in personal income from 1967 to 1971. Because real property tax rates were increased, there is a divergence between the total percent increase and the automatic percent increase. (To calculate this figure, the effective property tax rate for 1967 was applied to the base in 1971.) Since there were no discretionary changes for the other taxes over this period, all revenue growth is considered automatic. It is evident that the automatic component of income tax revenue growth far outpaced that of the other taxes, and, in fact, only the income tax is elastic with respect to income. Revenues from this tax grew by 53 percent—or 1.58 times faster than total personal income between 1967 and 1971. However, as will be discussed below, the elasticity of this tax has varied greatly from year to year. Sales tax yields were second in automatic growth, increasing at a rate about 11 percent slower than income. The slowest automatic growth is found in the yields of the property tax and other corporation and public

TABLE 2.2

Increases in Personal Income and Major
Tax Revenues in New York City, 1967-71

	Percent Increase 1967-71		Ratio of Revenue Increase to Income Increase		Rank in Income Elasticity
	Total	Automatic	Total	Automatic	
Personal income	33.56	—	—	—	—
Property tax	37.02	19.83	1.10	0.59	4
Resident income and commuter earnings tax	52.91	52.91	1.58	1.58	1
Business income tax					
General corporation tax	24.63	24.63	0.73	0.73	3
Other corporation taxes	13.66	13.66	0.41	0.41	5
Sales tax	30.02	30.02	0.89	0.89	2

Sources: Property tax revenue based on figures from Reports of the Finance Administrator to the Council of the City of New York for the Fiscal Years 1966/67-1970/71 (New York: Council of the City of New York, 1966-71). "Personal Income, New York City" (unpublished tables, Bureau of Labor Statistics). Comptroller of the City of New York, Annual Report (New York: Office of the Comptroller, 1967-1971).

utilities taxes, both of which increased by less than 20 percent, a rate less than two-thirds that of the growth of income.

It was noted above that there were discretionary changes in 1972 for certain of these taxes. The revenue effects of these discretionary actions may be estimated by assuming that the automatic growth rate of each tax between 1971 and 1972 remained equal to that observed for the 1967-71 period. The results of this analysis are presented in Table 2.3. As was also true in the earlier period (during which rates were constant), relative income tax revenue increases are greatest. In this instance, revenues increased by 122 percent, of which 27 percent may be allocated to automatic growth and 95 percent to the increase in the tax rate. The other corporation and public utilities taxes and the general corporation tax revenues increased

71

by 36 percent and 31 percent, respectively. Automatic and discretionary growth of the general corporation tax was 7 percent and 24 percent, while for the other corporation and public utilities taxes, automatic growth was 29 percent and discretionary growth, 7 percent. Only a small rate increase occurred for the property tax, and none for the sales tax. For these two taxes, the respective increases in yield for the year were both 5 percent.

The overall impact of these differential growth rates among city tax yields, as well as of the substantial rate increases, has caused the gradual, but consistent, diminution of the relative importance of the property tax. However, the effects of the increase in the property tax limits in 1969 are reflected in the increase in the proportion of total locally raised revenues produced by this tax in 1971.[5] Over the five-year life-span of the income tax, the proportion of total city tax revenues yielded by the property tax has fallen by 3.6 percentage points, from 52.4 percent to 47.8 percent of total revenue—half the amount of total decrease over the past two decades. (See Table 2.4.) With respect to the income tax, the powerful impact of rate increase and progressive rate structure can be easily seen. As a result of tax base growth, the yields from this tax increased from 4.3 percent to 4.9 percent of total revenue between 1967 and 1971. Between 1971 and 1972, however, they jumped from 4.9 percent to 9.6 percent of total revenues.

In summary, the income tax, even considering its relatively short life, has proved to be the most dynamic element in the city tax system. This can be attributed to both the automatic and the discretionary components of income tax revenue growth, which, on the one hand, impose increasing average tax rates as income grows and, on the other hand, have increased the entire family of rates. However, since the income tax in New York City is a relatively minor revenue source and constitutes less than 10 percent of total city government receipts, its dynamic performance is not reflected in the performance of the whole city government revenue structure.

Although the property tax is still the city's major locally raised revenue producer, its dominance is gradually declining. This is because the base has grown more slowly than income and because legal tax limits have restricted discretionary rate increases. Revenue from both the sales and the general corporation taxes have declined as a proportion of total revenues since 1967. For the general corporation tax, this decline occurred in spite of a revenue increase due to discretionary changes in the tax rate in 1972. The sales tax declined as a proportion of revenues throughout the period, while the special corporation (including public utilities) tax surpassed its 1967 proportion in 1972, following discretionary changes in some rates. In total, the share of total locally raised revenue associated

TABLE 2.3

Automatic and Discretionary Components of Tax Revenue Growth in New York City, 1971-72

	Revenue (in millions of dollars)		Percent Increase		
	1971	1972	Automatic	Discretionary	Total
Property tax	2,080.0	2,188.0	4.95	0.24	5.19
Resident income and commuter earnings Tax	199.4	443.2	26.97	95.23	122.20
Business income Tax					
General corporation Tax	183.3	239.9	7.43	23.45	30.88
Other corporation taxes	100.5	136.8	28.80	7.29	36.09
Sales Tax	493.6	519.7	5.29*	0.00	5.29

*Actual increase.

Sources: Property tax revenue based on figures from Reports of the Finance Administrator to the Council of the City of New York for the Fiscal Years 1970/71-1971/72 (New York: Council of the City of New York, 1971-72); Comptroller of the City of New York, Annual Report (New York: Office of the Comptroller, 1971-72).

TABLE 2.4

Major Taxes as Percentages of Locally Raised Revenues in New York City, 1967-72

Fiscal Year	Property Tax	Sales Tax	Resident Income and Commuter Earnings Tax	General Corporation Tax	Other Corporation Taxes*	Total
1967	52.4	12.6	4.3	6.1	2.9	78.3
1968	49.7	12.4	5.1	6.0	2.4	75.6
1969	49.6	12.7	5.8	6.0	2.7	76.8
1970	48.6	12.0	5.3	5.2	2.6	73.7
1971	50.9	12.1	4.9	4.5	2.5	74.9
1972	47.8	11.3	9.6	5.2	3.0	76.9

*includes taxes on financial, transportation, insurance, and public utilities corporations.

Source: Comptroller of the City of New York, Annual Report (New York: Office of the Comptroller, 1961-72).

with these taxes declined between 1967 and 1971 but increased again as a result of discretionary rate changes in 1971.

Comparisons with Other Large Cities

The historical data presented above give some picture of the revenue performance of the New York City government over the past decade. This performance is now placed in context through comparison with other governments in large cities in the United States. Unfortunately, the more detailed income elasticity estimates may not be replicated here, and so comparison centers around the levels of the relevant variables and on growth rates in aggregate measures.

A comparison of the revenue performance of the governments of the 10 largest cities in the United States is given in Table 2.5. These data are subject to a major comparability problem—which relates primarily to education finance. Of these 10 cities, seven have independent school districts; in the remaining three—New York City, Baltimore, and Washington, D.C.—school finances are a responsibility of city government. Naturally, city government revenues in those cities with dependent school systems are greater than the average of per capita revenues in all 10 cities—that is, $763 as compared to $373. Among the cities with dependent school systems, per capita general revenues in New York City ($838), while greater than those in Baltimore ($618), were less than those in Washington, D.C. ($908). While per capita revenues in the three cities with dependent school systems generally increased at a more rapid rate than those in cities with independent school districts, the rate of growth in New York City (16.2 percent) was lower than that in both Baltimore (21.1 percent) and Washington, D.C. (18.5 percent) and was also exceeded by the growth rate of revenues in Philadelphia (16.6 percent).

With regard to per capita revenues raised from own sources, similar differences exist between cities with dependent and independent school districts. Own source revenues in New York ($454), Baltimore ($285), and Washington, D.C. ($581) in 1970 were high in relation to the other cities. However, the rate of increase in per capita revenues raised from own sources in New York City (7.6 percent) was lower than that in any of the other nine largest cities.

The percent of total revenues raised from own sources declined between 1960 and 1970 in New York City, Baltimore, Washington, D.C., Los Angeles, and Chicago; however, the decline was greatest in New York City.

While the property tax remains a principal source of revenue in all cities, its importance declined in all cities except Chicago. The fact that the cities with dependent school systems are least reliant

TABLE 2.5

Comparison of Per Capita General Revenues for 10 Largest U.S. Cities, 1966 and 1970

City	Per Capita Total General Revenues (dollars)		Average Annual Percent Increase 1966-70	Per Capita General Revenues Raised from Own Sources (dollars)		Average Annual Percent Increase 1966-70	Percent of Total General Revenues Raised from Own Sources		Percent of Total General Revenues from Property Taxes	
	1966	1970		1966	1970		1966	1970	1966	1970
New York City*	509	838	16.2	348	454	7.6	68.4	54.2	35.1	27.9
Baltimore*	335	618	21.1	184	285	13.7	55.2	46.1	41.8	26.3
Washington, D.C.*	526	908	18.4	385	581	12.7	73.4	64.0	22.1	18.6
Chicago	132	183	9.7	105	139	8.1	80.1	75.8	18.5	36.3
Los Angeles	130	188	11.2	110	156	10.5	84.8	82.8	34.4	31.3
Philadelphia	166	276	16.6	142	241	17.4	86.1	87.1	30.5	20.9
Detroit	185	272	11.8	131	197	12.6	70.7	72.6	36.5	30.6
Houston	84	112	8.3	76	108	10.6	91.2	96.3	60.2	46.9
Dallas	89	142	14.9	87	137	14.4	98.5	96.0	64.8	50.7
Cleveland	127	194	13.2	100	170	17.5	76.5	87.4	51.1	38.6
Averages	228	373	14.1	167	247	12.5	73.4	76.2	39.5	32.8

*Cities with dependent school districts.

Sources: U.S. Department of Commerce, Bureau of the Census, City Government Finances, 1965-66 and 1969-70, Series GF-No. 12 and GF70-No.4 (Washington, D.C.: U.S. Government Printing Office, 1966 and 1970). The 1970 population figures used to calculate per capita revenues were obtained from the 1969-70 volume. The 1966 population figures used to calculate per capita revenues were interpolated from 1960 and 1970 Census of Population data, which were taken from both volumes.

on the property tax as a source of general revenues results primarily from the inclusion of federal and state school aid in the general revenues of these cities. From these data, it is clear that the government of New York City, like those of Baltimore and Washington, D.C., raises more revenue per capita and relies less on the property tax and more on external funding than the other seven cities.

In order to evaluate the relative tax effort in New York City, it is necessary to consider revenues raised for education and non-education purposes on a comparable basis. The data in Table 2.6 allow a comparison of the tax effort of overlapping local governments in the 10 largest cities in 1970. (The measures of tax effort should be interpreted as no more than a rough indication of performance relative to ability. They do not necessarily indicate the incidence of taxation—that is, upon whom the ultimate burden rests—nor do they make adjustments for underlying differences in the fiscal capacities of cities.) The data in this table show comparisons of tax-income ratios by classes of tax. They indicate that, relative to the average of the 10 largest cities, tax effort in New York City is high. However, total tax effort in Cleveland and Washington, D.C. was higher. For the property tax, New York City is above the average in school, non-school, and total property tax effort. However, school property tax effort in New York City (2.63) is exceeded by that in Cleveland (4.49) and Los Angeles (3.11), while nonschool property tax effort in New York City (6.23) is exceeded by that in Cleveland (8.52), Philadelphia (8.25), and Los Angeles (7.01). In terms of total property tax effort, New York City (8.86) ranks fourth behind Cleveland (13.01), Los Angeles (10.12), and Philadelphia (9.86).

The importance of nonproperty taxes in New York City, relative to other cities, can be seen in its high nonproperty tax effort (3.96), which exceeds that of all other large cities except Washington, D.C. (9.01). Moreover, a comparison of nonproperty tax to total tax effort clearly indicates the relative importance of nonproperty taxes in New York City; about one-third of New York City's total effort can be attributed to its nonproperty tax efforts, whereas, in all other cities except Washington, D.C., nonproperty tax effort accounts for less than 25 percent of total tax effort.

This brief comparison suggests that, while both per capita total revenues and per capita own source revenues are high in New York City, total revenues have increased at the more rapid rate. Moreover, when tax effort rather than revenues are compared among the 10 largest cities, New York City ranks third in total effort, fourth in property tax effort, and second in nonproperty tax effort.

TABLE 2.6

Comparison of Tax Effort for 10 Largest U.S. Cities, 1970

City	Nonschool Property Tax Effort	School Property Tax Effort	Total Property Tax Effort	School Nonproperty Tax Effort	Total Nonproperty Tax Effort	Total Effort
New York City	6.23	2.63	8.86	0	3.96	12.82
Baltimore	5.65	2.49	8.14	0.90	2.04	11.08
Washington, D.C.	4.37	1.39	4.76	2.85	9.01	14.79
Chicago	4.51	2.33	6.84	0	1.81	8.65
Los Angeles	7.01	3.11	10.12	0	1.35	11.47
Philadelphia	8.25	1.61	9.86	0.62	2.26	12.74
Detroit	5.89	2.42	8.31	0	2.04	10.35
Houston	4.45	2.00	6.45	0	0.59	7.04
Dallas	4.76	2.06	6.82	0	0.91	7.73
Cleveland	8.52	4.49	13.01	0	1.86	14.87
Average	5.96	2.45	7.84	0.99	2.58	11.15

Sources: Tax effort calculations derived from Seymour Sacks et al., "Competition Between Local School and Non-School Functions for the Property Tax Base" (paper presented to the American Association for the Advancement of Sciences, Philadelphia, December 1971). Personal income data taken from "Personal Income, New York City" (unpublished tables, Bureau of Labor Statistics).

TAX BASE AND REVENUE IMPLICATIONS OF CHANGES IN THE COMPOSITION OF ECONOMIC ACTIVITIES IN NEW YORK CITY

The performance of the four principal forms of taxation in New York City is considered in this section with the objective of identifying and measuring the implications of changes in the structure of city economic activity for the base and revenue growth of each of these taxes. To this end, the four parts of this section are concerned with the four principal forms of taxation—property, corporation, personal income, and retail sales. The historical performance of each tax is reviewed relative to its yield and its rate and base structure. The detailed description of the tax structure seems necessary because of the importance of a thorough understanding of the operation of each tax for the purposes at hand. The principal focus, however, is on the variation in the distribution of tax base and tax revenues among industries, and on the revenue implications of changes in the city's economic structure—that is, on changes in the relative importance of these industries in the city economy.

The accuracy of an analysis such as this is heavily dependent on the availability of accurate data showing relationships between tax base and yield and the activities of individual industries. It should be noted at the outset that, unlike previous inquiries into the questions posed in this analysis, this research has benefited from the availability of such data from unpublished state and city government sources. Because the results here do not rely exclusively on inferences from aggregate data, some specific conclusions may be reached about the relative fiscal effects of declines in particular industries. Important is the development of disaggregated data on the base, rates, and revenues of the property, corporate, and personal income taxes.

While these data have greatly facilitated the analysis, there are major limitations, many of which are discussed at some length. Others, particularly those of a more technical nature, have been considered elsewhere and are noted in the text. In general, a major problem is the unevenness of the accuracy of the results, which arises because the data are more accurate and detailed for some taxes than for others. The important point, however, is that, despite these limitations, some measure of success has been achieved in a disaggregated evaluation of the base and rate performance of the principal forms of taxation and an exploration of the implications of a changing economic structure for tax revenues.

The Property Tax

The purpose here is to examine the factors underlying the growth of New York City property tax revenues and to identify and measure the property tax revenue implications of changes in the industrial composition of the city's economic base. To this end, the analysis centers around a discussion of

1. the institutional framework of property taxation as it relates to the definitions of the tax base and the determination of the tax rate;

2. changes that have occurred in statutory and real property tax base—that is, assessed and market values of property, as classified by land use;

3. a methodology by which property values by land-use class may be identified in terms of industrial sectors;

4. variations in property tax base, tax rates and tax revenue by industrial sector; and

5. the implications of these variations for the response of the property tax base and revenues to changes in the composition of the city's economic structure.

More specifically, the first of the discussions provides an overview of the property tax system by briefly describing the process of taxation. The second examines historical trends of components of the property tax system: assessed values, market values, assessment ratios, and statutory and real tax rates. The third is concerned with the changes in the composition of land use and analyzes the changes in property values that occurred between 1961 and 1971 and their effect on the tax base and tax revenues. It focuses on the land-use shifts that have occurred and that have resulted in changes in the level and distribution of tax base and tax liability among the various classes of property and land use.

The fourth item focuses on the problem that arises from the fact that, by convention, statistics related to the taxation of property are collected by land-use, rather than industrial, categories. Specifically, the concern is with the methods to be employed in the identification and measurement of the contribution of the city's industries to the base and revenues of the property tax. This discussion is technical in nature and may be omitted by those not concerned with technical methods. Nonetheless, the methodology described in this subsection permits the components of the property tax system (that is, the tax base, tax rates, and tax revenues) to be related to the industrial composition of the city.

Finally, the fifth discussion reports on the measurement of tax base, tax rates, and tax revenue resulting from the application of this methodology. It focuses on differentials in property tax rates, assessment ratios, and per-employee property tax base and revenues that exist among the city's industries and explores the implication of these differentials for the response of the property tax to changes in the composition of the city's economic structure. Finally, the section closes with a brief summary and evaluation of the findings.

An Overview

Any analysis of the relationship between the composition of economic activities and the yields of the property tax must consider, in some detail, the factors underlying the relationship between tax revenues and the tax base—that is, the value of property. This relationship can be expressed as follows:

$$TR = r(av/mv)(MV) \tag{1}$$

where:

TR	=	tax revenue
r	=	the citywide statutory tax rate
(av/mv)	=	the assessment ratio
MV	=	the market (or full) value of real property

By state law, market (or full) value is the value of property upon which the property tax is applied. This being the case, it is the market value of taxable property that constitutes the actual base of the property tax.[6] However, the tax assessor usually assesses property for purposes of taxation at some level that is lower than the market value. The assessment ratio (av/mv) represents the proportion of market value the tax assessor enters on the tax roll.

It is assessed value upon which the statutory tax rate (r) is levied, and the product of the tax rate times assessed value yields the amount of revenue raised through property taxation. Although the property tax is levied on assessed values, the practice of assessing property at less than full market value in no way constrains the amount of revenues that may be raised, because the level at which the statutory tax rate is set is determined by the total market, rather than the assessed, value of property.[7] For this reason, the statutory tax rate is misleading with regard to the size of the "burden" imposed by property taxation.* A more appropriate measure of the property tax burden is the <u>real tax rate</u>, the rate at which the market value

---

*As used here, "burden" refers to the liabilities imposed by the taxation of property in relation to the value of property. It is not meant to imply anything about the question of incidence—that is, to whom the actual liability of the property tax accrues.

of property is taxed. In equation (1), the real tax rate is given as the product of the statutory tax rate (r) and assessment ratio (av/mv). Tax revenue may therefore be viewed either as the application of the real tax rate to market value or as the application of the statutory tax rate to assessed value.

In spite of the operational ease of increasing the statutory tax rate, the city cannot raise unlimited amounts of revenue through property taxation, since the total amount of revenue that the city can raise is legally limited in two ways.[8] First, to finance operating expenditures in any year, the city is allowed to levy taxes in an amount not exceeding 2.5 percent of a five-year average of full values, less the amount that is used to service short-term budget anticipation notes, revenue anticipation notes, and tax anticipation notes.* The service of long-term debt is not included in operating expenditures; hence, property tax levies for debt service expenditures are allowed over and above the tax limit. Thus, in any given year, the nominal tax rate is determined by dividing the constitutionally limited general revenue levies plus revenues for debt service by the assessed value of property, net of exemptions. However, the amount of total debt is limited to an amount equal to 10 percent of a five-year average of full values. This limit on debt provides the second (indirect) limit on property tax revenues. (Technically, the limit refers to the amount of revenue which may be raised. However, because assessed value is fixed in any one year, the tax rate—the ratio of tax revenue to assessed value—is also limited.)

The first part of the tax limit—that on operating expenditures and temporary debt—has existed since 1884 and was increased several times before it reached its current level of 2.5 percent of a five-year average of full value.† The second part of the tax limit is indirect, because, rather than limiting tax collections, it limits the amount of debt for which the city may contract—that is, it places a limit on the amount of debt to be serviced from operating resources. However, it should be noted that, in addition to debt controlled by the debt limit,

————————————

*Constitutionally, the city must subtract the service of these notes from its tax limit. Operationally, the effect of this practice is to move this sort of debt finance into the operating expenditure column. The city must also subtract the service of pension fund bonds (for pension systems on a nonactuarial basis) from the total limit, but, because it does not fund pension systems in this manner, this transaction does not apply to the city.[9]

†Full value is defined as equalized full value, which is the total market value of the statutory tax base (assessed value), as estimated by the New York State Board of Equalization and Assessment.[10]

there exists a group of enumerated purposes, generally outlays for capital purchases, for which debt may be contracted outside the debt limit.[11]

Historical Trends

Between 1961 and 1971, the total property tax levy increased by 102 percent from $1.026 billion to $2.08 billion. (See Table 2.7.) During this period, the tax limit increased by 110 percent, while the tax levies under the limit and outside the limit increased by 111 percent and 87 percent respectively. As a percentage of total property tax levy, debt outside the tax limit increased from 35.97 percent in 1961 to a high of 37.2 percent in 1967 and declined to 33.13 percent in 1972. That the city has remained close to its tax limit can be seen in Column (5) of Table 2.7. Of the years shown in Table 2.7, those in which the city was not within 2 percent of its tax limit were 1969 and 1971; however, it was during 1969 that a legal change concerning the calculation of the tax limit was made. As a result of this change, the tax limit was increased. Since that time, the ratio of tax levy to tax limit has increased rapidly and will probably reach the 1961 level again within a short time.

Table 2.8 shows property tax revenues, assessed values, full values, and five-year average full values (in current dollars) for the years 1961 to 1972. During this period, revenue yields grew by $1.17 billion, an increase of 115 percent, or about 10 percent per year. Of this increase, approximately $496 million can be attributed to growth in assessed values. This growth accounts for only slightly less than one-half of the total revenue increase—some 42 percent.* The remaining tax revenue growth is attributable to increases in the statutory tax rate.

It should be noted that only a portion of the rate increases can be associated with an increase in tax burden. This is because, while assessed value increased by only 46 percent, full value increased by 113 percent, and five-year average full value (on which tax limits are calculated) increased by 121 percent—that is to say, the ratio of assessed to full value dropped from 82 percent in 1961 to 57 percent in 1972. Had tax rates remained constant, the relative tax burden with respect to full valuation would have fallen. A portion of the tax rate increase was, therefore, necessary so that tax yields could keep pace with the equalized market value of the tax base.

_____

*This proportion has been calculated by applying the 1961 tax rate to the 1972 assessed value and dividing the result by the actual increase in revenues.

TABLE 2.7

Property Tax Levies, Debt, and Tax Limits for New York City, 1961-72
(dollar figures in thousands of current dollars)

Fiscal Year	Total Levy	Levy Under Tax Limit*	Levy Outside of Limit	Tax Limit*	Levy Under Limit as Percent of Tax Limit	Levy Outside of Limit as Percent of Total Levy
1961	$1,026,833	$ 657,531	$369,352	$ 662,186	99.28	35.97
1963	1,132,680	755,899	376,781	762,785	99.09	33.26
1965	1,311,956	887,473	424,483	888,638	99.87	32.35
1967	1,572,976	987,692	585,284	1,003,571	98.42	37.20
1969	1,737,682	1,122,409	615,273	1,215,237	92.36	35.40
1971	2,080,384	1,390,295	690,089	1,394,794	94.90	33.17
1972	2,188,669	1,463,390	725,279	1,464,790	98.09	33.13

*Expenditures for temporary debt have been included in levy under tax limit and tax limit calculations.

Source: Reports of the Committee on Finance to the Council of the City of New York with Respect to the Budget Tax Levy and Tax Rates for the Fiscal Years 1960/61-1971/72 (New York: Council of the City of New York, 1960-72).

TABLE 2.8

Property Tax Revenues[a], Assessed Values, Full Values, and Five-Year Average Full Values for New York City, 1961-72
(in millions of current dollars)

Fiscal Year	Revenue	Assessed Value	Full Value	Five-Year Average Full Value
1961	1,014	24,994	30,227	26,487
1962	1,052	26,084	33,633	28,390
1963	1,116	27,236	35,122	30,511
1964	1,119	28,557	38,366	33,178
1965	1,292	29,770	40,327	35,545
1966	1,382	30,851	42,942	38,078
1967	1,518	31,734	43,995	40,142
1968	1,615	32,485	51,067[b]	46,367
1969	1,695	33,304	53,182[b]	48,609
1970	1,853	34,292	56,546[b]	51,114
1971	2,080[c]	35,329	61,261[b]	55,791
1972	2,188[c]	36,665	64,667[b]	58,591

[a]Property tax revenues differ from property tax levies (Table 2.7) because the tax levy represents the expected amount of revenues, while actual revenues include delinquent tax payment but are generally not fully collected on a current basis.

[b]Change in definition.

[c]Estimated revenues.

Sources: Reports of the Finance Administrator to the Council of the City of New York for the Fiscal Years 1960/61-1969/70 (New York: Council of the City of New York, 1960-70). This is the source for all revenue figures for 1961-70. Reports of the Committee on Finance to the Council of the City of New York with Respect to the Budget Tax Levy and Tax Rates for the Fiscal Years 1960/61-1971/72 (New York: Council of the City of New York, 1960-72). This is the source for all other figures.

Table 2.9 shows the consistently defined assessment ratios (equalization rates) for both the individual boroughs and the city.[12] It is important to note that in each case, the ratio declined. This means that, over time, the average percentage of market value at which the city assesses property has fallen. In addition, in a given year, a good deal of variation is visible among the boroughs, which is at least partially due to the fact that the city assesses different types of property at different rates and that the composition of land use varies among the boroughs. One- and two-family dwellings that comprise a greater proportion of property in some boroughs than in others tend to be assessed at the lowest rates. (See Table 2.10.) Thus, Manhattan, with the least proportionate amount of this type of property, possesses the highest equalization rate. Richmond, on the other hand, which is largely residential, possesses the lowest equalization rate. That is, on the average, property is assessed at a smaller percentage of its market value in Richmond than is true in the other boroughs.

Table 2.10 shows the variation in equalization rates between different classes of property for the years 1961 and 1969.[13] In both years, the greatest variation exists between residential properties and the other property types. Public utility properties in both years were assessed at the highest proportion of full value, while in both years commercial and industrial properties were assessed similarly. The impact of assessing property at consecutively lower percentages of full value may be seen by comparing the growth rates of assessed values and full value. (See Table 2.8.) Over the 1961-71 period, assessed value grew by 41 percent, while full value (including the definitional change) grew by 103 percent. This means that, unless the assessed values are transformed to full market values through the use of the equalization rate, the real growth of the tax base will be understated by the amount by which the equalization rate changes.

Table 2.11 illustrates the divergence between assessed and market values in terms of tax rates. Column (1) shows statutory tax rates (the actual rates levied upon assessed values), while Columns (3) and (5) show real tax rates, using constantly defined full values and the modified concept of full value respectively.* Using the constantly defined equalization rate, an increase in real tax rates can be observed; for the modified rate, tax burden (in terms of assessed value) appears to have fallen. In this case, the constant equalization rate is the proper benchmark to use, and, when we apply this rate,

---

*The equalization rate used for purposes of state aid did not change in definition over the period. This rate is presented in Column (4), Table 2.11.

TABLE 2.9

Borough and City-wide Equalization Rates for New York City, 1961-72

Fiscal Year	Manhattan	Bronx	Brooklyn	Queens	Richmond	City-wide
1962	0.85	0.95	0.74	0.68	0.66	0.78
1963	0.85	0.87	0.73	0.68	0.67	0.77
1964	0.83	0.82	0.69	0.65	0.65	0.74
1965	0.83	0.81	0.68	0.64	0.64	0.74
1966	0.82	0.77	0.65	0.63	0.63	0.72
1967	0.83	0.76	0.65	0.63	0.64	0.72
1968	0.83	0.77	0.65	0.63	0.64	0.72
1969	0.83	0.75	0.63	0.61	0.62	0.71
1970	0.83	0.74	0.62	0.60	0.60	0.70
1971	0.77	0.73	0.59	0.57	0.54	0.67
1972	0.74	0.72	0.57	0.55	0.51	0.64

Note: The ratios shown are defined consistently and are comparable over the period shown. For this reason, they do not correspond directly to the rate used to calculated the tax limit, the definition of which was changed in 1969.

Sources: Unpublished tables, Bureau of School Financial Aid, Board of Education, City of New York.

TABLE 2.10

City-wide Equalization Rates by Class of Property for New York City, 1961 and 1969

Survey Year	Public Utility Property	Vacant Land	Residential Property	Commercial Property	Industrial Property
1961	0.83	0.64	0.51	0.77	0.75
1969	0.88	0.59	0.36	0.65	0.62

Source: Unpublished data, Board of Equalization and Assessment, State of New York.

TABLE 2.11

Nominal and Effective Property Tax Rates and Equalization
Rates for New York City, 1961-71

Fiscal Year	Nominal Tax Rate (percent)	Constantly Defined Equalization Rate (city-wide)	Constant Effective Tax Rate (percent)	Equalization Rate with Tax Limit Modifications	NonConstant Effective Tax Rate (percent)
1961	4.12	0.82	3.38	0.82	3.38
1963	4.16	0.77	3.20	0.77	3.20
1965	4.41	0.74	3.26	0.74	3.26
1967	4.95	0.72	3.56	0.72	3.56
1969	5.22	0.71	3.70	0.63	3.28
1971	5.89	0.67	3.94	0.58	3.41

Sources: Unpublished data, Board of Education, City of New York. (This is the source for the city-wide, constantly defined equalization rate for 1969 and 1971 only.) Reports of the Committee on Finance to the Council of the City of New York with Respect to the Budget Tax Levy and Tax Rates for the Fiscal Years 1960/61-1970/71 (New York: Council of the City of New York, 1960-71). (This is the source for all other figures.)

86

an increase of 0.56 percentage points (from 3.38 percent to 3.94 percent) is found in the effective tax rate, an increase of only 16.6 percent over the 10-year period.

Changes in Property Values and Relative Tax Shares by Land-Use Class

This subsection reports on changes that have occurred over the 1961-71 period in market and assessed values of real property in New York City. Market and assessed values are analyzed below in terms of the land-use classes used by the City Assessor. The intent here is to describe and analyze: (1) growth in market value of real property; (2) growth in assessed value of real property, as a component of market value; and (3) the distribution of the total city property tax burden among land-use classes. The analysis therefore focuses both on the distribution of market values and the distribution of the total tax liability. Because the city-wide tax rate is levied on assessed values rather than market values and because the relation between assessed and market values is not the same for all land-use classes, the distributions of market values and tax liabilities among land-use classes differ. To illustrate these differences, the analysis considers the contribution of each land-use class to the real property tax base as defined by law (market value), as well as the contribution to total tax receipts (the product of the tax rate multiplied by assessed value). From this it is possible to show how the relative tax burdens of the various land-use classes have shifted over the 10-year period. (It should be stressed that tax burden, as used in this section, refers to the tax impact—that is, the tax liability levied on the land-use class—rather than the actual incidences of the tax. Tax incidence refers to the party who finally pays the tax bill and may differ from the party upon whom the tax is originally levied. When impact and incidence differ, the tax burden is said to have been shifted.)

Two principal findings emerge: (1) growth in the market value of a single land-use class does not ensure a corresponding growth in the assessed value of that property classification; and (2) when the market value and assessed value of a single property class grow at different rates, the relative shares of the total tax levy borne both by the single class and by all other classes of land-use change.

Columns (1) and (2) of Table 2.12 present a comparison of the growth rates of market and assessed values of ordinary real property by land-use class. (Because of their special nature, tax-exempt and special-franchise and public-utility properties have been omitted from this discussion. For a discussion of the growth in the value of those properties, see Chapter 1, section entitled "Changes in Property Values and Land Use," above.) These data show the differential

TABLE 2.12

Growth Rates of Market and Assessed Values and
Proportions of Total Increase in Market and Assessed Values
by Land-Use Class for New York City, 1961-71
(percent)

| | Percent Increase | | Contribution to Total Increase in * | |
	Market Value	Assessed Value	Market Value	Assessed Value
One-family dwelling	68.7	10.3	15.1	3.2
Two-family dwelling	104.1	29.9	18.4	7.6
Walkup apartment	25.0	12.8	5.4	5.5
Elevator apartment	103.2	77.7	24.8	37.9
Warehouse	87.7	48.4	1.3	1.5
Factory	78.8	41.1	3.2	3.6
Garage	32.9	18.0	0.9	1.0
Hotel	70.2	40.6	1.5	1.7
Theater	-7.2	-20.3	-0.1	-0.3
Store	48.8	32.5	3.0	4.1
Loft	33.3	9.0	2.2	1.3
Miscellaneous	68.8	49.9	2.9	4.1
Office building	128.6	87.8	20.5	28.3
Vacant land	32.5	9.2	1.0	11.2
Total			100.0	100.0

*Columns may not add to total due to rounding.

Sources: City of New York Tax Commission, Annual Report (New York: Tax Commission, 1961 and 1971); market values calculated from unpublished information from the New York State Department of Equalization and Assessment.

88

effects of the growth in property values by land-use class on the property tax limit and on the statutory base of the property tax.* The deviation between growth in market and assessed values among land-use classes illustrates the existence of significant variations in the degree to which different land-use classes have contributed to the growth in the property tax limit and revenues and in the tax base. With the exception of theaters, whose market and assessed values both declined, the estimated growth in market value in all land-use classes exceeded the growth in assessed values. However, between land-use classes, the difference in the ratios of market to assessed value have grown.

The most rapidly growing sectors of land use (those whose market value grew at a rate greater than that of the city as a whole) were office buildings, two-family dwellings, elevator apartments, warehouses, factories, and miscellaneous buildings. Of these, office buildings, elevator apartments, warehouses, factories, and miscellaneous buildings experienced relatively large increases in assessed values. The largest differences between the rates of growth in market and assessed values occurred in the categories of one- and two-family dwellings; the smallest occurred in office and miscellaneous buildings.

The relative contributions of each land-use class to the total increase in the property tax limit and to property tax revenues are given in Column (3), and the relative share of each class in the total increase in tax liability is given in Column (4). These columns illustrate vividly the impact of differential market and assessed value growth rates on the property tax system.

With one exception—theaters—all land-use classes contributed to the increase in the property tax limit and therefore to the growth in tax revenues. However, as can be seen in the table, the growth in four land-use classes—elevator apartments, office buildings, and one-family and two-family dwellings—accounted for 78.8 percent of

---

*While the tax liability is the product of the tax rate and tax base, the fact that the same tax rate is applied to all land-use classes renders unnecessary consideration of tax rate changes in the relative comparisons of market and assessed values among land use classes (see note 15). Also omitted from the discussion is consideration of the five-year average in determining the contribution of each land-use class to tax limit increases. While this analysis treats the market value change between 1961 and 1971 as the tax limit change, in actuality the change in the tax limit should be calculated by the average of the difference for each class in 1961 and 1971, and the four preceding periods (that is, 1960 and 1970, 1959 and 1969, and so on).

the total market value of ordinary real estate. If walkup apartments are added to the list, the five largest contributors accounted for 84.8 percent of the increase in the market value of ordinary real estate. Since it is the total market value of property that places the limit on the amount of revenue that may be raised through the property tax for current operating expenditures and since the city has taxed property close to the limit, it is clear that the major increase in tax revenues can be attributed to residential and office building properties.

The percentage of growth in assessed values that is allocated to each land-use class indicates the extent to which the liability associated with the revenue increase has been imposed in each land-use class. As indicated in the table, the greatest share of the increased tax liability was imposed on elevator apartments (37.9 percent), office buildings (28.3 percent), and vacant land (11.2 percent). As the share of assessed value increase in these three classes was greater than their share of market value increase, the tax liability imposed on them exceeded their contribution to the limits and revenues of the property tax. On the other hand, the share of the increase in tax liability that accrued to one- and two-family dwellings (3.2 and 7.6 percent, respectively) clearly indicates that revenue increases attributable to these classes greatly exceeded their liability increases. To a much lesser extent, this experience was shared by two classes of property, lofts and theaters. As a result, the tax treatment of these four classes has imposed a tax liability on all other classes of property that exceeds their contribution to the increase in tax base, tax revenues, and tax limits.

The implications of these differential revenue and liability shares are important. Assuming taxation is at the limit, when market values for a property class increase more rapidly than assessed values, the class tends to increase tax limits and therefore tax revenues to a greater extent than its tax liability. As a result, a portion of the revenue increase brought about through the market value increase is shifted to other classes through an increase in the city-wide tax rate.

The effects of the differential growth rates and shares of growth in market and assessed values on the contribution of each land-use class to property tax revenues and liabilities can be seen in Table 2.13, which shows the proportion of total city market and assessed values contained in each land-use class in 1961 and 1971. Because an equal statutory tax rate is levied on all classes of property (the city-wide tax rate), the proportion of total city assessed values accounted for by an individual class is also equal to the proportion of total city property tax revenues for which the class is liable. Of particular interest is the relationship between the proportion of market value contained in a given class and the corresponding proportion

TABLE 2.13

Proportions of Market Value and Assessed Value of Total Relative Tax Shares by Use Class for New York City, 1961 and 1971

	Proportion of Market Value		Proportion of Assessed Value		Relative Tax Share*	
	1961	1971	1961	1971	1961	1971
One-family dwelling	16.59%	15.94%	12.59%	9.84%	0.76	0.62
Two-family dwelling	16.34	15.51	10.44	9.61	0.78	0.62
Walkup apartment	16.18	11.52	17.65	14.10	1.09	1.22
Elevator apartment	18.20	21.05	20.08	25.27	1.10	1.20
Warehouse	1.11	1.19	1.28	1.35	1.15	1.13
Factory	3.06	3.11	3.61	3.61	1.18	1.16
Garage	2.01	1.52	2.20	1.84	1.09	1.21
Hotel	1.57	1.52	1.73	1.72	1.10	1.13
Theater	0.64	0.34	0.70	0.40	1.09	1.18
Store	4.71	3.99	5.20	4.88	1.10	1.22
Loft	5.09	3.87	5.60	4.36	1.10	1.13
Miscellaneous	3.19	3.07	3.47	3.68	1.09	1.20
Office building	12.04	15.67	13.28	17.66	1.10	1.13
Vacant land	2.26	1.70	2.18	1.69	0.96	0.99
Total	100.00	100.00	100.00	100.00		0.99

Note: Columns may not add to total due to rounding.

*Columns (5) and (6) are the result of dividing Columns (3) and (4) by Columns (1) and (2), respectively.

Sources: City of New York Tax Commission, Annual Report (New York: Tax Commission, 1961 and 1971). Market values calculated from unpublished information from the New York State Department of Equalization and Assessment.

of assessed value. The relative tax share is used to illustrate this relationship. This is the proportion of total city property tax revenues for which a given land-use class is liable relative to (divided by) the proportion of the total city market value of property tax base, which is contained in that class—that is, its contribution to tax limits and revenues. The relative tax share, shown in Columns (5) and (6), gives a measure of the rate at which the market value of property in a property class is taxed—the real rate—relative to the average real rate at which the market value of real property is taxed in all use classes.[14] Relative tax shares change as differential changes occur in the rates of assessed and market value growth.[15]

The differential rates of growth in assessed and market values have led to changing proportions of total assessed and market value among land-use classes and, therefore, to significantly changing relative tax shares and real tax rates. Table 2.13 shows that elevator apartments have increased from 18.2 percent of total city market values in 1961, to 21.05 percent in 1971. For assessed values, the increase was from 20.08 percent in 1961 to 25.27 percent in 1971, resulting in an increase from 1.1 to 1.2 in its relative tax share. This means that, in 1961, elevator apartments were subject to a tax liability that was 10 percent higher than that of the city as a whole. As a result of the growth in market values and assessed values for elevator apartments, and value changes in the remaining land-use classes, the relative tax liability borne by elevator apartments in 1971 stood at 1.2, 20 percent higher than it would have been if property in all use classes were taxed at the same real tax rate—that is, if all property had been assessed at the same proportion of market value. Office buildings are similarly affected. The office building share of market value increased from 12.04 percent to 15.67 percent of total values between 1961 and 1971; its assessed value share rose from 13.28 to 17.66, in turn increasing its relative tax share from 1.1 in 1961 to 1.13 in 1971.

Both one-family and two-family dwellings decreased as a proportion of the assessed value total over the 1961-71 period. One-family dwellings dropped from 16.59 percent of total market value in 1961 to 15.94 percent in 1971, and from 12.59 percent of total assessed value in 1961 to 9.84 percent in 1971. The two-family dwelling class increased from 13.34 percent of the total market value in 1961 to 15.51 percent in 1971; its share of assessed value dropped from 10.44 percent in 1961 to 9.61 percent in 1971. As a result of these changes, relative tax shares in both classes dropped. The one-family dwelling category sank from 0.76 in to 0.62 in 1971; for two-family dwellings, the decrease was only slightly more abrupt, from 0.78 in 1961 to 0.62 in 1971. In 1971, both one- and two-family dwellings were liable for tax payments that were 38 percent lower than would have been the case if their proportionate share of city-wide assessed and market values in these classes had been equal.

Factories and warehouses also experienced decreasing tax shares. The warehouse class increased its total share of both potential and statutory values, but because market values grew somewhat more rapidly than assessed values, its relative tax share decreased from 1.15 in 1961 to 1.13 in 1971. The value of factory property increased as a proportion of the total market value but remained constant as a proportion of assessed value. The relative tax share for the factory land-use class decreased from 1.18 in 1961 to 1.16 in 1971.

Only three land-use classes (one- and two-family dwellings and vacant land) possessed relative tax shares of less than unity. ("Unity" means that the proportion of market and assessed value are equal.) In the case of vacant land, the relative tax shares increased over the decade to a level nearly equal to unity. The relative tax shares of warehouses and factories remained well above unity, even while declining over the decade. The remaining classes of land use—walkup apartments, garages, hotels, theaters, store buildings, loft buildings, and miscellaneous buildings—all experienced increasing tax shares over the decade. Thus, real tax rates (tax liability as a proportion of market value) on one- and two-family dwellings and warehouse and factory property declined between 1961 and 1971 relative to those of other classes. Alternatively, the relative real tax rate imposed on all other classes of property increased.

Thus, one- and two-family dwellings, which together have accounted for 33.5 percent of the increase in tax limit and growth in property tax revenues (Table 2.8), have experienced a decline in the real rate of taxation and in their relative contributions to tax liabilities. Office buildings and elevator apartments, the other major contributors to the increase in tax limit and tax revenues, experienced relative increases both in their real tax rates and their share of tax liabilities.

The Value of Property by Industrial Use[16]

While the analysis thus for sheds light on the historic performance of the property tax, the categorization of the data by land-use classes precludes identification of the relationship between components of the property tax and the industrial structure. The purpose of this subsection is to describe briefly the procedures by which the property tax base and revenues can be related to specific industries.

First, the relationship between industrial activity and the tax base (the market value of property) must be specified. Incorporated into this discussion is a consideration of the factors underlying differences in amounts of interindustry tax base contributions. Then the estimation and measurement of the tax base on an industry basis is considered, with a discussion of the data underlying these estimates and an examination of their variations among industries.[17]

Identifying the Industrial Property Tax Base. The relation between the market and assessed value of real property and employment can be expressed by the following identities:

$$MV_i = (Ps)_i(S/E)_iE_i \qquad (2)$$

$$AV_i = (av/mv)_i(Ps)_i(S/E)_iE_i \qquad (3)$$

where:

AV_i = assessed value

$(av/mv)_i$ = the assessment ratios—that is, assessed value divided by the market value

Ps_i = the market value per square foot of the average amount of taxable property with which an employee in the industry works $\left(\text{that is,} = \dfrac{MV_i}{S_i}\right)$

$(S/E)_i$ = the quantity (number of square feet) of taxable property that a worker in the industry has to work with on the average

E_i = employment

i = the industry.

Consider the right-hand side of equations (2) and (3). The component Ps (subscript omitted) represents the price per square foot of space in a given industrial sector. The term $[(S/E)(E)]$, the product of the quantity of space per employee and the level of employment, can be reduced simply to (S), the quantity of space. In the simplest terms, therefore, equations (2) and (3) present a price-times-quantity relationship, which determines the value of a given quantity of floorspace. When (Ps)(S/E)(E) is multiplied by (av/mv), the assessment ratio, the market value of property is translated into assessed value.

The quantity of space has been stated on a per-employee basis for four reasons. First, the activity of an industry is performed by employees within the confines of a structure located on a parcel of land. Structure and land are the principal (property) taxable inputs in the production process of an industry. The (S/E) term simply represents the proportion in which two-inputs—taxable property (that is, structure and land) and labor—are combined in the performance of the industry's operation. When stated on a per-employee basis and multiplied by price (Ps), this term allows a comparison of property tax base—the market value of property—per employee by industry.

Second, employment provides a useful measure of economic activity since, unlike the available alternatives (some of which may be conceptually superior), it is consistently defined and generally available at a detailed level for all industries. Operationally, this means that information regarding employment by industry is readily available; other measures, such as income, are not.

Third, employment is the measure commonly used in the analysis of economic structure. Its use here, therefore, allows a comparison of this with other studies of the urban economy. As was noted, the term Ps, the average value per unit of taxable capital per worker, when multiplied by (S/E), translates the quantity of taxable property into dollar terms—that is, the market value of taxable property per worker in the industry.

Finally, the tax base has been identified in this manner because it provides a means of indirectly estimating the amount of tax base in each industry from data that, while not readily available in published form, can be estimated from information contained in the records of various departments of the New York City government.

The tax liability of an industry can be obtained by multiplying both sides of equation (3) by the nominal tax rate (r). Thus, the total amount of property tax revenues for which an industry is liable (TR_i) may be stated as

$$TR_i = r(av/mv)_i Ps_i (S/E)_i E_i \qquad (4)$$

From equations (2) and (4), the factors underlying differences in property tax base and liabilities among industries can be identified. In general, the larger (smaller) the amount of physical capital associated with the typical worker in an industrial sector—that is, $(S/E)_i$—the larger (smaller) will be the industry's tax base. Similarly, the larger (smaller) the value placed on floorspace in any industry— that is, $(Ps)_i$—the larger (smaller) will be the industry's tax base. Finally, the larger (smaller) the number of employees (that is, E_i), the larger (smaller) will be the tax base of the industry. It is clear, however, that various combinations of differences in the size of these variables may cause substantial differences in interindustry tax base—for example, a small number of workers working with large quantities of high-priced real property may contribute more to the tax base than a large number of workers processing smaller amounts of low-priced real property.

With regard to equation (4), the statutory tax rate (r) is not a source of variation in the contribution of different industries to tax liability because it is levied equally on the assessed value of all taxable property. However, the rate at which the market value of property is taxed, the real tax rate—r multiplied by $(av/mv)_i$—will differ among industries to the extent they are assessed at different rates of market value. This means that assessment policy (or assessment error) enters into the tax system as a separate source of tax liability variation.[18] It should be noted that, in the previous subsection, it was found that the variation in assessment ratios is greater between residential and nonresidential properties (and among types of residential property) than among nonresidential property uses.

The tax liability of any industry can change only when one or more of the component variables of equation (4) changes. In this instance, it is useful to consider two sets of variables: policy variables, determined by city fiscal policy, and private market variables, determined by industrial behavior. When the property tax is levied in amounts less than its limit, the city may increase tax revenues independent of private sector activity, by modifying either the statutory tax rate or the assessment ratio. The most common case is for both to be somewhat adjusted in each fiscal year. In fact, the assessment ratio has fallen consistently since 1961 (that is, assessments have failed to keep pace with market value) and the statutory tax rate has been increased annually. Thus, it appears that the city adjusts the statutory tax rate largely to correct for the changing assessments ratio.[19] The point to be made, however, is that, when the tax is levied below limit, both total revenues and the distribution of tax liabilities among industries can be changed by changes in assessment ratios and the tax rate. However, when the tax is levied at (or very near to) its limits, as it has been, changes in the tax rate or assessment ratio cannot be used to increase the amount of revenues for ordinary operating expenses.

Under these conditions, revenues for operating expenses can be increased only if there is an increase in the tax base—that is, the market value of property. It should be noted, however, that when the property tax is levied at its limit, changes in the tax rate and assessment ratios, although not affecting total revenues, will alter the distribution of tax liabilities among industries. Relative tax burden is then distributed in direct relation to the size of the assessment ratio of the individual industry. Differences in property tax revenues accounted for by the market-determined industrial base appear in equations (2) through (4) as differences in space per worker and differences in price per square foot of space. While some observers prefer to view this portion of the tax base (indeed, of the overall urban economy) as a mutually determined configuration of economic behavior, it is analytically useful to separate these variables in order to analyze differences in the tax base associated with various industries, which can be accounted for by differences in price and quantity of real property.

Because productive techniques differ among industries, different industries are likely to employ workers and taxable capital in different physical amounts. In addition, the market values of any physical amount of property are likely to vary among industries, depending on the nature of the activity for which it is used. As indicated in equation (2), industrial differences in the market value can be attributed to differences in the quantity and/or value of taxable property in the industry. As it is the market value of taxable property that underlies the tax limit, differentials among industries in the amount and/or value of taxable property result in underlying differential industry contributions to the property tax revenues. It should be noted, however, that the contribution of an industry to tax revenues through its contribution to the tax base (that is, the market value of property) may differ from its direct contribution to tax revenues (that is, its tax liability or tax payments). Tax liability for any given statutory tax rate is determined by assessed rather than market value of property. As the assessment ratio may differ among industries, the tax liabilities of individual industries may differ from their contribution to the tax base, tax limits, and therefore overall tax revenue. (For example, an increase in market value accompanied by a zero increase in assessed value will add to the overall tax base but will not increase the tax liability of the firm. However, due to the increase in market value, the tax limit will increase and, if the city increases the overall tax rate in response to the tax limit change, the revenue contribution of the firm will increase, as will the tax liabilities of all other firms.)

Interindustrial Variations in the Property Tax System. We now turn to the questions of variation in the tax base (market value of taxable property) among industries. Table 2.4 presents the estimated value of the components of the property tax base as described in equation (2). Column (1) of Table 2.14 shows the estimated amount of floorspace per worker in each sector, and Column (2) shows the estimated value of one square foot of floorspace in this use. Both square feet and prices have been calculated from disaggregated data sets; hence, manufacturing as shown here is the weighted average of the two-digit-level SIC (Standard Industrial Classification) manufacturing industries.[20] The values calculated for the price of floorspace are also composite in a vertical sense—that is, they represent a summary from a broader data set but have also been aggregated horizontally in order to consider the various uses of space in each industry.

Underlying interindustry variations in tax base and tax liability per employee are significant differences in both the usage of space (with respect to intensity) and the price of the space used. Such sectors as mining, finance, and insurance, all of which are primarily office functions in New York City, possess similar prices. Real estate, too, is an office activity, and its somewhat lower price is representative of the fact that this activity is spread throughout the city, while the others (mining, finance, and insurance) are primarily based in Manhattan. Outside Manhattan, the value of office space is less than in the central borough.

Conversely, manufacturing, transportation, and services all possess relatively low values of floorspace. This is because their space is generally used for production or warehousing and is subject to much less intense use than would be true in, for example, finance. Because, ultimately, the use to which it is put determines the value

TABLE 2.14

Estimated Floorspace per Worker and Market
Value per Square Foot of Floorspace in
New York City by Industry, 1969

Industry	Floorspace per Worker (in square feet)	Market Value per Square Foot of Floorspace (in dollars)
Agriculture	227	18.07
Mining	227	30.44
Manufacturing	310	10.13
Transportation	1,257	9.05
Wholesale trade	705	14.24
Retail trade	239	19.49
Finance	173	28.62
Insurance	145	27.57
Real estate	1.041	23.66
Services	429	10.70

Source: Calculated from unpublished data, Department of City Planning and Department of Real Property Assessment, City of New York.

of floorspace, those industries that use space less intensively carry on activities in lower-priced facilities. This is evident from the fact that the relationship between floorspace per worker and price of floorspace is generally one of inverse proportions. Using the quantity of floorspace per worker to serve as a measure of intensity in use—Column (1), Table 2.14—reveals that office-oriented industries tend to use rather small amounts of high-priced space, while production- and warehouse-oriented industries use larger amounts of lower-priced space. This, of course, should not be unexpected, it the relationships shown in equations (2) and (3) describe the workings of the city land market.

This also points to the fact that viewing either prices of space or quantities of space separately will bring about misleading conclusions regarding the property tax base contributions of workers in different sectors. In those cases where relatively large amounts of space and high prices are combined, such as in real estate and transportation, individual contributions will be high. Where both intensity of use and price are low, such as in manufacturing, the property tax base contribution of workers is low. Ultimately, it is the interactions of both intensity and price that will determine the tax base contribution of workers in different industrial sectors.

Table 2.15 shows the variation of effective or real tax rates (the rate at which market value is taxed) and assessment ratios (the proportion of market value at which real property is assessed) among industries. As indicated there, transportation is assessed at the smallest proportion of market value (62.13 percent). Therefore, the real tax rate for this sector is correspondingly the lowest of all sectors. This is because an equal nominal tax rate is levied on all sectors—that is, assessed value in all sectors is taxed at the same rate. All variations in the rate at which market value is taxed may, therefore, be attributed to variations in the rate at which the market value of property is assessed. Following transportation, services is assessed at the second smallest proportion of market value (63.4 percent) and taxed at the second lowest real rate (3.31 percent). Retail trade is assessed at the highest proportion of market value (67.73 percent) and incurs the highest real tax rate (3.54 percent), with agriculture second (with an assessment ratio of 67.49 percent and a real tax rate of 3.52 percent).

The point to be made here is that slight differences in assessment translate directly into differential rates of taxation. Thus, while a 6.2 percent difference in rate of assessment seems perfectly defensible, and, indeed, perhaps unavoidable, the resulting differential tax rates (again a 6.2 percent differential) are certainly undesirable, unless resulting from explicit policy.

TABLE 2.15

Estimated Effective Property Tax Rates and
Assessment Ratios in New York City by Industry, 1969
(as percent)

	Effective Tax Rate*	Assessment Ratio
Agriculture	3.52	67.49
Mining	3.39	64.98
Manufacturing	3.41	65.39
Transportation	3.24	62.13
Wholesale trade	3.38	64.84
Retail trade	3.54	67.73
Finance	3.40	65.21
Insurance	3.41	65.37
Real estate	3.45	66.06
Services	3.31	63.40

*The effective tax rate (that is, the rate levied on market value) was calculated by applying the assessment ratio in Column (2) to the 1969 city-wide tax rate (0.0522).

Source: David J. Bjornstad, "Components of the Real Property Tax Base: Model Development with Empirical Application to Selected Industries in New York City" (unpublished dissertation, Syracuse University, Syracuse, N.Y., 1973).

Tax liabilities and tax base per employee are included in Table 2.16 for the 10 industries in which data were available. As indicated in the first column of that table, real estate contributes the largest amount of tax liability per employee ($860), while manufacturing contributes the least ($107). In fact, insurance, incurring the second lowest liability per employee ($136), contributes $29 more per employee in tax payments than manufacturing. Services, incurring the fourth lowest liability ($152), paid $45 more per employee than manufacturing.

A similar pattern is evident in the case of tax base (market value) per employee. Real estate registers the largest base ($24,926) and manufacturing the smallest ($3,141) per employee. Again, both insurance ($3,997) and agriculture ($4,103), the second and third smallest industries in terms of tax base per employee, contain significantly larger tax bases per employee than does manufacturing.

TABLE 2.16

Estimated Property Tax Liability and Base
per Employee in New York City by Industry, 1969
(dollars)

Industry	Property Tax Liability	Property Tax Base
Agriculture	144	4,103
Mining	234	6,910
Manufacturing	107	3,141
Transportation	369	11,377
Wholesale trade	243	7,192
Retail trade	165	4,657
Finance	168	4,952
Insurance	136	3,997
Real estate	860	24,926
Services*	152	4,592

*Includes only business services.

Source: David J. Bjornstad, "Components of the Real Property Tax Base: Model Development with Empirical Application to Selected Industries in New York City" (unpublished dissertation, Syracuse University, Syracuse, New York, 1973).

Having identified the contributions of each industry to the property tax base and liability of the property tax, the analysis turns now to the question that ultimately is raised when analyzing the industrial composition of tax liability and tax revenue—that is, what is the effect of the changing composition of economic activities on the base and revenues of the tax? Table 2.17 allows an estimation of this effect to be made. The coefficients in the table indicate the number of jobs in the column industry that would be necessary to replace a job in the corresponding row industry and still maintain constant nonresidential property tax liabilities. Explained for manufacturing (the third row), they indicate that the replacement of a manufacturing job requires the addition of 0.74 agricultural jobs, 0.46 mining jobs, 0.29 transportation jobs, 0.65 retailing jobs, 0.12 real estate jobs, and 0.71 service sector jobs.

The variation in replacement requirements is quite large among industries. The easiest jobs to replace are those in manufacturing,

101

TABLE 2.17

Estimated Employment Replacement Requirements for Constant Nonresidential Property Tax Liabilities in New York City by Industry, 1969

Replaced Industry	Replacing Industry									
	Agriculture	Mining	Manufacturing	Transportation	Wholesale Trade	Retail Trade	Finance	Insurance	Real Estate	Services
Agriculture	1.00	0.62	1.35	0.39	0.59	0.88	0.86	1.06	0.17	0.95
Mining	1.62	1.00	2.19	0.64	0.96	1.42	1.39	1.72	0.27	1.54
Manufacturing	0.74	0.46	1.00	0.29	0.44	0.65	0.64	0.79	0.12	0.71
Transportation	2.55	1.57	3.44	1.00	1.52	2.24	2.19	2.71	0.43	2.43
Wholesale trade	1.68	1.04	2.27	0.66	1.00	1.48	1.44	1.78	0.28	1.60
Retail trade	1.14	0.70	1.54	0.45	0.68	1.00	0.98	1.21	0.19	1.08
Finance	1.17	0.72	1.57	0.46	0.69	1.02	1.00	1.24	0.20	1.11
Insurance	0.94	0.58	1.27	0.37	0.56	0.83	0.81	1.00	0.16	0.90
Real estate	5.95	3.67	8.02	2.33	3.53	5.22	5.10	6.30	1.00	5.65
Services	1.05	0.67	1.42	0.41	0.62	0.92	0.90	1.11	0.18	1.00

Note: Figures in the columns indicate the number of jobs in the respective sectors necessary to replace a job in the row sectors and still maintain constant property tax revenues.

Source: Calculated from Table 2.16.

TABLE 2.18

Estimated Employment Replacement Requirements for Constant Nonresidential Property Tax Base in New York City by Industry, 1969

Replaced Industry	Replacing Industry									
	Agriculture	Mining	Manufacturing	Transportation	Wholesale Trade	Retail Trade	Finance	Insurance	Real Estate	Services
Agriculture	1.00	0.59	1.31	0.36	0.57	0.88	0.83	1.03	0.16	0.89
Mining	1.68	1.00	2.20	0.61	0.96	1.48	1.40	1.73	0.28	1.50
Manufacturing	0.77	0.45	1.00	0.28	0.44	0.67	0.63	0.79	0.13	0.68
Transportation	2.77	1.65	3.62	1.00	1.58	2.44	2.30	2.85	0.46	2.48
Wholesale trade	1.75	1.04	2.29	0.63	1.00	1.54	1.45	1.80	0.29	1.57
Retail trade	1.14	0.67	1.48	0.41	0.65	1.00	0.94	1.17	0.19	1.01
Finance	1.21	0.72	1.58	0.44	0.69	1.06	1.00	1.24	0.20	1.08
Insurance	0.97	0.58	1.27	0.35	0.56	0.86	0.81	1.00	0.16	0.87
Real estate	6.08	3.61	7.94	2.19	3.46	5.35	5.03	6.24	1.00	5.43
Services	1.12	0.66	1.46	0.40	0.64	0.99	0.93	1.15	0.18	1.00

Note: Figures in the columns indicate the number of jobs in the respective sectors necessary to replace a job in the row sectors and still maintain constant property tax base.

Source: Calculated from Table 2.16.

while the most difficult are those in real estate. The results of the employment trend out of manufacturing and wholesaling and into services are quite interesting. Specifically, the replacement of a manufacturing job requires 0.71 service sector jobs, while wholesaling requires 1.6 service sector jobs in order to maintain constant property tax liabilities.

Table 2.18 allows a similar analysis for property tax base per employee. It should be noted, however, that, since it is the tax base that determines the tax limit and the amount of revenues that can be raised, the coefficients of Table 2.18 refer to both the tax base and tax limit and, when the tax is levied at or close to its limit, to tax revenues. The interpretation of the coefficients follows as before. For manufacturing, the replacement of one job requires the addition of 0.45 mining jobs, 0.67 retailing jobs, 0.13 real estate jobs, and 0.68 service sector jobs, to maintain a constant nonresidential property tax base.

Manufacturing is the easiest industry to replace, while real estate is the most difficult. Further, the present trend of a shift in employment from manufacturing and wholesaling into services appears a mixed blessing. While these coefficients suggest that the replacement of a manufacturing job requires 0.68 service employees, they also suggest that the replacement of a wholesaling job requires the addition of 1.57 service sector jobs.

Summary and Implications. This analysis suggests that property tax revenues from the taxation of nonresidential property are sensitive to changes in the structure of employment. The clearest cases are manufacturing, where an employee is most easily replaced, and real estate, where replacement is most difficult. Applied to the shifts that have been occurring in the New York City economy, the implications are not for buoyancy in property tax receipts. For example, the loss of a manufacturing job is easily replaced, but the loss of a job in either wholesale or retail trade is more difficult to replace. In terms of "gaining" sectors, a services job is "superior" to only manufacturing, insurance, and agriculture. The biggest "gaining" sector—government, (not shown here)—is "inferior" to all other jobs in that property held by government for its own use is exempt from local property taxation. Quantification of the effects of employment restructure are considered (for all taxes) in the concluding section of this chapter.

Corporation and Public Utilities Taxes

The goal of this section is to evaluate the revenue implications of changes in the industrial composition of the city's economic base for those taxes imposed directly on corporations and public utilities. The analysis centers on a review of the performance of these taxes and on the estimation of (1) differential contribution by the city's industries to corporation and public utilities tax revenues, (2) differential tax rates among industries, (3) industry differentials in per employee tax base and tax revenue, and (4) the implications of these differentials for the response of the corporate tax revenues to structural changes in the city's economic base. Accordingly, this analysis is presented in five steps. In the first, the growth in corporation and public utilities tax revenues is considered. In the second, the derivation of statistics on the distribution of actual tax yields is described, and these data are analyzed on an industry-by-industry basis. In the third, the array of effective tax rates and tax payments as a proportion of the tax base, as among industries, will be presented and discussed. In the fourth, interindustry differentials in tax revenues per employee will be analyzed and their implications explored. The fifth considers the effect of changing employment patterns on tax base and revenue.

An Overview

In 1967 and 1972, total (general, financial, transportation, and insurance) corporation and public utilities taxes accounted for 9 percent and 8.2 percent of the locally raised revenues of the New York City government. (See Table 2.4.) Of the total amount of these taxes, the general corporation tax accounted for 62.5 percent and 63.7 percent in 1967 and 1972, respectively. (See Table 2.19.)

The revenue yields of the taxes on corporations and public utilities and their relation to personal income during the period between 1961 and 1971 are given in Table 2.19. The total revenues of the taxes on corporations and public utilities increased greatly, following the change in tax rates imposed in 1971. However, total revenues from these taxes increased by 59 percent between 1967 and 1972. For the period following the 1966 change in the tax structure, but prior to the 1971 change in the general corporation tax rate, the growth in tax revenues was 21 percent. During the period 1967 to 1970, revenues from the general corporation tax increased by 24.6 percent, while the combined revenues of the insurance, finance, transportation, and public utilities taxes increased by 13.6 percent. Thus, the revenues from the general corporation tax have accounted for more than 60 percent of the combined revenues from these taxes.

As a proportion of city income, the revenues yielded by the financial, insurance, transportation, and public utilities taxes and the general corporation tax have declined from 0.24 percent to 0.2 percent and 0.4 percent to 0.37 percent, respectively, between 1967

TABLE 2.19

Corporation and Public Utilities Tax Revenues and City Income in New York City, 1967-72
(dollar figures in millions of dollars)

Fiscal Year	All Corporation* and Public Utilities Tax Revenues	General Corporation Tax Revenues	Public Utilities Finance Transportation, Insurance Tax Revenues	General Corporation Tax as Percent of All Corporation and Public Utilities Tax Revenues	City Personal Income	Finance, Transportation Insurance, and Public Utilities Tax Revenues as Percent of City Income	General Corporation Tax Revenues as Percent of City Income	All Corporation* and Public Utilities Tax Revenues as Percent of City Income
1967	$235.52	$147.09	$ 88.43	62.5	$36,268	0.24	0.40	0.64
1968	280.23	199.55	80.68	71.2	38,404	0.21	0.51	0.72
1969	305.99	211.76	94.23	69.2	42,097	0.22	0.50	0.72
1970	301.56	202.47	99.09	67.1	45,342	0.21	0.44	0.65
1971	283.82	183.31	100.51	64.6	48,439	0.20	0.37	0.57
1972	376.70	239.91	136.78	63.7	N.A.	N.A.	N.A.	N.A.

N.A.: Not available

*Includes general finance, insurance, and transportation corporation taxes.

Sources: Comptroller of the City of New York, Annual Report (New York: Office of the Comptroller, 1967-72). Personal income data are taken from "Personal Income, New York City" (Unpublished tables, Bureau of Labor Statistics). The income figures shown for each fiscal year are for calendar year, that is, 1966/67 = 1966.

and 1970. In total, then, the sum of these two tax sources have declined from 0.64 in 1967 to 0.57 in 1972. (See Column [8], Table 2.19.) This clearly indicates that the growth in the revenues from the general corporation income tax and in those from the taxes on other corporations and public utilities combined has not kept pace with the growth of city income. (For the period 1967 to 1971, the crude income elasticity of the general corporation income tax and the other taxes are 0.90 and 0.85 respectively.)

Interindustry Distribution of Tax Revenues

For purposes of this analysis, it would be desirable to have data showing the distribution of business income tax revenues and taxable income by industry class. By their nature, the public utilities and the transportation, finance, and insurance corporation taxes are levied upon firms in specific industries. Thus, tax revenues reported in the New York City Comptroller's Report identify the industrial source of these taxes.

For the general corporation income tax, it is not possible to identify the industrial source of tax revenues from any available source. However, for purposes of this study, the distribution of general corporation tax liabilities and taxable income by industrial class was estimated for 1969 and 1971 from a special tabulation of the general corporation income tax returns performed by the New York City Department of Finance and Administration. It should be noted that in the discussion of the industrial distribution of tax revenues, the revenues are those that correspond to the old and not the new tax rate, which became effective in 1971.

An additional limitation of these data is the exclusion of the tax revenues attributable to the taxation of firms that file combined returns for the parent and subsidiary components. Regrettably, there is no way to determine either the amount of tax revenue or its distribution among industries that is associated with the filing of combined corporate income tax returns. While it is unfortunate that the analysis is based on data subject to such limitations, no other data identifying the industrial distribution of general corporation tax revenues are available.

Column (1) of Table 2.20 gives the percentage distribution of corporation tax yield among industries. In 1969, the manufacturing sector was a major contributor to general corporation tax revenues— it accounted for 41.6 percent. Next in order of importance are services (18 percent) and wholesale trade (14 percent). Within the manufacturing sector, the major identifiable components are apparel (8.59 percent), printing-publishing (8.32 percent), and chemicals (4.69 percent), which appear to contribute a greater fraction of tax revenue than the other two-digit industry classes.

TABLE 2.20

Structure of Corporation and Public Utilities Income Tax
Payments, and Percent Distribution of Tax Payments
Among Industries in New York City, 1969

	Interindustry Distribution of General Corporation Income Tax	Interindustry Distribution of All Corporate Income Taxes, Including Public Utilities[a]
Manufacturing	41.6	23.0
Ordnance	0	0
Food and kindred	2.98	1.67
Tobacco	0.53	0.30
Textiles	2.98	1.64
Apparel	8.59	4.81
Lumber and wood products	7.20	0.40
Furniture	7.42	0.23
Paper	1.18	0.66
Printing and publishing	8.32	4.66
Chemicals	4.69	2.63
Petroleum	0.41	0.23
Rubber	0.53	0.30
Leather	0.60	0.34
Stone, clay, and glass	0.28	0.15
Primary metal	0.45	0.25
Fabricated metal	2.16	1.21
Machinery, except electrical	1.59	0.89
Electrical machinery	1.69	0.95
Transportation equipment	0.79	0.44
Instruments	0.86	0.48
Miscellaneous manufacturing	2.40	1.34
Transportation and communication[b]		2.0
Public utilities		15.0
Wholesale trade	14.0	8.0
Retail trade	9.0	5.0
Finance		22.0
Insurance		5.0
Real Estate	14.0	8.0
Services	18.0	10.0
Other	4.0	2.0

[a]All corporate tax revenues include those from the finance, transportation, public utilities, insurance, and general corporation taxes.

[b]Includes general income tax on communications industry.

Sources: Finance, transportation, and insurance corporation tax revenues from Comptroller of the City of New York, Annual Report (New York: Office of the Comptroller, 1970); general corporation income tax liabilities from Special Tabulation, Department of Finance Administration, City of New York.

The data in Table 2.20 allow speculation concerning the distributional effects of possible tax rate increases. For example, approximately 41 percent of any increase in the general corporation income tax rate would come from manufacturing firms, 18 percent from service firms, 14 percent from both wholesale trade and real estate, and 9 percent from retail trade. An increase in the rates of any other corporation tax or in the public utilities tax rate would reduce the relative contributions of those sectors in which rates remained constant and increase those to which the rate increase is applied. Clearly, any attempt to increase tax revenues by changing specific tax rates will alter the relative tax contributions of all sectors.

Average Industry Tax Rates

The above discussion dealt only with the distribution of tax payments by type of industry. These figures can better be placed in perspective by examining the relation of tax payment to tax base. In each case, tax base is defined as net corporation income allocated to the City of New York.

Table 2.21 gives the average rate (calculated as the ratio of tax payments to allocated net income) at which allocated net income was taxed under the general corporation income tax for 1969. The manufacturing sector shows an effective rate of 5.76 percent. This is lower than the effective rate for any of the other four major sectors. Real estate has the highest effective rate (6.79 percent), while services, retail trade, and wholesale trade tend to cluster around the 6 percent level. Within the manufacturing sector, there is little variation in the effective tax rate. Only ordnance at 7.17 percent falls outside the range (5.6 percent to 5.9 percent) within which all the other components of manufacturing tend to lie.

Per-Employee Tax Revenues and Tax Base

For planning purposes, a basic unit of economic base measurement is employment. It not only provides a useful gauge as to changes in activity in particular economic sectors but is probably more easily measured than any alternative indicator of economic activity. Accordingly, the data in Table 2.22 are an attempt to link tax payments in a particular industry sector to employment in that sector, by expressing tax liability on a per employee basis. Corporate income and public utilities tax revenues per employee are given in Table 2.22 by industrial sector (includes the financial, transportation, insurance, and general corporation tax revenues). The interindustry variation is greater than was the case in either the tax revenue or effective

TABLE 2.21

General Corporation Income Taxes as
Proportion of Allocated New Income of
Corporations in New York City, 1969

Industry	Average Tax Rate
Manufacturing	5.76
Ordnance	7.17
Food and kindred	5.70
Tobacco	5.74
Textiles	5.79
Apparel	5.79
Lumber and wood products	5.98
Furniture	5.97
Paper	5.74
Printing and publishing	5.74
Chemicals	5.66
Petroleum	5.58
Rubber	5.92
Leather	5.80
Stone, clay, and glass	5.98
Primary metal	5.91
Fabricated metal	5.78
Machinery, except electrical	5.86
Electrical machinery	5.76
Transportation equipment	5.68
Instruments	5.75
Miscellaneous manufacturing	5.81
Wholesale trade	5.85
Retail trade	5.92
Real estate	6.79
Services	6.10

Sources: Finance, transportation, and insurance corporation
tax revenues from Comptroller of the City of New York, Annual Report (New York: Office of the Comptroller, 1970); general corporation
income tax liabilities from Special Tabulation, Department of Finance
Administration, City of New York.

TABLE 2.22

Corporation Income and Public Utilities Tax Revenues
per Employee in New York City by Industry, 1969
(dollars)

Industry	Revenue
Manufacturing	79.40
Ordnance	—
Food and kindred	76.60
Tobacco	285.80
Textiles	134.60
Apparel	60.60
Lumber and wood products	55.30
Furniture	38.80
Paper	71.80
Printing and publishing	104.20
Chemicals	175.60
Petroleum	80.30
Rubber	68.20
Leather	31.70
Stone, clay, and glass	52.90
Primary metal	54.00
Fabricated metal	90.90
Machinery, except electrical	88.70
Electrical machinery	53.60
Transportation equipment	146.90
Instruments	62.00
Miscellaneous manufacturing	55.00
Transportation and communication	16.70
Public utilities	1,687.30
Wholesale trade	77.40
Retail trade	32.70
Finance	254.90
Insurance	116.40
Real estate	201.90
Services	36.10

Sources: Finance, transportation, and insurance corporation tax revenues from Comptroller of the City of New York, Annual Report (New York: Office of the Comptroller, 1970); general corporation income tax liabilities from Special Tabulation, Department of Finance Administration, City of New York

tax rate statistics shown above. Per-employee tax payments in the public utilities group clearly place this sector in a class by itself. In 1969, this industry paid taxes totaling $1,687 per employee, an amount five times greater than per-employee payments in any of the remaining sectors. The finance sector provides the next largest per-employee tax payment in 1969 ($254.90).

Within the manufacturing sector, tobacco, chemicals, and textiles show the highest tax revenue per employee, while ordnance, leather, and furniture have the lowest tax revenue per employee. In general, a dichotomy between the service sectors and manufacturing is difficult to draw precisely. While public utilities, finance, and insurance all exhibit a greater tax payment per employee than the manufacturing sector, the ratio is smaller for services, retail trade, and transportation.

Table 2.23 presents a breakdown by industry class of the general corporation income tax base per employee for 1969. Real estate ($3,071) has the highest general corporation income tax base per

TABLE 2.23

General and Financial Corporate Income
Tax Base per Employee in New York City
by Industry, 1969
(dollars)

Industry	Amount
Manufacturing	1,378.80
Wholesale trade	1,323.90
Retail trade	551.30
Finance*	1,422.80
Real estate	3,071.40
Services	588.70

*Tax base is defined as allocated net income. The tax base of the financial corporation tax is estimated on the assumption that tax revenues equal the product of the statutory tax rate and the tax base.

Sources: Finance, transportation, and insurance corporation tax revenues from Comptroller of the City of New York, Annual Report (New York: Office of the Comptroller, 1970); general corporation income tax liabilities from Special Tabulation, City of New York, Department of Finance Administration.

employee, while finance, manufacturing, and the wholesale trade tend to cluster around the middle range of $1,300-$1,400 of corporate income tax base per employee. On the other hand, the service sector and retail trade clearly have the least general corporate income tax base per employee.

The Effect of Changing Employment Patterns on Tax Base and Revenue

The policy question immediately posed by such variations is clear: What would be the responsiveness of tax revenues and tax base to changes in the structure of employment? Most pertinent in the central-city case is the question of how many service sector jobs are needed to replace the loss of a single manufacturing job, in order to keep corporate tax revenues or the corporate tax base constant, assuming no change in net income per employee.

The estimation process in the case of revenue per employee is simple to illustrate. By use of the estimates of revenue per employee shown in Table 2.22, it is possible to estimate the effect of employment shifts on tax revenues by computing the ratio of tax revenue per employee between any pair of industry classes. These ratios are contained in Table 2.24. The first row indicates that, in order to keep revenues constant, the loss of a manufacturing job would necessitate the gain of 1.03 wholesale jobs, 2.43 retail jobs, 0.31 finance jobs, 0.39 real estate jobs, and 2.19 service sector jobs. Other rows can be interpreted similarly.

The comparison of these coefficients among industry classes provides some interesting results. The industry classes that show a relatively low revenue yield per employee, and therefore require the least employment replacement, are retail trade and transportation and communication. On the other hand, those sectors that require the most employment replacement to compensate for the loss of one job are real estate, finance, and public utilities.* When these results are viewed against the trend in New York City employment away from manufacturing and the wholesale trade, and toward government and services, the revenue implications are disturbing—particularly with respect to shifts to general business and personal services, and retail trade.

_____

*However, public utilities, because of their character (high capital intensity relative to labor and extensive regulation) put this category in a class not easily, or appropriately, compared to the other categories.

112

TABLE 2.24

Estimated Employment Replacement Requirements for Constant Corporation and Public Utilities Income Tax Revenues in New York City by Industry, 1969

Replaced Industry	Manufacturing	Transportation and Communication	Public Utilities	Replacing Industry					
				Wholesale Trade	Retail Trade	Finance	Insurance	Real Estate	Services
Manufacturing	1.00	4.75	0.05	1.03	2.43	0.31	0.68	0.39	2.19
Transportation and communication	0.21	1.00	0.01	0.22	0.51	0.07	0.14	0.08	0.96
Public utilities	21.25	101.02	1.00	21.80	51.59	6.62	14.49	8.39	46.73
Wholesale trade	0.97	4.63	0.05	1.00	2.36	0.30	0.66	0.38	2.14
Retail trade	0.41	1.96	0.02	1.10	1.00	0.13	0.28	0.16	0.91
Finance	3.21	15.26	0.15	3.29	7.79	1.00	2.19	1.26	7.06
Insurance	1.47	6.97	0.07	1.50	3.56	0.46	1.00	0.58	3.22
Real estate	2.54	12.09	0.12	2.61	6.17	7.92	1.73	1.00	5.59
Services	0.45	2.16	0.02	0.46	1.10	0.14	0.31	0.18	1.00

Note: Figures in the columns indicate the number of jobs in the respective sectors necessary to replace a job in the row sectors and still maintain constant corporation and public utilities income tax revenues.

Sources: Finance, transportation, and insurance corporation tax revenues from Comptroller of the City of New York, Annual Report (New York: Office of the Comptroller, 1970); general corporation income tax liabilities from Special Tabulation, Department of Finance Administration, City of New York.

TABLE 2.25

Estimated Employment Replacement Requirements for Constant General and Financial Corporation Income Tax Base in New York City by Industry, 1969

Replaced Industry	Manufacturing	Replacing Industry				
		Wholesale Trade	Retail Trade	Finance	Real Estate	Services
Manufacturing	1.00	1.04	2.50	0.96	0.45	2.34
Wholesale trade	0.96	1.00	2.40	0.93	0.43	2.25
Retail trade	0.39	0.42	1.00	0.38	0.18	0.94
Finance	1.03	1.07	2.58	1.00	0.46	2.42
Real estate	2.23	2.32	5.57	2.16	1.00	5.22
Services	0.43	0.45	1.07	0.41	0.19	1.00

Note: Figures in the columns indicate the number of jobs in the respective sectors necessary to replace a job in the row sectors and still maintain constant general and financial corporation income tax base.

Sources: Financial corporation tax revenues taken from Comptroller of the City of New York, Annual Report (New York: Office of the Comptroller, 1970); general corporation income tax liabilities taken from Special Tabulation, City of New York, Department of Finance Administration.

Table 2.25 presents the data that enable a comparison of effects on the corporation income tax base of substitution of jobs among industry classes. These results indicate that the replacement of a manufacturing job requires the addition of 1.04 wholesale jobs, 2.50 retail jobs, 0.96 finance jobs, 0.45 real estate jobs, and 2.34 service sector jobs in order to keep the tax base constant. Variation in replacement requirements among industry classes can be seen to be relatively large. By far the most difficult jobs to replace in terms of corporation income tax base per employee are in real estate, followed by the wholesale trade and manufacturing. The easiest positions to replace are in the retail trade and services.

The effect on the tax base of general movement away from manufacturing and wholesale trade jobs, and toward service sector jobs, is worthy of particular attention because of the historical trend in that direction in New York City. According to the results in Table 2.25, in order to keep tax base constant it would be necessary for the city to gain 2.34 service sector jobs for each lost manufacturing job and 2.25 service sector jobs for each lost wholesale job. The major sector of employment increase—state and local government—is again omitted since this sector is not subject to corporate income taxation—that is, if a government job replaces a manufacturing job, then presumably the entire $79.40 in tax revenues is lost.

Summary and Conclusions

With respect to variations in tax payments among industries, the largest fraction of corporation income taxes (in 1969) was paid by the manufacturing sector (23 percent), followed by finance, public utilities, and services. With respect to the industrial pattern of income tax rates, the average for manufacturing (5.76 percent) is smaller than that for the wholesale trade (5.85 percent), the retail trade (5.92 percent), real estate (6.7 percent), and services (6.1 percent).

Tax revenues and tax base per employee also show a substantial variance among industrial sectors. In 1969, tax revenues per employee in manufacturing ($79.4) were larger than those in the retail trade ($32.7), services ($36.1), and transportation ($16.7), but less than all other industries—the largest revenue yield being collected from public utilities ($1,687). However, the tax base per employee in manufacturing in 1969 ($1,378) was reported to be lower than only finance ($1,422) and real estate ($3,071).

An analysis of the possible effects on tax revenues and tax base of a changing structure of employment suggests that the replacement of a manufacturing job requires 2.19 service sector jobs to maintain constant revenue and 2.34 service sector jobs to maintain a constant tax base. Further, the replacement of a wholesaling job requires 2.14 service sector jobs to maintain constant revenues and 2.25 service sector jobs to maintain a constant tax base.

The Personal Income Tax

The purpose of this section is to consider the factors underlying the growth in New York City's personal income tax revenues and to explore the revenue implications of changes in the composition of the city's economic base. To this end, the analysis centers around the following:

1. the institutional framework of personal income taxation as it relates to the definition of the tax base and tax rates;
2. changes that have occurred in the factors that determine the revenue yield of the resident income tax, for example, the income distribution of taxpayers, average tax rates;
3. the automatic responses of resident income tax yields attributable to the progressivity of the rate structure and the response of taxable income to changes in total income;
4. variation in personal income tax base and revenues by industrial class; and
5. the implication of these variations for the response of the personal income tax base and revenues to changes in the composition of the city's economic and residential structure.

Accordingly, the following subsection briefly outlines the structure of the personal income tax and examines its historical performance. The second subsection examines the historical trends of the resident income tax in terms of its components—that is, the distribution of taxpayers, the size distribution of taxable income, average tax rates, and tax liabilities by income class. Included here is a discussion of the automatic responsiveness of the tax structure to changes in income. The third subsection is concerned with differences among industries in per-employee tax base and tax revenues, and explores the implications of the differential effects of the response of the personal income tax to changes in the city's economic and residential structure. The fourth presents a brief summary and evaluation of the findings.

It should be noted that this kind of analysis of the personal income tax system in New York City has always been hampered by the unavailability of data. In essence, the only readily available data consist of annual revenues reported for the resident income and commuter earnings taxes combined. Aggregate data of this variety preclude virtually any detailed analysis of the operation of the tax system. Fortunately, for the purpose of this study, three types of information not generally available were obtained. The first set—estimated dollar amounts of the commuter earnings tax—was provided by the Department of Finance Administration of the City of New York. The second was obtained from the Bureau of Tax Statistics of the New York State Department of Taxation and Finance. These data include detailed statistics on the distribution of taxpayers, their wages and salaries, and their income by income class. Though these data were collected from the New York State income tax files, the similarity between the state and city tax systems allows them to be used, after certain modifications, for the analysis of the New York City tax system.[21] The third set of data was obtained from the Bureau of Economic Analysis of the U.S. Department of Commerce. It contains the personal income and earnings data that underlie the analysis of interindustry differentials in the resident income and commuter earnings tax base discussed in the third part of this section.

An Overview

Taxation of resident personal income and commuter earnings in New York City was initiated in 1966. By design, the city tax system resembles that of New York State, which in turn resembles the federal system. While the tax rates applied by the city differ from those of the state, the definitions of total and taxable income were similar until 1970. The difference between the state and city systems increased in 1970, when the state, but not the city, modified its system in conformity with changes introduced in the federal system.

The Personal Income Tax Base. The law requires that the income of each New York City resident, resident estate, and resident trust be taxed under the resident income tax. Income from partnerships may also be taxed, but associations that are taxable as corporations under federal law (as well as other organizations that are eligible for exclusion from the federal income tax) are excluded from income taxation by the city.

For residents, taxable income for city income tax purposes is adjusted federal gross income with certain modifications. These modifications consist of personal exemptions ($600 per person), plus a number of adjustments.[22] For nonresidents, the tax base consists of all city-earned net income of self-employed persons and the total city-earned wages and salaries of those not self-employed. No tax is imposed on gross incomes totaling less than $3,000. Other than applying the appropriate exemption, the nonresident taxpayer makes no adjustments to total wages and salaries or total net income.

Personal Income Tax Rates. The maximum rate at which the city can tax income is set by the state. For residents, a schedule has been adopted that applies to all taxpayers and that provides for mild progressivity (that is, a high-income taxpayer incurs a proportionately [to income] higher tax liability than a lower-income taxpayer). On nonresidents, a flat rate is imposed; however, the rate differs as between self-employed and non-self-employed persons. Under no circumstances may a nonresident be taxed for a greater amount than he would be if he were a resident.[23]

The nonresident tax levy on adjusted incomes is 0.45 percent and 0.65 percent for self-employed and non-self-employed persons, respectively. These rates went into effect for the tax year beginning January 1, 1971. Prior to the rate increase, the respective rates on self-employed and non-self-employed persons were 0.26 percent and 0.36 percent. The new and old rates applied to residents are shown in Table 2.26.

The existence of a progressive tax rate structure, whether by increasing rates (as in the case of the resident income levy) or by decreasing exclusion (as in the case of the nonresident income levy), ensures that tax yields will be responsive to economic growth. This is because, as an individual's income grows, he finds himself moving into tax brackets in which higher rates are applied, and thus to proportionately higher tax liabilities. In other words, as income grows, the average effective tax rate of the tax system increases.

TABLE 2.26

Current and Old Income Tax Rates in New York City

Taxable Income	Old Rate	Current Rate
Less than $1,000	0.4%	0.7%
Less than $3,000 but greater than $1,000	$4 + 0.6%	$7 + 1.1%
Less than $6,000 but greater than $3,000	16 + 0.8	29 + 1.4
Less than $10,000 but greater than $6,000	40 + 1.0	71 + 1.8
Less than $15,000 but greater than $10,000	80 + 1.2	143 + 2.1
Less than $20,000 but greater than $15,000	140 + 1.4	248 + 2.5
Less than $25,000 but greater than $20,000	210 + 1.6	373 + 2.8
Less than $30,000 but greater than $25,000	290 + 1.8	513 + 3.2
Over $30,000	380 + 2.0	673 + 3.5

Note: In each case, the percentage rate is paid on the marginal amount—for example, if an individual earns $6,500, under the new rate he would pay $71 plus 1.8 percent of the increment that was greater than $6,000—in other words, 1.8 percent of $500.

Source: David J. Bjornstand, "The Structure and Performance of the New York City Tax System," Working Paper no. 2, Maxwell Research Project on the Public Finances of New York City, July 1972.

Revenue Performance

The data in Table 2.27 show a time series of revenues yielded by the personal income tax and the commuter earnings tax, as well as gross city personal income and the proportion of tax yield to personal income. For the short period of time during which the personal and commuter earnings taxes have been in effect, the growth in revenues has been impressive. For the period 1967 through 1971, when the rates were constant, revenues grew by 53 percent, although most of the increase—31 percent—occurred between 1967 and 1968. During this period, personal income grew by 33.6 percent, a relative rate about two-thirds that of income tax revenues. In 1972, both the resident income and commuter earnings tax rates were raised. This increase was accompanied by a marked increase in yield for this year—from $199.4 million in 1971 to $443.2 million in 1972—an absolute growth of $243.8 million.

The revenues of the commuter earnings tax account for a small and roughly constant proportion of total income tax revenues—that is, about 11 percent of the combined total revenues from the personal income tax and the commuter earnings tax. Among the main reasons for the relatively smaller size of commuter earnings tax revenues are the lower statutory rate and the exclusion of certain income sources from the tax base. Further, Columns (5) and (6) of Table 2.27 show that both taxes are small proportions of total city income. The slight decline from 1969 to 1971 is analyzed in the following subsection with other indicators of the tax response to changes in the base.

Historical Trends and the Responses of
Resident Income Tax Revenues to Changes
in Income

The factors determining the revenues generated by the taxation of personal income by New York City's government are the distribution of taxpayers, income, taxable income, average tax rates, and revenues by income class. It should be noted that, for New York City as well as for most cities, analyses of this kind have been hampered by a lack of data at a level of disaggregation that would allow an examination of the sources of change in tax revenues. Fortunately, the similarity in the structures of the New York City and the New York State personal income tax systems and a tabulation of data from New York State tax returns allow an evaluation of both the revenue performance of the city personal income tax and the factors underlying this performance. However, as the data from the state were not available for the years prior to 1964, the changes that have occurred

TABLE 2.27

Personal Income and Commuter Earnings Tax Revenues in
New York City, 1968-72

Fiscal Year	Total Resident Income and Commuter Earnings Tax Revenues (in millions of current dollars)	Resident Income Tax Revenues	Commuter Earnings Tax Revenues (estimated)	Commuter Earnings Revenues as Percent of Total Resident Income and Commuter Earnings	Commuter Earnings Tax Revenues as Percent of City Income	Total Resident Income and Commuter Earnings Tax Revenues as Percent of City Income
1967	130.4	N.A.	N.A.	N.A.	N.A.	0.359
1968	170.3	150.3	20.0	11.74	0.052	0.443
1969	201.5	177.7	23.8	11.81	0.057	0.479
1970	205.9	183.9	22.0	10.68	0.049	0.454
1971	199.4	177.6	20.8	10.43	0.043	0.412
1972	443.2	392.6	50.6	11.42	N.A.	N.A.

N.A.: Not available.

Sources: Total revenue figures from Comptroller of the City of New York, Annual Report (New York: Office of the Comptroller, 1968-1972); commuter earnings tax figures from unpublished estimates of the Department of Financial Administration, City of New York; personal income data from "Personal Income, New York City" (unpublished tables, Bureau of Labor Statistics). (The income figures shown for each fiscal year are for calendar year—that is, 1966-67 = 1966.)

119

in the components of the tax system can be considered only since that date.

The Distribution of Taxpayers, Taxable Income, Tax Liability and Average Tax Rates by Income Class. In 1964 and 1970, there were rough similarities in the distribution of taxpayers in that there is a small proportion of total taxpayers in higher income brackets (for example, 2.1 percent and 3.9 percent above $20,000 in 1964 and 1970, respectively) and the majority of taxpayers report incomes of less than $10,000 (89.5 percent and 75.3 percent in 1964 and 1970, respectively). (See Table 2.28.)

However, it is clear that between 1964 and 1970 there was a shift in the distribution of taxpayers among income classes. The proportion of taxpayers reporting incomes less than $7,000 was less in 1970 than in 1964. Except for the two highest income classes (those above $500,000), which contain a negligible proportion of total taxpayers, all income classes above $7,000 had a larger proportion of total taxpayers in 1970 than in 1964.

In 1964, the majority of taxpayers (52 percent) reported incomes of less than $5,000; 36.9 percent reported incomes in that range in 1970. The proportion with incomes from $5,000 to $9,999 was similar in both years—37.5 percent in 1964 and 38.4 percent in 1970. Thus, in 1964, 89.5 percent of taxpayers had incomes less than $10,000, while in 1970 this figure was 75.3 percent.

The decline from 1964 to 1970 in the proportion of taxpayers reporting less than $5,000 of total income was accompanied by an increase in the proportion of taxpayers with incomes from $10,000 to $19,999 (from 8.4 percent in 1964 to 20.9 percent in 1970). In income classes of $20,000 and above, there is only a small proportion of taxpayers (2.1 percent in 1964 and 3.9 percent in 1970).

Changes similar to those in the distribution of taxpayers occurred in the distribution of total income by income class. (See Table 2.29.) Here, too, there was a shift away from the lower-income classes between 1964 and 1970. Those income classes less than $9,000 showed declines and those above $9,000 had increases (excepting the two highest income classes). Income classes less than $5,000 had 24.2 percent of total income in 1964 and 12.5 percent in 1970. Income classes from $5,000 to $9,999 accounted for 42.6 percent and 34.5 percent of total income in the two years. Thus, in 1964 about two-thirds (66.8 percent) of total income was reported by taxpayers whose total income was less than $10,000, while in 1970 it was less than half (47 percent). Of course, there was a corresponding increase in total income in the classes of $10,000 and above. In income classes from $10,000 to $19,999, the proportion of total income was 17.4 percent in 1964 and 33.8 percent in 1970. The increase was less pronounced for income classes of $20,000 and above, which made up

TABLE 2.28

Distribution of Resident Income Taxpayers in New York
City by Income Class, 1964 and 1970

| Income Class | Percent of Total Taxpayers | |
(dollars)	1964	1970
1 — 999	5.5	4.5
1,000 — 1,499	4.9	3.9
1,500 — 1,999	4.9	3.8
2,000 — 2,499	5.2	3.9
2,500 — 2,999	5.8	3.7
3,000 — 3,499	6.2	4.2
3,500 — 3,999	6.3	4.2
4,000 — 4,499	6.8	4.3
4,500 — 4,999	6.4	4.4
5,000 — 5,999	11.3	9.2
6,000 — 6,999	9.5	8.8
7,000 — 7,999	7.4	7.9
8,000 — 8,999	5.6	6.8
9,000 — 9,999	3.7	5.7
10,000 — 10,999	2.6	4.9
11,000 — 11,999	1.6	3.9
12,000 — 12,999	1.2	3.3
13,000 — 13,999	0.8	2.4
14,000 — 14,999	0.6	1.8
15,000 — 19,999	1.6	4.6
20,000 — 24,999	0.7	1.5
25,000 — 49,999	1.0	1.7
50,000 — 99,999	0.3	0.5
100,000 — 499,999	0.1	0.2
500,000 — 999,999	0.0*	0.0*
1,000,000 plus	0.0*	0.0*
Total	100.0	100.0

*Less than 0.05 percent.

Source: Calculated from "New York State Personal Income Tax
Analysis of Major Items by Total Income Class," for New York City Residents (unpublished tables, Bureau of Tax Statistics, Office of Tax Research,
New York State Department of Taxation and Finance). For a discussion of
these data, see Metropolitan and Regional Research Center, New York
City: Economic Base and Fiscal Capacity, Report prepared for the Temporary State Commission to Study the Governmental Operation of New York
City, April 1973 (New York: State Study Commission on New York City,
1973), Appendix II-1.

TABLE 2.29

Distribution of Reported Total Income by Income
class as Reported by Resident Income Taxpayers
in New York City: Estimated for 1964 and 1970

Income Class (dollars)	Percent of Total Income	
	1964	1970
1 — 999	0.5	0.3
1,000 — 1,499	1.0	0.6
1,500 — 1,999	1.4	0.8
2,000 — 2,499	1.9	1.1
2,500 — 2,999	2.6	1.3
3,000 — 3,499	3.3	1.7
3,500 — 3,999	3.8	1.9
4,000 — 4,499	4.7	2.2
4,500 — 4,999	5.0	2.6
5,000 — 5,999	10.1	6.3
6,000 — 6,999	10.0	7.1
7,000 — 7,999	9.0	7.3
8,000 — 8,999	7.8	7.1
9,000 — 9,999	5.7	6.7
10,000 — 10,999	4.4	6.4
11,000 — 11,999	3.0	5.6
12,000 — 12,999	2.4	5.0
13,000 — 13,999	1.8	4.0
14,000 — 14,999	1.4	3.2
15,000 — 19,999	4.4	9.6
20,000 — 24,999	2.5	4.2
25,000 — 49,999	5.6	6.8
50,000 — 99,999	3.2	3.8
100,000 — 499,999	3.2	3.3
500,000 — 999,999	0.6	0.5
1,000,000 plus	0.6	0.6
Total	100.0	100.0

Source: See Source for Table 2.28, above.

TABLE 2.30

Distribution of Total Taxable Income by Income Class
as Reported by Resident Income Taxpayers in New
York City: Estimated for 1964 and 1970

Income Class (dollars)	Percent of Total Taxable Income	
	1964	1970
1 — 999	0.1	0.0
1,000 — 1,499	0.4	0.1
1,500 — 1,999	0.8	0.2
2,000 — 2,499	1.2	0.7
2,500 — 2,999	1.9	0.9
3,000 — 3,499	2.6	1.3
3,500 — 3,999	3.2	1.5
4,000 — 4,499	4.2	1.8
4,500 — 4,999	4.5	2.2
5,000 — 5,999	9.4	5.6
6,000 — 6,999	9.6	6.6
7,000 — 7,999	8.8	7.1
8,000 — 8,999	7.6	7.1
9,000 — 9,999	5.9	6.8
10,000 — 10,999	4.7	6.6
11,000 — 11,999	3.3	5.7
12,000 — 12,999	2.7	5.2
13,000 — 13,999	2.0	4.3
14,000 — 14,999	1.7	3.4
15,000 — 19,999	5.3	10.5
20,000 — 24,999	3.2	4.8
25,000 — 49,999	7.3	8.0
50,000 — 99,999	4.2	4.5
100,000 — 499,999	4.1	3.8
500,000 — 999,999	0.7	0.5
$1,000,000 plus	0.06	0.7
Total	100.0	100.0

Source: See Source for Table 2.28, above.

TABLE 2.31

Distribution of Tax Liability by Income Class for Resident Income Tax in New York City: Estimated for 1964 and 1970

Income Class (dollars)	Percent of Total Tax Liability 1964	1970
1 — 999	0.0	0.0
1,000 — 1,499	0.2	0.0
1,500 — 1,999	0.4	0.1
2,000 — 2,499	0.7	0.4
2,500 — 2,999	1.1	0.5
3,000 — 3,499	1.6	0.8
3,500 — 3,999	2.0	0.9
4,000 — 4,499	2.7	1.1
4,500 — 4,999	3.1	1.4
5,000 — 5,999	6.7	3.8
6,000 — 6,999	7.3	4.8
7,000 — 7,999	6.9	5.3
8,000 — 8,999	6.2	5.5
9,000 — 9,999	5.0	5.5
10,000 — 10,999	4.2	5.6
11,000 — 11,999	3.1	5.0
12,000 — 12,999	2.6	4.7
13,000 — 13,999	2.0	4.0
14,000 — 14,999	1.7	3.3
15,000 — 19,999	5.9	10.9
20,000 — 24,999	4.0	5.6
25,000 — 49,999	11.2	11.3
50,000 — 99,999	8.4	8.4
100,000 — 499,999	9.3	8.1
500,000 — 999,999	1.7	1.2
1,000,000 plus	1.5	1.5
Total	100.0	100.0

Source: See Source for Table 2.28.

TABLE 2.32

Distribution of Average Tax Rate by Income Class for
Resident Income Tax in New York City: Estimated
for 1964 and 1970

Income Class (dollars)	Average Tax Rates 1964	1970
1 — 999	0.05	0.01
1,000 — 1,499	0.19	0.07
1,500 — 1,999	0.25	0.12
2,000 — 2,499	0.32	0.36
2,500 — 2,999	0.38	0.41
3,000 — 3,499	0.43	0.46
3,500 — 3,999	0.47	0.48
4,000 — 4,499	0.51	0.52
4,500 — 4,999	0.54	0.54
5,000 — 5,999	0.58	0.63
6,000 — 6,999	0.63	0.70
7,000 — 7,999	0.67	0.75
8,000 — 8,999	0.70	0.80
9,000 — 9,999	0.77	0.85
10,000 — 10,999	0.84	0.90
11,000 — 11,999	0.91	0.93
12,000 — 12,999	0.96	0.97
13,000 — 13,999	0.99	1.03
14,000 — 14,999	1.06	1.05
15,000 — 19,999	1.18	1.17
20,000 — 24,999	1.39	1.38
25,000 — 49,999	1.73	1.71
50,000 — 99,999	2.29	2.31
100,000 — 499,999	2.55	2.57
500,000 — 999,999	2.64	2.72
1,000,000 plus	2.32	2.64
Total	0.87	1.03

Source: See Source for Table 2.28, above.

15.7 percent of total income in 1964 and 19.2 percent in 1970. While this trend reflects to some extent the general growth in per capita incomes that has occurred nationwide, the fact that the major change occurred in the lowest income brackets most likely reflects such things as changes in legal minimum wages and increased social security payments.

While the distributions of total income and total taxable income (total income less deductions and exemptions) appear essentially similar, a major difference occurs in the distribution of the two shares among the higher income classes. Also, those income classes of less than $9,000 have shares of taxable income (Table 2.30) that are smaller than their shares of total income. The proportion of all total income reported in the income classes above $9,000 is less than the proportion of taxable income.

There is a clear similarity in the upward shift in the two distributions between 1964 and 1970. The fact that, on both years, the lower (higher) income classes accounted for a smaller (larger) proportion of taxable income than of total income indicates that, on the average, deductions and exemptions as a proportion of total income are larger (smaller) among the lower (higher) income classes.

Accompanying the changes in the distributions of taxpayers, total income, and taxable income has been a shift in proportion of tax liability (Table 2.31) imposed on taxpayers in the various income classes.* As might be expected with a progressive rate structure, the largest tax liabilities relative to their proportion of total income (Table 2.28) are among the higher income classes and the converse holds for the lower income classes.

While 66.8 percent and 47 percent of total income were contained in tax returns reporting less than $10,000 of income in 1964 and 1970 respectively, 43.9 percent and 30.1 percent of tax liabilities were associated with those returns. Further breakdown shows that 11.8 percent and 5.2 percent of total tax liability were in income classes less than $5,000 in 1964 and 1970, respectively. In the income classes between $5,000 and $9,999, the tax liability was 32.1 percent of the total in 1964 and 24.9 percent in 1970. The percent of total tax liability in income classes of $20,000 and above has remained unchanged in the two years—36.1 percent. This corresponds to 15.7 percent and 19.2 percent of all total income for those income classes in 1964 and 1970. The major increases in the proportion of tax

---

*The tax liability is based upon the application of current (beginning January 1, 1971) statutory rates to taxable income. While there was no personal income tax in 1964, it is possible to simulate its behavior, had it been in existence, from state data for New York City.

liability occurred primarily in income classes from $9,000 to $19,000. For income classes from $10,000 to $19,999, the percent of total tax liability was 19.5 percent in 1964 and 33.5 percent in 1970.

The progressive rate structure is also reflected in average tax rates,* which consistently increase with income class except for the very highest income classes, where the marginal tax rate is constant (Table 2.32). The general increase in average tax rates, as well as the decline in average tax rates for the lowest income class, between 1964 and 1970 can be attributed to changes in deductions, exemptions, and/or the distribution of income within an income class. Thus, it appears that, due both to the progressive rate and the declining importance of deductions and exemptions, the rate at which income is taxed under the current structure has increased over time for virtually all but the lowest-income residents. For the city as a whole, this pattern is reflected in the average tax rate (assuming the 1971 tax rate structure), which increased from 0.87 percent in 1964 to 1.03 percent in 1970. This implies that, if the city had imposed the resident income tax at the rates current in 1971 during the 1964-70 period, tax liabilities would have increased from 0.87 percent of reported income in 1964 to 1.03 percent in 1970.

It should be noted that the average tax rate increased each year from 1964 to 1968 but declined somewhat between 1968 and 1970. (See Table 2.33.) The explanation for this decline lies in part in a slight redistribution of income toward lower income classes, which have lower average tax rates, and in part to an increase in the growth of deductions and exemptions relative to total income. Of course, the income tax did not come into existence until 1966, and the city imposed a lower rate tax structure between 1966 and 1970. This being the case, the actual levels of average tax rates were lower than indicated above.

Confirmation of these results can be found in Table 2.27. While the average resident income tax rate is not given, it can be calculated from the data presented there. The sixth column in Table 2.27 gives the sum of resident income and commuter earnings tax revenues as a proportion of total income. Subtracting from that the commuter earnings tax revenues as a proportion of total income, an average tax rate for the income tax (not shown) is obtained. This average tax rate follows a pattern of increases in value up to 1969 and declines thereafter, which is similar to the trends shown in Table 2.33. As mentioned previously, the individual values in Table 2.27 are less than those in Table 2.33 because the latter uses the current rate in

_____

*Average tax rates are calculated as the ratio of tax liability to total income multiplied by 100.

TABLE 2.33

Average Tax Rates for Resident Income Tax
in New York City, 1964-70

Fiscal Year	Average Tax Rates (percent)
1964	0.873
1965	0.924
1966	0.947
1967	1.014
1968	1.059
1969	1.038
1970	1.031

Source: See Source for Table 2.28, above.

the calculation of the average rates. In addition, Table 2.27 is based
on actual fiscal year data for tax revenues rather than simulated
revenues, and the income data are personal income earned rather
than income reported.

An alternative aggregate measure of the responsiveness of a
tax system is that of elasticity. The elasticity of a tax is a measure
of the change in tax liability resulting from a change in total income.
More specifically, it is the percent change in tax liability divided by
the percent change in total income. This is an important indicator
of the behavior of the tax system under changing economic conditions.

The structure of the tax is the determinant of its elasticity.
The New York City income tax is a progressive tax; the marginal
rate ranges from 0.7 percent to 3.5 percent. However, as previously
explained in the computation of taxable income, the city allows deductions and exemptions from total income, so that the tax base is
not total income, but taxable income. This suggests the necessity
of separate estimation of rate and base elasticities to obtain the total
elasticity of the tax.

The base elasticity is a measure of the automatic growth of
the taxable income in response to growth in total income. It is determined by the amount of deductions and exemptions allowed against
total income and by automatic changes in the level of deductions resulting from changes in income. If deductions and exemptions remain
at a constant absolute level between income classes, then taxable
income will grow relative to total income as income rises. Consequently, the base elasticity will be greater than unity. If, as income

rises, deductions and exemptions increase relative to income, then taxable income will grow at a rate slower than income.

The rate elasticity is a measure of the automatic growth of tax liability in response to growth in taxable income. The rate elasticity of the income tax is determined by the degree of progressivity in the tax rate structure and by the distribution of income. The lower the maximum marginal tax rate, the faster will the rate elasticity become insignificant as income grows. The highest marginal rate for the city income tax is 3.5 percent, which is applied to income above $30,000. Since the marginal tax rate is applied to a high income class, it is reasonable to expect the rate elasticity to be larger than unity, but not much larger because the rates are not steeply graduated. However, if the distribution of taxable income should change from the higher tax rate brackets to the lower brackets, the elasticity could be less than unity. With a shift in taxable income toward lower rate income brackets, a given change in taxable income produces a smaller change in tax liability.

Table 2.34 contains the base, rate, and overall elasticities of the New York City resident income tax.[24] The most striking feature is the decline in all three elasticities. In particular, the rate elasticities for 1968 to 1969 and 1969 to 1970 were quite low (less than one). This indicates that the percent growth of tax liability has been less than the percent growth of taxable income.

It appears that the decline was the result of a change in the relative distribution of taxable income downward among income

TABLE 2.34

Resident Income Tax, Base Rate, and Overall Elasticities
in New York City, 1964/65-1969/70

| Years | Elasticities | | |
	Base (EB)	Rate (ER)	Overall (ET)
1964/65	1.399	1.328	1.858
1965/66	1.504	1.168	1.756
1966/67	1.373	1.303	1.789
1967/68	1.257	1.277	1.605
1968/69	0.960	0.535	0.514
1969/70	1.034	0.713	0.737

Source: See Source for Table 2.28, above.

129

classes. Thus, while total income continues to grow, it has grown less rapidly relative to the number of taxpayers in the higher income groups for the last three years of the period (1968 to 1970). In addition there has been a slight downward shift in the distribution of income among some of the middle income brackets. This shift probably reflects a cyclical downturn in the economy that occurred in the late 1960s.

Similarly, the decline in the base elasticities indicates that taxable income has not increased in proportion to the growth in total income. The implication of this pattern is that deductions and exemptions have increased more rapidly than total income. Again, this can most probably be attributed to the cyclical decline in the economy and an attendant increase in deductions for capital losses.

In combination, the decline in the base and rate elasticities produces the decline in the overall elasticity. The fact that the overall elasticity has declined implies that tax revenues will grow at a rate less than income. Moreover, the fact that the rate elasticity has consistently had a lower value than the base elasticity implies that due to the rate structure, revenues will grow at a slower rate than the tax base—that is, taxable income. Should the overall elasticity continue to have a value less than one, as in 1969-70, tax revenues will not grow as fast as total income. Moreover, the fact that the rate elasticity has more often had a lower value than the base elasticity indicates that the growth of revenues is primarily attributable to the overall trend in deductions and exemptions, which have not grown as fast as total income. That the overall elasticity of the tax is less than one implies a declining average tax rate.

Employment by Industry and the Tax Base

Employment is crucial to the personal income tax base because wages and salaries are a very large component of total income. The average earnings of employed individuals by type of industry are given in Table 2.35. Clearly, earnings per employee for some types of industries are considerably larger than others.* From this, it follows that certain industries provide more (individual) income tax base per employee than others and that a structural change in city employment could affect the overall level of the individual income tax base and yield. Table 2.35 shows the higher earnings industries to be mining, contract construction, transportation, communications, and public

---

*Mining has relatively few employees, of which most are in administrative capacities. This could account for the unusually high wages and salaries per employee for that industry.

TABLE 2.35

Earnings per Employee in New York City by Industry, 1970

Industry	Earnings (dollars)
Farm	9,191
Government	10,456
Manufacturing	9,698
Mining	18,671
Contract construction	13,232
Transportation, communication, and public utilities	12,142
Wholesale and retail trade	9,337
Finance, insurance, and real estate	10,220
Services	8,726
Other	10,264

Sources: "Earnings by Broad Industrial Sector, New York City" (unpublished tables, Regional Economics Information System, Bureau of Economic Analysis, U.S. Department of Commerce). Government figures calculated from average October earnings of full-time equivalent employment multiplied by 12 from U.S. Department of Commerce, Bureau of the Census, Government Employment in Selected Metropolitan Areas and Large Counties: 1970, Series GE70-No.3 (Washington, D.C.: U.S. Government Printing Office, 1971).

TABLE 2.36

Estimated Average Tax Base and Tax Liability
Per Employee in New York City by Industry, 1970
(dollars)

Industry	Average Tax Base per Employee	Tax Liability per Employee
Farm	10,062	87
Government	11,537	107
Manufacturing	10,649	95
Mining	32,015	544
Construction	15,230	169
Transportation and communication	13,535	140
Wholesale and retail trade	10,230	89
Finance, insurance, and real estate	11,265	103
Services	9,529	80
Other	11,317	104

Source: See Source for Table 2.28, above.

utilities. Services is the lowest in earnings per employee, with farm, wholesale trade and retail trade only slightly higher.

The first column of Table 2.36 presents estimates of resident personal income tax base (total income) and average tax liability per employee by industry. Among industries, the relative amount of tax base per employee is similar to that of the average earnings per employee shown in Table 2.35. The high-wage industries generate larger amounts of tax base per employee, and, conversely, the low-wage industries generate lower amounts of tax base per employee.

Through a comparison of the per-employee tax base of one industry with that of another, inferences may be made concerning the effect of changes in the share of employment of industries. For example, for each manufacturing job lost in the city, an average of $10,649 of tax base (total income) is lost. If an accompanying growth of one employee occurred in the service sector, which has an average tax base per employee income of $9,549, a net loss in tax base equal to $1,100 would result. The loss of tax base associated with the loss of a manufacturing job could be exactly offset by the addition of 1.118 service sector jobs (that is, $10,649 ÷ $9,549).*

A complete set of replacement requirements necessary to replace each lost employee or, in other words, to maintain constant resident income tax base is given in Table 2.37. Each cell in the table contains the number of employees in the industry named in the column required to replace one job lost in the industry named in the row. For example, on the average, for each manufacturing job lost, a gain of 0.923 government employees, 0.699 construction employees, 0.787 transportation and communication employees, 0.945 finance, insurance, and real estate employees, or 1.118 service employees is required, if constant tax base is to be maintained.

With regard to tax liabilities, comparison of the relative per-employee tax liabilities shows the higher-income (higher-wage) industries to have the higher average tax liabilities and the lower-income (lower-wage) industries, lower average tax liabilities. Clearly, in order to maintain a constant level of tax liabilities, the higher-wage industries require more replacement employees than the lower-wage industries. Also, the higher-wage industries can replace lost jobs with relatively fewer employees than can the lower-wage industries. Two industries experiencing declining employment in the

---

*Note that the assumption behind this example and the following discussion is that the employees considered contributed to the base of the resident income tax base—that is, they are residents of New York City. For a consideration of the effects of commuting on the resident income tax base, see below.

TABLE 2.37

Estimated Employment Replacement Requirements for Constant
Resident Income Tax Base per Employee in New York City
by Industry, 1970

Replaced Industry						Replacing Industry				
	Farm	Govern- ment	Manu- fac- turing	Mining	Con- struc- tion	Transportation and Communication	Trade	FIRE*	Services	Other
Farm	1.000	0.872	0.945	0.314	0.661	0.743	0.984	0.893	1.056	0.889
Government	1.147	1.000	1.083	0.360	0.758	0.852	1.128	1.024	1.211	1.019
Manufacturing	1.058	0.923	1.000	0.300	0.699	0.787	1.041	0.945	1.118	0.941
Mining	3.182	2.775	3.006	1.000	2.102	2.365	3.130	2.842	3.360	2.829
Construction	1.514	1.320	1.430	0.476	1.000	1.125	1.489	1.352	1.598	1.346
Transportation and com- munication	1.345	1.173	1.271	0.423	0.889	1.000	1.323	1.202	1.421	1.196
Trade	1.017	0.887	0.961	0.320	0.672	0.756	1.000	0.908	1.074	0.904
FIRE*	1.120	0.976	1.058	0.352	0.740	0.832	1.101	1.000	1.182	0.995
Services	0.947	0.826	0.895	0.298	0.626	0.704	0.931	0.846	1.000	0.842
Other	1.125	0.981	1.063	0.354	0.743	0.836	1.106	1.005	1.188	1.000

*Finance, insurance and real estate.

Source: Calculated from Table 2.35.

TABLE 2.38

Estimated Employment Replacement Requirements for Constant
Resident Income Tax Liabilities in New York City
by Industry, 1970

Replaced Industry						Replacing Industry				
	Farm	Govern- ment	Manu- fac- turing	Mining	Con- struc- tion	Transportation and Communication	Trade	FIRE	Services	Other
Farm	1.000	0.811	0.915	0.160	0.513	0.621	0.974	0.841	1.089	0.835
Government	1.233	1.000	1.129	0.197	0.633	0.766	1.202	1.037	1.344	1.030
Manufacturing	1.092	0.885	1.000	0.174	0.561	0.678	1.064	0.919	1.190	0.912
Mining	6.264	5.077	5.734	1.000	3.215	3.888	6.103	5.267	6.821	5.230
Construction	1.948	1.579	1.784	0.311	1.000	1.209	1.898	1.638	2.122	1.627
Transportation and com- munication	1.611	1.306	1.475	0.257	0.827	1.000	1.570	1.355	1.755	1.345
Trade	1.026	0.832	0.940	0.164	0.527	0.637	1.000	0.863	1.118	0.857
FIRE	1.189	0.964	1.089	0.190	0.610	0.738	1.159	1.000	1.295	0.993
Services	0.918	0.744	0.841	0.147	0.471	0.570	0.895	0.772	1.000	0.767
Other	1.198	0.971	1.096	0.191	0.615	0.743	1.167	1.007	1.304	1.000

Source: Calculated from Table 2.35.

133

city are construction and manufacturing, of which the former has relatively large replacement requirements. For each manufacturing job lost, the maintenance of a constant personal income tax liabilities requires, on the average, 0.885 government employees, 0.676 employees in transportation, communication and public utilities, 1.064 wholesale and retail trade employees, 0.919 finance employees, or 1.190 service employees. (See Table 2.38.)

Resident and Nonresident Employment and Tax Revenues

The preceding analysis has examined the effects of changes in the industrial composition of employment on personal income tax revenues. This subsection analyzes the revenue effects of changes in employee place of residence, given the existing industrial structure. Specifically, this analysis is directed to the following question: If a resident employee becomes a nonresident employee, what will be the implication for city income tax revenues? This is particularly important given the differential nonresident/resident income tax rate and the continuing trend toward suburbanization.

The resident personal income tax revenues lost will exceed the gain from the nonresident earnings tax, if an employee in any given industry moves his residence to the suburbs. Under the current rate structure, the lowest resident income tax rate (that applied to taxable income less than $1,000) is 0.7 percent, but this still exceeds the 0.65 percent applied to nonresident commuter earnings. It is possible for an individual taxpayer with a given level of earnings to pay less tax as a resident than as a nonresident only if his deductions and exemptions are so large that he has little or no taxable income. For the average taxpayer, who is the subject of analysis here, the loss of revenue from the change of residence is a certainty.

For example, in Table 2.37, it is shown that, in order to keep income tax revenues constant, the loss of one manufacturing job must be compensated for by the addition of 1.041 trade jobs. Now the issue is, if the manufacturing job in the city is not lost, but the employee moves to the suburbs, how many additional trade jobs are required to keep the level of personal income taxes constant? The ratios in Table 2.39 indicate the average number of resident employees that must be added in one industry to replace exactly the loss of tax liability resulting from the change from resident to nonresident by one average employee in another industry. As in Tables 2.37 and 2.38, the replaced industry is named in a row and the replacing industry is named in a column. To follow the example above, the third row indicates that, on the average, for each manufacturing employee who moves from the city to the suburbs, the number of resident employees

134

TABLE 2.39

Estimated Employment Replacement Requirements for Constant Total Tax Liability from Resident Income Tax and Nonresident Earnings Tax in New York City by Industry, 1970

Industry of Resident Employee Becoming Nonresident Employee	Replacing Industry									
	Farm	Government	Manufacturing	Mining	Construction	Transportation and Communication	Trade	FIRE	Services	Other
Farm	0.536	0.435	0.491	0.086	0.275	0.333	0.522	0.451	0.584	0.448
Government	0.600	0.487	0.550	0.096	0.308	0.373	0.585	0.505	0.654	0.501
Manufacturing	0.591	0.479	0.541	0.094	0.303	0.367	0.575	0.497	0.643	0.493
Mining	5.015	4.065	4.591	0.801	2.574	3.113	4.886	4.217	5.462	4.187
Construction	1.107	0.897	1.013	0.177	0.568	0.687	1.079	0.931	1.206	0.924
Transportation and communication	0.851	0.690	0.779	0.136	0.437	0.528	0.830	0.716	0.927	0.711
Trade	0.552	0.447	0.505	0.088	0.283	0.342	0.538	0.464	0.601	0.461
FIRE	0.574	0.465	0.525	0.092	0.294	0.356	0.559	0.482	0.625	0.479
Services	0.489	0.397	0.448	0.078	0.251	0.304	0.477	0.411	0.533	0.409
Other	0.579	0.469	0.530	0.092	0.297	0.359	0.564	0.487	0.630	0.483

Source: Calculated from Table 2.35.

135

in the trade sector who need to be added in order to maintain an un-
changing level of tax liability is 0.575. All the values of Table 2.39
are less than those of Tables 2.37 and 2.38 because the loss of tax
liability due to a change of residence is not as great as the loss due
to the loss of a job.

Summary and Conclusions

A general upward shift in the distribution of taxpayers, total
income, and taxable income by income class has occurred, However,
the growth in tax liability is less than proportionate to the growth in
the tax base.

As in the case of the taxes above, there are replacement requirements necessary to maintain a constant tax base and tax liability when
jobs in an industry are lost, or when jobs remain in the city, but
employment moves to the suburbs. In both these cases, the results
show that employment in high-wage industries, such as construction
and government, is more difficult to replace than employment of low-
wage industries, such as trade and services.

The Sales Tax

This section is divided into four parts. The first briefly describes the sales tax and its historical performance. The second
describes the method by which tax revenues are identified by industry.
In the third, the variation of the sales tax base and sales tax revenue
by industry is investigated for 1968 and 1970. Finally, the response
of the sales tax base and sales tax revenue to the changing composition
of economic activity is considered.

An Overview

New York State currently levies a 4 percent tax on retail sales.
Within New York State, counties and the City of New York may add
up to an additional 3 percent to the state rate. Revenues generated
by the tax are returned to the respective county in which the tax was
collected. For New York City, revenues are paid to the city's general
fund. The general form of the sales tax is quite simple, but, because
of numerous changes that have occurred in its legal structure, the
revenue yields that the city has received have varied substantially.
Prior to August 1, 1965, the tax was administered locally, and a 4
percent rate on taxable items was levied by the city. Since this date,
the tax has been administered by the State Tax Commission, and the
city's share of the total levy has been limited to 3 percent. For this
reason, a corresponding loss in local revenue has occurred.

It should be pointed out that the sales tax, while usually considered a tax on solely local retail activity, also possesses a nonlocal component. This portion, called the compensating use tax, is levied on goods that are purchased outside the taxing jurisdiction, but that are brought into the taxing jurisdiction by local residents. It is therefore levied in lieu of the payment that would have been imposed had the goods been purchased in the jurisdiction and serves to discourage the evasion of local sales taxes by local residents. In practice, because the information necessary to levy the use tax is seldom available to tax officials, it is commonly evaded. It makes up a relatively small proportion of sales tax revenue.

The discontinuous revenue increases that were brought about by substantial rate increases in the property, income, and corporation taxes are not evident in the case of the sales tax. On the contrary, in 1965, the change in the tax rate allocated to local governments left New York City with a smaller proportion of total sales tax revenues than it had previously enjoyed and, in absolute terms, a smaller amount of revenue. At that time, revenue dropped from $441.9 million to $382.1 million and did not rise above the 1965 level until 1969. (See Table 2.40.) In revenue terms, therefore, the yield from the

TABLE 2.40

Sales Tax Revenue in New York City, 1961-72
(in thousands of current dollars)

Fiscal Year	Revenues
1961	303,000
1962	318,031
1963	326,327
1964	417,403
1965	441,853
1966	382,121
1967	379,621
1968	409,889
1969	444,240
1970	466,907
1971	493,601
1972	519,704

Source: Comptroller of the City of New York, Annual Report (New York: Office of the Comptroller, 1961-72).

sales tax grew more slowly over the decade than would have been true had the decrease not occurred. Between 1966 and 1972, revenues increased by 36 percent, an average yearly increase of 6 percent.

Relating Sales Tax Revenues to the Tax Base

The purpose of this subsection is to discuss the method by which the change in sales tax revenues can be attributed to changes in the economic base. This consists of two parts: First, the changes in tax revenues must be related to changes in the tax base; and, second, changes in the tax base must be related to the changes in the composition of economic activities.

The revenue response of a tax to change in its base can be, and usually is, evaluated by examining the change in revenues relative to the change in the base. As was indicated in the discussion of the resident income tax, this relationship can be expressed as rate and base elasticities. Rate elasticities indicate that portion of the change in tax revenues that can be attributed to the rate structure of the tax. The base elasticity indicates that portion of the change in tax revenues that can be attributed to changes in income. When the tax is imposed at a flat rate, the change in revenues can be related directly to changes in the base. Under these circumstances, the behavior of revenues can be related directly to the behavior of the tax base. Thus, it is possible to express the revenue response to changes in the tax base as follows:

$$\Delta SR = \eta_{bs} \frac{SR_1}{SB_1} \Delta SB \tag{8}$$

where: ΔSR = the change in tax revenues

η_{bs} = the base elasticity of the sales tax

ΔSB = the change in sales tax base—total personal income

SR_1 = tax revenues in the initial period

SB_1 = the sales tax base in the initial period.

The empirical estimation of the response to the change in the sales tax base requires only total revenues, total tax base, the base elasticity, and the change in the tax base. As the tax is imposed on the purchase of goods and services, and as the latter is closely related to income, the tax base and base elasticity required for this analysis are those of personal income.

The relation between the base of the sales tax and the composition of economic activities is similar to that of the income tax described above. However, unlike the income taxes, the sales tax rate and base are not differentially defined for residents and commuters. This being the case, and since the objective is to evaluate the effect of changes in the composition of the city's economy for the tax base, the tax base (personal income earned in New York City) and employment in each industry can be related directly to each other. As indicated in the foregoing discussion, data on tax bases by industry are generally not readily available. However, for the purpose of this analysis, the unpublished estimates of earnings produced by each industry in New York City and earnings as a percent of personal income, made available by the U.S. Department of Commerce, provide the data that identified each industry's contribution to the base (personal income) of the sales tax.[25]

Industrial Variation in Tax Base and Tax Revenue

In 1968, manufacturing represented the largest amount of the total base, followed by services and trade. (See Table 2.41.) Construction, on the other hand, contained the smallest amount. However, by 1970, services replaced manufacturing in terms of aggregate sales tax base, although the other industries maintained their relative shares.

As was the case with the sales tax base, manufacturing maintained the largest share of the total sales tax revenues in 1968, followed by services and trade (Table 2.42).* However, by 1970, services had replaced manufacturing as the industry with the most revenue paid. In sum, in 1968, manufacturing had the largest aggregate base as well as tax payments of any industry. By 1970, services had replaced manufacturing as the largest industry for both aggregate sales tax base and revenues raised.

Although manufacturing clearly dominates most other industries in terms of aggregate sales tax base and revenues, when these measures are calculated on a per employee basis, its relative position is different. (See Table 2.43.) The construction industry registers the largest base per employee ($17,103) and revenue per employee ($173), while services is lowest in both categories ($11,366 in base per

––––––––––

*Sales tax revenues generated by each industry were estimated on the basis of the city-wide relationship (that is, the ratio) of tax revenues to tax base.

139

TABLE 2.41

Estimated Total Sales Tax Base in New York City by Industry, 1968 and 1970
(in thousands of dollars)

Industry	1968	1970
Manufacturing	9,135,112	9,687,218
Construction	1,515,502	1,889,007
Transportation and communication	4,251,826	5,134,225
Wholesale and retail trade	8,040,582	9,009,113
Finance, insurance, and real estate	5,514,745	6,199,819
Services	8,251,069	9,832,526
Government	N.A.	7,591,440

N.A.: Not available.

Sources: "Earnings by Broad Industrial Sector" and "Earnings as a Percent of Personal Income" (unpublished tables, Regional Economics Information System, Bureau of Economic Analysis, U.S. Department of Commerce).

TABLE 2.42

Estimated Total Sales Tax Revenue in New York City by Industry, 1968 and 1970
(in thousands of dollars)

Industry	1968	1970
Manufacturing	95,919	97,841
Construction	15,913	19,086
Transportation and communication	44,644	51,856
Wholesale and retail trade	84,426	90,992
Finance, insurance, and real estate	57,905	62,618
Services	86,636	99,309
Government	N.A.	76,404

Sources: "Earnings by Broad Industrial Sector" and "Earnings as a Percent of Personal Income" (unpublished tables, Regional Economics Information System, Bureau of Economic Analysis, U.S. Department of Commerce).

TABLE 2.43

Estimated Sales Tax Base and Revenue per Employee in New York City by Industry, 1970
(dollars)

Industry	Base per Employee	Revenue per Employee
Manufacturing	12,633	128
Construction	17,102	173
Transportation and communication	15,853	160
Wholesale and retail trade	12,179	123
Finance, insurance, and real estate	13,319	135
Services	11,366	115
Government	13,489	136

Source: "Earnings by Broad Industrial Sector" and "Earnings as a Percent of Personal Income" (unpublished tables, Regional Economics Information System, Bureau of Economic Analysis, U.S. Department of Commerce).

employee and $115 in revenue per employee). Manufacturing is third lowest in both categories—$12,633 in base per employee and $128 in revenue per employee.

Response of the Sales Tax to Employment Changes

After noting the industrial variation in sales tax base and revenue, the question that immediately arises concerns the effect on each of shifts in the composition of total employment. In particular, what would be the effect on sales tax revenues or on the sales tax base of the replacement of a manufacturing job with one in the service sector or the trade sector? Because of a lack of data, the city-wide relationship between tax base and tax revenue was employed to determine tax revenues for each industry; therefore, the coefficients in Table 2.44 relate to the effect of employment shifts on either base or revenue per employee.

Each coefficient in Table 2.44 indicates the number of jobs in the column sector necessary to replace one job in the corresponding row sector. Specifically, they indicate that the replacement of one job in manufacturing requires the addition of 0.73 construction jobs, 0.8 transportation jobs, 1.04 trade sector jobs, 0.94 finance jobs, 1.11 service sector jobs, or 0.94 government sector jobs, in order to maintain constant sales tax revenues and sales tax base.

The easiest jobs to replace appear to be those in the service sector, requiring only 0.89 manufacturing jobs, 0.93 trade jobs, or 0.85 finance jobs, in order to keep sales tax revenues and base constant. On the other hand, construction jobs are the most difficult to replace. One construction job requires the addition of 1.35 manufacturing jobs, 1.08 transportation jobs, 1.4 trade jobs, 1.28 finance jobs, 1.5 service sector jobs, or 1.27 government sector jobs, in order to maintain constant sales tax base and revenues.

Finally, a word about the implications for sales tax revenues and base of the past trend of employment changes is in order. The replacement of manufacturing and wholesale jobs requires the addition of 1.11 service sector jobs for the former and 1.06 for the latter, in order to maintain constant sales tax revenues and base.

Summary and Conclusions

Manufacturing maintains a larger aggregate sales tax base and furnishes larger amounts of sales tax revenue than the other industries (except for services), though its per-employee share of each is second lowest. Both manufacturing and trade jobs are among the most difficult to replace and require 1.11 and 1.06 service sector jobs respectively to offset the loss in sales tax base and revenue that would accompany their movement out of the city.

141

TABLE 2.44

Estimated Employment Replacement Requirements for Constant Sales Tax Revenues or Base in New York City by Industry, 1970

Replaced Industry	Replacing Industry						
	Manufacturing	Construction	Transportation and Communication	Wholesale and Retail Trade	Finance, Insurance, and Real Estate	Services	Government
Manufacturing	1.00	0.73	0.80	1.04	0.94	1.11	0.94
Construction	1.35	1.00	1.08	1.40	1.28	1.50	1.27
Transportation and communication	1.25	0.92	1.00	1.30	1.18	1.39	1 78
Wholesale and retail trade	0.96	0.71	0.76	1.00	0.91	1.06	0.90
Finance, insurance, and real estate	1.05	0.78	0.84	1.09	1.00	1.17	0.99
Services	0.89	0.66	0.71	0.93	0.85	1.00	0.85
Government	1.06	0.79	0.85	1.11	1.00	1.18	1.00

Sources: "Earnings by Broad Industrial Sector" and "Earnings as a Percent of Personal Income" (unpublished tables, Regional Economics Information System, Bureau of Economic Analysis, U.S. Department of Commerce).

TABLE 2.45

Estimated New Residential Property, Business Income, Personal Income, and Sales Tax Revenues per Employee in New York City by Industry[a] (dollars)

Industry	Nonresidential Property Tax	Corporate Income Tax[b]	Personal Income Tax	Commuter Earnings Tax	Retail Sales Tax	Total Tax Revenues[c] per Employee
Manufacturing	79	79	95	44	128	374
Wholesale and retail trade	274	53	89	41	123	530
FIRE	241	163	103	53	135	622
Services	115	36	80	37	115	338
Government	—	—	107	55	136	234

[a]Calculated from business income, property, and sales tax revenues per employee in 1969 and personal income tax revenues per employee in 1970.
[b]Includes general corporation income tax, financial corporation income tax, and insurance corporation tax.
[c]Personal income and commuter earnings tax revenues per employee included in total tax revenues are calculated as the weighted average of personal income and commuter earnings tax per employee. The weights employed are resident and commuting employees as a percent of total employment in each industry.

Sources: For tax revenues per employee, see Tables 2.16, 2.22, 2.36, and 2.43. For employment weights applied to the personal income and commuter earnings tax revenues see Table 1.1, above, and U.S. Department of Commerce, Bureau of the Census, Census of Population and Housing: 1970, New York Standard Metropolitan Statistical Area PHC(1)-45, Part 1 (Washington, D.C.: U.S. Government Printing Office, 1971).

SUMMARY: THE REVENUE IMPLICATIONS OF
CHANGING ECONOMIC STRUCTURE

The main objective in this chapter has been to report the revenue implications of interindustry differences in tax base and revenue contribution, so as to infer the revenue implications of changes in the composition of the city's economic base. The importance of this question is underlined by the great changes the composition of the city's employment base has undergone since 1961 and the more acute job losses which occured between 1969 and 1971.

Using a variety of methods and data sources, the analysis above attempts to establish a linkage between economic structure and tax revenues by estimating the tax payments that lie behind workers in different sectors. The taxes that respond directly to such employment changes are the corporate income tax and the business property tax (through direct employer payments) and the individual income and retail sales taxes (through individual payments). Resident property taxes are not included in this discussion, on the assumption that employment structure changes will not markedly affect residential assessed values and, therefore, revenues—this omission may require further research. (Moreover, the indirect effects of industrial activities on the property tax base and revenues, which may result from, for example, property value increases resulting from the reduction in land available for competitive use because of land use by industry, have been neglected.)

The findings derived from separate analyses of each principal tax base can be summarized in the form of the intersector variance in revenues per employee for the taxes considered. (See Table 2.45.) However, there are comparability problems with these analyses. In particular, the performance of the different taxes has been evaluated for different years (1969 and 1970), and data are not available to cover the same set of employment sectors for every tax. The number of sectors included in the specific tax analyses are greater than the number shown in this summary table because aggregation of sectors was necessary in order to make the analysis common.

These limitations notwithstanding, the analysis underscores a growing imbalance between the structure of the New York City tax system and changes in the city's economic base. This imbalance can be seen in the estimated revenues per employee in each industry for each of the four taxes considered in this analysis. (See Table 2.45.) Per-employee total tax revenues are lowest in government and services, the two activities that have experienced the largest employment increase during the period under discussion. In fact, during the 1960s, three out of every four new employees were in the government sector.

143

The relatively low value of tax revenues per government employee is directly attributable to the fact that government activities are not liable for property or business income taxation. The relatively low contribution per employee in the service industry can be traced to its relatively low average wages and the relatively large proportion of nonprofit enterprises in this sector. In the most rapidly declining sector, manufacturing, a moderate level of personal income and commuter earnings tax revenues per employee, coupled with low per-employee tax revenues, yields an overall level of per-employee tax revenues that exceeds only that in the service and government sectors. Among the employment sectors considered here, the trade industries, in which employment has declined slightly, combine the highest level of property tax revenues with relatively low corporate income, personal income, and commuter earnings tax revenues per employee to generate the second highest level of per employee tax revenues.

It is possible to use the per-employee total tax revenue data (Table 2.45) in conjunction with actual changes in employment by industrial sector to explore the revenue implications of the changes in the composition of employment that occurred between 1960 and 1970. It must be emphasized that such an explanation should be considered hypothetical, in that it does not pretend to estimate the actual changes in tax revenues that occurred between 1960 and 1970. In fact, due to the major changes in the structure of taxation—that is, the introduction of personal income taxation and the substitution of corporate income taxes for the gross receipts tax—estimation of the actual changes in tax revenues is not possible within the present context.

However, it is possible to estimate what the effects of the changes in the level and composition of employment would have been, if (1) the structure of the nonresidential property tax, the business income tax, the resident personal income and commuter earnings taxes, and the sales tax had existed and been constant throughout the 1960-70 period; and (2) the amount of per-employee tax revenues in each employment sector from these taxes had remained constant at the levels given in Table 2.45. Clearly, these are questionable assumptions. Still, tentative indications of the response of tax revenues to the changes in New York City employment that have occurred between 1960 and 1970 can be derived. (See Table 2.46.)

Applying the 1960-70 employment changes to these revenue response coefficients reveals that, in total, the revenue response is positive—that is, the net effect of the employment change between 1960 and 1970 on revenues is toward an increase. This response, however, is the combined result of the net negative effects of manufacturing and wholesaling that are more than offset by the revenue growth contributed by the growing sectors.

144

TABLE 2.46

Hypothetical Revenue Response to Changes in Composition
of Employment in New York City, 1960-70
(in thousands of dollars except column 1)

	Employment[a]	Property Tax[b]	Business Income Tax	Personal Income and Commuter Earnings Tax[c]	Sales Tax	Total Tax Revenues[c]
Manufacturing	-180.6	-13,027	-14,267	-15,893	-23,117	-66,304
Wholesale and retail trade	-9.3	-2,121	-492	-744	-1,144	-4,501
FIRE	74.7	4,168	12,176	6,200	10,084	32,628
Services[d]	176.0	6,636	6,336	12,672	20,240	45,884
Government	154.6	0	0	15,151	21,026	36,177
Estimated revenue loss due to employment loss		-15,148	-14,759	-16,637	-24,261	-70,805
Estimated revenue gain due to employment increase		10,804	18,512	34,023	51,350	114,689
Estimated total change in tax revenues		-4,344	3,752	17,386	27,089	43,884

[a] In the estimation of property tax revenues per employee (discussed earlier in this section), parts of some industries were not included because of insufficient data. In order to allow for such omissions, the employment data used in calculation of the revenue response of the property tax are those reported in David J. Bjornstad, "A Method for Estimating Interindustrial Variation in the New York City Property Tax System" (Internal Working Paper No. 18, Maxwell Research Project on the Public Finances of New York City, Syracuse University, Syracuse, N.Y. May 1973).

[b] For the property tax, the revenue response has been calculated on the assumption that the tax is levied at the tax limit. Thus, the data reported in this column refer to the effect of employment change on the tax limit.

[c] Personal income and commuter earnings tax revenues per employee included in total tax revenues are calculated as the weighted average of personal income and commuter earnings tax per employee. The weights employed are resident and commuting employees as a percent of total employment in each industry.

[d] Includes only business services for the property tax.

Sources: For tax revenues per employee, see Tables 2.16, 2.22, 2.36, and 2.43. For employment weights applied to the personal income and commuter earnings tax revenues see Table 1.1, and U.S. Department of Commerce, Bureau of the Census, Census of Population and Housing: 1970, New York Standard Metropolitan Statistical Area PHC(1)-45, Part 1 (Washington, D.C.: U.S. Government Printing Office, 1971).

145

An examination of this revenue response on a tax-by-tax basis clearly underscores the weaknesses and strengths of the New York City tax system in the face of a shift of employment out of goods-handling activities, manufacturing and trade, and into government and the services. As indicated, the increase in hypothetical nonresidential property tax revenues attributable to the growth sectors is not sufficient to compensate for the revenue loss due to the decline in manufacturing. The net decline in property tax revenues can be traced to the fact that the second largest sector of employment growth, the government, is not generally liable for the property tax. The response of corporate tax revenues, while positive, suffers a deficiency similar to the property tax—that is, the exemption of the government sector. In fact, the major factor underlying the positive response of the business income taxes is the large contribution of the finance, insurance, and real estate sector.

The major contribution to the hypothetical revenue response considered here is made by the sales tax. In this case, as in the case of the personal income and commuter earnings tax, the growth sectors, particularly government and services, make large contributions to the increase in hypothetical tax revenues. In fact, it is through the income and sales taxes that the government sector makes its total contribution to tax revenues. Clearly, changes in the composition of employment that incorporate a growth in government and services and a decline in manufacturing imply difficulties for any city that relies heavily on revenues from the taxation of nonresidential property and business income.

To this point, the analysis examined the hypothetical response of tax revenues to the changes in the level of each industry's employment that occurred between 1960 and 1970. It indicates clearly that the additional tax revenues attributable to the sectors with growing employment not only offset the decrease in revenues associated with the declining employment sectors but were sufficient to allow for an absolute growth in tax revenues. This growth in revenues, however, reflects both the differential growth in employment among industries and the net growth in total employment.

In addition to the overall response of tax revenue to growth and change in the composition of employment, it is possible to isolate the effects of changes in the composition of employment on tax revenues. To do this, it is only necessary to compare the revenue yield of each tax from each industry in 1970 with that which would have been forthcoming, if the structure of employment in 1970 had been the same as it was in 1960. A comparison of the estimated revenue yields of the four major forms of taxation from the major employment sectors in 1970 (Table 2.47) with the revenue yields that would have occurred, if total employment in 1970 had been distributed among

TABLE 2.47

Estimated Revenue Yield in New York City by Industry
and by Type of Tax, 1970
(in thousands of dollars)

Industry	Nonresidential Property Tax	Personal Income and Commuter Earnings Tax	Corporate Income Tax*	Retail Sales Tax	Total Tax Revenues
Manufacturing	60,530	67,452	60,530	98,074	286,586
Wholesale and retail trade	201,527	58,840	38,982	90,467	389,816
FIRE	110,764	38,147	74,915	62,046	285,872
Services	29,337	56,419	28,210	90,114	204,080
Government	0	55,154	—	76,541	131,695
Total	402,158	276,012	202,637	417,242	1,298,049

*Includes general corporation, financial corporation, and insurance corporation taxes.

Sources: For tax revenues per employee, see Tables 2.16, 2.22, 2.36, and 2.43. For employment weights applied to the personal income and commuter earnings tax revenues see Table 1.1 and U.S. Department of Commerce, Bureau of the Census, Census of Population and Housing: 1970, New York Standard Metropolitan Statistical Area PHC(1)-45, Part 1 (Washington, D.C.: U.S. Government Printing Office, 1971).

TABLE 2.48

Estimated Constant Employment Tax Revenues in New
York City by Industry and by Type of Tax, 1970
(in thousands of dollars)

Industry	Nonresidential Property Tax	Personal Income and Commuter Earnings Tax	Corporate Income Tax*	Retail Sales Tax	Total Tax Revenues
Manufacturing	79,277	88,309	79,277	128,449	375,312
Wholesale and retail trade	216,296	63,152	41,838	97,096	418,382
FIRE	98,598	33,957	66,687	55,231	254,473
Services	24,093	45,958	22,979	73,405	166,435
Government	0	42,405	—	58,847	101,252
Total	418,264	273,781	210,781	413,028	1,315,854

*Includes general corporation, financial corporation, and insurance corporation taxes.

Sources: For tax revenues per employee, see Tables 2.16, 2.22, 2.36, and 2.43. For employment weights applied to the personal income and commuter earnings tax revenues see Table 1.1, and U.S Department of Commerce, Bureau of the Census. Census of Population and H̶ ̶ ̶

TABLE 2.49

Estimated Revenue Response to Change in Industrial Composition
of Employment in New York City, 1970
(in thousands of dollars)

Industry	Nonresidential Property Tax	Personal Income and Commuter Earnings Tax	Corporate Income Tax*	Retail Sales Tax	Total Tax Revenues
Manufacturing	-18,742	-20,857	-18,747	-30,375	- 88,721
Wholesale and retail trade	-14,769	- 4,312	- 2,856	- 6,629	- 28,566
FIRE	12,166	4,190	8,228	6,815	31,399
Services	5,244	10,461	5,231	16,709	37,645
Government	—	12,749	—	17,694	30,443
Estimated gross revenue loss due to employment change	-33,511	-25,169	-21,603	-37,004	-117,287
Estimated gross revenue gain due to employment change	17,410	27,400	13,459	41,218	99,487
Estimated net revenue change due to employment change	-16,101	2,231	- 8,144	4,214	-17,800

*Includes general corporation, financial corporation, and insurance corporation taxes.

Sources: For tax revenues per employee, see Tables 2.16, 2.22, 2.36, and 2.43. For employment weights applied to the personal income and commuter earnings tax revenues see Table 1.1, and U.S. Department of Commerce, Bureau of the Census, Census of Population and Housing: 1970, New York Standard Metropolitan Statistical Area PHC(1)-45, Part 1 (Washington, D.C.: U.S. Government Printing Office, 1971).

industries as it was in 1960 (Table 2.48), indicates that total tax revenues would have been larger in 1970, had the composition of employment not changed between 1960 and 1970. (See Table 2.49.) That is
to say, the net revenue response of the four principal forms of taxation
to the changes in the composition of employment that occurred between
the two years is negative. It is clear that the net revenue loss can
be traced to the nonresidential property tax and the corporation income
taxes and the small positive contribution to these taxes of those sectors whose share of employment increased during the 1960s—government and the services. Alternatively, both the personal income (including the commuter earnings tax) and the retail sales taxes responded
positively to the compositional changes in employment.

While the previous analysis (Tables 2.46-2.49) casts revenue
responses in terms of the changes in the level and composition of
employment that occurred between 1960 and 1970, it is also possible
to develop revenue measures for any level of job trade-offs between
sectors—that is, the employment replacement requirements necessary
to maintain constant total tax revenues (personal and business income,
sales, and nonresidential property taxes). These coefficients indicate,
for example, that the replacement of a manufacturing job requires
the addition of 0.71 wholesale or retail trade jobs, 0.6 finance, insurance, and real estate jobs, 1.10 service jobs, and 1.61 government
jobs. (See Table 2.50.)

The largest replacement requirements are in the finance, insurance, and real estate and transportation and communication industries, and in wholesale and retail trade. The most easily replaced
employees are those in government. The gain of a government or
a service sector job is more than offset by the loss of one job in all
other sectors. For the city employment structure to be changing
toward government and services and for the net revenue response
to be positive, the government and service sector gains must be
relatively great indeed. Such was the case in the decade of the 1960s.

The findings of this analysis, tentative as they must be, indicate
that a continuation of past trends in the changing composition of employment implies a continuation of growth in tax revenues, only if
total employment expands. However, it appears that those changes
in the composition of employment that have occurred in themselves
do not hold potential for major growth in revenues. In fact, if total
employment falls as it has in the recent past, the implications derived
from this are that a continuation of the shift out of manufacturing and
into government and the services will certainly aggravate rather than
alleviate revenue shortfalls.[26] Therefore, there may be a need for
compensating structural reform in the tax system.

Since the analysis presented in this study has been limited in
the scope of taxes considered, a comprehensive tax reform package

149

cannot be suggested. However, if an increasingly larger proportion of city employment occurs in those activities that either are not subject to, or make relatively small contributions to, the business income and property tax revenues—that is, government and services—alternative revenue sources will have to be cultivated. Of the two remaining forms of taxation considered in this study, one, the retail sales tax, is both high and at its legal limit. An increase in the retail sales tax rate would not be palatable because of its already high rate and the fact that, by nature, it tends to be regressive, placing a relatively greater burden on the poor.

The other form of taxation—that on income earned in the city—is not subjected to the limitation associated with the property tax—that is, exemption of whole sectors of employment. Moreover, the income tax is a progressive tax that places a relatively smaller burden on the poor and that tends to grow more rapidly than income. Moreover, a relatively large and growing proportion of income earned in the city, such as commuter earnings, is subject to a relatively low rate of taxation. Perhaps herein lies an area of potential tax revenue growth through structural change in the tax system.

APPENDIX: REVENUE RESPONSE TO FUTURE CHANGES IN THE STRUCTURE OF EMPLOYMENT

The purpose of the analysis presented in Chapter 2 is to establish a linkage between the structure of the New York City tax system and the structure of the city's economic base. While an analysis and projection of trends in tax payments by industry has not been the objective of the study, the tax revenues per employer coefficients in Table 2.45 do provide a means of exploring the revenue response of the city's tax system to future changes in the composition of the city's economic base. To this end, projections of locally raised revenues for 1979 are presented in Table 2.A-1 of this appendix.

These forecasts are obtained, first, by estimating the amount of revenue that would be generated by the four forms of taxation (nonresidential property, business income, personal income, and retail sales) in 1979, assuming a constant amount of tax revenue per employee (Table 2.A.1) and given varying assumptions about the growth of employment between 1970 and 1979. These estimates are then adjusted (that is, multiplied by the ratio of all locally raised revenues in 1969 to revenues from the four forms of taxation in 1969) to obtain an estimate of total locally raised revenues and inflated by a price index to allow for price changes. The price index for 1979 is estimated by assuming that prices would continue to grow at the same annual average rate as they did between 1965 and 1972.

TABLE 2.50

Estimated Employment Replacement Requirements for Constant
Tax Revenues from Taxation of Nonresidential Property,
Business Income, Personal Income, and Retail Sales*

Replaced Industry	Replacing Industry				
	Manufacturing	Wholesale and Retail Trade	FIRE	Services	Government
Manufacturing	1.00	0.71	0.60	1.11	1.61
Wholesale and retail trade	1.42	1.00	0.85	1.57	2.28
FIRE	1.66	1.17	1.00	1.84	2.68
Services	0.90	0.64	0.54	1.00	1.46
Government	0.62	0.44	0.37	0.69	1.00

*Calculated from business income, property, and sales tax figures for 1969 and personal income tax figures for 1970.

Sources: For tax revenues per employee, see Tables 2.16, 2.22, 2.36, and 2.43. For employment weights applied to the personal income and commuter earnings tax revenues see Table 1.1, and U.S. Department of Commerce, Bureau of the Census, Census of Population and Housing: 1970, New York Standard Metropolitan Statistical Area PHC(1)-45, Part 1 (Washington, D.C.: U.S. Government Printing Office, 1971).

TABLE 2.A-1

New York City Locally Raised Revenue Projections
for 1979

	Amount (in millions of dollars)	Percent Change 1972-79
Low	6,274.7	22.7
Intermediate	6,747.3	31.9
High	6,917.3	35.2
1972	5,115.7	—

Source: Comptroller of the City of New York, Annual Report
(New York: Office of the Comptroller, 1972).

The low projection of locally raised revenues was estimated on
the assumption that the level of total employment (private and public)
in 1979 would be the same as that in 1970, while the change in the job
composition that occurred between 1960 and 1970 would continue.
The intermediate projection was obtained by assuming that the job
structure in 1970 would be maintained in 1979 but that employment
in each industry would increase at a rate equal to the increase in
total employment between 1960 and 1970. Finally, the high revenue
forecast is based on projecting the rates of growth (or decline) in
each industry for the 1960-70 period forward to 1979.

Based on these assumptions, forecasts of locally raised revenues
for 1979 range between $6.27 billion and $6.9 billion—that is, an increase in revenues over 1972 of between 22.7 percent and 35.2 percent.
As can be seen, a continuation of the trends of change in the structure
of employment that occurred between the years 1960 and 1970, un-
accompanied by an increase in total employment, would generate a
revenue increase of about 23 percent. Alternatively, a continuation
of the employment experience of that decade—that is, a growth in total
employment composed of rapid growth in the government and service
sectors and declines in the manufacturing and trade sectors—would
lead to an increase in locally raised revenue of about 35 percent.
Given the recent fall in employment between 1969 and 1972 in all the
major employment sectors, even these forecasts, which cannot be
considered high, would seem to overstate the revenue possibilities
for 1979. However, it should be noted that these forecasts are based
on an assumed constancy in the amount of tax revenues per job in each

industry. A number of factors, such as changes in profits, personal income, property, and retail sales per employee, as well as structural changes in the tax system itself, could lead to changes in per-employee tax revenues and thereby alter the revenue projections.

NOTES

1. Alexander Ganz and Thomas O'Brien, "The City: Sandbox, Reservation or Dynamo?" (Cambridge: Massachusetts Institute of Technology, 1972; mimeographed).

2. U.S. Department of Commerce, Bureau of the Census, Compendium of City Government Finances (Washington, D.C.: U.S. Government Printing Office).

3. Comptroller of the City of New York, Annual Report (New York: Office of the Comptroller).

4. For a comprehensive discussion of the changes introduced into the tax structure of New York City, see David J. Bjornstad, "The Structure and Performance of the New York City Tax System" (Internal Working Paper No. 2, Maxwell Research Project on the Public Finances of New York City, Syracuse University, Syracuse, N.Y., July 1972).

5. For a discussion of property tax limits, see David J. Bjornstad, "The New York City Property Tax Base: Definition, Composition and Measurement" (Internal Working Paper No. 7, Maxwell Research Project on the Public Finances of New York City, Syracuse University, Syracuse, New York, October 1972).

6. For a discussion of the legal structure of the property tax, see ibid. The rationale underlying the use of the term, market value, rather than the more commonly cited full value, is also covered in this paper.

7. For an analysis of the procedures involved in the assessment of property and the determination of the property tax rate, see ibid.

8. McKinney's Consolidated Laws of New York, New York State Constitution, Article VIII, sec. 6.

9. See ibid., sec. 5 subparagraph D.

10. For discussion of the tax limit and the manner in which it is calculated, see Bjornstad, "Structure and Performance of New York City Tax System," op. cit. and "New York City Property Tax Base," op. cit.

11. McKinney, New York State Constitution, Article VIII, Sec. 11, subparagraph A. Under the State Constitution, the city may exclude from the operating tax limit certain capital items that it chooses to finance in the current budget. Though this "pay-as-you-go" option requires the city to issue short-term capital notes, it gains a net advantage by avoiding the service changes of longer-term notes.

(This section should not be confused with Subparagraph B of sec. 11, which allows jurisdictions other than New York City to exclude from the tax limit current expenditure items for which there is a legally established "period of probable usefulnees.")

12. For the definition of the consistently defined equalization rate, see Bjornstad, "Structure and Performance of New York City Tax System," op. cit., pp. 34-36.

13. These figures have been calculated from the worksheets from which the city-wide equalization rate is calculated by the State Board of Equalization and Assessment.

14. The real tax rate is defined as the ratio of tax liability or tax revenue to the market value of property. Thus, for the ith property class the real tax,

$$r_i^* = \frac{TR_i}{MV_i} = \frac{rAV_i}{MV_i}$$

For the city as a whole, the real tax rate,

$$r^* = \frac{TR}{MV} = \frac{rAV}{MV}$$

Dividing r_i^* by r^* yields

$$\frac{r_i^*}{r^*} = \frac{rAV_i}{MV_i} \div \frac{rAV}{MV} = \frac{AV_i}{AV} \div \frac{MV_i}{MV}$$

where

TR_i = tax revenue or liability of the ith class

MV_i = market value of the ith class

AV_i = assessed value of the ith class

A = ΣAV_i

TR = ΣTR_i

MV = ΣMV_i

r = nominal tax rate (effective tax rate on assessed value)

r^* = real tax rate (effective tax rate on market value).

15. Because an equal tax rate is levied on all property, it is possible to avoid the use of revenues in the calculation of the relative tax shares (RTS) by substituting a class's assessed value for its revenue liability. This can be easily shown for the ith uses class, where the variables are defined as in note 14.

$$RTS_i = TR_i/TR \div MV_i/MV$$

since: $$TR_i = rAV/_i \text{ and } TR = rAV_i$$

$$RTS_i = rAV_i/rAV \div MV_i/MV$$

which becomes:

$$RTS_i = AV_i/AV \div MV_i/MV.$$

16. The material considered in this subsection has been discussed in detail in David J. Bjornstad, "Components of the Real Property Tax Base: Model Development with Empirical Application to Selected Industries in New York City" (unpublished dissertation, Syracuse University, Syracuse, New York, 1973).

17. The successful completion of this task was greatly facilitated by the helpful cooperation of Mr. Philip Click, Chief Assessor in New York City, who made available from the files of his office a large part of the information required for this study.

18. In this analysis, the assessment ratio is treated as exogenously determined by tax policy. For a more detailed treatment of this topic in which the assessment ratio is endogenously determined by tax policy and market forces, see J. T. Romans, "On the Measurement of Assessment Error," National Tax Journal 23 (March 1970): 89-91

19. For a discussion of the effects on revenue of discretionary changes in the property tax, see section of this chapter entitled "Intercity Comparisons and Historical Trends."

20. Underlying the data contained in Table 2.14 are three sets of sample data. The first, provided by the New York City Department of City Planning, pertains to total amount of space per employee and the distribution of space among use, such as offices, warehouses, and factories; the second pertains to the value per foot of space by type of use and was obtained from the New York City Real Property Assessment Department. As the assessment records give assessed values, the third set of data, equalization rates by property class, was required for the estimation of the market value per square foot of space. These data were provided by the New York State Department of Equalization and Assessment. For a discussion of these data sets, and the procedures underlying the estimates presented in Table 2.14, see Bjornstad, "Components of the Real Property Tax Base," op. cit.

21. For a discussion of these data and the modifications applied to them, see Metropolitan and Regional Research Center, New York City: Economic Base and Fiscal Capacity, Report prepared for the Temporary State Commission to Make a Study of the Governmental Operation of the City of New York, April 1973 (New York: State Study Commission on New York City, 1973), Appendix II-1.

22. For a comprehensive discussion of the past and recent (1971) structure of the personal income tax, see Bjornstad, "Structure and Performance of New York City Tax System," op. cit.

23. McKinney's Consolidated Laws of New York, Model Local Law, sec. 25M2.

24. The overall elasticity, ET is defined as the product of the rate, ER, and base, EB, elasticities where

$$ER = \frac{\Delta TL/(TL_1 + TL_2)}{\Delta TI/(TI_1 + TI_2)}$$

$$EB = \frac{\Delta TI/(TI_1 + TI_2)}{\Delta TY/(TY_1 + TY_2)}$$

where

TL = tax liability

TI = taxable income

TY = total income

Δ represents a change in the associated variable between years 1 and 2.

25 "Earnings by Broad Industrial Categories" and "Earnings as a Percent of Personal Income," (unpublished tables, Regional Economics Information System, Bureau of Economic Analysis, U.S. Department of Commerce).

26. Estimates of tax revenues for the year 1979, based on various plausible assumptions about employment growth, are given in the appendix to this chapter.

The goal of this chapter is to identify the factors affecting the historical growth of New York City government expenditures, to measure the sensitivity of expenditures to changes in these factors, and to use this information to project the future pattern and level of city expenditures. To accomplish this, the model links historical expenditure increases to the rate of inflation—over which the city government has no discretionary control—and to increases in city government employment levels, real wage rates, and pension and fringe benefit contribution rates—over which the city does have a measure of discretionary influence.

This study is more concerned with a measurement of the relative importance of the basic factors affecting expenditures than with an analysis and projection of trends in each of these factors. To the extent the determinants of changes in these factors are amenable to quantitative analysis, such an analysis is presented in the next chapter. The model around which this analysis is built is described in this chapter. It is then applied to New York City fiscal data to analyze the growth in city government expenditures over the 1965-72 period and thereby provide a basis for estimating the sensitivity of city government expenditures to changes in the four basic factors outlined above. This sensitivity and its implications for the future level of New York City expenditures are then discussed. However, before the expenditure analysis is discussed, an attempt is made to place it in an appropriate context by describing the historical growth in New York City government expenditures and by comparing the expenditure level and structure of New York City with those of a selected group of other large cities.

The scope of the analysis is limited both by its time frame and by the expenditure details that are considered. Though the years 1965 to 1972 comprise the time span most often studied, the boundary

157

years for any particular segment of the analysis were chosen primarily on a basis of the availability of comparable data. The expenditure analysis is confined to a consideration of current expenditures, taken here to be those expenditure items included in the expense budget. Capital expenditures are excluded from this study, primarily because they respond to an entirely different set of factors than do current expenditures; hence an entirely different kind of model would be required for the analysis. The major reason for this difference is the typical long-term trend in capital expenditures. It is well known that capital expenditures are "lumpy" and that time series will not show clear "trends" of increase or decrease—that is, the level of capital spending in any given year reflects such influences as a considerable period of past planning and current money market considerations.

THE HISTORICAL GROWTH IN NEW YORK CITY GOVERNMENT EXPENDITURES

The purpose of this section is to trace the historical growth in New York City government expenditures. In order to determine possible causes for growth in aggregate current expenditures, the following analysis will focus, in turn, on the objects of expenditure (what factors of production, such as labor, equipment, were bought by the city government) and the functions of these expenditures (how the funds were distributed among city government activities). It should be noted at the outset that the specific concern here is the finances of the New York City government, to the exclusion of other local governments that overlap the New York City area.

Growth in Expenditures by Object

City government expenditures are disaggregated by object of expenditure for a seven-year period in Table 3.1. The data show that between 1965 and 1972, total current expenditures increased from $3.3 billion to over $8.5 billion—by an average annual rate of 14.3 percent. The largest component of current expenditures, when viewed by object, was personal services, or direct labor costs, which increased from $1.7 billion in 1965 to more than $3.2 billion in 1972— by a yearly rate of 9.7 percent. However, while direct labor costs still dominated city government expenditure requirements (38.5 percent of total current expenditures in 1972), their relative importance diminished over the seven-year period. The annual rate of increase in total current expenditures was a full five percentage points higher than that in direct labor costs, primarily because the rate of increase

TABLE 3.1

New York City Government Expenditures by Object, 1965-72
(in millions of dollars)

Year	Personal Services	Supplies, Materials, and Equipment	Contractual Services	Social Welfare Contributions	Retirement System Contributions	Debt Service	Other Current Expenditures*	Total Current Expenditures
1965	1,709.3	105.6	141.2	469.7	312.5	472.5	136.0	3,346.8
1966	1,916.5	132.7	200.5	559.8	218.2	552.9	198.2	3,778.8
1967	2,081.6	151.0	287.4	719.5	364.4	638.0	254.9	4,469.8
1968	2,300.9	166.7	412.2	1,039.8	396.1	655.1	325.2	5,296.0
1969	2,485.5	187.1	425.3	1,446.6	376.9	672.4	472.6	6,066.4
1970	3,015.4	159.0	485.7	1,498.4	423.0	705.8	417.7	6,705.0
1971	3,082.8	110.1	450.2	1,870.9	388.5	781.8	782.4	7,466.7
1972	3,271.4	125.8	449.1	2,149.4	489.6	847.4	1,175.4	8,508.1
Total increase	1,562.1	20.2	307.9	1,679.7	177.1	374.9	1,039.4	5,161.3
Average annual increase	9.7%	2.5%	18.0%	24.3%	6.6%	8.7%	38.2%	14.3%

*"Other Current Expenditures" include payment primarily for health insurance for city employees, social security taxes, the transportation of school children, rent and allowances for uniforms, certain employee welfare and pension payments, and unallocated appropriations, which consist primarily of unallocated appropriations for the Health and Hospitals Corporation, the interdepartmental appropriations for other than personal services, the Cash Imprest Fund, and Community School Districts.

<u>Source</u>: Comptroller of the City of New York, <u>Annual Report</u> (New York: Office of the Comptroller, 1965-72).

in total current expenditures was dominated by a 24 percent per year increase in transfer payments.

Second in importance as a component of total current expenditures were social welfare contributions. These transfer payments rose from slightly less than $470 million in 1965 to more than $2.1 billion in 1972. This translates into a yearly rate of increase of about 24.3 percent, which is larger than that for any other object category except the "other current expenditure" grouping. It should be noted that increases in transfer payments are not necessarily indicative of a drain on city revenues raised from own sources. However, when state and federal reimbursements are removed, the rate of increase in locally supported welfare expenditures is 23.6 percent per year.

Debt service expenditures increased from about $470 million in 1965 to almost $850 million in 1972—by a yearly rate of 8.7 percent. Debt service payments might be interpreted as being analogous to other transfer payments, in that they represent the cost of capital assets purchased by the city government. As may be seen from the data in Table 3.1, such capital payments represent less than 26 percent of total direct labor payments in 1972 and are growing at a slower rate.

Retirement system contributions by the city government accounted for the next largest fraction of the budget (5.8 percent in 1972) and increased from $312.5 million in 1965 to $489.6 million in 1972—a yearly rate of 6.6 percent. Therefore, the growth in retirement system costs over the eight years since 1965 averaged about two-thirds of the percentage increase in direct labor costs and grew at a rate substantially below that of total current expenditures.

Finally, expenditures for supplies, materials, and equipment and contractual services displayed an erratic pattern of growth over the period. The growth in expenditures for supplies, materials, and equipment between 1965 and 1969 was substantial—from $105.6 million to $187.1 million. Between 1969 and 1971, expenditures declined but then rose again in 1972. Expenditures for contractual services grew even more rapidly between 1965 and 1970—from $141.2 million to $485.7 million—but decreased in both 1971 and 1972. The growing importance of contractual services as a component of city government expenditures deserves underlining. It now accounts for about the same fraction of the expense budget as retirement system costs, and it is growing faster. In part, this rapid growth can be attributed to the growth in local government support of privately provided social welfare-type programs, such as private antipoverty, on-the-job training, and mental health agencies and programs to combat addictive drugs, which, along with expenditures for special services clinics, accounted for approximately 40 percent of contractual service expenditures in 1971.

Growth in Expenditures by Function

Quite apart from the question of how the expense budget is distributed among objects of expenditure is the issue of how the city government has allocated its resources among functional expenditure areas. Such a breakdown enables estimation of the extent to which the growth in particular functional areas of expenditure is dominating overall expenditure growth. New York City government expenditures are shown by function in Table 3.2 for the 1965-72 period. The social service component is the single most important fraction of the city expense budget. Between 1965 and 1972, expenditures for this function rose from $562.1 million to $2.5588 billion, or at a yearly rate of 24 percent. Only higher education, of the departments noted in Table 3.2, increased at a greater rate: from $77.4 million to $371.8 million over the period, by an average yearly rate of 25.1 percent. Expenditures for public schools increased from $878.9 million in 1965 to $1.9158 billion in 1972—which amounts to an 11.8 percent increase yearly. Health services expenditures rose from $314.6 million to $753.4 million, an average rate of 13.3 percent a year.

Of significantly less budgetary importance are the police, fire, and environmental protection (including sanitation) functions. For police (the largest of the three), expenditures rose from $318 million in 1965 to $599.1 million in 1972; the yearly rate of growth was 9.5 percent. Expenditures on fire increased from $163.9 million to $269.5 million, at a yearly rate of only 7.4 percent—the smallest increase of any of the larger departments. Environmental Protection Administration (EPA) expenditures increased more rapidly than was the case for fire—from $125.7 million to $281.6 million over the period, averaging 12.2 percent per year.

The remaining functions listed in Table 3.2 increased at rates generally smaller than the larger departments. For libraries, parks and recreation, and cultural expenditures, the yearly rate of increase was 7.1 percent; for general government and legislative, 6.7 percent; and for correction and judicial, 11.1 percent. Expenditures for other functions increased from $640.6 million in 1965 to $1.3091 billion in 1972—a yearly increase of 10.8 percent.

Growth in Expenditures: Summary

In summary, New York City government current expenditures increased by 14.3 percent per year between 1965 and 1972. The dominant force on this rate of increase was welfare expenditures. When viewed as objects of expenditure, transfer payments increased faster than any class of factor payment, and when viewed by function,

TABLE 3.2

New York City Government Expenditures by Function, 1965-72
(in millions of dollars)

Year	Police	Fire	EPA	Public Schools	Higher Education	Social Services	Health Services	Libraries, Parks and Recreation, Cultural	General Government and Legislative	Correction and Judicial	Other Current Expenditures	Total Current Expenditures
1965	318.0	163.9	125.7	878.9	77.4	562.1	314.6	73.3	138.7	53.6	640.6	3,346.8
1966	332.8	169.1	132.9	953.2	89.2	716.8	349.0	82.4	150.9	56.2	746.3	3,778.8
1967	390.5	189.3	139.1	1,124.7	113.2	938.8	386.0	89.4	156.3	57.7	911.8	4,496.8
1968	421.8	199.6	147.4	1,234.6	142.2	1,403.3	466.3	93.3	168.1	66.6	952.8	5,296.0
1969	461.6	236.9	227.0	1,392.6	187.8	1,826.7	533.7	98.9	190.4	73.8	837.0	6,066.4
1970	568.0	251.4	243.3	1,563.6	250.1	1,871.4	610.6	103.0	230.3	91.5	921.8	6,705.0
1971	571.5	257.4	273.9	1,821.7	319.6	2,256.8	634.0	110.6	220.4	102.1	898.7	7,466.7
1972	599.1	269.5	281.6	1,915.8	371.8	2,558.8	753.4	118.4	218.8	111.8	1,309.1	8,508.1
Total increase	281.1	105.6	155.9	1,036.9	294.4	1,996.7	438.8	45.1	80.1	58.2	668.5	5,161.3
Average annual increase	9.5%	7.4%	12.2%	11.8%	25.1%	24.0%	13.3%	7.1%	6.7%	11.1%	10.8%	14.3%

Source: Comptroller of the City of New York Annual Report (New York: Office of the Comptroller, 1965-72).

expenditures for social services exhibited a growth rate substantially above that for total expenditures.

On the basis of object of expenditure, direct labor costs grew faster than any materials-supplies-equipment expenditures, retirement system contributions, or debt service. From this, it might be argued that if transfer payments are excluded, an increasingly greater share of each expenditure dollar is being spent directly for wages and salaries. (It is left for a later section of this study to show how this increase in direct labor costs is attributable to employment increase, wage rate increase, and inflation.)

The significant feature of the distribution and growth of New York City expenditures on a functional basis is the dominance of the social expenditure functions, particularly education and welfare. Spending for these two functions has all but determined both the level and the trend in New York City government total expenditures over this period. Conversely, the housekeeping functions grew at generally lower rates, with the notable exceptions of the EPA and Criminal Courts and Justice.

A COMPARISON OF NEW YORK CITY GOVERNMENT EXPENDITURES WITH THOSE OF THE OTHER NINE LARGEST CITIES IN THE UNITED STATES

While the data above highlight the level and rate of increase in New York City government expenditures, they give little indication of their "normality"—that is, whether New York City is the same as or in some way different from other cities in the United States. To this end, New York City is compared here with the nine largest cities in the nation, with the specific purpose of determining whether the patterns of growth in expenditures that took place in New York City between 1966 and 1971 also occurred in other large U.S. cities.[1]

Before making such comparisons, it should be noted that some differences in the scope of services provided by different local governments prevent exact comparison. The city government in Washington, D.C., unlike any other city government, is not located within the jurisdiction of a state government. As a consequence, many services and public functions that in most cities are provided by the state or county governments are the responsibility of the city government in Washington, D.C. Similarly, in both New York City and Baltimore, the city government encompasses activities that in other cities are provided by the county. The most notable outcome of such peculiarities in the government structures of these cities is the responsibility for the provision of welfare services on the part of these cities' governments. In addition to welfare, New York City, Washington, D.C., and Baltimore, are unique among the 10 largest cities in that in all three, the government, rather than independent school districts, has responsibility for the education function. Only in New York City, however, does the provision of education extend to the college level. In addition, New York City stands alone in the degree to which it is responsible for the provision of health and hospital services.

Finally, before proceeding, it should be noted that differences among data sources prevent exact comparison of those categories of expenditure that were reported in the previous section. That is, in order to obtain comparable data among cities, it is necessary to use data from the annual Department of Commerce publication, City Government Finances,[2] which are not comparable with the data contained in New York City financial reports. There are a number of possible explanations for the differences that exist between data reported in the New York City Comptroller's Annual Report[3] and those reported by the U.S. Census. The most important are the definitional differences that exist between the two sources—that is, how a particular subfunction is classified. However, it should be noted that the Census data, as reported in City Government Finances, are uniform, as among cities, and therefore the comparative analysis presented here is internally consistent.

Comparison by Expenditure Object

Table 3.3 shows a comparison of expenditures by object for the 10 largest cities in the United States in the years 1966 and 1971. In order to compare these data independently of the effects of city size, all expenditures are expressed in per capita terms.

On average, the largest category of expenditure is personal service—that is, direct wage and salary payments to government employees. In 1966, per capita personnel expenditures in New York City were greater than in any city studied, and, in 1971, the per capita level in New York City was second only to Washington, D.C. in this group. As both cities perform functions not usually provided by city governments, the high level of per capita expenditures is not surprising. However, while direct labor expenditure per resident in New York City was still almost $280 greater than the average for the other nine cities, the rate of growth for the New York City government over this period was below the average.

Per capita transfer expenditures were over two times larger in New York City than in any of the other cities studied, and more than 10 times larger than the other nine cities combined in 1971. This disparity is not particularly surprising since these transfers are largely for public welfare, and none of the cities in the comparison,

TABLE 3.3

Per Capita Expenditures by Object for 10 Largest U.S. Cities, 1966 and 1971
(dollars)

	Personal Service		Transfers		Retirement Contribution		Interest on Debt		Capital		Other		Total Expenditures		Average Annual Increase	
	1966	1971	1966	1971	1966	1971	1966	1971	1966	1971	1966	1971	1966	1971	Dollars	Percent
New York	299.1	477.0	71.9	255.8	44.9	78.1	17.2	30.5	60.8	124.7	88.9	240.8	582.9	1,206.6	124.7	15.7
Other nine (average)	108.3	195.3	11.4	20.5	12.8	21.7	7.1	12.8	38.1	69.0	38.4	73.1	216.1	392.3	35.2	12.7
Chicago	75.1	149.5	5.4	5.8	7.6	9.4	6.6	9.9	24.0	41.4	21.5	39.9	140.2	256.0	23.2	12.8
Los Angeles	121.5	180.3	0.2	0.1	20.6	36.1	3.3	6.6	31.5	67.9	60.5	73.4	237.6	364.5	25.4	8.9
Philadelphia	86.9	176.6	8.9	17.6	8.4	22.0	11.8	20.0	37.9	84.8	35.9	65.0	189.7	385.8	39.2	15.3
Detroit	104.6	181.9	16.5	11.8	23.6	39.0	6.5	13.1	25.0	55.0	29.9	75.7	206.1	376.5	34.1	12.8
Houston	53.3	68.0	—	3.0	3.2	5.8	7.9	10.8	52.0	30.4	23.0	42.7	139.4	160.8	4.3	2.9
Baltimore	183.9	378.6	57.4	120.8	17.4	27.3	10.0	18.4	54.6	143.4	44.7	99.7	268.0	788.2	84.0	16.5
Dallas	71.1	110.5	2.6	2.4	6.7	10.1	9.0	16.6	66.1	80.0	5.0	26.3	160.6	245.9	17.1	8.9
Washington	291.8	582.0	43.9	126.5	20.8	38.1	6.5	20.3	92.5	154.1	96.0	278.6	551.4	1,199.6	129.6	16.8
Cleveland	91.4	172.1	4.2	0.1	3.0	0.1	5.8	12.0	33.9	46.6	45.6	75.8	183.9	306.8	24.6	10.8
All 10 cities*	176.9	296.3	33.1	105.0	24.4	41.9	10.8	19.2	46.3	89.0	56.5	133.3	348.0	684.7	67.3	14.8

*The figures in this row are weighted averages obtained by dividing the expenditures of all 10 cities combined by the total population in the 10 cities.

Source: U.S. Department of Commerce, Bureau of the Census, City Government Finances, 1965-66 and 1970-71, Series GF-No. 12 and GF71-No. 4 (Washington, D.C.: U.S. Government Printing Office, 1967 and 1972).

165

except Baltimore and Washington, D.C., have a major financial responsibility for welfare expenditures. Still, among these three cities, New York City exhibited the greatest percentage increase in transfer payments.

Per capita retirement contribution expenditures by the New York City government were significantly greater than those observed in any other city in the comparison, and almost four times the average for the other nine cities. Notwithstanding this relatively high level of per-resident retirement cost, the rate of growth in New York City government contributions to retirement systems is about equal to that of the other nine cities combined.

With respect to capital expenditures, New York City shows a higher level than do most cities—with the notable exceptions of Washington, D.C. in 1966 and both Washington, D.C. and Baltimore in 1971. Expenditures by Washington, D.C. in "other purposes" areas were greater in both years than were those for New York City.

In sum, total expenditures per capita were greater in New York City than in any of the other large cities examined here. In 1966, New York City spent 67.5 percent more per resident than did the average city, and by 1971, this disparity had grown slightly, to 76.2 percent. New York City's annual percent rate of growth (15.7 percent) was exceeded only by that in Washington, D.C. (16.8 percent) and Baltimore (16.5 percent), the only other two cities in the group that perform the welfare function. When these differences in aggregate expenditure performance by the New York City government are examined by expenditure object, it may be seen that they are primarily explainable by differences in transfer payments, retirement contributions, and capital expenditures, where New York City's expenditures grew faster than the average for the other nine cities. It is also notable that New York City's higher rate of expenditure growth is not solely due to the growth in direct labor costs. A final note to be added here is that these expenditure comparisons are presented on a per capita basis, and, if such expenditures do respond in a direct way to population change, then the different rates of growth in per capita expenditures may be partially a function of changes in population size. Over the 1960-70 period, New York City's population grew by 1.5 percent, while the other nine cities show a range from -16.8 percent for Cleveland to 31.4 percent for Houston, with an average of 1.6 percent.

One problem with the comparison above is that the 10 cities have different ranges of service responsibility. In order to abstract comparative problems from this and focus more sharply on intercity expenditure differences on an object basis, the data in Table 3.4 present a breakdown of personnel expenditures for a group of "common functions"—functions that are generally provided by city

166

TABLE 3.4

Employment per 10,000 Population and Per Capita Labor Costs and
Average Wages in Common Functions for 10 Largest U.S. Cities, 1966 and 1971

| City | Employment per 10,000 Population | | Per Capita Average Wages | | Per Capita Labor Costs | | Average Annual Increase in Per Capita Labor Cost | |
	1966	1971	1966	1971	1966	1971	Dollars	Percent
New York	123.4	123.8	$8,090	$11,992	$99.8	$148.5	9.7	8.3
Other Nine (Average)	104.9	115.6	7,102	10,709	74.5	123.8	9.9	10.7
Chicago	93.1	106.1	7,523	11,829	85.6	125.5	8.0	8.0
Los Angeles	96.9	94.6	8,836	12,111	70.0	114.6	8.9	10.4
Philadelphia	121.0	139.8	6,505	10,788	78.7	150.8	14.4	13.9
Detroit	99.3	107.0	7,393	11,274	73.4	120.7	9.5	10.5
Houston	78.4	73.7	5,834	8,296	45.7	61.1	3.1	6.0
Baltimore	133.5	159.9	5,453	7,758	72.8	124.1	10.3	11.5
Dallas	104.4	109.5	5,456	8,032	57.0	87.9	6.9	9.1
Washington	151.6	203.8	7,511	11,250	113.9	229.5	23.1	15.0
Cleveland	106.1	119.7	6,123	9,906	65.0	118.6	10.7	12.5
All 10 Cities*	111.5	118.4	7,494	11,191	83.6	132.5	9.9	9.7

*The figures in this row are weighted averages obtained by dividing the expenditures of all 10 cities combined by the total population in the 10 cities.

Source: U.S. Department of Commerce, Bureau of the Census, City Employment, 1966 and 1971, Series GE-No. 3 and GE71-No. 2 (Washington, D.C.: U.S. Government Printing Office, 1967 and 1972).

government in all cities. The specific intent here is to examine the most important component of expenditures—direct labor costs—in more detail in order to study the difference among these cities in the level and growth in average wage payments and relative employment levels. Employment per 10,000 population by the New York City government is greater than that for the combined average of the other cities—123.4 versus 104.9 in 1966 and 123.8 versus 115.6 in 1971. However, in 1966, higher levels of employment per 10,000 population were registered by both Baltimore (133.5) and Washington, D.C. (151.6); similarly, in 1971, larger amounts of employment occurred in Philadelphia (139.8), Baltimore (159.9), and Washington, D.C. (203.8).

It would be difficult to determine, theoretically, what the level of employment should be. However, if such a norm were established on a basis of what other very large cities do, New York City's employment level is clearly in the "normal" range and growing at "normal" rates. There are possible errors in such comparisons, the most important being that these cities have different scopes of service, and, therefore, the comparison will show city governments that "do more things"—such as that of Washington, D.C.—to have higher employment levels and cities that make substantial use of special districts to have lower employment levels. Comparative expenditure growth rates might be similarly distorted. However, New York City has long been known to have responsibility for a substantial number of public functions that, aside from Washington, D.C. and, to a lesser extent, Baltimore, are not commonly provided by city governments. This would suggest that, if anything, there is an upward bias on New York City government employment in this comparison, and the earlier conclusion about the normality of New York City employment would still hold.

The second facet of comparative labor cost analysis is the levels of average wages paid to city government employees. Ideally, wages paid to comparable classes of government employees would be matched —for example, policemen and teachers. However, such data are not readily available on a comparable basis for all the cities. Instead, average wage levels are estimated as the ratio of total personal service expenditures to employment. When measured in this fashion, average wages paid to New York City government employees are higher than the average for all 10 cities combined.* In 1966, the average wage paid in New York City ($8,090) was 14 percent above

---

*Where the comparison is of average wages in the common municipal functions, it is likely that some of the elements of the common functions generally provided by states or counties, such as state police, are provided by the city government in Washington, D.C.

the average for the other cities, and, in 1971, it was $11,992, or 12 percent above the average. However, in both years, higher average wages were paid to public employees in Los Angeles—$8,836 in 1966 and $12,111 in 1971—and the average wage in Chicago in 1971 was only slightly lower than that in New York City. When correction is made for the effects of inflation over the period, the average wage in New York City for Public employees ($9,311) is only 4.5 percent above the average ($8,910) and is below those paid in Chicago ($9,594) and Los Angeles ($9,919).[4]

Labor costs per city resident were also larger in New York City than in the other cities combined—$99.80 versus $74.50 in 1966 and $148.50 versus $123.80 in 1971. However, in 1966, per capita labor costs were greater in Washington, D.C. than in New York City, and, in 1971, they were higher in both Washington, D.C. and Philadelphia. Further, growth in per capita labor costs in New York City was less than the yearly average for the other cities combined—8.3 percent per year versus 10.7 percent. In fact, per capita labor costs in the common functions included here grew more slowly in New York City than in any of the cities examined, with the exceptions of Chicago and Houston.

Comparison by Expenditure Function

City government expenditures may be compared by function, first, for those functions that are commonly performed by city governments, and, second, for those functions that are more variable in the sense that they are often financed through special districts or by higher levels of government.

A comparison of city government expenditures for "common functions" is provided in Table 3.5. The three functions that represent the largest fraction of common function expenditures of city governments are police, fire, and sanitation and sewerage. For all three functions, per capita expenditures by the New York City government were above the average for the other cities in both 1966 and 1971. For police, per capita expenditures for New York City were greater than for every city except Washington, D.C. in 1966 and Washington, D.C. and Philadelphia in 1971.

These same relationships also held true for parks and recreation, libraries, financial administration, and general control. In all cases, New York City expenditures were greater than the average for all the other cities, but in no case were they the highest. In the case of parks and recreation, Philadelphia, Detroit, Washington, D.C., and Cleveland spent more per capita in at least one of the two years than did New York City. Baltimore and Washington, D.C. both spent more for

TABLE 3.5

Per Capita Expenditures for Common Functions for 10 Largest U.S. Cities, 1966 and 1971
(dollars)

	Highways		Parks and Recreation		Libraries		Financial Administration		General Control		Water Supply		Police		Fire		Sanitation and Sewerage		Common Functions and Expenditures Total		Average Annual Increase	
	1966	1971	1966	1971	1966	1971	1966	1971	1966	1971	1966	1971	1966	1971	1966	1971	1966	1971	1966	1971	Dollars	Percent
New York	16.8	21.4	9.9	15.4	4.3	8.2	4.3	6.3	10.3	17.2	9.8	14.1	37.4	65.1	17.4	28.4	27.4	41.8	137.7	217.9	16.0	9.6
Other nine (average)	17.7	24.6	8.1	12.3	3.0	4.8	3.0	5.7	5.0	8.9	16.3	22.2	25.2	52.0	12.4	20.9	16.7	29.5	107.3	180.8	14.7	11.0
Chicago	16.3	17.4	1.4	2.3	2.1	4.0	1.7	3.4	3.6	2.4	13.6	15.4	25.9	54.8	10.0	19.0	12.0	22.5	86.7	141.2	11.0	10.2
Los Angeles	17.0	28.2	9.6	10.6	3.4	4.0	2.8	6.1	3.2	4.9	21.0	23.3	28.2	47.7	15.6	22.0	15.2	18.8	115.9	165.5	9.9	7.4
Philadelphia	10.1	11.6	10.7	21.2	3.0	5.1	4.1	7.2	9.2	18.1	9.7	15.9	23.9	53.5	10.0	18.1	17.0	27.0	97.5	177.5	16.0	12.7
Detroit	10.6	13.0	10.8	17.5	3.4	5.2	3.5	5.6	3.0	5.5	19.9	37.2	24.1	49.6	10.1	16.4	17.5	50.9	102.9	200.8	19.6	14.3
Houston	14.4	15.6	5.2	71.2	1.4	2.2	2.3	3.3	1.9	2.3	15.0	32.0	13.9	20.8	11.2	18.9	25.1	21.8	90.6	124.0	6.7	6.5
Baltimore	20.0	44.2	8.4	23.0	4.8	8.0	4.1	9.8	5.9	14.9	12.9	16.4	28.8	64.1	18.0	28.4	13.1	30.3	116.0	239.2	24.6	15.6
Dallas	28.4	30.1	8.1	14.6	3.0	6.5	2.1	4.1	2.0	4.1	27.2	21.5	16.4	31.5	13.3	19.4	20.4	25.3	121.1	157.1	7.2	5.3
Washington	52.4	88.3	19.6	17.3	7.9	12.9	7.5	13.8	16.4	42.3	13.6	18.3	38.5	108.3	18.1	29.3	28.5	61.6	202.5	391.8	37.8	14.1
Cleveland	15.0	16.3	10.4	15.3	—	—	0.8	2.5	3.6	7.5	18.7	28.6	19.6	47.6	11.4	24.9	17.2	41.5	96.7	184.1	17.5	13.7
All 10 cities*	17.4	23.5	8.7	13.4	3.5	6.0	3.5	5.9	6.9	11.9	14.0	19.3	29.6	56.7	14.2	23.6	20.5	33.9	118.2	194.2	15.2	10.4

*The figures in this row are weighted averages obtained by dividing the expenditures of all 10 cities combined by the total population in the 10 cities.

Source: U.S. Department of Commerce, Bureau of the Census, City Government Finances, 1965–66 and 1970–71, Series GF-No. 12 and GF71-No. 4 (Washington, D.C.: U.S. Government Printing Office, 1967 and 1972).

libraries and financial administration than did New York City in at
least one of the years in question, and, in the case of general control,
Washington, D.C. spent a higher amount than did New York City.

Expenditures per capita by New York City on highways and water
supply were less than the average for the other cities in both years.
In fact, New York fell behind Los Angeles, Baltimore, Washington,
D.C., and Dallas in highway expenditure, and behind every other city
in water supply expenditure.

In the aggregate, common function expenditures for New York
City were higher than the average for the other cities in both years—
$137.70 versus $107.30 in 1966 and $217.90 versus $180.80 in 1971.
However, the growth in common function expenditures by the New
York City government was less than the average for the other cities
combined (9.6 percent per year versus 11.0 percent per year). In
fact, growth in common function expenditures per capita for New York
City (9.6 percent) was less than that for Chicago (10.2 percent),
Philadelphia (12.7 percent), Detroit (14.3 percent), Baltimore (15.6
percent), Washington, D.C. (14.1 percent), and Cleveland (13.7 percent). Only in Los Angeles, Dallas, and Houston did per capita common function expenditures grow more slowly.

Although an analysis of common function expenditures provides
some insight into such a fiscal comparison of city governments as is
required here, it is also necessary to compare expenditures for the
"variable" functions (that is, education, welfare, health, and hospitals).
The data presented in Table 3.6 allow such a comparison to be made.
For each of the functions shown, New York City expenditures were
greater than the average for the other cities. New York City expenditures on education were greater than any city studied in 1966; however, Washington, D.C. spent more than New York City on education
in 1971. Only New York City, Baltimore, and Washington, D.C. had
any responsibility for educational expenditure in either year. Welfare
expenditures per capita in New York City were the highest of any of
the cities studied, but, again, only New York City, Washington, D.C.,
and Baltimore appear to bear any great responsibility for welfare
expenditures. For health and hospital expenditures, New York City
spent the most of any city studied in 1966, but Washington, D.C.
spent more in 1971. Finally, New York City spent more per capita
on housing than did any of the other cities in both years.

In the aggregate, variable function expenditures in New York
City were higher than the average of the other cities as well as higher
than any other city studied. However, of all these cities, only Baltimore, which, like New York, performs services generally provided
by county governments, and Washington, D.C., which unlike any other
area is not a state-chartered corporation, (and perhaps Philadelphia)
have responsibility for anywhere near as wide a scope of functions as

171

TABLE 3.6

Per Capita Expenditures for Variable Functions for 10 Largest U.S. Cities, 1966 and 1971
(dollars)

	Common Functions		Education		Welfare		Health and Hospitals		Housing		Variable Functions Other		Total		Average Annual Increase	
	1966	1971	1966	1971	1966	1971	1966	1971	1966	1971	1966	1971	1966	1971	Dollars	Percent
New York	137.7	217.9	131.2	252.8	71.6	253.9	58.6	128.0	26.3	61.8	157.5	292.2	445.2	988.9	108.7	16.8
Other nine (average)	107.3	180.8	14.9	32.6	9.3	17.3	9.8	22.7	8.1	19.0	66.7	119.9	108.8	211.2	20.5	14.2
Chicago	86.7	141.2	—	—	2.8	3.1	5.4	10.4	5.3	11.1	39.9	90.3	53.5	114.8	12.3	16.5
Los Angeles	115.9	165.5	—	—	0.1	0.1	1.4	1.0	2.7	5.7	117.5	192.3	121.7	199.0	15.5	10.4
Philadelphia	97.5	127.5	1.4	3.3	5.7	10.5	14.1	31.2	16.5	45.8	54.6	117.7	92.2	258.3	33.2	22.9
Detroit	102.9	200.8	2.6	4.7	11.6	3.1	14.4	24.3	12.0	20.4	62.5	123.3	103.2	175.7	14.5	11.3
Houston	90.6	124.0	—	—	—	—	11.6	4.9	—	—	37.3	31.8	49.8	36.8	-2.6	-5.3
Baltimore	116.0	239.2	119.9	244.9	56.4	120.0	23.4	49.8	10.8	49.3	49.4	85.0	272.0	549.0	55.4	16.9
Dallas	121.1	157.1	—	—	—	—	2.0	3.1	—	—	37.4	85.6	39.5	88.8	9.8	17.6
Washington	202.5	391.8	123.6	282.5	43.9	124.9	29.5	154.8	12.0	43.4	139.9	202.4	348.9	797.8	89.8	18.3
Cleveland	96.7	184.1	—	0.1	2.1	—	4.7	7.3	16.2	15.9	64.2	99.4	87.2	122.7	7.1	7.1
All 10 cities*	118.2	194.2	56.7	111.7	31.7	102.3	27.3	60.5	14.7	34.4	99.3	181.7	270.2	490.5	44.1	13.0

*The figures in this row are weighted averages obtained by dividing the expenditures of all 10 cities combined by the total population in the 10 cities.

Source: U.S. Department of Commerce, Bureau of the Census, City Government Finances, 1965-66 and 1970-71. Series GF-No. 12 and GF71-No.4 (Washington, D.C.: U.S. Government Printing Office, 1967 and 1972).

172

the City of New York. Further, in terms of average yearly growth of variable function expenditures, New York City expenditures grew slightly more rapidly than was the case for the combined average of the other cities—16.8 percent versus 14.2 percent. However, the cities that share functional responsibility similar to that of New York City all registered yearly expenditure growth rates in excess of the 16.8 percent for New York City: Philadelphia, 22.9 percent; Baltimore, 16.9 percent; and Washington, D.C., 18.3 percent.

In summary, two points should be emphasized when comparing New York City to the other nine largest cities in the United States. First, although New York City spent a higher amount than the average in most of the common function areas, these expenditures were less than those of some other cities in the case of every function and, in the aggregate, grew less rapidly over the period than those of all but three of the cities studied. Secondly, in terms of the functional responsibility assigned to New York City, variable function expenditures were higher than for any other of the cities studied, though growth in these expenditures was less than that registered by the three cities that appear to share similar functional responsibilities.

From this, it might be concluded that the explanation of New York City's high annual growth rate in per capita expenditures lies in its higher growth rate for variable function expenditures. Part of this explanation, then, is simply intercity differences in the assignment of functions among local governments, and, therefore, the incomparability of city government financial data for the variable functions.

Expenditure Comparison: Summary

As noted above, intercity expenditure comparisons are difficult and, when not interpreted cautiously, can lead to misleading inferences. With these problems in mind, one can draw a number of conclusions from the above analysis. New York City spends more per capita than does any of the other cities examined here, but the growth rate in this spending is not substantially above the average. The higher level of spending may be traced primarily to social service costs—terms of expenditure objects, a high level of transfer payments, and, in terms of expenditure functions, a high level of welfare expenditures. With respect to the other objects of expenditure, and with respect to the "common municipal functions," expenditures by the New York City government appear relatively "normal" in terms of both per capita level and growth rate. Labor costs, a focus of growing concern in all cities, also do not appear "abnormal" in New York City, as compared with the other cities. Both the ratio of city government employees per city resident and the average level of wages appear well within normal limits, as defined in this comparison.

In sum, the above-average level of expenditures by the New York City government is largely attributable to its provision of a variety of services, particularly welfare, not usually provided by local governments. When these functions are netted out, the New York City government's expenditure performance does not deviate substantially from that of the other nine largest cities in the nation.

A MODEL TO EXPLAIN THE GROWTH IN NEW YORK CITY'S EXPENDITURES

When the total expenditures of the New York City government are viewed in terms of objects of expenditure, the level of its current expenditures may be stated as follows:

$$X = L + N + R + T \tag{1}$$

where: L = direct labor expenditures

N = nonlabor expenditures (such as materials and supplies)

R = pension and fringe benefit expenditures

T = transfer payments.

It follows that the increase in current expenditures between any two periods (ΔX) may be described as:

$$\Delta X = \Delta L + \Delta N + \Delta R + \Delta T \tag{1a}$$

The increments in labor and pension expenditures may be further broken down and attributed to increases in the number of employees, increases in real wage rates, and increases in inflation rates. The increase in nonlabor costs is broken down in a comparable manner—that is, into expenditure increase due to real quantity increases (which are eventually attributed to employment increase) and that due to inflation rates.

The following subsections deal with the methods used to relate each of the four components to the underlying factors as described above. In a final subsection, these individual components are combined and the complete model is presented.

174

Direct Labor Expenditures

The intention here is to devise a method to separate empirically from the total change in direct labor expenditures (ΔL) that which is due to increased employment (ΔE), that which is due to increased real wage rates ($\Delta W'$), and that which is due to inflation, or price level changes (ΔP). Therefore, the goal is to measure the increase in direct labor expenditures in terms of the following identity:

$$\Delta L = Z_1 \Delta E + Z_2 \Delta P + Z_3 \Delta W'$$

where: Z_1 = the change in direct labor cost per new employee

           Z_2 = the change in direct labor cost per unit change in the price level

           Z_3 = the change in direct labor cost per dollar change in real wages.

The initial step to be taken in deriving the Z_i coefficients in equation (2)—that is, to derive the partitioning of total direct labor cost changes into changes due to employment and changes due to wage increases, may be described quite simply. First, the amount attributable to employment increase may be defined as the amount by which labor costs would have risen, if all new employees had been hired at the old (1965) wage rate.* This amount (the employment effect) may be estimated by multiplying the number of new employees by the average annual wage rate in 1965. Second, the amount attributable to wage rate increases may be defined as the amount by which labor costs would have risen, if all employees (as of the terminal year, 1972) received a raise equaling the difference between average wages in 1965 and 1972.† This amount (the amount attributable to money wage increases) may be estimated by multiplying the total number of employees in 1972 by the increase in average annual wages over the period. It can be partitioned further into a real wage and a price level component. The amount of direct labor expenditure

---

*New employees here refers to anyone hired between 1965 and 1972.
†It is clear that these definitions assume existing employment growth before estimating the wage rate effects. There are other a priori alternatives for this estimation, but the assumptions made here would would seem to fit the goals of expenditure analysis more closely.

increase attributable to price increases (inflation) is defined as the amount by which labor costs would have risen, if money wages (for all employees as of 1972) had increased commensurate with the increase in the general price level. This amount (the price effect) may be estimated by multiplying the price level increase (the price index times the average wage in 1965 minus the average wage in 1965 minus the average wage in 1965) by the total number of employees in 1972. Finally, the amount attributable to real wage changes is simply the amount by which labor costs have risen as a result of wage increases in excess of those attributable to inflation. This amount (the real wage effect) can be estimated by multiplying the the increase in real wages (the average wage in 1972 minus the inflated 1965 average wage) by the total number of employees in 1972.

This procedure can be explained more clearly in a simple algebraic formula. Begin with the following identity:

$$E_2 W_2 - E_1 W_1 = W_1(E_2 - E_1) + E_2(W_2 - W_1) \quad (3)$$

where: E_1 = employment level in 1965

E_2 = employment level in 1972

W_1 = average wage rate in 1965

W_2 = average wage rate in 1972.

In other words, the total change in labor costs—$E_2 W_2 - E_1 W_1$— may be viewed as being composed of an employment effect—$W_1(E_2 - E_1)$—and a money wage effect—$E_2(W_2 - W_1)$. The employment effect is the product of the added employees $(E_2 - E_1)$ and the old wage rate (W_1); the wage effect is the product of the wage increase $(W_2 - W_1)$ and the total number of old and new employees (E_2). The wage effect can in turn be divided into two effects:

$$E_2(W_2 - W_1) = E_2(W_1 P_2 - W_1) + E_2(W_2 - W_1 P_2) \quad (4)$$

where: P_2 = an index of prices in 1972 with 1965 as a base year.*

---

*The value of the consumer price index on July 1, 1964 was estimated as the average for the months of June and July of that year. The estimate for June 30, 1972 was obtained by averaging values for the months of June and July. When the index for July 1, 1964 is set at 100.0, the index for June 30, 1972 is 141.3.

In other words, the increase in labor costs due to money wage increases—$E_2(W_2 - W_1)$—is made up of a price effect—$E_2(W_1P_2 - W_1)$—and a real wage effect—$E_2(W_2 - W_1P_2)$. The price effect is the product of the price level increase $(W_1P_2 - W_1)$ and the total number of employees in 1972 (E_2). The real wage effect is the product of the increase in real wages $(W_2 - W_1P_2)$ and the total number of old and new employees (E_2).

Substituting equations (3) and (4) into equation (2) and simplifying, it may be seen that the change in total labor expenditures can be estimated from

$$\Delta L = W_1(E_2 - E_1) + E_2P_2(W_2/P_2 - W_1) + E_2W_1(P_2 - P_1) \tag{5}$$

$$= W_1\Delta E + E_2P_2\Delta W' + E_2W_1\Delta P \tag{5a}$$

where:

P_1 = an index of prices in 1965.

Empirically, such an estimate may be made if only average wage rates, employment levels, and price level increases are known.

Retirement System Expenditures

An analysis of changes in retirement system expenditures by the city may be approached in a similar fashion. More specifically, the basic approach taken here involves estimation of three components of the increase: (1) that due to the growth in employment, (2) that due to the growth in aggregate salaries, and (3) that due to the combined effects of salary increases in excess of the rate of growth assumed in the actuarial tables used to derive the initial city contribution rate, and to improvements in retirement benefits furnished to employees. In other words,

$$R = E \cdot P \cdot W' \cdot C \tag{6}$$

where: R = retirement system expenditures of the city government

C = city government retirement system contribution rate.

The increase in total retirement cost expenditures (ΔR) may then be written as:

177

$$\Delta R = r_1 \Delta E + r_2 \Delta P + r_3 \Delta W + r_4 \Delta C \qquad (6a)$$

where the r_i are presented in a fashion analogous to the Z_i presented in equation (2). Assume that the city government contribution rate may be easily measured as some percentage (C) of the average wage (W); hence for any given year (t), city government retirement system expenditures are computed from:

$$R_t = C_t W_t E_t \qquad (7)$$

The change in city contributions between any two years, say years 1 and 2, may be written as:

$$\Delta R = R_2 - R_1 = C_2 W_2 E_2 - C_1 W_1 E_1 \qquad (8)$$

Assuming for the moment that the contribution rate has not changed (that is, $C_2 = C_1$), then equation (8) may be rewritten as:

$$\Delta R = C(W_2 E_2 - W_1 E_1) = CW_1 \Delta E + CE_2 \Delta W \qquad (9)$$

where $CW_1 \Delta E$ might be termed a pure employment effect and $CE_2 \Delta W$, a wage rate effect, with the same set of assumptions and limitations as attended the analysis of direct labor costs above. If the assumption that the city contribution rate remains constant is dropped, equation (9) may be written as:

$$\Delta R = C_2 W_2 E_2 - C_1 W_1 E_1$$
$$= C_1 W_1 (E_2 - E_1) + W_1 E_2 (C_2 - C_1) +$$
$$E_2 C_2 (W_2 - W_1) \qquad (10)$$

Finally, as before, the wage rate effect—$E_2 C_2 (W_2 - W_1)$—may be partitioned into a real and monetary component:

$$E_2 C_2 (W_2 - W_1) = E_2 C_2 (W_2 - W_1 P_2) +$$
$$E_2 C_2 (W_1 P_2 - W_1) \qquad (11)$$

The existence of a price, or inflation, effect on city government retirement contributions deserves further consideration. As noted in the section above, the increase in the wage rate may be seen as including an increase that is just adequate to offset price level increases and that, therefore, may be attributed to inflation. Any wage rate increment over and above this amount may be viewed as an increment in real wages. To the extent that wage rates do increase because of increases in the general price level, the corresponding increase in

retirement system costs may be attributed to the inflation factor.
For example, if the city were contributing to a retirement system at
a rate of 10 percent of wages, and if wages rose by $1,000 because
of inflation, then retirement costs would be assumed to rise by $100
because of inflation. It should be noted, however, that no attempt is
made to ascribe changes in the statutory city contribution rate (that
is, ΔC) to changes in the price level.

Equations (10) and (11) now may be combined, and the terms
rearranged, to obtain the estimating equation for the change in retirement system costs:

$$\Delta R = C_1 W_1 (E_2 - E_1) + E_2 C_2 P_2 (W_2/P_2 - W_1) + E_2 C_2 W_1 (P_2 - P_1) + E_2 W_1 (C_2 - C_1) \tag{12}$$

$$= C_1 W_1 \Delta E + E_2 C_2 P_2 \Delta W' + E_2 C_2 W_1 \Delta P + E_2 W_1 \Delta C \tag{12a}$$

As before, expenditure increase is a function of increases in employment, real wages, and an inflation effect. In addition, changes in
retirement cost expenditures may also be attributed to changes in
the effective contribution rate of the city government.

Nonlabor Expenditures[5]

Since total nonlabor expenditures (N)* are equal to the price
per unit purchased $(P')^\dagger$ times the quantity of units purchased, that
is

$$N = P'Q \tag{13}$$

then

$$\Delta N = n_1 \Delta Q + n_2 \Delta P' \tag{13a}$$

---

*It is clear that both the price and quantity terms in this section
should be subscripted for different types of purchases, but for ease
of presentation, the subscripts are dropped.

†The price term is written P' throughout in this section to emphasize that it may not indicate simply a consumer index but sub-
components of the wholesale price index.

When both prices and quantities change, the problem is to divide the total expenditure change $(P_2'Q_2 - P_1'Q_1)$ into a price and a real quantity component. This can be achieved quite simply in a fashion analogous to that employed in partitioning labor cost changes described in equation(3)

$$P_2'Q_2 - P_1'Q_2 = P_1'(Q_2 - Q_1) + Q_2(P_2' - P_1'). \quad (14)$$

The term $P_1'(Q_2 - Q_1)$ is the amount by which nonlabor costs have risen as the result of increases in the quantities purchased, while $Q_2(P_2' - P_1')$ is the amount by which nonlabor costs have risen because of increases in the prices of the products.

In terms of equation (13a),

$$\Delta N = P_1'(Q_2 - Q_1) + Q_2(P_2' - P_1') \quad (15)$$

$$= P_1'\Delta Q + Q_2\Delta P' \quad (15a)$$

In other words, changes in nonlabor costs can be divided into changes due to quantity $(P_1'\Delta Q)$ as well as price-level changes $(Q_2\Delta P')$.

It would not seem unreasonable to assume a relationship between the physical quantities of such objects as materials and supplies and the level of employment and, therefore, between increases in physical quantities purchased. Assume that between 1965 and 1972, g_1 units of physical quantity were needed for every unit of employment increase —that is, that:

$$(Q_2 - Q_1) = g_1(E_2 - E_1) \quad (15b)$$

Then:

$$\Delta N = g_1 P_1'(E_2 - E_1) + Q_2(P_2' - P_1') \quad (15c)$$

or

$$\Delta N = g_1 P_1'\Delta E + Q_2\Delta P' \quad (15d)$$

Now, only g_1, P_1', and Q_2 need be estimated.

The Complete Model

The complete model can now be obtained by the substitution of equations (5), (12), (15), and (18) into equation (1). After combining the terms:

$$\Delta X = \Delta E(W_1C_1 + W_1 + g_1P_1') + \Delta P(E_2W_1 + W_1E_2C_2) + \Delta P'(Q_2)$$ (16)

$$+ \Delta W'(E_2P_2 + E_2C_2P_2) + \Delta C(E_2W_1) + \Delta T$$

where: ΔE = change in employment

ΔP = change in price level

ΔC = change in pension contribution rate

$\Delta W'$ = change in real wages

ΔT = change in transfer payments.*

Simplifying still further:

$$\Delta X = x_1'\Delta E + x_2'\Delta P + x_3'\Delta P + x_4'\Delta W + x_5'\Delta C + \Delta T$$ (17)

where: $x_1' = W_1C_1 + W_1 + g_1P_1'$

$x_2' = E_2W_1 + W_1E_2C_2$

$x_3' = Q_2$

$x_4' = E_2P_2 + E_2C_2P_2$

$x_5' = E_2W_1$

In order to determine the sensitivity of expenditures to changes in any of the independent variables, the following relationships may be derived:

$$\frac{\Delta X}{\Delta E} = x_1'$$ (18a)

$$\frac{\Delta X}{\Delta P} = x_2'$$ (18b)

---

*Because of data unavailability, the components of transfer payments will not be dealt with in this analysis.

$$\frac{\Delta X}{\Delta P'} = x'_3 \qquad (18c)$$

$$\frac{\Delta X}{\Delta W'} = x'_4 \qquad (18d)$$

$$\frac{\Delta X}{\Delta C} = x'_5 \qquad (18e)$$

These values can then be used to estimate what would happen to total expenditures (as well as each of the components of aggregate expenditure) as a result of changes in any of the independent (exogenous) variables. For example, for every one employee added in any given department, expenditures will rise by x'_1, which is a composite of the wage, pension, and materials-equipment costs that may be attributed to the new employee.

From these coefficients, the responsiveness of city government expenditures to any given set of price, real wage, inflation, employment, pension contribution rate, and transfer payment increases may be estimated.

Limitations and Assumptions

The use of this model to forecast possible expenditure trends in the future requires close examination of the assumptions implicit to the model. Basic to the partitioning procedure outlined in previous subsections is a partitioning of changes in costs that could be interpreted as overstating the effect of changes in wage rate and understating the effect of changes in employment. This possible bias grows out of the desire to estimate the employment effect as the costs that would have been saved, had wage rates remained at their 1965 level and only employment levels had changed. It follows that the wage rate increase between 1965 and 1972 for new employees is assigned completely to the wage rate effect, and therein lies the possible bias. The choice of this allocation method was made on the basis of what it was desired to show for purposes of expenditure policy analysis.

This allocation problem might be made clear with an example. Changes in labor costs can be attributed to changes in employment and wages according to the following formula

$$E_2W_2 - E_1W_1 = E_1(W_2 - W_1) + W_1(E_2 - E_1) + (E_2 - E_1)(W_2 - W_1) \qquad (19)$$

The first term—$E_1(W_2 - W_1)$—represents increases due to changes only in wages, the second—$W_1(E_2 - E_1)$—represents changes due to employment change, while the third—$(E_2 - E_1)(W_2 - W_1)$—represents changes due to both wages and employment changes.

Since it is desirable to divide the total change in costs into only two components, a decision must be made about how to allocate the third term, $(E_2 - E_1)(W_2 - W_1)$. Allocation of the term to wage changes yields:

$$E_2W_2 - E_1W_1 = E_2(W_2 - W_1) + W_1(E_2 - E_1) \tag{20}$$

while allocation to employment produces:

$$E_2W_2 - E_1W_1 = E_1(W_2 - W_1) + W_2(E_2 - E_1) \tag{21}$$

If both E and W are increasing functions of time (as is the case in the present study), the allocation in equation (20) (that used in this study) might be construed as overstating the effect of wage rate change and understating the effect of employment change. The opposite result is produced by the allocation in equation (21). In the forecasts that follow, the effect of this allocation procedure should be kept in mind.

AN ANALYSIS OF THE HISTORICAL TREND IN NEW YORK CITY GOVERNMENT EXPENDITURES

Using the model described above, the historical pattern of expenditures by the New York City government may be analyzed. The specific objective here is to attribute the expenditure increase, on a function-by-function basis, to increases in employment level, real wage rates, price level, and the city government contribution rate for its retirement systems. In terms of our simple formulation in equation (17) above:

$$\Delta X = x_1' \Delta E + x_2' \Delta P + x_3' \Delta P' + x_4' \Delta W' + x_5' \Delta C + \Delta T \tag{22}$$

where each x_i coefficient shows the responsiveness of expenditures to a change in the factor under consideration, holding all other factors constant. For example, the coefficient x_1 describes the change in expenditures that would have occurred, if city government employment had changed but real wage rates, price level, and pension contribution rates had not changed. These coefficients may be estimated for each function, using a methodology similar to that described above.

The analysis is presented below, first, on a function-by-function basis with careful attention to an analysis of each expenditure component (for instance, direct labor costs, retirement costs). Then the functions are aggregated to present an analysis of the pattern of total current expenditures.

The data requirements for an empirical analysis such as this are substantial, and, accordingly, a number of assumptions and empirical shortcuts have been taken. First, detailed city government employment and wage rate data are available in the Executive Budget[6] but not in the Comptroller's Annual Report. Therefore, the relative importance of the sources of direct labor cost growth must be estimated from budgeted rather than from actual expenditure data, though the coefficients derived will be applied to the actual data. This is tantamount to an assumption that the budgeted shortfall (or overestimate) for direct labor costs is proportionate to that for retirement contribution, nonlabor, and other costs. A second general limitation is that the data used in deriving estimates of employment, real wage, and other effects did not include certain expenditures that could not be classified as direct labor, retirement system contributions, or materials-equipment-supplies. For example, among the excluded items are expenditures that are classified in the budget as "other" or "miscellaneous." These limitations will be repeated below in more detail with respect to the specific function in question.

A third shortcoming is that all city government functions have not been considered in the detailed analysis. Specifically, the functions studied were police, fire, environmental protection (sanitation), social services, health services, public schools, and higher education. These seven functions together account for about two-thirds of the total expense budget of the city government in 1972. The analysis of these seven functions is used to generate expenditure inferences for the remaining functions. The direction and magnitude of the possible error that arises in making this assumption is dealt with below.

Police Department Expenditures

The historical trend of expenditure increase for the Police Department may be analyzed with the model described above. Direct labor expenditures, retirement cost expenditures, and nonlabor expenditures are related to changes in employment, real wages, prices, and the pension contribution rate in the three sections that immediately follow.* The fourth section aggregates these individual expenditure

---

*The transfer payment component of the model does not apply to the Police Department analysis and is therefore omitted.

components to a consideration of the effects of these factors on total expenditures.

Direct Labor Costs[7]

In order to determine if there are differences in labor cost trends for different job categories, Police Department labor costs are broken down into five relatively homogeneous classifications: executive, uniformed, clerical, laborer, and other.* (See Appendix Tables 3.A.1-3.A.6.) The executive category includes top-level management, to the exclusion of lower-level administrative personnel. Uniformed personnel are policemen. The clerical category refers to occupations such as stenographers, clerks, and typists. The laborer category is made up of general maintenance as well as skilled personnel. The "other" category includes everything else—attorneys, accountants, photographers, assistant administrators.[8]

Wages paid to (authorized for) each employee in the department were aggregated by job category, and this total was divided by the number of employees in that job category in order to calculate an average wage rate. (It should be noted that the focus here is on labor costs rather than wage policy. Thus, the intent is to determine the cost per employee of producing police services, rather than the wage paid for a particular job to be performed. As a result, no attempt has been made to compare growth in wages for specific grades of job categories.) This procedure was followed for both 1965 and 1972, and percentage changes in average wage rates and employment levels were calculated. The results of this breakdown of the sources of labor cost change in 1965 and 1972 are summarized in Appendix Tables 3.A.1-3.A.4.

Direct labor costs by job category are shown in Appendix Table 3.A.1.[†] Between 1965 and 1972, direct labor costs of the Police Department more than doubled, with 94 percent of the increase being directly attributed to uniformed personnel cost increases. These data serve to emphasize the overwhelming importance of uniformed personnel in the Police Department labor cost structure—over 95 percent of total direct labor costs. Still, the relative growth in labor costs is greater for the nonuniformed Police Department personnel.

---

*Direct labor costs for the other six departments analyzed are also broken down into these five categories.

†After excluding pensions, fringe benefits, debt service, and capital expenditures, direct labor costs were 96 percent of total costs for police. When capital budget items are included, direct labor costs still represented about 93 percent of total police costs.

185

A summary of Police Department employment trends over the 1965-72 period is presented in Appendix Table 3.A.2. Police Department employment increased by only 23.6 percent, or by 6,622. When compared to the 100 percent increase in direct labor costs, these statistics would seem to suggest that much of the reason for increasing police expenditures in New York City is to be found in the area of rising wage rates. Before turning to that issue, it is useful to note that, of the total departmental employee increase of 6,622, approximately 78 percent was uniformed personnel. Of the remaining 22 percent, the bulk of the increase was in the "laborer" and "other" categories. The more complete breakdown of the "other" category shown in Appendix Table 3.A.3 reveals that a large share of that increase was "administrative aides and assistants."

Average annual wages are presented in Appendix Table 3.A.4. It should be reemphasized that these wage rates are not inclusive of pension and other fringe benefits. It should be noted that, for the department as a whole, average wage rates have increased by more than 60 percent, the departmental average rising from $8,554 to $13,979. In percentage terms, the largest raises are to be found in the administrative and uniformed personnel categories.

In sum, direct labor cost increases for the Police Department over the 1965-72 period may be characterized by (1) a cost and employment structure dominance by uniformed personnel; (2) no noticeable change in this dominance, though the employment of nonuniformed personnel did increase more rapidly than the employment of uniformed personnel; (3) relatively greater increases in average wages than in total employment; and (4) a markedly greater increase in average wages for the uniformed personnel than for all lower-paid occupation classes.

Having described the level and composition of increases in total direct labor costs, it remains to estimate the marginal effects on direct labor costs of increases in employment (ΔE), real wages ($\Delta W'$), and inflation (ΔP). The result of applying the model developed in the preceding section to the Police Department is as follows:[9]

$$\Delta L = \$8,554\Delta E + \$296,695,490\Delta P + \$49,010\Delta W' \quad (23)$$

Subject to the assumptions outlined above, direct labor costs rose by $8,554 for each new employee hired over the period, by $296,695,490 for each 100 percent increase in the price level (or $2.96 million per 1 percent rise), and by $49,010 for a $1 increase in average real wages.

Substituting observed values for ΔE, ΔP, $\Delta W'$, and ΔL into equation (23), it may be concluded that, of each $1 increase in direct labor costs over the 1965-72 period, 23.1 cents was due to increases in employment, 51.3 cents to inflation, and 25.6 cents to increases in real wages.*

Appendix Table 3.A.5 presents a breakdown of the percentages of expenditure increase attributable to changes in employment, prices, and real wages for each of the job categories used in this analysis. Since uniformed personnel quantitatively dominate Police Department employment, it is not surprising that the total and uniformed analyses are approximately parallel. (See also Appendix Table 3.A.6.) It is interesting to note, however, that in the laborer and clerical occupation classes—which are the lowest-paid occupations in the Police Department—wage increases over the 1965-72 period were less than the increase in the general price level.

Though these interpretations would seem to argue a stronger effect of inflation than on either employment or real wages, it should be noted that the three determining variables are measured in different units—that is, employees, price index numbers, and dollar wage rates. Consequently, the size of the coefficients presented in equation (2) may not be compared to this end. A comparable set of coefficients might be calculated by translating the coefficients in equation (2) into elasticities, or percent increases, as below:

---

*In terms of the (budgeted) total direct labor expenditure, the total $244,797,589 increase may be allocated as follows: $56,548,243 to employment increases, $125,581,163 to inflation, and $62,668,183 to real wage increases.

It is important to emphasize here that the real wage effect described above refers to the proportion of total direct labor costs that may be attributed to increases in real wages. It does not describe the percentage increase in real wages. The former, the proportion of total labor cost increase attributable to real wages, is, of course, influenced by the amounts of cost increase attributable to other factors: A large increase in number of employees will inevitably decrease the proportion of total cost increase attributable to wage increase. For example, uniformed police show a real wage effect of 29.6 percent of total cost increase, while associate professors at the City University of New York (CUNY) show a real wage effect of 18.2 percent, despite the fact that the total wage increase for the two categories was almost exactly the same—66.8 percent and 65.6 percent. The difference in the proportion of the most increase attributable to real wage increase results primarily from the difference in the increase in total employees—19.3 percent for police and 130.6 percent for associate professors at CUNY.

$$\eta_E \;=\; Z\frac{E}{1L} \;=\; 1.00 \tag{24a}$$

$$\eta_P \;=\; Z\frac{P}{2L} \;=\; 1.23 \tag{24b}$$

$$\eta_{W'} \;=\; Z\frac{W'}{3L} \;=\; 1.75 \tag{24c}$$

These elasticities show that a 1 percent change in employment will produce a 1 percent change in labor costs; a 1 percent change in prices will yield a 1.23 percent change in labor costs; and a 1 percent change in real wages will result in a 1.75 percent change in labor costs. In other words, the greatest relative impact on labor costs is caused by real wage changes, followed by price changes and employment changes.

Before we proceed further, it is important to note that the method employed here will necessarily yield an elasticity coefficient of unity for the employment effect. This is a direct result of the partitioning procedure described above. A different procedure would lead to a different elasticity coefficient for employment (as well as for the other variables). Since a primary reason for calculating these coefficients was to determine the relative importance among departments of the three effects, the fact that the employment coefficient will always equal unity is not our concern. The important thing is the size of the other coefficients relative to that of employment.

Retirement System Costs[10]

The membership of the Police Pension Fund (Article 2) consists of all members of the police force in the competitive class who received permanent appointments after March 29, 1940. Although other choices are available, almost all members have chosen the fund's 20-year plan described below.[11]

1. Eligibility: Eligibility is after 20 years of service.
2. Benefits: Benefits equal 50 percent of the annual earnable compensation on the date of retirement. For all service beyond 20 years, a member receives 1/60 of annual average earnings from the date of minimum service until the date of retirement for each year of additional service, plus payments for life that are the actuarial equivalent of any excess member contributions and excess reserve for ITHP (Increased Take-Home Pay).

A second basic type of retirment system operated and supported in large part by New York City government contributions is the non-actuarial system. These have been closed to new members for many

188

years, and most of them have been superseded by one of the actuarial systems described above. They are financed by a so-called pay-as-you-go method* whereby the city's annual contribution in any given period equals the benefits that the city is obligated to provide to beneficiaries during that period. Hence, none of these systems accumulates reserves to finance ultimate payments to beneficiaries. The one exception is the BMT-IRT Transit Plans, which were required to build reserves by 1968 sufficient to discharge all future obligations.[12] (The cost to the city government of supporting the nonactuarial portion of the police retirement system is not considered here.) Despite a very large relative increase in city contributions between 1971 and 1972, the cost of this system is very near the maximum it is ever likely to reach, because membership is frozen. Unless there is some dramatic improvement in benefits provided to beneficiaries, the fact that membership cannot grow means that once all present members are retired and collecting benefits, the city's annual maximum liability will be at its upper limit. Moreover, as deaths of beneficiaries receiving payments begin to outnumber substantially the number of new beneficiaries, the cost to the city of supporting these systems will begin to decline. Indeed, the relative importance of expenditures for the nonactuarial systems has already fallen significantly. While the nonactuarial systems accounted for $29.7 million, or 11 percent, of total city spending on retirement benefits and social security in 1961, the $35.9 million spent in 1972 accounted for less than 5 percent of the 1972 total. In view of these trends and the fact that membership is frozen, this analysis of Police Department retirement costs will focus on the actuarial system.

Appendix Table 3.A.7 to this chapter describes the annual city contribution to (or expenditures for) each retirement system between fiscal years 1961 and 1972. As noted above, the main emphasis here is on the police actuarial system, and the object is to attribute the increase that has taken place between 1965 and 1971 ($33.6 million) to increased employment, increased real wages, inflation, and increases in the city's legal contribution rate.

The data in Table 3.7 contain several quantitative measures, which, when viewed together, provide a summary of the major trends exhibited by the police retirement system between 1961 and 1971.

---

*This is an ironic use of a term frequently employed in connection with the issue of whether to limit expenditures for any purpose to no more than current income or to finance some by borrowing. In the general case, pay-as-you-go would be the fiscally conservative approach. In the case of funding retirement programs, it would be considered a fiscally questionable practice.

TABLE 3.7

New York City Police Department Pension Fund (Article 2), 1961-71

(dollar figures in millions of dollars)

Fiscal Year	Number of Active Members	Salaries of Active Members	Employee Contributions	Employer Contributions	Number of Beneficiaries	Payments to Beneficiaries	Assets	Liabilities[a]	Investment Income[b]
1961	22,405	$148.1	$14.4	$23.2	486	$1.8	$237.2	$648.6	$7.0
1962	23,132	173.8	17.5	24.2	667	2.4	276.7	804.7	9.0
1963	24,596	194.2	20.1	26.7	799	2.8	319.2	1,075.5	10.9
1964	25,265	206.8	17.9	30.6	1,442	5.6	359.9	1,263.3	12.7
1965	25,803	232.2	19.9	46.7	1,756	7.2	420.2	1,412.5	15.2
1966	27,219	245.0	22.7	56.4	2,079	9.0	492.7	1,525.1	18.5
1967	27,927	275.5	25.2	68.4	3,225	14.6	576.1	1,440.1	22.4
1968	29,359	293.8	24.1	75.7	3,941	18.4	657.0	1,582.4	27.4
1969	30,742	324.1	17.8	47.1	5,030	25.2	710.9	1,791.3	31.4
1970	32,129	369.1	19.8	85.0	5,330	27.4	796.0	2,018.4	36.7
1971	31,761	371.1	21.1	80.3	5,816	31.3	888.3	1,994.1	42.0
Average Annual Increase[c]	4.2%	15.0%	4.7%	24.6%	109.7%	163.9%	27.4%	20.7%	50.0%

[a]Equal to present value of future benefits including both those already accrued and those expected to be earned by present active members.

[b]Excludes gains or losses on the sale of securities.

[c]Calculated from total percent increase over 1961-71 period divided by the number of years (10).

Sources: Records of the City Actuary; Annual Report to the Superintendent of Insurance of the State of New York (Albany, N.Y.: Office of the Superintendent of Insurance, 1961-71); Comptroller of the City of New York, Annual Report (New York: Office of the Comptroller, 1961-1971), Appendix A.

These data show the increase in membership to parallel almost exactly the total employment increase in the Police Department and the increase in average salary rates of members to be about four times greater than the rate of increase in members. The contribution rates by employers and employees shown in Table 3.7 suggest that the system is moving closer and closer to being noncontributory—that is, whereas the city government accounted for about 62 percent of total employer plus employee contributions in 1961, the percentage had risen to 80 by 1971. This trend is amplified by the data on employer contributions per member and by employer contributions as a percentage of salaries shown in Appendix Table 3.A.8. The city government contribution to the Police Department pension rose from 15.7 percent of salaries in 1961 to 21.6 percent in 1971.

In sum, these data show that city government contributions to the Police Pension Fund have increased substantially in the last decade. For purposes of comparison, it should be noted that the $33.6 million increase in city government contribution to the Police Pension Fund is equivalent to about 20 percent of the direct labor cost increase that took place over the 1965-71 period. It is further clear from these data that this increase is partly attributable to each of the factors considered here—that is, employment increase, real wage rates, inflation, and changes in the employer contribution rates.

A further explanation of the inflation effect seems called for here. Theoretically, there are two components of the effect of price-level increases on retirement system contributions by the city government. First, as the price level rises, there are built-in increases in the level of retirement cost. It has not been possible to isolate such increases here, and these are spread out over the employment, wage rate, and contribution rate effects. The second component of the price-level effect on retirement system costs is the price-level effect on real wages. It was possible to estimate this effect and to allocate it to the price-increase term. Since only the second of these components is so treated, the total effect of price level change on retirement system costs is understated.

In order to determine the impact of changes in each of these variables, the model previously described can be applied:[13]

$$\Delta R = \$1,809 \Delta E + \$64,785,484 \Delta P + 10,172 \Delta W' + \$295,824,127 \Delta C \tag{25}$$

These results indicate that the hiring of an additional Police Department employee (that is, $\Delta E = 1$) increases retirement costs by $1,809; an increase in average real wages of $1 ($\Delta W' = 1$) increases retirement costs by $10,172; a 100 percent change in the price level ($\Delta P = 100$) increases costs by $64,785,484; and a 100 percentage point increase in the contribution rate (ΔC) will increase costs by $295,824,127. By substituting values for the independent variables into equation (25) above, it may be shown that changes in the contribution rate have been responsible for 12.8 percent of the increase in retirement costs to the city; employment increases accounted for 32.1 percent; and price increases for 65.6 percent of the increase in retirement costs. It also appears that the decrease in average real wages of members of the police retirement system* that occurred over the period 1965-71 had a dampening effect on retirement costs equivalent to 10.5 percent of the total increase in retirement costs to the city. In other words, had the wages of members of the retirement system kept pace with the cost of living, total retirement costs would have been still higher than they actually were in 1971.

The substantial importance of the discretionary city government actions in the wage and employment areas vis-à-vis the contribution rate is not surprising, given the data presented above, which show the drastic decline in the employees' share of total contributions.

Again, the coefficients presented in equation (25) are not independent of units; hence they must be standardized in order for us to compare their relative importance.[14]

$$\eta_E = 1.00 \tag{26a}$$

$$\eta_{W'} = 1.79 \tag{26b}$$

$$\eta_{P'} = 1.32 \tag{26c}$$

$$\eta_C = 1.23 \tag{26d}$$

These elasticity coefficients indicate that changes in real wages have the greatest impact on retirement costs, followed by changes in prices, changes in the contribution rate, and changes in the level of employment. Again, as with labor costs, the importance of the elasticity coefficient is that it enables measurement of the relative magnitudes of the reaction of retirement costs to changes in the independent, exogenous variables.

---

*Data collected on the average salaries of members of the Police Department Actuarial Retirement System (92 percent of total Police Department employees in 1965) show that average salaries did not increase as fast as the Consumer Price Index. However, for all Police Department employees, there was a 15.7 percent increase in real wages.

Nonlabor Costs[15]

Nonlabor costs are defined here to include expenditures for city government purchases of materials, equipment, supplies, and contractual services. Expenditures for such purchases by the Police Department are presented in Table 3.8, in total and by object. These expenditures are relatively small by comparison with other objects of police expenditures—0.3 percent of direct labor costs and 12.7 percent of retirement costs in 1972. The largest components of this increase are in the "supplies" and "contractual services" categories.

In the context of the model being used here, where expenditure increase is related to employment, real wage, and price-level changes, the consideration on nonlabor expenditures requires some modification. Consider, first, the price-level term. The impact of inflation on nonlabor expenditure can be shown in two ways. Laspeyres price indexes have been developed for each object of expenditure and are shown in Table 3.9, and the resulting deflated real expenditures by object are presented in Table 3.10.

Using these price indexes (P') and deflated real expenditures (Q'), the change in nonlabor expenditures might be partitioned as follows:

$$\Delta N = {}^1\Delta Q + \$10,138,384\,\Delta P' \tag{27}$$

which implies that the purchase of one more dollar of supplies (in real terms) (ΔQ) will increase nonlabor costs by \$1 and that an increase in the prices of supplies and materials $(\Delta P')$ of 100 percent will raise nonlabor costs by \$10,138,384. If we substitute the observed valued for ΔP and ΔQ, 27.8 percent of the increase in nonlabor expenditures over the 1965-72 period is found to be attributable to inflation and 72.2 percent to an increase in real purchases.

As noted above, by assuming a relationship between the quantity of supplies purchased (Q) and the employment level (E), it is possible to show the relationship between nonlabor costs and employment levels.[16] Accordingly, equation (27) may be rewritten as:

$$\Delta N = \$716\,\Delta E + \$10,138,384\,\Delta P'. \tag{28}$$

To compare the relative effects, elasticities must be computed as above.

$$\eta E = 2.89 \tag{29a}$$

$$\eta P' = 1.68$$

$$\eta Q = 1.00 \tag{29c}$$

193

TABLE 3.8

New York City Police Department Annual Nonlabor Expenditures, 1965-70
(in thousands of dollars)

Object Class	1965	1966	1967	1968	1969	1970
Total	5,396.0	6,228.8	7,491.3	8,636.3	9,435.7	8,964.6
		(15.4)*	(20.3)	(15.3)	(9.3)	(-5.0)
Supplies	1,668.3	2,143.1	1,704.0	3,024.7	3,117.9	3,452.8
		(28.5)	(-20.5)	(77.5)	(3.1)	(10.7)
Materials	434.0	428.1	543.6	611.6	587.7	664.6
		(-1.4)	(27.0)	(12.5)	(-3.9)	(13.1)
Equipment	892.5	1,152.5	2,712.3	2,035.1	2,639.5	1,304.6
		(29.1)	(135.3)	(-25.0)	(29.7)	(-50.6)
Contractual services	2,401.2	2,505.1	2,531.4	2,964.9	3,090.6	3,542.7
		(4.3)	(1.1)	(17.1)	(4.2)	(14.6)

Note: Years used are fiscal years.

*Figures in parentheses are annual percentage changes.

Source: Compiled from the Comptroller of the City of New York, Annual Report (New York: Office of the Comptroller, 1965-70), Part 2A, Statement 8.

TABLE 3.9

Laspeyres Price Index for New York City Police
Department Nonlabor Goods and Services, 1965-70

Object Class	1965[a]	1966	1967	1968	1969	1970	1971
Total	100.0	101.4	103.6	105.7	108.2	111.2	115.6
		(1.4)[b]	(2.2)	(2.0)	(2.3)	(2.8)	(4.0)
Supplies	100.0	101.9	105.2	107.3	108.1	108.7	111.3
		(1.9)	(3.2)	(2.0)	(0.7)	(0.6)	(2.4)
Materials	100.0	101.7	103.7	102.8	107.3	110.7	114.8
		(1.7)	(2.0)	(-0.9)	(4.4)	(3.2)	(3.7)
Equipment	100.0	101.6	103.8	105.6	107.6	110.6	112.6
		(1.6)	(2.2)	(1.7)	(2.0)	(2.7)	(1.8)
Contractual services	100.0	100.8	102.2	104.9	108.5	113.6	120.0
		(0.8)	(1.4)	(2.7)	(3.3)	(4.7)	(5.7)

Note: Years used are fiscal years.

[a]Base year: 1965 = 100.
[b]Figures in parentheses are annual percentage changes.

Source: Compiled by the author.

TABLE 3.10

Laspeyres Deflated Real Expenditures for New York City Police
Department Nonlabor Goods and Services, 1965-70
(in thousands of dollars)

Object Class	1965[a]	1966	1967	1968	1969	1970
Total	$5,396.0	$6,145.4	$7,229.7	$8,169.9	$8,723.6	$8,060.0
		(13.9)[b]	(17.6)	(13.0)	(6.8)	(-7.6)
Supplies	1,668.3	2,102.1	1,619.3	2,818.3	2,883.9	3,175.9
		(26.0)	(-23.0)	(74.0)	(2.3)	(10.1)
Materials	434.0	421.1	524.3	595.0	547.6	600.1
		(-3.0)	(24.5)	(13.5)	(-8.0)	(9.6)
Equipment	892.5	1,134.6	2,612.3	1,927.4	2,452.0	1,179.9
		(27.1)	(130.3)	(-26.2)	(27.2)	(-51.9)
Contractual services	2,401.2	2,486.3	2,476.8	2,825.1	2,849.5	3,119.8
		(3.5)	(-0.4)	(14.1)	(0.9)	(9.5)

Note: Years used are fiscal years.

[a]Base year: 1965 = 100.
[b]Figures in parentheses are annual percentage changes.

Source: Compiled by the author.

Total Police Department Expenditures

The objective here is to combine the three analyses presented above to estimate the sources of increase in total Police Department expenditures over the 1965-72 period. In order to use the above analysis to this end, a number of assumptions are made. First, since the goal is to estimate actual expenditure changes, it must be assumed that the estimates developed above from budget data may be properly applied to actual expenditures as presented in the Comptroller's Annual Reports. Second, about 15 percent of Police Department expenditures were not included in the above analysis. It is assumed that, had these expenditures been included, the results would not have been affected. Finally, a somewhat arbitrary classification of all current expenditures into direct labor, nonlabor, and retirement costs has been made. In previous sections, changes in a particular type of cost (labor, nonlabor, and retirement) have been related to changes in four independent variables—employment (E), prices (P), real wages (W'), and the employer contribution rate (C). For the Police Department as a whole, total expenditures could then be expressed as a function of these components. However, due to the less than complete coverage of the Police Department system, there is a difference in the employment and wage components when comparing direct labor costs to retirement costs. Further, there is a difference between the change in the price level as it affects workers' wages and the change in prices of supplies and other equipment purchased.

In order to explain past changes in total expenditures fully, it is necessary to incorporate these considerations in an expanded version of the model for the department as a whole. The estimation of this model follows in the same fashion as explained previously.

$$\Delta X = \$9,270 \Delta E + \$1,809 \Delta E_R + \$361,480,974 \Delta P + \$10,138,384 \Delta P' + 49,010 \Delta W' + 10,172 \Delta W'_R + \$295,824,127 \Delta C \qquad (30)$$

where: ΔE = change in employment for whole department

ΔE_R = change in retirement system membership

$\Delta W'$ = change in real wage for whole department

$\Delta W'_R$ = change in real wage for retirement system membership

ΔP = change in price level for consumers

$\Delta P'$ = change in price level for nonlabor costs.

As before, these results can be interpreted to indicate that a change of one unit in departmental employment will raise costs by \$9,270, a change in retirement system membership by one member will raise costs by \$1,809, and so on.

When observed changes in the exogenous variables are substituted in the equation above, it is possible to determine the impact of changes in employment, real wages, and so forth on total costs. The results indicate that 21.4 percent of the increase in expenditures between 1965 and 1972 resulted from increased general employment, 3.7 percent from increased retirement membership employment, 22.8 percent from increased average real wages of all employees, -1.4 percent from wages of retirement system members, 51 percent from increases in consumer prices, 0.6 percent from increases in prices of supplies, and 1.8 percent from increases in the contribution rate.

In order to compare the marginal effects of the seven variables, elasticity coefficients must be calculated. Using the procedure developed above, these coefficients were as follows:

$$\eta E \quad = \quad 0.89 \tag{31a}$$

$$\eta E_R \quad = \quad 0.16 \tag{31b}$$

$$\eta P \quad = \quad 1.23 \tag{31c}$$

$$\eta P' \quad = \quad 0.03 \tag{31d}$$

$$\eta W' \quad = \quad 1.43 \tag{31e}$$

$$\eta W'_R \quad = \quad 0.31 \tag{31f}$$

$$\eta C \quad = \quad 0.20 \tag{31g}$$

The coefficient ηE_R, for example can be interpreted to indicate that a 1 percent increase in retirement system membership will produce a 0.16 percent increase in total expenditures.

Fire Department Expenditures

The historical trend in Fire Department expenditures, as in the case of police, will be analyzed in terms of the employment, real wage, price, and pension contribution rate components of changes in the three types of expenditures (direct labor, retirement contribution, nonlabor). In the first section, the components of direct labor cost change will be presented. In the second section, retirement costs will be analyzed; in the third, nonlabor costs will be investigated. Finally, the last section will present an analysis of total fire expenditures.

Direct Labor Costs

The structure of labor costs in 1965 and 1972 for the Fire Department is shown in Appendix Tables 3.A.1-3.A.4. The dominance of uniformed personnel in the department totals is clear. (See Appendix Tables 3.A.1 and 3.A.2.) In 1972, 95 percent of labor costs and 92.5 percent of employment was accounted for by uniformed personnel. On the other hand, the growth in uniformed employment has been less rapid than in other department occupations. Between 1965 and 1972, uniformed employment grew by only 2.3 percent as opposed to 5 percent for the entire Department. From the data in Appendix Table 3.A.3, it is apparent that the large growth in "other" employment (70.9 percent) was partially the result of growth in the inspector and dispatcher categories (from 190 to 351 employees).

Again, the dominance of uniformed personnel can be seen in the disparity in average wages, shown in Appendix Table 3.A.4. Wages for these employees was slightly greater than the departmental average in both years. Further, growth in wages for these employees was greater (85.6 percent) than that for any other job category.

In summary, these results indicate that, although uniformed employment was the largest single category, growth was slower than for nonuniformed employment. On the other hand, wages for uniformed employees were higher than for all other job categories (except executive) and grew faster than for any other job category.

The relative impact of changes in employment, real wages, and prices on direct labor costs can be determined through the application of the model described previously.

Thus:

$$\Delta L = \$8,507 \Delta E + \$125,052,900 \Delta P + 20,771 \Delta W' \qquad (37)$$

The coefficients indicate that an increase of one employee (ΔE) yields an increase in direct labor cost of \$8,507, a \$1 increase in real wages (ΔW) raises labor costs by \$20,771, and an increase of 100 percent in the price level (ΔP) raises costs by \$125,052,900.

When observed values for ΔE, ΔP, and $\Delta W'$ are substituted into the equation above, the results indicate that, for the entire department, 5.5 percent of the increase in labor costs was due to employment increases, 48.5 percent to price increases, and 46 percent to real wage changes. The percentage components for each job category are included in Appendix Table 3.A-5 and show that uniformed personnel registered a relatively larger real wage component and smaller employment component than was the case for nonuniformed personnel.

In order to measure the marginal significance of changes in each of the independent variables (E, P, and W), it is necessary to employ elasticity coefficients:

$$\eta E = 1.00 \tag{33a}$$

$$\eta P = 1.05 \tag{33b}$$

$$\eta W' = 1.48 \tag{33c}$$

These coefficients suggest that a 1 percent change in employment will produce a 1 percent change in direct labor costs; a 1 percent change in prices will result in a 1.05 percent change in costs; and a 1 percent change in real wages will produce a 1.48 percent change in costs.

Retirement System Costs

The membership of the Fire Pension Fund (Article 1-B) consists of all persons in the uniformed force of the Fire Department in positions in the competitive class, who were appointed medical officers or firemen after March 29, 1940. Although other choices are available, almost all members have chosen the 20-year retirement plan.[17]

1. Eligibility: Eligibility is after 20 years of service.
2. Benefits: Benefits equal 50 percent of annual compensation earnable upon the date of retirement. For all service beyond 20 years, a member receives 1/60 of annual average earnings from the date of minimum service until the date of retirement for each year of additional service.

Appendix Table 3.A-8 shows the growth in the Fire Department Pension Fund in relation to other funds between 1961 and 1972.

The chief explanation for the recent slow growth in the city's contribution to the Fire Pension Fund is simply that an impasse exists between the city and representatives of the firemen as to the interpretation of a particular section of the City Administrative Code regarding the method by which actuarial funding deficiencies are to be made up. The net result of the impasse is that the Fire Pension Fund is not being funded as the Code requires and the city's contributions, as reported in Appendix Table 3.A.8, understate the costs that have accrued and that will have to be paid eventually. However, in the long run, contributions to the Fire Pension Fund by the city are apt to increase at a rate similar to that of the other systems.

In Table 3.11, a breakdown of the important aspects of the Fire Department Pension Fund is provided. Over the 1961-71 period, membership increased from 9,781 to 13,603 and aggregate salaries from $64.1 million to $158.9 million. Particularly interesting is the trend in employer-employee contributions. While the aggregate contribution of employers has more than tripled (from $9.5 million to $32 million) between 1961 and 1971, employees contributions have shown a marked decline (from $3.9 million to $600,000) over the same period. This trend toward a noncontributary plan is evidenced by the growth in the effective employer contribution from 14.8 percent (of aggregate salaries) in 1961 to 20.1 percent in 1971, as shown in Appendix Table 3.A.8. Further, the trend in the contribution rate for the Fire Department roughly parallels that for the Police Department, although since 1965, the police rate has been higher in every year except 1969.

The relative effect of employment, wages, and contribution rates on fire pension costs can be analyzed in the manual described in the section of this chapter beginning on page 174. Thus:

$$\Delta R \;=\; \$1,634 \,\Delta E \;+\; \$25,973,837 \Delta P \;+\; 4,043 \Delta W' \;+ \$126,701,646 \Delta C \tag{34}$$

where the symbols are defined as previously. The coefficients suggest that an increase in employment of 1 increases pension costs by $1,634 and an increase in the price level of 100 percent increases pension costs by $25,973,837; if real wages rise by $1, pension costs will increase by $4,043; and, if the contribution rate rises by 100 percentage points, pension costs will rise by $126,701,646.

Substituting actual changes in the independent variables into the above equation allows the determination of percentage shares of increased costs due to each independent variable. Of the total change in pension costs between 1965 and 1971, 24 percent was due to employment change, 68.7 percent to changes in the price level, and 20.1 percent to a change in the contribution rate. Because of the actual decline in the average real wages of pension fund members, the real wage component was -12.8 percent, indicating that, had wages kept up with the cost of living, costs would have risen even more rapidly than they did.

In order to compare the coefficients obtained with respect to their relative importance, elasticity coefficients can be calculated.[18]

TABLE 3.11

New York City Fire Department Pension Fund (Article 1-B), 1961-71
(dollar figures in millions of dollars)

Fiscal Year	Number of Active Members	Salaries of Active Members	Employee Contributions	Employer Contributions	Number of Beneficiaries	Payments to Beneficiaries	Assets	Liabilities[a]	Investment Income[b]
1961	9,781	$ 64.1	$ 3.9	$ 9.5	428	$ 1.4	$ 89.5	$366.1	$ 2.7
1962	10,276	77.4	4.5	11.7	641	2.2	107.6	451.8	3.7
1963	11,240	89.1	5.4	13.0	874	3.1	128.1	542.1	4.6
1964	11,659	96.2	3.3	14.9	1,070	4.0	150.9	638.4	5.3
1965	11,709	106.3	4.0	19.1	1,189	4.7	177.4	696.9	6.4
1966	12,026	111.0	4.3	22.9	1,276	5.2	207.3	739.8	7.7
1967	12,190	124.3	4.8	23.5	1,426	6.2	238.6	702.9	9.2
1968	12,294	126.2	4.9	22.3	1,725	8.2	272.4	740.8	10.8
1969	12,937	139.7	0.9	31.3	1,923	9.4	306.9	822.5	12.8
1970	13,494	155.9	0.5	31.9	2,184	11.7	341.7	940.8	15.4
1971	13,603	158.9	0.6	32.0	2,416	13.9	379.0	961.2	17.8
Average annual increase[c]	3.9%	14.7%	-8.5%	23.7%	46.4%	89.3%	36.5%	16.3%	55.9%

[a]Equal to present value of future benefits including both those already accrued and those expected to be earned by present active members.

[b]Excludes gains or losses on the sale of securities.

[c]Calculated from total percent increase over 1961-71 period divided by the number of years (10).

Sources: Records of the City Actuary; Annual Report to the Superintendent of Insurance of the State of New York (Albany, N.Y.: Office of the Superintendent of Insurance, 1961-71), Comptroller of the City of New York, Annual Report (New York: Office of the Comptroller, 1961-71), Appendix A.

As defined here, the employment coefficient indicates that a 1 percent
change in employment yields a 1 percent change in pension costs, a
1 percent change in contribution rates yields a 1.16 percent change
in pension costs, a 1 percent change in prices yields a 1 percent change
in pension costs, and a 1 percent change in real wages produces a
1.76 percent change in pension costs.

Nonlabor Costs

Nonlabor costs—that is, expenditures on supplies, materials,
equipment, and contractual services, are presented in Table 3.12.
Total nonlabor expenditure increased from $1,488,500 in 1965 to
$2,411,800 in 1970. The areas of greatest expenditure were supplies
($960,500 in 1970) and contractual services ($767,500 in 1970). In
the aggregate, nonlabor costs in the Fire Department represent a
small fraction of expenditures in relation to other components of
expenditure—8.7 percent of retirement costs and only 1.4 percent of
direct labor costs in 1972.

In order to assess the impact of inflation on nonlabor expenditures,
the determination of Laspeyres price indexes may be used. Such
indexes for nonlabor costs are shown in Table 3.13. Using 1964-65
as a base, the index for nonlabor costs in the aggregate was 118.3.
Not surprisingly, the area of nonlabor cost showing the largest increase was contractual services—an index of 125.9 in 1971. The
area where inflation has had the least impact is equipment—an index
of 110.7 in 1971. Deflated real expenditures yield a measure of the
effect of increased purchases of nonlabor commodities and services.
Such a series is shown in Table 3.14. Expenditures in real terms
increased by about 50 percent (from $1.5 million to $2.1 million) as
opposed to be more than 60 percent increase in money expenditures.

To determine the marginal effects of price and real quantity
changes on nonlabor costs, it is helpful to return to the model. When
we make the necessary calculations,[19]

$$\Delta N = \$1,285\,\Delta E + \$2,393,010\,\Delta P'.$$

These coefficients indicate that a change in employment of 1 will increase nonlabor costs by $1,285, and that a 100 percent increase in
the price level will increase nonlabor costs by $2,393,010. When
the values of the independent variables ($\Delta P'$ and ΔQ or ΔE) are substituted into the above equations, it is possible to determine the fraction of the total change in nonlabor costs attributable to each variable.
Specifically, 31.7 percent of the total increase in labor costs can be
attributed to price changes, and the remaining 68.4 percent, to changes
in real quantities purchased (or employment).

TABLE 3.12

New York City Fire Department Annual NonLabor Expenditures, 1965-70
(in thousands of dollars)

Object Class	1965	1966	1967	1968	1969	1970
Total	1,488.5	1,516.4	1,527.7	1,750.1	2,119.0	2,411.8
		(1.9)*	(0.7)	(14.6)	(21.1)	(13.8)
Supplies	716.4	775.7	773.3	856.5	1,052.7	960.5
		(8.3)	(-0.3)	(10.8)	(22.9)	(-8.8)
Materials	232.3	233.4	251.3	305.2	321.1	313.0
		(0.5)	(7.7)	(21.4)	(5.2)	(-2.5)
Equipment	71.0	73.1	75.6	105.1	152.3	370.8
		(3.0)	(3.4)	(39.1)	(44.8)	(143.5)
Contractual services	468.7	434.2	427.4	483.3	592.9	767.5
		(-7.4)	(-1.6)	(13.1)	(22.7)	(29.4)

Note: Years used are fiscal years.

*Figures in parentheses are annual percentage changes.

Source: Compiled from Comptroller of the City of New York, Annual Report (New York: Office of the Comptroller, 1965-70), Part A, Statement 8.

TABLE 3.13

Laspeyres Price Index for New York City Fire Department
Nonlabor Goods and Services, 1965-70

Object Class	1965a	1966	1967	1968	1969	1970	1971
Total	100.0	101.8	104.2	107.1	109.8	114.0	118.3
		(1.8)b	(2.3)	(2.8)	(2.5)	(3.8)	(3.8)
Supplies	100.0	102.2	104.6	108.4	109.2	112.6	115.6
		(2.2)	(2.4)	(3.6)	(0.7)	(3.1)	(2.7)
Materials	100.0	101.7	103.7	102.6	107.1	110.4	114.5
		(1.7)	(2.0)	(-1.1)	(4.4)	(3.0)	(3.8)
Equipment	100.0	100.4	102.5	104.8	106.5	109.0	110.7
		(0.4)	(2.1)	(2.3)	(1.6)	(2.3)	(1.5)
Contractual services	100.0	101.5	103.8	107.4	112.8	118.9	125.9
		(1.5)	(2.3)	(3.5)	(5.0)	(5.4)	(5.8)

Note: Years used are fiscal years.

aBase year: 1965 = 100.
bFigures in parentheses are annual percentage changes.

Source: David Greytak and Robert Dinkelmeyer, "The Components of Change in New York City's Non-Labor Costs—Fiscal Years 1965-1970: Supplies, Materials, Equipment and Contractural Services," Working Paper no. 13, Maxwell Research Project on the Public Finances of New York, 1972.

TABLE 3.14

Laspeyres Deflated Real Expenditures for New York City Fire
Department Nonlabor Goods and Services, 1965-70
(in thousands of dollars)

Object Class	1965a	1966	1967	1968	1969	1970
Total	1,488.5	1,488.9	1,466.4	1,633.6	1,929.1	2,115.9
		(0.0)b	(-1.5)	(11.4)	(18.1)	(9.7)
Supplies	716.5	759.0	739.0	789.9	964.2	853.2
		(5.9)	(-2.6)	(6.9)	(22.1)	(-11.5)
Materials	232.3	229.5	242.3	297.5	299.9	283.6
		(-1.2)	(5.6)	(22.8)	(0.8)	(-5.4)
Equipment	71.0	72.8	73.8	100.3	142.9	340.1
		(2.6)	(1.4)	(35.9)	(42.5)	(137.9)
Contractual services	468.7	427.8	411.6	449.9	525.5	645.3
		(-8.7)	(-3.8)	(9.3)	(16.8)	(22.8)

Note: Years used are fiscal years.

aBase year: 1965 = 100.
bFigures in parentheses are annual percentage changes.

Source: David Greytak and Robert Dinkelmeyer, "The Components of Change in New York City's Non-Labor Costs—Fiscal Years 1965-1970: Supplies, Materials, Equipment and Contractural Services," Working Paper no. 13, Maxwell Research Project on the Public Finances of New York, 1972.

The elasticity coefficients, when calculated, enable a comparison to be made of the relative impact of the independent variables.

$$^{\eta}E \;\; = \;\; 13.00 \tag{36a}$$

$$^{\eta}Q \;\; = \;\; 1.00 \tag{36b}$$

$$^{\eta}P' \;\; = \;\; 1.65 \tag{36c}$$

The coefficients show that a 1 percent change in real quantities purchased will yield a 1 percent increase in expenditures, while a 1 percent increase in the price level will produce a 1.65 percent increase in nonlabor expenditures, and a 1 percent increase in employment will increase nonlabor costs by 13 percent.

Total Fire Department Expenditures

The purpose of this section is to combine the analysis of Fire Department expenditures presented above in order to explain the relative importance of the factors determining the increases in total fire expenditures between 1965 and 1972. Since changes in each component of expenditure have been attributed to changes in employment, real wages, prices, and the pension contribution rate, it is possible, as before, to show the relation between changes in these variables and changes in total Fire Department expenditures. As explained previously, because of the difference in employment and wage levels for members and nonmembers of the Fire Pension Fund, as well as the distinction between consumer prices and the price index applicable to supplies and equipment, the equation describing total departmental expenditures must take such differences into account. Therefore, for the Fire Department as a whole, the calculation provides the following result:

$$\Delta X \; = \; \$9,792 \Delta E \;\; + \;\; \$1,634 \; E_R \;\; + \;\; \$151,026,737 \, \Delta P \;\; + \\ \$2,393,010 \Delta P' \;\; + \;\; 20,771 \Delta W' \;\; + \;\; 4,043 W\dot{R} \;\; + \\ \$126,701,646 \Delta C \tag{37}$$

Again, the interpretation of the coefficients indicates that an increase of one employee increases direct labor and nonlabor expenditures by \$9,792; the addition of one employee to the retirement system adds \$1,634 to total expenditures. Similarly, an increase of \$1 in real wages raises departmental direct labor costs by \$20,771 and pension costs by \$4,043. Other coefficients can be interpreted in an analogous fashion.

The substitution of observed changes in the independent variables enables the determination of the percentages of labor costs attributable to each. After substitution, the results show that 5.6 percent of the increased expenditure resulted from increased departmental employment, 2.5 percent from increased membership in the retirement system, 40.7 percent from increased real wage rates, -1.4 percent from changes in real wages of pension fund members, 50.1 percent from increases in consumer prices, 0.4 percent from equipment price changes, and 2.1 percent from increases in the pension contribution rate.

To compare the relative marginal effects of the independent variables, elasticity coefficients were calculated:

$$\eta E \quad = \quad 0.98 \tag{38a}$$

$$\eta E_R \quad = \quad 0.14 \tag{38b}$$

$$\eta P \quad = \quad 1.08 \tag{38c}$$

$$\eta P' \quad = \quad 0.02 \tag{38d}$$

$$\eta W' \quad = \quad 1.27 \tag{38e}$$

$$\eta W'_R \quad = \quad 0.26 \tag{38f}$$

$$\eta C \quad = \quad 0.16 \tag{38g}$$

These coefficients indicate that changes in real wages have the greatest effect on Fire Department costs, followed by changes in consumer prices and changes in employment.

Environmental Protection Administrative Expenditures

In this section, the expenditures of the Environmental Protection Administration will be analyzed in terms of growth in direct labor, retirement and nonlabor (such as supplies and materials) costs. The growth in each will be attributed to changes in employment, prices, real wages, and retirement contribution rate for pensions.

Direct Labor Costs

Tables 3.A-1 through 3.A-4 record the level and composition of direct labor costs for EPA. Labor costs and employment of uniformed personnel, as shown in Appendix Tables 3.A.1 and 3.A.2, represent about 60 percent of the department total. Although this is the largest of any job category in EPA, these workers are not as important relatively as in the Police and Fire Departments. On the other hand, growth in uniformed labor costs and employment was smaller than for all job categories except laborer, as well as for the departments as a whole.

In Appendix Table 3.A.3, the absolute growth in "other employment" (508 employees) is disaggregated. Although in relation to other occupation categories, the percentage growth in employment of engineers was not large, this category accounted for 301 of the employees that were added to the department.

Average wage rates are the subject of Table 3.A-4. Although wages for uniformed personnel are greater than the departmental average, they are less than those for the executive and other groups, and not much higher than those of the laborer category. This relative position of uniformed personnel differs from the Police and Fire Departments, where wages of uniformed personnel were higher than all categories except executives.

As before, growth in direct labor costs can be attributed to employment, wages, and inflation, that is:

$$\Delta L = \$7,330 \Delta E + \$150,939,360 \Delta P + 29,097 \Delta W' \tag{39}$$

In other words, the addition of an employee will increase costs by $7,330, an increase in the price level of 100 percent will increase costs by $150,939,360, and an increase in real wages of $1 will increase costs by $29,097. Substitution of the observed changes in E, P, and W' into the equation produces the result that 11.1 percent of the increase in costs was due to increased employment, 54.4 percent to increased prices, and 34.5 percent to increased real wages. These components for all job categories are shown in Appendix Tables 3.A.5 and 3.A.6. Again, the dominance of uniformed personnel is evident, but not to the extent that existed for police and fire.

The elasticity coefficients, η_E, η_2, and $\eta_{W'}$, may be calculated using the method explained above.

$$\eta_E = 1.00 \tag{40a}$$

$$\eta_P = 1.29 \tag{40b}$$

$$\eta_{W'} = 1.82 \tag{40c}$$

205

These indicate that a 1 percent increase in employment yields a 1 percent increase in labor costs; a 1 percent increase in prices, a 1.29 percent rise in costs; and a 1 percent rise in real wages, a 1.82 percent increase in direct labor costs.

Retirement System Costs

Most EPA employees who are members of a pension system belong to the New York City Employees Retirement System (NYCERS). The membership of NYCERS consists of the vast majority of general government employees other than policemen, firemen, and teachers and other permanent employees of the Board of Education. Also included in this system are employees of New York City's Housing Authority, Transit Authority, and Triborough Bridge and Tunnel Authority, as well as the employees of a few other small city public authorities.

NYCERS serves as an umbrella for several specific plans designed for separate employee groups. Although a complete description of all the features of each plan is beyond the scope of this report, a brief summary of the basic retirement plans selected by most employees is presented below.[20]

1. Career Pension Plan
    a. Eligibility: The earliest eligibility is at age 55 (or 50 for certain positions classified as physically taxing) after 20 years of service. Benefits are not payable until the date on which the member would have completed 25 years of service.
    b. Benefits: Benefits are 2.2 percent of salary base —e.g., earnings in the year prior to retirement (or the average salary earned in any three-year span, if higher) —for each of the first 25 years of service. In addition, 1.7 percent (or 1.2 percent, if it was before July 1, 1968) of salary base is paid for each year of service over 25 as well as the actuarial equivalent of deductions accumulated in excess (i.e., member contributions) and ITHP contributions.
2. Increased Service Fraction Plan
    a. Eligibility: The age of eligibility is 55.
    b. Benefits: Benefits are 1.53 percent (1.2 percent for years prior to July 1, 1968) of salary base for each year of service plus additional lifetime payments that are the actuarial equivalent of the member's accumulated contributions and the reserve for ITHP.

3. Department of Sanitation and Transit Authority Twenty-Year Plans

a. Eligibility: Eligibility and payability are after 20 years of service for the Sanitation Department. Eligibility is after 20 years' service, but payability is after age 50 and 20 years service for Transit Authority employees.

b. Benefits: Benefits are: (1) 50 percent of final years' salary (annual salary based on last day's pay rate for sanitation workers); plus (2) 1/100 of the average of the last five years' salary for all years in excess of 20; plus (3) 1/200 of the average of the last five years' salary for all years in excess of 20 and after July 2, 1965 (Sanitation) or July 1, 1968 (Transit Authority); plus (4) lifetime payments that are the actuarial equivalent of excess member contributions and all reserves for ITHP paid for service in excess of 20 years.

As is clear in Appendix Table 3.A.7, both the absolute size and growth of NYCERS were greater than for any other pension system covering New York City employees. In Appendix Table 3.A.9, the important parts of the retirement system are presented. The number of active members has increased by an average of 4.8 percent, and the salaries of members, by 15.3 percent. At the same time, employee contributions grew by only 1.9 percent yearly between 1961 and 1971, while employer contributions grew by 22.7 percent per year. Appendix Table 3.A.8 shows that, though growth in the NYCERS contribution rate was greater than for Teachers Retirement and Board of Education Retirement Systems, in every year the NYCERS contribution was lower than that of any of the other retirement systems. Taking these factors into consideration, retirement contribution can be expressed as follows:

$$\Delta R = \$550 \Delta E + \$19,923,996 \Delta P + 3841 \Delta W' + \$150,939,360 \Delta C, \tag{41}$$

where the interpretation of the coefficients is the same as before. (Since the wages and the membership of EPA employees in NYCERS were not known, estimated retirement costs of these employees were determined by assuming that all EPA employees were members of the system and by using budgeted employment and wage figures together with the average NYCERS rate.) Substitution of observed changes in E, P, W, and C into the above equation indicates that 4.3 percent of the increase was due to employment, 35.6 percent to increased prices, 24 percent to real wages increases, and 36.1 percent to increases in the contribution rate.

The elasticity coefficients were determined to be the following:

$$\eta E \;=\; 1.00 \tag{42a}$$

$$\eta P \;=\; 1.88 \tag{42b}$$

$$\eta W' \;=\; 2.55 \tag{42c}$$

$$\eta C \;=\; 1.09 \tag{42d}$$

indicating that an increase in prices of 1 percent results in a 1.88 percent increase in retirement costs of EPA employees.

Nonlabor Costs

Table 3.15 shows the effect of increased prices on the various categories of EPA nonlabor expenditures. For department expenditures as a whole, prices rose by 17 percent between 1965 and 1971. The largest rise in prices was registered in the purchase of contractual services—30.1 percent—the smallest in supplies—12.3 percent. Considering these factors, the change in nonlabor costs can be expressed as follows:[21]

$$\Delta N \;=\; \$8354\Delta E \;+\; \$21{,}308{,}530\Delta P' \tag{43}$$

Therefore, the increase in employment of one increases nonlabor costs by $9,964 and the increase in prices of 100 percent raises costs by $21,308,530. In percentage terms, this indicates that 80.2 percent of the increase in nonlabor costs between 1965 and 1971 can be attributed to changes in quantities purchased (employment) and only 19.8 percent to increased prices.

The elasticity coefficients, ηE, $\eta P'$, ηQ, can be calculated to determine the relative impact of percent changes in the independent variables:

$$\eta E \;=\; 28.90 \tag{44a}$$

$$\eta Q \;=\; 1.00 \tag{44b}$$

$$\eta P' \;=\; 3.21 \tag{44c}$$

and can be interpreted as the percent change resulting from a 1 percent change in the independent variable.

TABLE 3.15

Laspeyres Price Index for New York City Environmental Protection
Administration Nonlabor Goods and Services, 1965-70

Object Class	1965a	1966	1967	1968	1969	1970	1971
Total	100.0	102.4	105.4	107.4	109.2	112.4	117.0
		(2.4)b	(2.9)	(1.9)	(1.7)	(2.9)	(4.1)
Supplies	100.0	102.8	106.3	108.9	107.7	109.6	112.3
		(2.8)	(3.4)	(2.5)	(-1.1)	(1.7)	(2.4)
Materials	100.0	101.7	103.7	102.6	107.0	110.2	114.5
		(1.7)	(1.9)	(-1.0)	(4.3)	(3.0)	(3.9)
Equipment	100.0	101.7	105.1	108.5	111.8	110.2	119.4
		(1.7)	(3.4)	(3.2)	(3.1)	(-1.4)	(8.3)
Contractual services	100.0	102.2	105.2	109.2	114.6	121.5	130.1
		(2.2)	(3.0)	(3.8)	(5.0)	(6.0)	(7.1)

Note: The expenditure weights include only the Department of Sanitation and the Department of Air Pollution Control. Years used are fiscal years.

aBase year: 1965 = 100.
bFigures in parentheses are annual percentage changes.

Source: David Greytak and Robert Dinkelmeyer, "The Components of Change in New York City's Non-Labor Costs—Fiscal Years 1965-1970: Supplies, Materials, Equipment and Contractual Services," Working Paper no. 13, Maxwell Research Project on the Public Finances of New York, 1972.

209

Total EPA Expenditures

In order to determine the relative effects of the variables for department costs as a whole, it is helpful to combine the results pertaining to labor, retirement, and nonlabor costs. It is then possible to explain the changes in total expenditures as a function of changes in employment, prices, real wages, and the pension contribution rate. To be consistent with previous sections, it is necessary to disaggregate employment, real wages, and prices into components that deal with different segments of the department. Therefore, the equation obtained after the addition of the coefficients of similar terms in the previous departmental equations is as follows:

$$\Delta X = \$15,684\,\Delta E + \$550\Delta E_R + \$170,863,356\,\Delta P +$$
$$\$21,308,530\,\Delta P' + 29,097\,\Delta W' + 3841\,\Delta W_R' +$$
$$\$150,939,360\Delta C \tag{45}$$

For EPA then, the addition of one employee raises departmental costs by \$15,684 and retirement costs by \$550; the increase in the consumer price level of 100 percent raises costs by \$170,863,356, while the increase in nonlabor prices of 100 percent raises costs by \$21,308,530. Other coefficients can be explained similarly.

When observed changes of the independent variables are substituted into the above equation, the percentage components are obtained. Of the total increase in EPA costs, 17.4 percent was due to increased general employment, 0.6 percent to increased pension system membership, 44.5 percent to increased consumer prices, 2.7 percent to increased nonlabor (wholesale) prices, 25.8 percent to increased general real wages, 3.4 percent to rising retirement system real wages, and 5.4 percent to the increased pension contribution rate.

The comparison of the marginal effects of the coefficients is possible through the use of elasticity coefficients.

$$\eta_E = 1.91 \tag{46a}$$

$$\eta_{E_R} = 0.07 \tag{46b}$$

$$\eta_P = 1.10 \tag{46c}$$

$$\eta_{P'} = 0.13 \tag{46d}$$

$$\eta_{W'} = 1.35 \tag{46e}$$

$$^\eta W_R = 0.18 \tag{46f}$$

$$^\eta C = 0.07 \tag{46g}$$

Public School Expenditures

As with other functions, the investigation of expenditures for public schools involves the analysis of direct labor, retirement, and nonlabor expenditures with respect to employment, real wage, price, and pension contribution rate components. After the separate analysis of each type of expenditure, the general model described above will be applied to total departmental expenditure.

Direct Labor Expenditure

The composition of labor costs for public schools is presented in Appendix Tables 3.A.10 through 3.A.12. As reported in Appendix Tables 3.A.10 and 3.A.11, delivery personnel account for more than 80 percent of the department total, in terms of both labor costs and employment. Further, between 1965 and 1972, wages for delivery personnel grew faster than those for any other job category (Appendix Table 3.A.12), but employment for teachers grew more slowly than any other category. Growth in labor costs for teachers was slightly greater than that for clerical employees but was slower than that for any other job category. Overall, the slow growth in delivery employment was enough to offset the relatively fast growth of wages for delivery personnel, resulting in the declining of share of total departmental costs represented by this job category between 1965 and 1972.

The assessment of the relative importance of changing employment and wage levels as a factor in changing departmental direct labor costs can be determined by use of the model. After calculation of the coefficients in the manner described earlier, the equation obtained is as follows:

$$\Delta L + \$8,540\,\Delta E + \$693,422,328\ \Delta P + 114,731\,\Delta W' \tag{47}$$

The interpretation of these coefficients follows that presented above. The increase of one employee raises direct labor costs by \$8,540; the increase of 100 percent in the price level raises costs by \$693, 422,238; and the increase in real wages of \$1 raises direct labor costs by \$114,731.

Substituting the observed changes in E, P, and W' into the above equation, it is possible to determine the fraction of the total increase

211

in labor costs attributable to changes in each variable. The results indicate that, of the total increase in direct labor costs for public schools, 31.8 percent was due to increases in employment, 49.6 percent changes in prices, and 18.6 percent to real wage changes. Tables 3.A-13 and 3.A-14 present these components for each job category. It is important to note that the real wage component for delivery personnel was greater than that for nondelivery personnel, while the employment component for nondelivery personnel was generally greater than that for delivery.

The comparison of the marginal effects of each of these components on direct labor costs requires the use of an elasticity coefficient, because the variables are measured in different units. The calculation of these coefficients follows as before:

$$\eta E \quad = \quad 1.00 \qquad\qquad (48a)$$

$$\eta P \quad = \quad 1.39 \qquad\qquad (48b)$$

$$\eta W' \quad = \quad 1.96 \qquad\qquad (48c)$$

These coefficients indicate that an increase in employment of 1 percent increases direct labor costs by 1 percent; the increase of prices by 1 percent increases labor costs by 1.39 percent; and the increase in real wages of 1 percent raises direct labor costs by 1.96 percent.

Retirement System Costs

There are two retirement systems that apply to public school employees: the Teachers Retirement System and the Board of Education Retirement System. The membership of the Board of Education Retirement System consists of all permanent employees in public schools other than those eligible for the Teachers Retirement System and members who transfer to other city employment and choose to remain in this system. The basic features of the retirement plans available are essentially the same as those of the NYCERS Career Pension Plan and the Increased Fraction Plan described above[22] and will not be repeated here.

The growth in both system is shown in Appendix Table 3.A-7. In the case of the Teachers Retirement System, the very large decline in city contributions from $140.7 million in 1971 to $26 million in 1972 is only a one-year deviation from the pattern of steady growth that has typified the system in most years since 1961. The reason for the decline is a legislatively mandated accounting modification that has delayed the full budgetary impact of recent improvements in teachers' retirement benefits. As is pointed out below in the section entitled "Forecasts of New York City Expenditures for 1979," the apparently precipitous decline in the cost of the Teachers Retirement System in 1972 will have turned into a startling increase in costs by 1973 or 1974.

Table 3.16 shows the important facts about the Teachers Retirement System (TRS). As shown there, there is a rather marked difference between growth exhibited in employer contributions and the dramatic decline in aggregate employee contributions. This is partly the result of the large increase in members' salaries—20 percent per year between 1961 and 1971. The contribution rate for the TRS over the 1961-71 period, as displayed in Appendix Table 3.A-8, has actually declined from 19.4 percent to 14.2 percent.

The Board of Education Retirement System, presented in Table 3.17, covers fewer members than the TRS and, unlike the TRS, exhibits growth in both employer and employee contributions. Further, the average yearly growth in both active members and aggregate salaries was less than that for TRS. The contribution rate, however, increased slightly between 1961 and 1971, although much year-to-year variation is evident. (See Appendix Table 3.A.8.)

In order to assess the relative importance of wage, price, employment, and contribution rate changes for pension costs in public schools, the model can again be applied. In the case of BERS (R_B), when substitution is made for the coefficients, the equation becomes:

$$\Delta R_B \;=\; \$939\,\Delta E \;+\; \$5,987,223\,\Delta P \;+\; 1,186\,\Delta W' \;+$$
$$\$40,454,208 \Delta C \tag{49}$$

Accordingly, for each employee added to the BERS, retirement costs increase $5,987,223, and so on. Substitution of changes in the independent variables into the equation suggests that 20 percent of increased BERS costs resulted from employment changes, 57.3 percent from price changes, 10.7 percent from real wage changes, and 11.9 percent from the increase in the contribution rate.

The analysis of the TRS for the public schools is made difficult because of the fact that some college teachers are also members of the system. Therefore, in order to estimate retirement costs for public school personnel only, it was assumed that all teachers in the public schools were members of the TRS. Thus, by use of the contribution rate shown in Appendix Table 3.A.8 for TRS and of employment figures and average wage figures estimated from the direct labor cost data, it is possible to estimate the cost of the TRS for education employees (R_T).

$$\Delta R_T \;=\; \$1,782\,\Delta E \;+\; \$76,143,145\,\Delta P \;+$$
$$12,237\,\Delta W' \;+\; \$536,219,332 \Delta C \tag{50}$$

TABLE 3.16

New York City Teachers Retirement System, 1961-71
(dollar figures in millions of dollars)

Fiscal Year	Number of Active Members	Salaries of Active Members	Employee Contributions	Employer Contributions	Number of Beneficiaries	Payments to Beneficiaries	Assets	Liabilities[a]	Investment Income[b]
1961	43,575	$329.9	$35.3	$ 64.1	16,461	$ 48.7	$1,127.0	$1,913.5	$35.2
1962	43,638	366.6	32.9	72.3	16,966	54.9	1,209.2	2,121.2	40.6
1963	44,698	385.3	35.8	90.9	17,320	58.6	1,309.7	2,239.5	54.6
1964	48,621	429.7	37.5	93.2	17,870	63.1	1,409.3	2,510.3	50.6
1965	50,867	460.1	50.3	97.3	18,215	66.9	1,536.6	2,673.7	56.7
1966	53,867	517.5	41.4	102.2	18,657	71.8	1,662.3	2,948.1	62.4
1967	57,470	557.9	51.9	99.2	19,122	76.9	1,788.5	2,614.5	69.6
1968	59,204	614.2	35.7	113.2	19,647	82.6	1,948.5	2,837.5	76.0
1969	61,745	715.3	30.1	103.5	20,068	86.2	2,046.8	3,050.9	75.3
1970	67,027	859.3	36.6	102.0	19,894	87.4	2,072.8	4,563.4	74.4
1971	74,339	989.5	22.1	140.7	21,274	108.8	2,335.6	5,108.7	75.4
Average annual change[c]	7.06%	20.0%	-6.3% (0.3)[d]	11.9%	2.92%	12.3%	10.7%	16.7%	11.4%

[a]Equal to present value of future benefits including both those already expected to be earned by present active members.
[b]Excludes gains or losses on the sale of securities.
[c]Calculated from total percent increase over 1961-71 period divided by number of years (10).
[d]Average percent increase for the 1961-70 period.

Sources: Records of the City Actuary; Annual Report to the Superintendent of Insurance of the State of New York (Albany, N.Y.: Office of the Superintendent of Insurance, 1961-71); Comptroller of the City of New York, Annual Report (New York: Office of the Comptroller, 1961-71), Appendix A.

TABLE 3.17

New York City Board of Education Retirement System, 1961-71
(dollar figures in millions of dollars)

Fiscal Year	Number of Active Members	Salaries of Active Members	Employee Contributions	Employer Contributions	Number of Beneficiaries	Payments to Beneficiaries	Assets	Liabilities[a]	Investment Income[b]
1961	4,226	$23.5	$2.8	$ 3.3	880	$ 2.0	$ 55.1	$ 90.9	$ 1.7
1962	4,316	25.2	2.5	3.0	921	2.1	58.5	97.7	1.9
1963	4,515	27.8	2.8	3.9	957	2.3	63.3	107.5	2.1
1964	4,872	32.3	3.4	4.9	1,017	2.5	69.4	121.1	2.3
1965	5,108	35.0	3.8	4.8	1,053	2.7	76.7	136.8	2.7
1966	5,207	38.2	4.0	5.6	1,131	2.9	84.2	150.0	3.1
1967	5,368	41.9	4.5	5.5	1,193	3.1	92.2	135.4	3.5
1968	5,664	44.4	4.5	5.9	1,247	3.4	100.5	175.7	4.0
1969	5,493	42.7	4.0	4.9	1,351	3.9	105.5	185.0	4.5
1970	5,688	51.3	4.5	6.1	1,448	4.5	105.6	211.9	4.8
1971	5,904	57.6	4.3	8.5	1,589	5.4	109.3	213.5	4.9
Average annual increase[c]	4.0%	14.5%	5.4%	15.7%	8.1%	17.6%	9.8%	14.1%	18.8%

aEqual to present value of future benefits including both those already accrued and those expected to be earned by present active members.

bExcludes gains or losses on the sale of securities.

cCalculated from total percent increase over 1961-71 period divided by number of years (10).

Source: Records of the City Actuary; Annual Report to the Superintendent of Insurance of the State of New York (Albany, N.Y.: Office of the Superintendent of Insurance, 1961-71); Comptroller of the City of New York, Annual Report (New York: Office of the Comptroller, 1961-71), Appendix A.

215

The coefficients can be interpreted in a similar fashion to that just explained.

Combining the costs of both systems yields an equation which estimates, for both systems, the retirement cost resulting from public school employees.

$$\Delta R = \$1,700\,\Delta E + \$71,957,707\,\Delta P + 12,259\,\Delta W' + \$575,661,658\,\Delta C \tag{51}$$

The increase in pension membership of one employee increases pension costs by \$1,700; the increase in the price level of 100 percent increases costs by \$71,957,707, and so on. In percentage terms, the aggregate equation suggests that 72.5 percent of the increase resulted from increased employment, 47.3 percent from the increase in real wages, and 81.7 percent from an increase in prices. The decrease in the contribution rate actually tended to cut costs by the amount of 101.5 percent of the actual increase.

To compare the marginal effects of the independent variables for retirement costs as a whole, elasticity coefficients need to be calculated.

$$\eta E = 1.00 \tag{52a}$$

$$\eta P = 0.88 \tag{52b}$$

$$\eta W' = 1.25 \tag{52c}$$

$$\eta C = 1.28 \tag{52d}$$

These coefficients indicate that a 1 percent increase in the price level will increase retirement costs by 0.88 percent; and 1 percent increase in real wages will increase costs by 1.25 percent; and a 1 percent increase in the contribution rate will raise costs by 1.28 percent.

Nonlabor Costs

Nonlabor expenditures between 1965 and 1970 are presented in Table 3.18. In 1965, the largest area of nonlabor expenditures was supplies. However, due to its factor growth rate, contractual services represented a larger fraction of the nonlabor budget in 1970 than did supplies. Over the period, expenditures on equipment actually declined from about \$3 million to slightly over \$2.3 million.

The Laspeyres price indexes presented in Table 3.19 enable a determination of the effects of inflation on nonlabor costs. For nonlabor

TABLE 3.18

New York City Public Schools Annual Nonlabor Expenditures, 1965-70
(in thousands of dollars)

Object Class	1965	1966	1967	1968	1969	1970
Total[a]	55,270.6	79,450.2	89,548.5	100,771.7	105,758.6	96,056.8
		(43.7)[b]	(12.7)	(12.5)	(4.9)	(-9.2)
Supplies	30,232.1	40,908.4	50,592.2	51,679.1	52,685.6	41,616.0
		(35.3)	(23.7)	(2.1)	(1.9)	(-21.0)
Equipment	3,018.4	8,070.8	6,913.6	5,796.6	9,816.1	2,363.6
		(167.4)	(-14.3)	(-16.2)	(69.3)	(-75.9)
Contractual services	22,020.1	30,470.9	32,042.6	43,296.0	43,257.0	52,077.1
		(38.4)	(5.2)	(35.1)	(-0.1)	(20.4)

Note: Years used are fiscal years.

[a]There is no "materials" account for public schools.
[b]Figures in parentheses are annual percentage changes.

Source: Compiled from Comptroller of the City of New York, Annual Report (New York: Office of the Comptroller, 1965-70), Part 2A, Statement 8.

TABLE 3.19

Laspeyres Price Index for New York City Public Schools
Nonlabor Goods and Services, 1965-70

Object Class	1965[a]	1966	1967	1968	1969	1970	1971
Total[b]	100.0	102.2	105.1	108.9	113.5	119.7	120.7
		(2.2)[c]	(2.9)	(3.6)	(4.2)	(5.5)	(0.9)
Supplies	100.0	102.1	104.7	107.5	111.1	116.9	107.6
		(2.1)	(2.6)	(2.6)	(3.4)	(5.2)	(-8.0)
Equipment	100.0	104.6	107.4	109.3	113.6	116.9	121.0
		(4.6)	(2.7)	(1.8)	(3.9)	(2.9)	(3.6)
Contractual services	100.0	102.0	105.2	110.0	115.3	122.1	129.8
		(2.0)	(3.1)	(4.6)	(4.8)	(5.9)	(6.3)

Note: Years used are fiscal years.

[a]Base year: 1965 = 100.
[b]There is no "materials" account for public schools.
[c]Figures in parentheses are annual percentage changes.

Source: David Greytak and Robert Dinkelmeyer, "The Components of Change in New York City's Non-Labor Costs—Fiscal Years 1965-1970: Supplies, Materials, Equipment and Contractural Services," Working Paper no. 13, Maxwell Research Project on the Public Finances of New York, 1972.

TABLE 3.20

Laspeyres Deflated Real Expenditures for New York City Public Schools
Nonlabor Goods and Services, 1965-70
(in thousands of dollars)

Object Class	1965[a]	1966	1967	1968	1969	1970
Total[b]	55,270.6	77,760.3	85,179.0	92,502.9	93,184.9	80,251.7
		(40.7)[c]	(9.5)	(8.6)	(0.7)	(-13.9)
Supplies	30,232.1	40,072.1	48,300.9	48,075.8	47,421.5	35,603.4
		(32.5)	(20.5)	(-0.5)	(-1.4)	(-24.9)
Equipment	3,018.4	7,715.9	6,437.3	5,303.4	8,640.9	2,021.9
		(155.6)	(-16.6)	(-17.6)	(62.9)	(-76.6)
Contractual services	22,020.1	29,873.5	30,458.8	39,360.0	37,516.9	42,651.2
		(35.7)	(2.0)	(29.2)	(-4.7)	(13.7)

Note: Years used are fiscal years.

[a]Base year: 1965 = 100.
[b]There is no "materials" account for public schools.
[c]Figures in parentheses are annual percentage changes.

Source: David Greytak and Robert Dinkelmeyer, "The Components of Change in New York City's Non-Labor Costs—Fiscal Years 1965-1970: Supplies, Materials, Equipment and Contractural Services," Working Paper no. 13, Maxwell Research Project on the Public Finances of New York, 1972.

costs. For nonlabor expenditures as a whole, prices between 1965 and 1971 rose by 20.7 percent. Prices of contractual services rose by 29.8 percent over the period, prices of equipment by 21 percent, and prices of supplies by only 7.6 percent. The deflated real expenditures on nonlabor costs for public schools are shown in Table 3.20 and give an indication of the relative growth in quantities purchased among the objects of nonlabor expenditure.

Applying the price and real expenditure variables to the model (See equation 13a), the equation obtained is as follows:[23]

$$\Delta N = \$796 \, \Delta E + \$72{,}749{,}542 \, \Delta P'$$ (53)

These coefficients suggest that an increase in employment of one increases nonlabor costs by $796, while an increase in prices of 100 percent raises nonlabor costs by $72,749,542. The substitution of actual changes in these independent variables into the above equation suggests that 50.2 percent of the change in nonlabor expenditures resulted from increases in prices and 49.8 percent from increases in the real quantities purchased.

The elasticity coefficients can now be calculated as before:

$$\eta E = 0.70$$ (54a)

$$\eta Q = 1.00$$ (54b)

$$\eta P = 1.26$$ (54c)

and indicate, for example, that a 1 percent increase in prices yields a 1.26 percent increase in nonlabor costs.

Total Public School Expenditures

Total expenditures in the public schools can be analyzed in the fashion used previously. Since changes in labor costs, retirement costs, and nonlabor costs have been linked to changes in employment, prices, real wages, and pension contribution rate, it is a simple matter to express expenditures for public schools as a whole with these same variables. The resulting equation is as follows:

$$\Delta X = \$9{,}336 \, \Delta E + \$1{,}700 \, \Delta E_R + \$765{,}379{,}945 \, \Delta P + $$
$$\$72{,}749{,}542 \, \Delta P' + 114{,}731 \, \Delta W' + $$
$$12{,}259 \, \Delta W'_R + \$575{,}661{,}658 \, \Delta C$$ (55)

These coefficients indicate that an increase in general employment of one will increase departmental costs by $9,336 and pension costs (if the new employee is a member) by $1,700. The other coefficients can be analyzed analogously.

The substitution of the observed changes in the independent variables into the equation above yields interesting results. Of the increase in public school expenditures over the period, 33.3 percent resulted from increased general employment, 4.1 percent from rising pension membership, 50 percent from increasing consumer prices, 2.9 percent from increasing nonlabor (wholesale) prices, 13.8 percent from rising average real wages of all employees, and 2 percent from rising real wages of pension fund employees; -7 percent was due to the decline in the contribution rate.

When the elasticity coefficients are calculated, it is possible to compare the marginal effects of these variables in percentage terms.

$$\eta_E = 0.84 \tag{56a}$$

$$\eta_{E_R} = 0.14 \tag{56b}$$

$$\eta_P = 1.18 \tag{56c}$$

$$\eta_{P'} = 0.11 \tag{56d}$$

$$\eta_{W'} = 1.51 \tag{56e}$$

$$\eta_{W'_R} = 0.18 \tag{56f}$$

$$\eta_C = 0.18 \tag{56g}$$

Higher Education Expenditures

Direct Labor Costs

Appendix Tables 3.A.10-3.A.12 present a breakdown of direct labor costs for several job categories in higher education. Appendix Table 3.A.10 indicates the dramatic growth in labor costs for higher education—323.8 percent for the department as a whole. In fact, direct labor costs grew by more than 200 percent for all categories. A basic reason for the rapid growth can be attributed to employment, which grew by 161 percent over the period. (See Appendix Table 3.A.11.) The only job category for which employment did not double the period

219

was "laborer," which grew by 91.7 percent. Wage growth, as shown in Appendix Table 3.A.12, was not as dramatic but still averaged 62.4 percent for the department as a whole. Wages in all delivery categories except "professors" grew by more than the departmental average.

By use of the model explained in the section beginning on page 174.

$$\Delta L = \$8,870\Delta E + \$151,854,400\Delta P + 24,191\Delta W' \tag{57}$$

suggesting, for example, that a change in employment of one will increase labor costs by $8,870. Substitution of observed changes in the variables E, P, and W' yields the conclusion that 49.4 percent of the increase in costs was due to changes in employment, 33.2 percent to changes in prices, and 17.4 percent to changes in real wages. The percentage components for each job category are shown in Appendix Tables 3.A.13 and 3.A.14.

In order to compare the marginal effect of changes in each of the independent variables, elasticity coefficients can be used.

$$\eta_E = 1.00 \tag{58a}$$

$$\eta_P = 2.61 \tag{58b}$$

$$\eta_{W'} = 3.69 \tag{58c}$$

These coefficients can be interpreted to indicate that a 1 percent change in employment yields a 1 percent change in direct labor costs; a 1 percent change in prices, a 2.61 percent change in labor costs; and a 1 percent change in real wages, a 3.69 percent change in direct labor costs.

Retirement System Costs

The employees of higher education are members of several retirement systems. The clerical and labor employees can be members of NYCERS; teachers can be members of the Teachers Retirement System. However, the Teachers Insurance and Annuity Association-College Retirement Equities Fund (TIAA-CREF), a privately operated, nonprofit national system for college teachers, is growing in importance as a pension plan. Eligible employees of the city's colleges and universities have been given the option of joining TIAA-CREF instead of joining the Teachers Retirement System. The city contributes 12 percent of that part of a member's salary subject to social security tax and 15 percent on the balance of the salary. City college and university faculty have been eligible for membership in TIAA-CREF only since 1967. Since then, about 75 percent of all new faculty have chosen TIAA-CREF, apparently because its superior vesting provisions are attractive to college teachers.[24] Thus, it is reasonable to expect that city outlays for TIAA-CREF will grow, provided that the number of faculty in city colleges and universities continues to increase at recent rates.

The growth in these three retirement systems is shown in Appendix Table 3.A.7. As indicated there, expenditures on TIAA-CREF have increased fivefold. The figures for TRS include contributions for public school personnel and so cannot be used to infer directly anything about higher education retirement costs. For the purpose of estimating the relative effect of employment, real wage, and price changes on retirement costs, the model is helpful:[25]

$$\Delta R = \$2,350 \, \Delta E + \$11,765,693 \Delta P +$$
$$1,668 \, \Delta W' + \$94,884,622 \, \Delta C \tag{59}$$

This indicates, for example, that an increase in employment of one will increase retirement costs by $2,350. After substituting values for changes in E, P, W', and C, it can be concluded that 87.9 percent of the increased costs resulted from employment increases, 40.2 percent from price changes, and 19.2 percent from real wage changes and that the decrease in contribution rates actually contributed toward a decline in retirement costs equivalent to 47.3 percent of the actual increase in costs.

The elasticity coefficients can be calculated or interpreted in the usual way.

$$\eta_E = 1.00 \tag{60a}$$

$$\eta_P = 1.72 \tag{60b}$$

$$\eta_{W'} = 2.33 \tag{60c}$$

$$\eta_C = 2.55 \tag{60d}$$

Nonlabor Costs

Tables 3.21-3.23 show the trend in the elements of nonlabor expenditure (such as equipment and supplies) for higher education. In Table 3.21, expenditures in each of the categories are shown for 1965 through 1970. Of the $30.4 million of nonlabor expenditure, $18.4 million was for contractual services, while only $300,000 was for materials. Supplies accounted for $5.2 million and equipment,

TABLE 3.21

New York City Higher Education Annual Expenditures, 1965-70
(in thousands of dollars)

Object Class	1965	1966	1967	1968	1969	1970
Total	3,789.3	5,466.4	8,916.0	12,025.6	19,500.5	30,389.4
		(44.3)*	(63.1)	(34.9)	(62.2)	(55.8)
Supplies	1,343.0	1,473.1	1,848.3	2,840.8	4,564.9	5,180.8
		(9.7)	(25.5)	(53.7)	(60.7)	(13.5)
Materials	119.8	127.4	138.5	163.4	276.4	300.4
		(6.3)	(8.8)	(18.0)	(69.1)	(8.7)
Equipment	1,127.5	1,840.7	3,143.3	4,281.4	5,490.6	6,489.6
		(63.3)	(70.3)	(36.6)	(28.2)	(8.2)
Contractual services	1,199.0	2,025.3	3,794.9	4,739.9	9,168.6	18,418.6
		(68.9)	(87.4)	(24.9)	(93.4)	(100.9)

Note: Years used are fiscal years.

*Figures in parentheses are annual percentage changes.

Source: Compiled from Comptroller of the City of New York, Annual Report, (New York: Office of the Comptroller, 1965-70), Part 2A, Statement 8.

TABLE 3.22

Laspeyres Price Index for New York City Higher Education Nonlabor Goods and Services, 1965-70

Object Class	1965a	1966	1967	1968	1969	1970	1971
Total	100.0	102.7	106.1	109.1	112.8	117.4	121.7
		(2.7)b	(3.3)	(2.8)	(3.5)	(4.0)	(3.7)
Supplies	100.0	101.5	105.4	107.9	109.4	112.0	111.5
		(1.5)	(3.9)	(2.3)	(1.4)	(2.4)	(-0.5)
Materials	100.0	101.1	104.0	105.4	111.1	117.1	118.6
		(1.1)	(2.8)	(1.4)	(5.4)	(5.3)	(1.3)
Equipment	100.0	105.4	108.5	110.8	115.4	119.2	123.4
		(5.4)	(3.0)	(2.1)	(4.1)	(3.3)	(3.5)
Contractual services	100.0	102.9	105.8	109.9	115.5	122.4	132.5
		(2.9)	(2.8)	(3.8)	(5.1)	(5.9)	(8.3)

Note: Years used are fiscal years.

aBase year: 1965 = 100.

bFigures in parentheses are annual percentage changes.

Source: Compiled by the author.

TABLE 3.23

Laspeyres Deflated Real Expenditures for New York City Higher Education
Nonlabor Goods and Services, 1965-70
(in thousands of dollars)

Object Class	1965[a]	1966	1967	1968	1969	1970
Total	3,789.3	5,321.3	8,404.6	11,027.4	17,283.0	25,893.8
		(40.4)[b]	(57.9)	(31.2)	(56.7)	(49.8)
Supplies	1,343.0	1,451.3	1,753.1	2,633.8	4,172.3	4,624.1
		(8.1)	(20.8)	(50.2)	(58.4)	(10.8)
Materials	119.8	125.9	133.2	155.0	248.7	256.7
		(5.1)	(5.8)	(16.3)	(60.5)	(3.2)
Equipment	1,127.5	1,747.0	2,888.9	3,864.9	4,759.8	5,444.6
		(54.9)	(65.4)	(33.8)	(23.2)	(14.4)
Contractual services	1,199.0	1,967.4	3,585.7	4,313.9	7,936.2	15,053.0
		(64.1)	(82.3)	(20.3)	(84.0)	(89.7)

Note: Years used are fiscal years.
[a]Base year: 1965 = 100.
[b]Figures in parentheses are annual percentage changes.

Source: Compiled by the author.

TABLE 3.24

Laspeyres Price Index for New York City Health Services
Administration Nonlabor Goods and Services, 1965-70

Object Class	1965[a]	1966	1967	1968	1969	1970	1971
Total	100.0	103.0	105.4	108.3	113.0	117.5	123.4
		(3.0)[b]	(2.4)	(2.7)	(4.3)	(4.0)	(5.1)
Supplies	100.0	100.8	103.1	104.0	105.8	107.0	109.7
		(0.8)	(2.2)	(0.8)	(1.8)	(1.1)	(2.5)
Materials	100.0	101.3	103.7	104.2	109.3	114.0	116.9
		(1.3)	(2.3)	(0.5)	(4.9)	(4.3)	(2.6)
Equipment	100.0	101.1	102.9	105.6	108.6	111.2	115.0
		(1.1)	(1.8)	(2.6)	(2.8)	(2.4)	(3.4)
Contractual services	100.0	104.1	106.7	110.6	116.7	122.9	130.5
		(4.1)	(2.5)	(3.6)	(5.5)	(5.3)	(6.2)

Note: Years used are fiscal years.
[a]Base year: 1965 = 100.
[b]Figures in parentheses are annual percentage changes.

Source: Compiled by the author.

$6.5 million. Table 3.22 and 3.23 show the effects of changes in prices and quantities on each of the categories. In Table 3.22, price indexes for each category are shown. Prices rose by 21.7 percent between 1965 and 1971 for nonlabor expenditures as a whole. The greatest rise was in contractual services (32.5 percent), while the least was in supplies (11.5 percent). In Table 3.23, deflated real expenditures are presented. In comparing these amounts with those of Table 3.21, it is possible to conclude that, of the $30.4 million in expenditure in current prices, $4.5 million was the result of increased prices, leaving a real expenditure in 1970 of $25.9 million.

When the model embodied in equation (13a)[26] is applied to non-labor costs and the coefficients are estimated,

$$\Delta N = \$3074 \, \Delta E + \$36,248,835 \, \Delta P' \tag{61}$$

When observed changes in the independent variables are substituted, it can be concluded that 79.7 percent of the increased nonlabor costs was due to change in the quantities purchased (employment) and 20.3 percent to changes in the prices of the products.

The elasticity coefficients calculated as previously are

$$\eta_Q = 1.00 \tag{62a}$$

$$\eta_{P'} = 6.71 \tag{62b}$$

$$\eta_E = 3.71 \tag{62c}$$

Total Higher Education Expenditures

Summarizing the above analysis, it is possible to analyze departmental expenditure changes according to the procedure outlined above; therefore,

$$\begin{aligned}
\Delta X = \ &\$11,944 \Delta E + \$2,350 \Delta E_R + \\
&\$163,620,093 \, \Delta P \quad \$36,248,835 \Delta P' \\
&+ 24,191 \Delta W' + 1668 \Delta W_R' + \\
&\$94,884,622 \, \Delta C
\end{aligned} \tag{63}$$

Substituting observed values for each of the independent variables, it can be concluded that 51.8 percent of the increase in costs was due to rising general employment, 5.6 percent to increased retirement system membership, 27.8 percent to rising consumer prices, 3.8 percent to increased nonlabor prices, 13.2 percent to rising general real wages, 1.1 percent to increased real wages of pension members, and -3.4 percent to the decline in the pension contribution rate.

The elasticity coefficients follow:

$$\eta_E = 1.11 \tag{64a}$$

$$\eta_{E_R} = 0.12 \tag{64b}$$

$$\eta_P = 2.31 \tag{64c}$$

$$\eta_{P'} = 0.51 \tag{64d}$$

$$\eta_{W'} = 3.03 \tag{64e}$$

$$\eta_{W'_R} = 0.26 \tag{64f}$$

$$\eta_E = 0.28 \tag{64g}$$

Health Services Administration Expenditures

Direct Labor Costs

Appendix Tables 3.A.15-3.A.17 report the structure and composition of direct labor costs for the Health Services Administration (HSA).* As indicated in Appendix Tables 3.A.15 and 3.A.16, labor costs and employment for delivery personnel represented about 30 percent of direct labor costs. Appendix Table 3.A.15 indicates that the wages of delivery personnel declined relative to other job categories, even though, in absolute terms, they increased between 1965 and 1972.

Returning to the model,

$$\Delta L = \$6065\,\Delta E + \$33,284,720\,\Delta P + 7755\,\Delta W' \tag{65}$$

which indicates that an increase on one employee increases labor costs by \$6,065, and so on. In percentage terms, the equation indicates that 21.5 percent of the increase in costs was due to employment increases, 56.3 percent to price increases, and 22.2 percent to real wage increases. The components for other job categories are shown in Appendix Tables 3.A.18 and 3.A.19.

The elasticity coefficients η_E, η_P, and $\eta_{W'}$, calculated in the usual fashion, can be shown as follows:

---

*The direct labor cost figures for HSA employees include only figures for those directly employed by the agency. Hospital workers were not included because of the unavailability of the necessary data.

$$\eta_E = 1.00 \qquad\qquad\qquad\qquad (66a)$$

$$\eta_P = 1.18 \qquad\qquad\qquad\qquad (66b)$$

$$\eta_{W'} = 1.66 \qquad\qquad\qquad\qquad (66c)$$

They indicate that an increase in employment of 1 percent increases costs by 1 percent; an increase in prices of 1 percent yields a 1.18 percent increase in costs; and a 1 percent increase in real wages produces a 1.66 percent increase in direct labor costs.

Retirement Costs

Because of the lack of specific data on the membership of HSA employees in NYCERS, estimates in this section are based on wage and employment data for the entire department as well as on the NYCERS aggregate contribution rate. Employing the model to evaluate estimated HSA retirement costs yields:

$$\Delta R = \$455\Delta E + \$4,393,583\Delta P + \\ 1,024\,\Delta W + \$33,384,720\,\Delta C \qquad\qquad (67)$$

indicating, for example, that the increase in employment of one increases retirement costs by \$455. Substitution of the actual changes in E, P, W', and C suggests that, since 1965, 7.9 percent of the increase in retirement costs has been due to increased employment, 37.6 percent to increased prices, 16.4 percent to rising real wages, and 38.1 percent to increased contribution rates.

The elasticity coefficients presented below can be interpreted in the usual fashion.

$$\eta_E = 1.00 \qquad\qquad\qquad\qquad (68a)$$

$$\eta_P = 2.02 \qquad\qquad\qquad\qquad (68b)$$

$$\eta_{W'} = 2.74 \qquad\qquad\qquad\qquad (68c)$$

$$\eta_C = 1.18 \qquad\qquad\qquad\qquad (68d)$$

Nonlabor Costs

Table 3.24 shows the price changes that occurred for the purchases of HSA nonlabor goods (such as supplies, materials). For total, nonlabor expenditures in all categories, prices rose by 23.4 percent. The prices of supplies increased less than any other category—9.7 percent—while those of contractual services increased the fastest—30.5 percent.

Making use of the model,[27]

$$\Delta N = \$32,198\,\Delta E + \$30,313,441\,\Delta P'$$ (69)

Substituting values for ΔN, ΔE, and $\Delta P'$ into this equation allows the determination of the relative percentage contribution of each of the total change in nonlabor costs. Specifically, 78.5 percent of the increase in nonlabor costs can be attributed to changes in employment (real quantities) and 21.5 percent to changes in prices.

The elasticity coefficients, calculated as before, are

$$\eta_Q = 1.00$$ (70a)

$$\eta_{P'} = 6.76$$ (70b)

$$\eta_E = 32.90$$ (70c)

and indicate that a 1 percent change in the price level yields a 6.76 percent change in nonlabor costs.

Total Health Services Administration Expenditures

To analyze total health service expenditures, the procedure follows exactly from that used above. Thus, after calculation of the coefficients, the equation obtained is as follows:

$$\Delta X = \$38,263\,\Delta E + \$455\,\Delta E_R + \$37,678,303\,\Delta P +$$
$$\$30,313,441\,\Delta P \quad 7,755\,\Delta W' + 1,024\,\Delta W'_R +$$
$$\$33,284,720\,\Delta C$$ (71)

The percentage components, obtained after substitution of observed changes into the above equation, suggest that 48.2 percent of the increase in health service expenditures was due to increased employment, 0.5 percent to added retirement system membership, 24.2 percent to increased consumer prices, 13.1 percent to added nonlabor (wholesale) prices, 9.3 percent to increased real wages, 1.2 percent to added real wages of retirement system members, and 3 percent to the increase in pension contribution rate.

The elasticity coefficients follow:

227

$$\eta_E \quad = \quad 5.19 \tag{72a}$$

$$\eta_{E_R} \quad = \quad 0.06 \tag{72b}$$

$$\eta_P \quad = \quad 1.09 \tag{72c}$$

$$\eta_{P'} \quad = \quad 0.88 \tag{72d}$$

$$\eta_{W'} \quad = \quad 1.37 \tag{72e}$$

$$\eta_{W'_R} \quad = \quad 0.18 \tag{27f}$$

$$\eta_C \quad = \quad 0.07 \tag{72g}$$

Social Services Department Expenditures

Direct Labor Costs

Appendix Tables 3.A.15-3.A.17 show the composition of labor costs in 1965 and 1972 for a group of job categories for social services. Growth in social services labor costs has been dramatic— 243.4 percent for the department as a whole. The smallest percentage increase was registered by delivery-investigation personnel (147.6 percent), while the largest absolute (dollar) increase was registered by clerical personnel ($71 million). Employment (See Appendix Table 3.A.16) has grown most in percentage terms for laborers (182.6 percent), but most in absolute terms for clerical personnel (8,500 employees). Average wages grew most for delivery-supervisor personnel—85.9 percent—and least for laborers—47.8 percent. (See Appendix Table 3.A.17.)

In order to determine the relative effect of changes in employment, real wages, and prices on labor costs, the model employed is as follows:

$$\Delta L \;=\; \$5,796\,\Delta E \;+\; \$180,692,912\,\Delta P \;+\; 44,046\,\Delta W' \tag{73}$$

After substituting observed values of ΔE, ΔP, and $\Delta W'$ into the above equation, it can be concluded that 43.6 percent of the rise in labor costs was due to employment change, 34.9 percent to price change, and 21.5 percent to real wage change. Appendix Tables 3.A.18 and 3.A.19 show these employment, real wage, and price components for each job category in the department.

The elasticity coefficients can be calculated as indicated previously

$$\eta_E = 1.00 \tag{74a}$$

$$\eta_P = 2.15 \tag{74b}$$

$$\eta_{W'} = 3.03 \tag{74c}$$

and can be interpreted in the usual fashion.

Retirement Costs

Because no specific figures were available for retirement system memberships for the Social Services Department, it was necessary to estimate the components of retirement system cost changes. Since most retirement system members belong to NYCERS, the contribution rate for this system, together with budgeted wage and employment figures for the whole Department were used for this estimation. As above, estimation of the coefficients of the model yields the following:

$$\Delta R = \$435\,\Delta E + \$23,848,824\,\Delta P + \$5,814\,\Delta W + \$180,672,912\,\Delta C \tag{75}$$

Substituting the observed changes in the independent variables into the above equation yields the conclusion that 23.4 percent of the increase was due to increased employment, 31.1 percent to increased prices, 14.1 percent to increased real wages, and 31.5 percent to the increased contribution rate.

The elasticity coefficients can be calculated and interpreted in the usual fashion:

$$\eta_E = 1.00 \tag{76a}$$

$$\eta_P = 3.69 \tag{76b}$$

$$\eta_{W'} = 5.01 \tag{76c}$$

$$\eta_C = 3.69 \tag{76d}$$

Nonlabor Costs

Although a specific price index for social service nonlabor expenditures was not calculated, it is possible to estimate the effect

229

of inflation on these expenditures by use of the price index for all New York City nonlabor expenditures. Such an index is shown in Appendix Table 3.A.20. For city government, nonlabor expenditures as a whole, between 1965 and 1971, prices rose by 21.5 percent—8.5 percent for supplies, 16.7 percent for materials, 21 percent for equipment, and 29.8 percent for contractual services.

When we employ the model described previously,[*]

$$\Delta N = \$950 \Delta E + \$23,376,444 \Delta P' \tag{77}$$

After substitution of the values of ΔE and ΔP observed over the period, it can be concluded that 73.7 percent of the increased cost was due to employment changes and 26.3 percent to price changes.

The elasticity coefficients can also be calculated:

$$\eta_Q = 1.00 \tag{78a}$$

$$\eta_{P'} = 2.51 \tag{78b}$$

$$\eta_E = 1.32 \tag{78c}$$

Total Social Services Department Expenditures[†]

When the general model is applied to social service expenditures, it is possible to determine the relative effects of change in the independent variables (E, P, W', and C) on departmental costs. As before,

$$\begin{aligned}
\Delta X = \ &\$6746 \Delta E + \$435 \Delta ER + \\
&\$204,521,736 \Delta P + \$23,376,444 \Delta P' + \\
&44,046 \Delta W' + 5,814 \Delta W'_R + \\
&\$180,672,912 \Delta C \tag{79}
\end{aligned}$$

Substituting observed values for changes in each of the parameters, (ΔER, ΔP, and so on), we can conclude that 43.4 percent of the increased cost was due to increased employment, 2.8 percent to increased pension membership, 32.2 percent to increased consumer prices, 2.3 percent to rising nonlabor (wholesale) prices, 13.3 percent to increased real wages, 1.7 percent to rising real wages of pension members, and 3.6 percent to the increase in the pension contribution rate.

---

[*]As indicated above, estimation of this model requires an estimate of g_1, which in this case is $950.

[†]This does not include transfer payments.

To compare the marginal effects of the independent variables, it is necessary to calculate elasticity coefficients. The calculation follows according to the procedure outlined above.

$$\eta_E = 1.00 \tag{80a}$$

$$\eta_{E_R} = 0.06 \tag{80b}$$

$$\eta_P = 2.08 \tag{80c}$$

$$\eta_{P'} = 0.24 \tag{80d}$$

$$\eta_{W'} = 2.60 \tag{80e}$$

$$\eta_{W'_R} = 0.34 \tag{80f}$$

$$\eta_C = 0.14 \tag{80g}$$

Transfer Payments

Table 3.25 shows the composition of transfer expenditures from the Social Services Department. Between 1965 and 1972, total transfers increased almost fivefold. The two largest areas of transfer—Aid to Families with Dependent Children (ADC) and Medical Assistance—also account for more than $1 billion of the almost $1.4 billion increase in expenditures over the period. Other large gains in absolute terms were registered in the areas of aid to the disabled ($45 million), old age assistance ($96.5 million), and home relief ($76,6 million).

When incorporating transfer expenditures into the model, a difficulty arises. Because of the dissimilarity between transfer expenditures and labor, nonlabor, and retirement expenditures, it is easier to incorporate transfers into the general model as if they represented a separate department. Further, it is difficult to decompose total transfer payments into components. Although it may at first seem logical to separate growth in transfer expenditures into that due to increases in the number of recipients and that resulting from increased average payment, the unavailability of adequate data precludes that possibility. Therefore, in the general model, only aggregate transfers will be included:

$$\Delta T = \$1,396,199,156 \tag{81}$$

TABLE 3.25

New York City Social Services Department Transfer Expenditures, 1965 and 1972
(dollars)

Category of Expenditure	1965	1972	Dollar Increase
Charitable institutions (not hospitals)	2,310,024	2,800,000	489,976
Foster home care	2,538,500	9,050,000	6,511,500
Old age assistance	3,421,000	99,938,500	96,517,500
Assistance to blind	2,509,000	4,802,700	2,293,700
ADC	188,146,000	799,094,000	610,948,000
Aid to disabled	25,243,000	170,479,000	145,236,000
Home relief	28,297,000	104,887,300	76,590,300
Medical assistance	34,529,000	467,645,900	433,116,900
Day care	6,900,000	61,450,000	54,550,000
Other	47,445,270	17,390,550	-30,054,720
Total	341,338,794	1,737,537,950	1,396,199,156

Source: Comptroller of the City of New York, Annual Report (New York: Office of the Comptroller, 1965 and 1972).

All Departments Combined

Method

The aggregation of departmental equations can be accomplished on two levels—by object and by function. By object, the aggregation of the appropriate equations for each department yields:[28]

$$\sum_i \Delta L^i = (\sum_i Z_1^i) \Delta E + (\sum_i Z_2^i) \Delta P + (\sum_i Z_3^i) \Delta W \tag{82}$$

$$\sum_i \Delta R^i = (\sum_i r_1^i) \Delta E_R + (\sum_i r_2^i) \Delta P +$$

$$(\sum_i r_3^i) \Delta W_R + (\sum_i r_4^i) \Delta C \tag{83}$$

$$\sum_i \Delta N^i = (\sum_i n_1^i g_1^i) \Delta E + (\sum_i n_2^i) \Delta P_C \tag{84}$$

$$\sum_i \Delta T^i = \sum_i \Delta T^i \tag{85}$$

where: i = each of the various departments studied.

The interpretation of the new coefficients for the variables E, P, W⁻, and C follows quite simply. In equation (81), $(\sum_i Z_1^i)$ shows the effect on total expenditures of increasing employment by one in each department. Each coefficient may be interpreted analogously, indicating the effect on the group of departments of equal changes in the given independent variable in each.

When aggregating by function, departmental expenditures have been divided in the following manner:

$$\Delta X = x_1' \Delta E + x_2' \Delta E_R + x_3' \Delta P' + x_4' \Delta P' + \\ x_5' \Delta W' + x_6' \Delta W_R + x_7' \Delta C \tag{86}$$

Aggregation by function can be accomplished by adding like coefficients from the model, equation (85), estimated for each department:

$$\sum_i \Delta X^i = (\sum_i x_1^i) \Delta E + (\sum_i x_2^i) \Delta E_R + (\sum_i x_3^i) \Delta P +$$

$$(\sum_i x_4^i) \Delta P' + (\sum_i x_5^i) \Delta W' + (\sum_i x_6^i) \Delta W_R' +$$

$$(\sum_i x_7^i) \Delta C + \sum_i \Delta T^i \tag{87}$$

This result can be seen to identical to that which is arrived at when the equations representing functions are combined. Again, the interpretation of the coefficient suggests that a unit increase in employment in each department will produce this effect on total expenditures.

Results

The results of this procedure in terms of objects of expenditure, as well as by function, are shown in Tables 3.26-3.28. For labor costs, 30.5 percent of the increase in labor costs was due to increased employment, 46.1 percent to increased prices, and 23.4 percent to increased real wages. (See Table 3.26.) For retirement costs, 34 percent was the result of membership increase, 50 percent, price increase, 12.2 percent, real wage increase, and 3.7 percent, increases in contribution rates. For nonlabor costs, 71.4 percent was the result of employment increase and 28.6 percent, the result of price increase. For all objects combined, 31.2 percent was the result of employment increase, 3.4 percent, retirement system membership increases,

233

TABLE 3.26

Explanation of Changes in Expenditures by Object for Seven New York City Departments

$$\Delta L = \$\; \underset{(30.5)^*}{53{,}662\,\Delta E} \;+\; \underset{(46.1)}{\$1{,}631{,}922{,}020\,\Delta P} \;+\; \$\; \underset{(23.4)}{289{,}601\,\Delta W'}$$

$$\Delta R = \$\; \underset{(34.0)}{89{,}330\,\Delta E_R} \;+\; \$\; \underset{(50.0)}{222{,}649{,}124\,\Delta P} \;+\; \$\; \underset{(12.2)}{38{,}821\,\Delta W'_R} \;+\; \$\; \underset{(3.7)}{1{,}457{,}969{,}045\,\Delta C}$$

$$\Delta N = \$\; \underset{(71.4)}{47{,}373\,\Delta E} \;+\; \$\; \underset{(28.6)}{196{,}528{,}186\,\Delta P}$$

$$\Delta T = \$1{,}396{,}199{,}156$$

$$\Delta X = \$\; \underset{(17.1)}{101{,}035\,\Delta E} \;+\; \$\; \underset{(2.0)}{8{,}933\,\Delta E_R} \;+\; \underset{(24.0)}{\$1{,}854{,}571{,}144\,\Delta P} \;+\; \underset{(1.1)}{\$196{,}528{,}186\,\Delta P'} \;+$$

$$ \$\; \underset{(10.2)}{289{,}601\,\Delta W'} \;+\; \$\; \underset{(0.5)}{38{,}821\,\Delta W'_R} \;+\; \$\; \underset{(0.5)}{1{,}457{,}969{,}045\,\Delta C} \;+\; \underset{(44.5)}{\Delta T}$$

*Figures in parentheses are percentage changes in object expenditures due to changes in the level of the independent variable (that is, employment, prices, real wages, and pension contribution rate).

Source: Compiled by the author.

44 percent, rising consumer prices, and 18.2 percent, increasing real wages. When transfers are included, the importance of each if the factors decreases proportionately, while the fraction of increased expenditure resulting from rising transfers is the most important—44.5 percent of the increased cost.

Table 3.27 shows the results discussed above for each function as well as an aggregate figure. As indicated elsewhere the effects of employment were smaller and of real wages, larger, for police, fire, and environmental protection than was the case for public schools, higher education, and social services. Also noteworthy are the negative contribution rate components for public schools and higher education, as well as the negative real wage components (for pensions) in both police and fire.

Table 3.28 shows the elasticity coefficients for each of the departments as well as for all departments combined. For all departments, the marginal effect of a 1 percent change in real wages is the largest, followed by general employment and consumer prices.

Table 3.29 shows these same elasticities for expenditures by object of expenditure. The elasticity of employment for nonlabor costs was greatest—10.7—and that for retirement system membership, the least—0.91.

FORECASTS OF NEW YORK CITY EXPENDITURES FOR 1979

The earlier sections of this chapter have placed almost complete emphasis on an explanation of the historical trend in New York City government expenditures between 1965 and 1972. The purpose of the present section is to forecast the future level of these expenditures, based on the model developed above, and to compare the results with the 1965-72 experience. Specifically, the subsection below presents forecasts of expenditures in 1979 for each of the seven departments studied, under alternative sets of assumptions, and the subsection after that shows an aggregation of these components to obtain a forecast of the size of the total expense budget, by objects of expenditure, in 1979. It should be noted that these forecasts, which are based on past expenditure growth, merely suggest the magnitude of 1979 expenditures, assuming no major governmental reorganization. The efffect of such a reorganization will be considered in a later chapter.

The forecasting model used here is a relatively simple identity, as presented in general form in equation (16) above. The forecast from this identity requires data on current employment, wage rates, pension contribution rates, and price levels and requires estimates of change over the forecast period in each of these variables. The

TABLE 3.27

Explanation of Changes in Total Expenditures for Each of Seven New York City Departments

Police	ΔX = $9,270ΔE+ (21.4)*	$1,809ΔE_R+ (3.7)	$361,480,974ΔP+ (51.0)	$10,138,384ΔP'+ (0.6)	$49,010ΔW'+ (22.8)	$10,172ΔW'_R+ (-1.4)	$295,824,127ΔC (1.8)
Fire	ΔX = 9,792ΔE+ (5.5)	1,634 E_R· (2.5)	151,026,737ΔP+ (49.6)	2,393,010ΔP'+ (0.4)	20,771ΔW'+ (40.9)	4,043ΔW'_R+ (-1.5)	126,701,646ΔC (2.5)
EPA	ΔX = 15,684ΔE+ (17.4)	5,500ΔE_R+ (0.6)	170,863,356ΔP+ (44.5)	21,308,530ΔP'+ (2.7)	29,097ΔW'+ (25.8)	3,841ΔW'_R+ (3.5)	150,939,360ΔC (5.4)
Public schools	ΔX = 9,336ΔE+ (33.3)	1,700ΔE_R+ (4.1)	765,379,945ΔP+ (50.9)	72,749,542ΔP'+ (2.9)	114,731ΔW'+ (13.8)	12,259ΔW'_R+ (2.0)	575,661,658ΔC (-7.0)
Higher education	ΔX = 11,944ΔE+ (51.8)	2,350ΔE_R+ (5.6)	163,620,093ΔP+ (27.8)	36,248,835ΔP'+ (3.8)	24,191ΔW'+ (13.2)	1,668ΔW'_R+ (1.1)	94,884,622ΔC (-3.4)
Social services	ΔX = 6,746ΔE+ (43.4)	4,350ΔE_R+ (2.0)	204,521,736ΔP+ (32.7)	23,376,444ΔP'+ (2.3)	44,046ΔW'+ (13.3)	5,814ΔW'_R+ (1.7)	180,672,912ΔC + ΔT (3.8)
Health services	ΔX = 38,263ΔE+ (48.7)	4,550ΔE_R+ (0.5)	37,678,303ΔP+ (24.2)	30,313,441ΔP'+ (13.1)	7,755ΔW'+ (9.3)	1,024ΔW'_R+ (1.2)	33,284,720ΔC (3.0)
Transfers	ΔT = $1,396,199,156						
Total	ΔX = $101,035ΔE+ (17.1)	$8,933ΔE_R+ (2.0)	$1,854,571,144ΔP+ (24.0)	$196,528,186ΔP'+ (1.1)	289,601ΔW'+ (10.2)	38,821ΔW'_R+ (0.5)	$1,457,969,045ΔC+ ΔT (44.5)

*Figures in parentheses are percentage changes in object expenditures due to changes in the level of the independent variable (that is, employment, prices, real wages, and pension contribution rate).

Source: Compiled by the author.

TABLE 3.28

Elasticity Coefficients by Department

Department	η_R	η_{E_R}	η_P	$\eta_{P'}$	$\eta_{W'}$	η_{W_R}	η_C	η_T
Police	0.88	0.16	1.22	0.03	1.43	0.29	0.20	—
Fire	0.99	0.14	1.07	0.02	1.27	0.24	0.16	—
EPA	2.10	0.07	1.10	0.13	1.35	0.17	0.07	—
Public schools	0.84	0.14	1.20	0.11	1.51	0.18	0.18	—
Higher education	1.01	0.12	2.36	0.36	3.03	0.30	0.32	—
Social services	0.96	0.06	2.08	0.19	2.60	0.34	0.14	—
Health services	4.62	0.06	1.09	0.78	1.37	0.18	0.07	—
Transfers	1.46	0.12	1.35	0.13	1.60	0.23	0.15	—
Average for all seven departments	1.17	0.10	1.08	0.10	1.27	0.10	0.12	0.20

Source: Compiled by the author.

TABLE 3.29

Elasticity Coefficients by Object

Object	η_E	η_{E_R}	η_P	$\eta_{P'}$	$\eta_{W'}$	η_{W_R}	η_C	η_T
Labor	0.96	—	1.40	—	1.90	—	—	—
Retirement	—	0.91	1.24	—	—	1.71	1.14	—
Nonlabor	10.70	—	—	2.06	—	—	—	—
Transfers	—	—	—	—	—	—	—	1.00
Average for all objects	1.17	0.10	1.08	0.10	1.27	0.19	0.12	0.20

Source: Compiled by the author.

237

assumed changes in the variables were based on the actual trends over the 1965-72 period. The relationship between explained and total current expenditure for 1972 was then used to determine total current expenditure in 1979. Since the forecasts were derived using a number of alternative sets of assumptions, a range of projections was derived. The most liberal of these is based upon the assumption that each of the variables (E, E_R, P, W', W_R, C, and Q) grew at the same rate between 1972 and 1979 that was observed between 1965 and 1972, while transfers grew at one-half the observed rate. The most conservative forecast assumes all variables to grow at 50 percent of the 1965-72 rate, with (welfare) transfers growing at one-quarter the observed rate. Other projections were made where single variables were assumed to grow at the slower rate, so as to show the marginal effect of such a slower growth on the level of 1979 expenditures.

It is important here to draw a distinction between variables that may be influenced by the city government and those that may not. It is assumed, therefore, that increases in employment, and the pension contribution rate are variables upon which city government can exert some influence and special attention is paid to the results of altering their growth rates.

Expenditure Forecasts by Function

Tables 3.30-3.36 present the forecasts of current expenditures (excluding debt service) for each of the departments analyzed in detail above. Table 3.37 shows the forecast for these seven departments combined.

Based on the 1965-72 trend,* New York City police expenditures will double between 1972 and 1979—from about $600 million to more than $1.2 billion. The single variable that has the greatest effect on increasing expenditures is prices—slow† growth in consumer prices will mean that expenditures by 1979 will only reach $1.05 billion. It should be noted that inflation has an important effect not only on the cost of materials purchased but also on cost-of-living wage increases that are assumed for all employees. On the other hand, if the growth in the major discretionary variables (E, C, and W') were slowed, expenditures would still climb to about $1.03 billion by 1979. Finally, if the present growth in all the independent variables were

---

*Between 1965 and 1972, prices grew at an annual rate of 5 percent.

†Throughout this analysis, "slow" will be taken to mean half of the 1965-72 rate of increase.

TABLE 3.30

New York City Expenditure Forecast for 1979: Police Department
(in millions of dollars)

Conditions	Type of Expenditure			Expenditures Accounted for	Total Expenditures
	Labor	Nonlabor	Retirement		
Present trend	979.5	26.8	234.1	1,240.4	1,232.4
Slow employment growth	886.0	20.5	211.8	1,118.3	1,111.6
Slow real wage growth	913.2	26.8	218.3	1,158.3	1,151.4
Slow price growth	836.3	24.7	199.9	1,060.9	1,054.5
Slow contribution rate growth	979.5	26.8	224.3	1,230.6	1,223.2
Slow real wage, employment, and contribution rate growth	826.0	20.5	189.2	1,035.7	1,029.5
Slow growth for all	705.3	18.9	161.5	885.7	880.4
1972 expenditure	484.9	12.0	106.2	603.1	599.1*

*Includes debt service and unallocated appropriations.

Sources: 1972 labor and total expenditure figures taken from New York City Executive Budget and Supporting Schedules (New York: Office of the City of New York, Annual Report (New York: Office of the Comptroller, 1972). 1972 nonlabor expenditure figure taken from Comptroller of the City of New York, Annual Report (New York: Office of the Comptroller, 1972). 1972 retirement expenditure figure derived from Bernard Jump, "The Cost of Providing Retirement and Social Security Benefits to New York City Employees: Trends, Causes, and Prospects, 1961-1972" (Internal Working Paper No. 9, Maxwell Research Project on the Public Finances of New York City, Syracuse University, Syracuse, N.Y., October 1972). (The derivation of all other figures, based on 1972 expenditures, is described in the accompanying text.)

cut in half, police expenditures would still rise to $880 million (an increase of 46 percent).

Table 3.31 presents similar forecasts for the Fire Department. Present growth in fire expenditures would result in almost a doubling of fire expenditures by 1979—to a level of $529 million. If price increases were held to one-half their current rate, expenditures in 1979 on fire protection would be $448 million, indicating again that price changes (excluding cost-of-living increases) have more effect on expenditures than any of the other variables. If all the variables (E, C, and W′) grew more slowly, expenditures in 1979 would still be $450 million. Finally, even if all the slower growth rates prevailed, fire expenditures in 1979 would exceed $384 million (an increase of 43 percent).

Forecasted expenditures for the Environmental Protection Administration appear in Table 3.32. If 1965-72 expenditure growth rates prevail between 1972 and 1979, EPA expenditures will increase to $606.2 million (an increase of 115.3 percent). Further, the effect of price changes appears to be larger than that of any other variable— a slower increase in prices results in expenditures for 1979 of $524.6 million. Control of the variables (W′, C, and E) appears to have some effect on expenditures, with a resultant rise to $495.7 million by 1979. Finally, control in growth of each of the variables involved in the model still yields a 1979 expenditure level of $427.8 million—an increase over 1972 of 51.9 percent.

Forecasts of expenditures for public schools are presented in Table 3.33. At the present rate of growth, public school expenditures will reach $3.81 billion in 1979—an increase of 99.5 percent. If the growth in prices were cut in half, expenditures would rise to $3.3 billion in 1979. Further, if it were possible to cut growth in each of the discretionary variables by half, expenditures would still rise to $3.21 billion in 1979. Finally, the achievement of slower growth rates in each of the variables would still produce public school expenditures in the neighborhood of $2.75 billion—an increase of 44 percent.

In contrast to public schools, forecasts of growth in higher education expenditures, as shown in Table 3.34, appear much larger. At present rates of increase, higher education expenditures will reach $2.2 billion by 1979 (increasing by more than 400 percent). If growth in employment were slowed on the other hand, expenditures in 1979 would only reach $1.23 billion (slightly more than 200 percent above 1972). Further, control of the variables (W′, E, and C) would produce expenditures of $1.18 billion in 1979, while a slowdown in all the variables would produce expenditures of $1.02 billion—still a 155 percent increase over 1972.

Forecasts of social service expenditures for 1979 are presented in Table 3.35. It should be emphasized here that this analysis is not

New York City Expenditure Forecast for 1979: Fire Department
(in millions of dollars)

Conditions	Type of Expenditure			Expenditures Accounted for	Total Expenditures
	Labor	Nonlabor	Retirement		
Present trend	437.4	5.7	98.4	541.5	527.0
Slow employment growth	426.9	4.6	96.1	527.6	511.8
Slow real wage growth	388.1	5.7	87.3	481.1	466.6
Slow price growth	373.4	5.2	84.0	462.7	448.8
Slow contribution rate growth	437.4	5.7	93.2	536.3	520.2
Slow real wage, employment, and contribution rate growth	378.8	4.6	80.7	464.1	450.2
Slow growth for all variables	323.4	4.2	68.9	396.5	384.6
1972 expenditure	228.2	2.9	45.9	277.0	269.5*

*Includes debt service and unallocated appropriations.

Sources: 1972 labor and total expenditure figures taken from New York City Executive Budget and Supporting Schedules (New York: Office of the Mayor, 1972). 1972 nonlabor expenditure figure taken from Comptroller of the City of New York, Annual Report (New York: Office of the Comptroller, 1972). 1972 retirement expenditure figure derived from Bernard Jump, "The Cost of Providing Retirement and Social Security Benefits to New York City Employees: Trends, Causes, and Prospects, 1961-1972" (Internal Working Paper No. 9 Maxwell Research Project on the Public Finances of New York City, Syracuse University, Syracuse, N.Y., October 1972). (The derivation of all other figures, based on 1972 expenditures, is described in the accompanying text.)

TABLE 3.32

New York City Expenditure Forecast for 1979: Environmental Protection Administration
(in millions of dollars)

Conditions	Type of Expenditure			Expenditures Accounted for	Total Expenditures
	Labor	Nonlabor	Retirement		
Present trend	472.3	91.8	109.6	673.6	606.2
Slow employment growth	451.9	60.5	104.8	617.2	555.5
Slow real wage growth	433.5	91.8	100.6	625.8	563.2
Slow price growth	403.2	86.1	93.5	582.9	524.6
Slow contribution rate growth	472.3	91.8	85.9	650.0	585.0
Slow real wage, employment and contribution rate growth	414.8	60.5	75.5	550.8	495.7
Slow growth for all	354.2	56.8	64.5	475.4	427.8
1972 expenditure	255.2	25.6	33.7	314.5	281.6*

*Includes debt service and unallocated appropriations.

Sources: 1972 labor and total expenditure figures taken from New York City Executive Budget and Supporting Schedules (New York: Office of the Mayor, 1972). 1972 nonlabor expenditure figure taken from Comptroller of the City of New York, Annual Report (New York: Office of the Comptroller, 1972). 1972 retirement expenditure figure derived from Bernard Jump, "The Cost of Providing Retirement and Social Security Benefits to New York City Employees: Trends, Causes, and Prospects, 1961-1972" (Internal Working Paper No. 9, Maxwell Research Project, on the Public Finances of New York City, Syracuse University, Syracuse, N.Y., October 1972). (The derivation of all other figures, based on 1972 expenditures, is described in the accompanying text.)

TABLE 3.33

New York City Expenditure Forecast for 1979: Public Schools
(in millions of dollars)

| Conditions | Type of Expenditure | | | Expenditures Accounted for | Total Expenditures |
	Labor	Nonlabor	Retirement		
Present trend	2,249.2	148.4	170.9	2,568.6	3,810.2
Slow employment growth	1,945.0	135.2	147.8	2,228.1	3,342.1
Slow real wage growth	2,157.8	148.4	164.0	2,470.3	3,705.4
Slow price growth	1,920.3	133.9	146.0	2,200.1	3,300.2
Constant contribution rate growth	2,249.2	148.4	281.1	2,678.8	4,018.2
Slow real wage, employment, and contribution rate growth	1,866.0	135.2	141.8	2,143.1	3,214.6
Slow growth for all	1,593.2	122.0	121.1	1,836.2	2,754.3
1972 expenditure	1,066.5	90.6	133.3	1,290.5	1,914.3*

*Includes debt service and unallocated appropriations.

Sources: 1972 labor and total expenditure figures taken from New York City Executive Budget and Supporting Schedules (New York: Office of the Mayor, 1972). 1972 nonlabor expenditure figure taken from Comptroller of the City of New York, Annual Report (New York: Office of the Comptroller, 1972). 1972 retirement expenditure figure derived from Bernard Jump, "The Cost of Providing Retirement and Social Security Benefits to New York City Employees: Trends, Causes, and Prospects, 1961-1972" (Internal Working Paper No. 9, Maxwell Research Project on the Public Finances of New York City, Syracuse University, Syracuse, N.Y., October 1972). (The derivation of all other figures, based on 1972 expenditures, is described in the accompanying text.)

TABLE 3.34

New York City Expenditure Forecast for 1979: Higher Education
(in millions of dollars)

Conditions	Type of Expenditure			Expenditures Accounted for	Total Expenditures
	Labor	Nonlabor	Retirement		
Present trend	1,035.6	547.9	75.6	1,659.1	2,197.6
Slow employment growth	716.2	302.6	52.3	1,071.1	1,231.8
Slow real wage growth	972.7	547.9	71.0	1,591.6	1,830.3
Slow price growth	884.2	492.1	64.5	1,440.8	1,656.9
Constant contribution rate growth	1,035.6	547.9	128.4	1,711.9	1,968.7
Slow real wage, employment, and contribution rate growth	672.7	302.6	49.1	1,024.4	1,178.1
Slow growth for all	574.4	271.7	41.9	888.0	1,021.2
1972 expenditure	246.7	45.6	30.6	322.8	371.8*

*Includes debt service and unallocated appropriations.

Sources: 1972 labor and total expenditure figures taken from New York City Executive Budget and Supporting Schedules (New York: Office of the Mayor, 1972). 1972 nonlabor expenditure figure taken from Comptroller of the City of New York, Annual Report (New York: Office of the Comptroller, 1972). 1972 retirement expenditure figure derived from Bernard Jump, "The Cost of Providing Retirement and Social Security Benefits to New York City Employees: Trends, Causes, and Prospects, 1961-1972" (Internal Working Paper No. 9, Maxwell Research Project on the Public Finances of New York City, Syracuse University, Syracuse, N.Y., October 1972). (The derivation of all other figures, based on 1972 expenditures, is described in the accompanying text.)

TABLE 3.35

New York City Expenditure Forecast for 1979: Social Services Department
(in millions of dollars)

Conditions	Type of Expenditure				Expenditures Accounted for	Total Expenditures
	Labor	Nonlabor	Retirement	Transfer		
Present trend	993.2	107.0	230.4	5,290.8	6,621.4	6,422.3
Slow employment growth	728.0	70.8	168.9	5,290.8	6,258.5	6,070.7
Slow real wage growth	935.1	107.0	216.9	5,290.8	6,549.8	6,353.3
Slow price growth	848.0	99.0	196.7	5,290.8	6,434.5	6,241.5
Slow contribution rate growth	993.2	107.0	180.8	5,290.8	6,567.8	6,370.7
Slow transfer growth	993.2	107.0	230.4	3,518.5	4,849.1	4,703.7
Slow real wage, employment, and contribution rate growth	685.4	70.8	124.7	5,290.8	6,171.7	5,986.6
Slow growth for all	585.2	65.5	106.5	3,518.5	4,275.7	4,147.4
1972 expenditure	289.1	29.4	38.2	1,737.5	2,094.2	2,031.7*

*Includes debt service and unallocated appropriations.

Sources: 1972 labor, transfer, and total expenditure figures taken from New York City Executive Budget and Supporting Schedules (New York: Office of the Mayor, 1972). 1972 nonlabor expenditure figure taken from Comptroller of the City of New York, Annual Report (New York: Office of the Comptroller, 1972). 1972 retirement expenditure figure derived from Bernard Jump, "The Cost of Providing Retirement and Social Security Benefits to New York City Employees: Trends, Causes, and Prospects, 1961-1972" (Internal Working Paper No. 9, Maxwell Research Project on the Public Finances of New York City, Syracuse University, Syracuse, N.Y., October 1972). (The derivation of all other figures, based on 1972 expenditures, is described in the accompanying text.)

specifically directed to explaining historical trends in transfer payments. Accordingly, the projection of the labor, nonlabor, and pension components of social service expenditures closely follows the reasoning outlined above, but the projections of transfer payments are little more than speculation. If past growth in the discretionary variables and in transfer payments is extended into the future, by 1979 social service expenditures will be $6.4 billion (an increase of more than 200 percent). If employment growth were cut in half, social service expenditures would still rise to $6 billion, while slower growth in each discretionary variable would still produce expenditures of $5.9 billion. On the other hand, if growth in transfers were cut, expenditures in 1979 would be $4.7 billion. Finally, if growth in all the variables were cut in half, expenditures in 1979 would be about $4.1 billion—an increase of almost 110 percent.

Forecasts of 1979 expenditures for health services appear in Table 3.36. Present growth in costs will produce expenditures of $685 million in 1979. If the growth in the variables (E, C, and W´) were cut in half, expenditures by 1979 would be $662 million. A slowdown in the growth of all the variables would still produce 1979 expenditures of $583 million—187 percent above 1972.

Table 3.37 contains forecasts of expenditures for 1979 for all seven departments. At the present rate, expenditures for these seven departments alone will reach $15.3 billion in 1979—an increase of more than 150 percent. Slowing of the rate of growth either in employment or in real wages would still yield 1979 expenditures of $13.7 billion and $14.7 billion, respectively. Even the control of the E, C, and W´ variables would mean 1979 expenditures of $13.1 billion. Control of growth in transfers produces somewhat poorer results— $13.3 billion in 1979. However, even the control of growth in all of the independent variables still results in 1979 expenditures of $10.1 billion—an increase of about 80 percent.

Total Expenditure Forecasts by Object

Tables 3.38 and 3.39 focus on growth in total New York City expenditures by object. In Table 3.38, actual growth in the objects of expenditure between 1965 and 1972 is presented; Table 3.39 includes proportions for each object of expenditure for 1979. The projected expenditures for departments other than the seven major ones considered here are based on the assumption that average real wage and nonlabor price figures for the seven departments correspond to average real wages and nonlabor prices for the remaining city department.

As indicated in Table 3.38, personal service, nonlabor, and retirement expenditures grew by 94.4 percent between 1965 and 1972.

TABLE 3.36

New York City Expenditure Forecast for 1979: Health Services Administration
(in millions of dollars)

Conditions	Type of Expenditure			Expenditures Accounted for	Total Expenditures
	Labor	Nonlabor	Retirement		
Present trend	99.3	376.8	23.0	499.0	1,048.0
Slow employment growth	91.9	213.1	21.3	326.3	685.2
Slow real wage growth	93.7	376.8	21.7	492.1	1,033.5
Slow price growth	84.7	335.8	19.7	440.2	924.5
Slow contribution rate growth	99.3	376.8	18.1	494.1	1,037.6
Slow real wage, employ- ment and contribution rate growth	86.7	213.1	15.8	315.1	661.8
Slow growth for all	74.0	189.9	13.5	277.4	582.6
1972 expenditure	53.0	38.7	7.0	98.7	202.9*

*Includes debt service and unallocated appropriations.

Sources: 1972 labor and total expenditure figures taken from New York City Executive Budget and Supporting Schedules (New York: Office of the Mayor, 1972). 1972 nonlabor expenditure figure taken from Comptroller of the City of New York, Annual Report (New York: Office of the Comptroller, 1972). 1972 retirement
expenditure figure derived from Bernard Jump, "The Cost of Providing Retirement and Social Security Benefits to New York City Employees: Trends, Causes, and Prospects, 1961-1972" (Internal Working Paper No. 9,
Maxwell Research Project on the Public Finances of New York City, Syracuse University, Syracuse, N.Y.,
October 1972). (The derivation of all other figures, based on 1972 expenditures, is described in the accompanying text.)

TABLE 3.37

New York City Expenditure Forecast for 1979: All Seven Departments
(in millions of dollars)

Conditions	Type of Expenditure				Expenditures Accounted for	Total Expenditures
	Labor	Nonlabor	Retirement	Transfer		
Present trend	6,004.6	1,273.9	960.7	5,290.8	13,530.0	15,288.9
Slow employment growth	5,193.0	786.7	822.2	5,290.8	12,092.8	13,664.8
Slow real wage growth	5,571.5	1,273.9	891.4	5,290.8	13,027.7	14,721.3
Slow price growth	5,126.6	1,152.7	820.3	5,290.8	12,390.3	14,001.1
Slow contribution rate growth	6,004.6	1,273.9	942.7	5,290.8	13,512.0	15,268.6
Slow transfers	6,004.6	1,273.9	960.7	3,518.5	11,757.7	13,286.2
Slow real wage, employment and contribution rate growth	4,768.4	786.7	748.6	5,290.8	11,594.5	13,101.8
Slow growth for all	4,071.2	711.8	639.2	3,518.5	8,940.7	10,103.0
1972 expenditure	2,623.6	242.5	395.9	1,737.5	4,999.6	5,671.1*

*Includes debt service and unallocated appropriations.

Sources: 1972 labor, transfer and total expenditure figures taken from New York City Executive Budget and Supporting Schedules (New York: Office of the Mayor, 1972). 1972 nonlabor expenditure figure taken from Comptroller of the City of New York, Annual Report (New York: Office of the Comptroller, 1972). 1972 retirement expenditure figure derived from Bernard Jump, "The Cost of Providing Retirement and Social Security Benefits to New York City Employees: Trends, Causes, and Prospects, 1961-1972" (Internal Working Paper No. 9, Maxwell Research Project on the Public Finances of New York City, Syracuse University, Syracuse, N.Y., October 1972). (The derivation of all other figures, based on 1972 expenditures, is described in the accompanying text.)

TABLE 3.38

Structure and Growth in Total New York City
Expenditures by Object, 1965-72
(dollar figures in millions of dollars)

	1965	1972	Percentage Growth
Personal service	$1,709.3	$3,271.4	91.4
Nonlabor	246.7	574.9	133.0
Retirement	363.2	662.5	82.4
Subtotal	2,319.3	4,508.8	94.4
Transfers	568.0	2,519.3	343.5
(Welfare)	(341.3)	(1,737.5)	409.0
Subtotal	2,887.3	7,028.1	143.4
Debt service and unallocated	459.5	1,479.9	222.1
Total	$3,346.8	$8,508.1	154.2

Source: Comptroller of City of New York, Annual Report (New York: Office of the Comptroller, 1965 and 1972.

Over the same period, transfers grew by 343.5 percent, with welfare transfers growing by 409 percent. When welfare and other transfer payments are added to personal service, nonlabor, and retirement costs, expenditures grew by 143.4 percent. Finally, when all items of expenditure are taken into account, New York City expenditures increased from $3.35 billion in 1965 to $8.51 billion in 1972—an increase of 154.2 percent.

Table 3.39 presents forecasts of possible 1979 expenditure levels in the four largest expenditure categories as well as the total budget. If present trends continue, current expenditures could reach $18.9 billion by 1979—an increase of more than 120 percent. A slowdown in price growth would cause total expenditures to rise to $17.5 billion, while restriction in real wage and employment growth would only limit expenditures to $18.3 billion and $17.9 billion, respectively. The control of the variables, E, W´, and C, would yield 1979 total expenditures of $17.3 billion. Slow growth of transfer payments would still produce expenditures of $16.3 billion in 1979. In fact, slow growth in all the variables over which the city government has influence—that is, Q, E, W´, P, T, and C, would produce expenditures in 1979 of $13.5 billion—an increase of about 60 percent. Even the elimination of

TABLE 3.39

New York City Expenditure Forecast for 1979: Expense Budget
(in millions of dollars)

Conditions	Type of Expenditure					Total Expense Budget
	Labor	Nonlabor	Retirement	Transfer	Total[a]	
Present trend	6,261.1	1,339.6	1,202.1	6,846.3	15,649.2	18,935.5
Slow employment growth	5,825.0	1,024.8	1,118.4	6,846.3	14,814.6	17,925.6
Slow real wage growth	5,816.8	1,339.6	1,116.8	6,846.3	15,119.6	18,294.7
Slow price growth	5,345.6	1,212.2	1,026.4	6,846.3	14,430.5	17,460.9
Constant contribution rate	6,261.1	1,339.6	1,264.7	6,846.3	15,711.8	19,011.3
Slow transfer growth	6,261.1	1,339.6	1,202.1	4,682.8	13,485.7	16,317.7
Excluding welfare	6,261.1	1,339.6	1,202.1	1,555.5	10,358.4	12,533.6
Slow real wage, employment and contribution rate growth	5,411.6	1,024.8	1,039.0	6,846.3	14,321.8	17,329.4
Slow growth for all	4,620.3	927.3	887.1	4,682.8	11,117.6	13,452.3
1972 expenditure	3,271.4	574.9	662.5	2,519.4	7,028.1	8,508.1[b]

[a]Excludes debt service and unallocated appropriations.
[b]Includes social security and city health insurance.

Source: All 1972 expenditure figures taken from Comptroller of the City of New York, Annual Report (New York: Office of the Comptroller, 1972). (The derivation of all other figures, based on 1972 expenditures, is described in the accompanying text.)

249

welfare from the New York City responsibility would still mean expenditures of $12.5 billion in 1979, if all other variables increased at their present rates.

Summary

In summary, the forecasts for expenditure growth in New York City between 1972 and 1979 are bleak indeed. At present rates, expenditures will more than double for most departments and objects. The largest single cause of increases in total current expenditures is the increasing burden of welfare. The next most important contributing factor is general price increases. It might be argued, however, that cost-of-living wage increments (part of the price effect in this model) are a discretionary variable—that is to say, while the city government may not be able to control inflation, it does have some control over whether the response to inflation should be to maintain the real income of city government employees.

These data could be used to suggest the longer-term budget relief that the city government might receive, if the responsibility for education and welfare financing were assigned to the state government. While total city expenditures in 1979 are projected here to rise to somewhere between $13 billion and $19 billion, the reassignment of education and welfare would reduce this range to between $6.1 billion and $8.8 billion. Assuming the maintenance of present state and federal aid proportions of total expenditures, such reassignment would reduce New York City's 1979 tax bill by an amount between $2.5 billion and $3.5 billion.[29]

APPENDIX: REPRESENTATIVE OCCUPATIONS
INCLUDED IN EACH JOB CATEGORY

Executive

Commissioner, Deputy Commissioner, Assistant Commissioner, Superintendent, Assistant Superintendent, President, Dean, Special Council, Director, Special Assistants

Uniformed

Police: Policeman
Fire: Fireman
Environmental Protection: Sanitationman
Social Services: Supervisor-Casework, Investigator-Casework
Public Schools: Principal, Teacher
Higher Education: Professor, Associate Professor, Assistant Professor, Instructor
Health Services: Doctor, Nurse, Public Health Consultant, Public Health Educator

Laborer

Motor Vehicle Operator, Auto Mechanic, General Laborer, Custodian, Cleaner, Electrician, Painter, Carpenter

Clerical

Stenographer, Typist, Clerk, Key Punch Operator, Telephone Operator, Secretary, Clerical Aide, Messenger

Other

Administrative Assistant, Engineer, Attorney, Clerk Grade 5, Accountant, Lab Technician, Photographer, Cook, Chaplain, Therapist, Dental Hygienist, Chemist

TABLE 3.A.1

New York City Direct Labor Costs* by Job Category for Police and Fire Departments and EPA, 1965 and 1972

Department Job Category	1965		1972		Percent Change 1965-72
	Dollar Amount	Percent of Departmental Total	Dollar Amount	Percent of Departmental Total	
Police Department					
Executive	156,504	0.1	372,710	0.1	138.1
Uniformed	232,452,130	96.8	462,126,655	95.3	98.8
Laborer	4,998,240	2.1	11,556,442	2.4	131.2
Clerical	1,711,464	0.7	4,541,252	0.9	165.3
Other	744,412	0.3	6,263,280	1.3	741.4
Departmental total	240,062,750	—	484,860,339	—	102.0
Fire Department					
Executive	70,500	0.1	179,274	0.1	154.3
Uniformed	113,550,997	95.4	217,009,872	95.1	91.1
Laborer	2,347,800	2.0	4,311,160	1.9	83.6
Clerical	1,058,176	0.9	1,759,330	0.8	66.3
Other	2,037,683	1.7	4,930,850	2.2	142.0
Departmental total	119,065,156	—	228,190,486	—	91.7
Environmental Protection Administration					
Executive	338,403	0.3	1,344,408	0.5	246.1
Uniformed	84,636,505	61.4	153,708,072	60.2	81.6
Laborer	40,491,558	29.4	70,327,104	27.6	73.7
Clerical	4,138,910	3.0	9,491,475	3.7	129.3
Other	8,276,449	6.0	20,353,858	8.0	145.9
Departmental total	137,931,825	—	255,224,917	—	85.0

*Direct labor costs exclude pensions and fringe benefits.

Source: New York City Executive Budget and Supporting Schedules, 1965-66 and 1972-73 (New York: Office of the Mayor, March 1965 and March 1972).

TABLE 3.A.2

New York City Employment Levels by Job Category for Police and Fire Departments and EPA, 1965 and 1972

Department Job Category	1965		1972		Percent Change 1965-72
	Number of Employees	Percent of Departmental Total	Number of Employees	Percent of Departmental Total	
Police Department					
Executive	8	—*	13	—*	62.5
Uniformed	26,734	95.3	31,395	92.0	19.3
Laborer	871	3.1	1,334	3.8	53.2
Clerical	348	1.2	691	2.0	98.6
Other	102	0.4	752	2.2	637.3
Departmental total	28,063	—	34,685	—	23.6
Fire Department					
Executive	4	—*	6	—*	50.0
Uniformed	13,199	94.3	13,592	92.5	2.3
Laborer	280	2.0	346	2.4	23.6
Clerical	224	1.6	262	1.8	17.0
Other	289	2.1	494	3.4	70.9
Departmental total	13,996	—	14,700	—	5.0
Environmental Protection Administration					
Executive	25	0.1	52	0.3	108.0
Uniformed	11,405	60.6	12,124	58.9	6.3
Laborer	5,525	29.4	5,629	27.3	1.9
Clerical	837	4.4	1,253	6.1	49.7
Other	1,026	5.5	1,534	7.4	49.5
Departmental total	18,818	—	20,592	—	9.4

*Less than 0.05 percent.

Source: New York City Executive Budget and Supporting Schedules, 1965-66 and 1972-73 (New York: Office of the Mayor, March 1965 and March 1972).

TABLE 3.A.3

Disaggregation of New York City "Other" Employment by Job Category for Police and Fire Departments and EPA, 1965 and 1972

Department Job Category	1965		1972		Percent Change 1965-72
	Number of Employees	Percent of Departmental Total	Number of Employees	Percent of Departmental Total	
Police Department					
Administrative aides and assistants	5	4.9	526	69.9	10,420.2
Engineers	3	2.9	6	0.7	100.0
Inspectors-investigators	–	–	–	–	–
Dispatchers-marshalls	–	–	–	–	–
Miscellaneous	94	92.2	220	29.6	134.0
Departmental total	102	–	752	–	637.2
Fire Department					
Administrative aides and assistants	6	2.1	10	2.0	66.6
Engineers	47	16.3	37	7.4	-21.3
Inspectors-investigators	60	20.7	140	28.3	133.3
Dispatchers-marshalls	130	44.9	211	42.7	62.3
Miscellaneous	46	15.9	96	19.4	108.7
Departmental total	289	–	494	–	70.9
Environmental Protection Administration					
Administrative aides and assistants	61	5.9	119	7.8	95.4
Engineers	337	32.8	638	41.6	89.3
Inspectors-investigators	470	45.8	453	29.5	- 3.6
Dispatchers-marshalls	–	–	–	–	–
Miscellaneous	158	15.4	324	21.1	105.1
Departmental total	1,026	–	1,534	–	49.5

Source: New York City Executive Budget and Supporting Schedules, 1965-66 and 1972-73 (New York: Office of the Mayor, March 1965 and March 1972).

TABLE 3.A.4

New York City Average Wage Rates* by Job Category for Police and Fire Departments and EPA, 1965 and 1972

Department Job Category	1965		1972		Percent Change 1965-72
	Salary	Percent of Departmental Average	Salary	Percent of Department Average	
Police Department					
Executive	$19,563	228.7	$28,670	205.1	46.6
Uniformed	8,685	101.5	14,489	103.6	66.8
Laborer	5,739	67.1	8,663	62.0	50.9
Clerical	4,918	57.5	6,572	47.0	33.6
Other	7,298	85.3	8,329	59.6	14.1
Departmental average	8,554	—	13,979	—	63.4
Fire Department					
Executive	17,625	207.2	29,879	192.5	69.5
Uniformed	8,603	101.1	15,966	102.9	85.6
Laborer	8,385	98.6	12,460	80.3	48.6
Clerical	4,724	55.5	6,715	43.3	42.1
Other	7,051	82.9	9,981	64.3	41.6
Departmental average	8,507	—	15,523	—	82.5
Environmental Protection Administration					
Executive	15,536	212.0	25,854	208.6	66.4
Uniformed	7,421	101.2	12,678	102.3	70.8
Laborer	7,329	100.0	12,494	100.8	70.5
Clerical	4,945	67.5	7,575	61.1	53.2
Other	8,067	110.1	13,268	107.1	64.5
Departmental average	7,330	—	12,394	—	69.1

*The figures reported are average wages in current dollars.

Source: New York City Executive Budget and Supporting Schedules, 1965-66 and 1972-73 (New York: Office of the Mayor, March 1965 and March 1972).

TABLE 3.A.5

Components of New York City Direct Labor Cost Change by Job Category for Police and Fire Departments and EPA, 1965-72

Department Job Category	Dollar Change	Percent of Departmental Total	Percent Due to Employmental Change	Percent Due to Price Level Change	Percent Due to Real Wage Change
Police Department					
Executive	216,206	0.1	45.2	49.8	5.0
Uniformed	229,674,525	93.8	19.5	51.0	29.6
Laborer	6,558,209	2.7	40.5	49.4	10.1
Clerical	2,829,788	1.2	59.6	50.8	-10.4
Other	5,518,868	2.3	86.0	42.1	-28.0
Departmental total	244,797,589	—	23.1	51.3	25.6
Fire Department					
Executive	108,774	0.1	32.4	41.1	26.5
Uniformed	103,458,875	94.8	3.3	47.8	48.9
Laborer	1,963,360	1.8	28.2	62.5	9.3
Clerical	701,154	0.6	25.6	74.7	- 0.3
Other	2,893,167	2.7	50.0	50.9	- 0.9
Departmental total	109,125,330	—	5.5	48.5	46.0
Environmental Protection Administration					
Executive	956,005	0.8	43.9	35.7	20.4
Uniformed	69,071,567	58.9	7.7	55.1	37.2
Laborer	29,835,546	25.4	2.6	58.5	39.0
Clerical	5,352,565	4.6	38.4	49.0	12.6
Other	12,077,409	10.3	33.9	43.3	22.7
Departmental total	117,293,092	—	11.1	54.4	34.5

Source: New York City Executive Budget and Supporting Schedules, 1965-66 and 1972-73 (New York: Office of the Mayor, March 1965 and March 1972).

TABLE 3.A.6

Components of New York City Direct Labor Cost Change for Uniformed and
Nonuniformed Personnel in Police and Fire Departments and
EPA, 1965-72

Department Job Category	Dollar Change	Percent of Departmental Total	Percent Due to Employment Change	Percent Due to Price Level Change	Percent Due to Real Wage Change
Police Department					
Uniformed	229,675,575	93.8	19.5	51.0	29.6
Nonuniformed	15,122,014	6.2	60.7	47.0	-7.7
Departmental total	244,797,589	–	23.1	51.3	25.6
Fire Department					
Uniformed	103,458,875	94.8	3.3	47.8	48.9
Nonuniformed	5,666,455	5.2	39.1	57.7	3.2
Departmental total	109,125,330	–	5.5	48.5	46.0
Environmental Protection Administration					
Uniformed	69,071,567	58.9	7.7	55.1	37.2
Nonuniformed	48,221,525	41.1	15.2	53.2	31.6
Departmental total	117,293,092	–	11.1	54.4	34.5

Source: New York City Executive Budget and Supporting Schedules, 1965-66 and 1972-73 (New York
Office of the Mayor, March 1965 and March 1972).

TABLE 3.A.7

Total Expenditures by New York City and Its Authorities for Retirement and Social Security Benefits, 1961-72
(in millions of dollars)

	1972	1971	1970	1969	1968	1967	1966	1965	1964	1963	1962	1961
Actuarial Retirement Systems												
Teachers Retirement System	25.9	140.7	102.0	103.5	113.2	99.2	102.2	97.3	93.2	90.9	72.3	64.1
N.Y.C. Employees Retirement System	295.3	222.4	157.7	128.4	109.9	109.7	96.1	68.4	80.1	67.7	70.4	68.0
Fire Department Pension Fund (Article 1-A)	33.3	32.0	31.9	31.3	22.3	23.5	22.9	19.1	14.9	13.0	11.7	9.5
Police Pension Fund (Article 2)	96.0	80.3	85.0	47.1	75.7	68.4	56.4	46.7	30.6	26.7	24.2	23.2
Board of Education Retirement System	9.4	8.5	6.0	4.9	5.9	5.5	5.6	4.8	4.9	3.9	3.0	3.3
Total	458.9	483.9	382.6	315.2	327.0	306.3	283.2	236.3	223.7	202.2	181.6	168.1
Nonacturial Retirement systems												
Police[a,b]	35.9	27.7	36.5	37.5	37.3	33.8	32.3	33.0	33.1	32.0	33.3	29.7
Fire[a]	30.6	14.9	19.3	20.6	19.0	18.0	14.9	14.8	15.6	14.3	16.4	13.1
Street cleaning	7.1	7.3	7.9	8.0	8.5	8.8	9.1	9.4	9.8	10.0	10.2	10.2
Health Department[a]	0.1	0.1	0.1	0.2	0.2	0.2	0.2g	0.2	0.2	0.2g	0.2g	0.2g
Courts[a]	0.1	0.1	0.1	0.1	0.1	0.1	0.1	0.1	0.1	0.1	0.1	0.1
Grady Law[c]	0.1	0.1	0.1	0.1	0.1	0.1	0.1	0.1	0.1	0.1	0.1	0.1
BMT and IRT (Transit)[d]	—	—	—	—	—	4.0	4.0	4.0	3.7	4.1	4.1	4.1
Total	73.9	50.2	64.0	66.5	65.2	65.0	60.7	61.6	62.6	60.8	64.5	57.5
Other retirement systems and programs												
City supplemental[a,c,e]	37.5	33.1	23.1	21.0	19.3	13.6	11.2	10.6	10.2	10.3	10.9	3.5
Teachers supplemental[c]	19.0	12.8	6.5	5.4	3.4	3.6	4.2	4.5	4.5	4.4	0.2	—
TIAA-CREF[c]	9.6	6.7	2.8	1.8	—	—	—	—	—	—	—	—
Cultural institutions[c]	3.9	2.6	1.8	1.1	0.8	1.1	1.1	1.1	0.8	0.4	—	—
Libraries[f]	5.1	3.6	2.8	3.0	2.9	2.9	2.7	2.6	2.3	2.1	1.5	1.0
Total	75.1	58.8	37.0	32.3	26.4	21.2	19.2	18.8	17.8	17.2	12.6	4.5
Total—all retirement systems	607.9	592.9	477.8	414.0	418.6	392.5	363.1	310.7	304.1	280.2	258.7	230.1
City share of social security taxes	146.0	125.2	118.5	98.6	81.0	72.7	48.6	44.6	42.8	37.2	31.7	30.7
Total	753.9	718.1	602.2	512.6	499.6	465.2	411.7	361.3	346.9	317.4	290.4	260.8

aPart 2A—Statements 5 and 8.

b1965-66 includes $5.9 million financed with serial bonds—Appendix B.

cPart 2A—Statement 7.

dPart 2B—Budget Notes: 1970-71 City Supplemental $26.2 million; 1962-63 Teachers Supplemental $4.4 million.

ePart 2B—Budget Notes: 1970-71 City Supplemental $26.2 million.

fAppendix B.

gLess than $50,000.

hEstimate.

Sources: The first six footnotes above all refer to Comptroller of the City of New York, *Annual Report* (New York: Office of the Comptroller, 1961–71). All city contributions to the five major actuarial systems except for 1971-72 are from annual reports issued by each system, annual statements to the Superintendent of Insurance of the State of New York, and Records of City Actuary. 1972 totals for all retirement systems are from the City of New York, *Expense Budget for the Fiscal Year 1972-1973* (New York, 1972), as finally adopted and certified. All social security data are from unpublished records of Department of ...

TABLE 3.A.8

New York City Actuarial Retirement System—Employer Contributions Per Member and as Percent of Salaries, 1961-71

Fiscal Year	Employer Contributions per Member (dollars)					Employer Contributions as Percent Salaries				
	N.Y.C. Employees Retirement System	Teachers Retirement System	Police Pension Fund— Article 2	Fire Department Pension Fund— Article A-1	Board of Education Retirement System	N.Y.C. Employees Retirement System	Teachers Retirement System	Police Pension Fund— Article 2	Fire Department Pension Fund— Article 1-A	Board of Education Retirement System
1961	532	1,471	1,471	971	781	10.0	19.4	15.7	14.8	14.0
1962	535	1,657	1,657	1,139	695	9.6	19.7	13.9	15.1	11.9
1963	504	2,034	1,086	1,157	864	8.6	23.6	13.8	14.6	14.0
1964	588	1,917	1,211	1,278	1,006	9.4	21.7	14.8	15.5	15.2
1965	483	1,913	1,810	1,631	1,077	7.5	21.1	20.1	18.0	15.7
1966	652	1,897	2,072	1,904	1,075	9.4	19.7	23.0	20.6	14.7
1967	717	1,726	2,449	1,927	1,025	9.9	17.8	24.8	18.9	13.1
1968	694	1,912	2,578	1,814	1,042	9.0	18.4	25.8	17.7	13.3
1969	759	1,676	1,532	2,419	892	9.3	14.5	14.5	22.4	11.5
1970	864	1,522	2,646	2,364	1,072	9.9	11.9	23.3	20.5	11.9
1971	1,714	1,893	2,528	2,352	1,439	12.9	14.2	21.6	20.1	14.8

Source: Calculated from Tables 3.7, 3.11, 3.16, 3.17, and 3.A.9.

TABLE 3.A.9

New York City Employees Retirement System (NYCERS), 1961-71
(dollar figures in millions of dollars)

Fiscal Year	Number of Active Members	Salaries of Active Members	Employee Contributions	Employer Contributions	Number of Beneficiaries	Payments of Beneficiaries	Assets	Liabilities[a]	Investment Income[b]
1961	127,793	$ 683.2	$65.4	$ 68.0	19,444	$ 33.5	$1,539.4	$2,048.4	$ 47.2
1962	131,656	735.4	61.0	70.4	21,032	37.8	1,645.8	2,317.4	54.7
1963	134,428	791.1	64.4	67.7	22,772	42.6	1,742.3	2,554.9	61.0
1964	136,214	850.8	65.5	80.1	24,043	46.6	1,865.3	2,759.3	67.0
1965	141,613	915.6	70.2	68.4	25,157	50.7	1,988.6	3,251.4	73.2
1966	147,439	1,020.8	76.5	96.1	26,312	55.4	2,138.6	3,550.7	80.3
1967	153,012	1,106.8	82.0	109.7	26,667	57.7	2,298.0	3,349.8	88.0
1968	158,395	1,227.4	85.6	109.9	30,534	72.1	2,463.2	4,545.8	96.9
1969	169,080	1,384.5	86.1	128.4	31,766	81.8	2,629.2	5,189.2	108.6
1970	182,520	1,587.2	87.7	157.7	35,722	104.4	2,737.8	5,720.3	120.2
1971	189,465	1,730.0	77.6	222.4	40,478	134.0	2,892.4	5,869.2	135.9
Average increase[c]	4.8%	15.3%	1.9% (3.8)[d]	22.7%	10.8%	40.0%	8.8%	18.7%	18.8%

[a] Equal to present value of future benefits, including both those already accrued and those expected to be earned by present active members.

[b] Excludes gains or losses on the sale of securities.

[c] Calculated from total percent increase over 1961-71 period divided by number of years (10).

[d] Average percent increase for the 1961-70 period.

Sources: Records of the City Actuary; Annual Report to the Superintendent of Insurance of the State of New York (Albany, N.Y.: Office of the Superintendent of Insurance, 1961-71); Comptroller of the City of New York, Annual Report (New York: Office of the Comptroller, 1961-71), Appendix A.

TABLE 3.A.10

New York City Direct Labor Costs by Job Category for
Public Schools and Board of Higher Education,
1965 and 1972

Department Job Category	1965 Dollar Amount	1965 Percent of Departmental Total	1972 Dollar Amount	1972 Percent of Departmental Total	Percent Change 1965-72
Public schools					
Executive	2,129,138	0.4	7,580,940	0.7	256.1
Delivery-principal	30,048,939	6.0	90,032,578	8.4	199.6
Delivery-teacher	415,309,988	83.0	842,700,176	79.0	102.9
Laborer	12,907,004	2.6	26,111,036	2.5	102.3
Clerical	14,364,474	2.9	43,150,118	4.1	200.4
Other	25,759,306	5.1	56,980,350	5.5	121.2
Departmental total	500,518,849	—	1,066,555,198	—	108.4
Board of Higher Education					
Executive	1,027,514	1.8	3,901,025	1.6	279.8
Delivery-professor	10,973,135	18.9	45,319,842	18.4	312.9
Delivery-associate professor	9,980,028	17.1	37,535,306	15.2	276.1
Delivery-assistant professor	12,195,527	21.0	50,123,534	20.3	311.0
Delivery-instructors	8,397,639	14.4	37,719,802	15.3	349.2
Laborer	5,500,570	9.5	16,611,781	6.7	202.0
Clerical	4,360,758	7.5	22,541,190	9.1	416.9
Other	5,766,461	9.9	32,932,196	13.4	471.0
Departmental total	58,201,632	—	246,675,676	—	323.8

Source: New York City Executive Budget and Supporting Schedules, 1965-66 and 1972-73 (New York: Office of the Mayor, March 1965 and March 1972).

TABLE 3.A.11

New York City Employment Levels by Job Category for
Public Schools and Board of Higher Education, 1965 and 1972

Department Job Category	1965		1972		
	Number of Employees	Percent of Departmental Total	Number of Employees	Percent of Departmental Total	Percent Change 1965-72
Public schools					
Executive	100	0.2	271	0.3	171.0
Delivery-principal	2,190	3.7	3,973	4.9	81.4
Delivery-teacher	49,182	83.0	63,503	78.2	29.1
Laborer	1,708	2.9	2,569	3.2	50.4
Clerical	2,654	4.5	5,713	7.0	115.3
Other	3,398	5.7	5,168	6.4	52.1
Departmental total	59,232	—	81,197	—	37.1
Board of Higher Education					
Executive	42	0.6	115	0.7	173.8
Delivery-professor	641	9.8	1,701	9.9	165.4
Delivery-associate professor	791	12.1	1,824	10.7	130.6
Delivery-assistant professor	1,239	18.9	3,075	18.0	148.2
Delivery-instructor	1,059	16.1	2,919	17.1	175.6
Laborer	1,062	16.2	2,036	11.9	91.7
Clerical	953	14.5	3,006	17.6	215.4
Other	773	11.8	2,444	14.3	216.2
Departmental total	6,560	—	17,120	—	161.0

Source: New York City Executive Budget and Supporting Schedules, 1965-66 and 1972-73 (New York: Office of the Mayor, March 1965 and March 1972).

TABLE 3.A.12

New York City Average Wage Rates by Job Category for Public
Schools and Board of Higher Education, 1965 and 1972

Department Job Category	Salary	Percent of Departmental Average	Salary	Percent of Departmental Average	Percent Change 1965–72
Public schools					
Executive	21,291	249.3	27,974	217.8	31.4
Delivery-principal	13,721	160.7	22,661	172.5	65.2
Delivery-teacher	8,444	98.9	13,270	101.0	57.2
Laborer	7,557	88.5	10,163	79.1	34.5
Clerical	5,412	63.4	7,553	58.8	39.6
Other	7,581	88.8	11,026	85.8	45.4
Departmental average	8,540	–	13,135	–	50.4
Board of Higher Education					
Executive	24,465	275.8	33,922	235.4	38.7
Delivery-professor	17,119	193.0	26,638	184.9	55.6
Delivery-associate professor	12,617	142.2	20,579	142.8	63.1
Delivery-assistant professor	9,843	111.0	16,300	113.1	65.6
Delivery-instructor	7,930	89.4	12,922	89.7	63.0
Laborer	5,179	58.4	8,159	56.6	57.5
Clerical	4,576	51.6	7,499	52.0	63.9
Other	7,460	84.1	13,475	93.5	80.6
Departmental average	8,870	–	14,409	–	62.4

Note: The figures reported are average wages in current dollars.

Source: New York City Executive Budget and Supporting Schedules, 1965–66 and 1972–73 (New York: Office of the Mayor, March 1965 and March 1972).

TABLE 3.A.13

Components of New York City Direct Labor Cost Change
by Job Category for Public Schools and Board of
Higher Education, 1965-72

Department Job Category	Dollar Change	Percent of Departmental Total	Percent Due to Employment Change	Percent Due to Price-Level Change	Percent Due to Real Wage Change
Public Schools					
Executive	5,451,802	0.1	66.8	43.7	-10.5
Delivery-principal	59,993,639	10.6	40.8	37.5	21.7
Delivery-teacher	427,390,188	75.5	28.3	51.8	19.9
Laborer	13,204,032	2.3	49.3	60.7	-10.0
Clerical	28,785,644	5.1	57.5	44.4	- 1.9
Other	31,221,044	5.5	43.0	51.8	5.2
Departmental total	566,036,349	—	31.8	49.6	18.6
Board of Higher Education					
Executive	2,873,511	1.5	62.2	40.4	- 2.6
Delivery-professor	34,337,707	18.2	52.8	35.0	12.1
Delivery-associate professor	27,555,278	14.6	47.3	34.5	18.2
Delivery-assistant professor	37,928,007	20.1	47.6	33.0	19.4
Delivery-instructor	29,322,163	15.6	50.3	32.6	17.1
Laborer	1,111,211	5.8	45.4	39.2	15.4
Clerical	18,180,432	9.6	51.7	31.2	17.1
Other	27,165,735	14.4	45.9	27.7	26.4
Departmental total	188,474,044	—	49.4	33.2	17.4

Source: New York City Executive Budget and Supporting Schedules, 1965-66 and 1972-73 (New York: Office of the Mayor, March 1965 and March 1972).

TABLE 3.A.14

Components of New York City Direct Labor Cost Change for
Delivery and Nondelivery Personnel in Public Schools
and Board of Higher Education, 1965-72

Department Job Category	Dollar Change	Percent of Departmental Total	Percent Due to Employment Change	Percent Due to Price Level Change	Percent Due to Real Wage Change
Public Schools					
Delivery	487,373,827	86.1	28.6	49.5	21.7
Nondelivery	78,662,522	13.9	51.0	50.0	-1.0
Departmental total	566,036,349	—	31.8	49.6	18.6
Board of Higher Education					
Delivery	129,143,155	68.5	49.9	33.9	16.2
Nondelivery	59,330,889	31.5	48.4	31.6	20.1
Departmental total	188,474,044	—	49.4	33.2	17.4

Source: New York City Executive Budget and Supporting Schedules, 1965-66 and 1972-73 (New
York: Office of the Mayor, March 1965 and March 1972).

TABLE 3.A.15

New York City Direct Labor Costs by Job Category for HSA and Social Services Department, 1965 and 1972

Department Job Category	1965 Dollar Amount	1965 Percent of Departmental Total	1972 Dollar Amount	1972 Percent of Departmental Total	Percent Change 1965-72
Health Services Administration					
Executive	707,950	2.5	2,258,629	4.3	219.0
Delivery-medical	8,464,324	30.0	13,648,202	25.7	61.2
Delivery-nonmedical	1,021,765	3.6	2,462,454	4.6	141.0
Laborer	2,054,696	7.3	4,185,998	7.9	103.7
Clerical	5,411,389	19.1	9,194,355	17.4	69.9
Other	10,665,483	37.7	21,268,643	40.1	99.4
Departmental total	28,325,607	—	53,018,281	—	87.2
Social Service Department					
Executive	394,114	0.4	1,235,508	0.4	213.5
Delivery-Supervisor	12,463,282	14.8	46,016,695	15.9	269.2
Delivery-investigator	33,085,736	39.3	81,907,720	28.3	147.6
Laborer	2,506,008	3.0	10,472,677	3.6	317.9
Clerical	23,110,071	27.5	94,848,750	32.8	310.4
Other	12,622,901	14.9	54,640,080	18.9	332.9
Departmental total	84,182,112	—	289,121,430	—	243.4

Source: New York City Executive Budget and Supporting Schedules, 1965-66 and 1972-73 (New York: Office of the Mayor, March 1965 and March 1972).

TABLE 3.A.16

New York City Employment Levels by Job Category for HSA and Social Services Department, 1965 and 1972

Department Job Category	1965		1972		Percent Change 1965-72
	Number of Employees	Percent of Departmental Total	Number of Employees	Percent of Departmental Total	
Health Services Administration					
Executive	37	0.8	77	1.4	108.1
Delivery-medical	1,313	28.1	1,440	26.2	9.7
Delivery-nonmedical	122	2.6	219	4.0	79.5
Laborer	422	9.0	538	9.8	27.5
Clerical	1,152	24.7	1,350	24.6	17.2
Other	1,624	34.8	1,864	34.0	14.8
Departmental total	4,670	—	5,488	—	17.5
Social Services Department					
Executive	26	0.2	50	0.2	92.3
Delivery-supervisor	1,594	11.0	3,165	10.2	98.6
Delivery-investigator	5,240	36.1	7,544	24.2	44.0
Laborer	484	3.3	1,368	4.4	182.6
Clerical	4,904	33.8	13,559	43.5	176.5
Other	2,276	15.7	5,486	17.6	141.0
Departmental total	14,524	—	31,172	—	114.6

Source: New York City Executive Budget and Supporting Schedules, 1965-66 and 1972-73 (New York: Office of the Mayor, March 1965 and March 1972).

267

TABLE 3.A.17

New York City Average Wage Rates by Job Category for HSA and Social
Services Department: 1965 and 1972

Department Job Category	1965		1972		Percent Change 1965-72
	Salary	Percent of Departmental Average	Salary	Percent of Departmental Average	
Health Services Administration					
Executive	19,134	315.5	29,333	303.6	53.3
Delivery-medical	6,447	106.3	9,478	98.1	47.0
Delivery-nonmedical	8,375	138.1	11,244	116.4	34.3
Laborer	4,869	80.3	7,781	80.5	59.8
Clerical	4,697	77.4	6,811	70.5	45.0
Other	6,567	108.3	11,410	118.1	73.7
Departmental average	6,065	—	9,661	—	59.3
Social Services Department					
Executive	15,148	261.4	24,710	266.4	63.1
Delivery-supervisor	7,819	134.9	14,539	156.8	85.9
Delivery-investigator	6,314	108.9	10,857	117.1	72.0
Laborer	5,178	89.3	7,655	82.5	47.8
Clerical	4,712	81.3	6,995	75.4	48.5
Other	5,546	95.7	9,960	107.4	79.6
Departmental average	5,796	—	9,275	—	60.0

Note: The figures reported are average wages in current dollars.

Source: New York City Executive Budget and Supporting Schedules, 1965-66 and 1972-73 (New York: Office of the Mayor, March 1965 and March 1972).

TABLE 3.A.18

Components of New York City Direct Labor Cost Change for HSA and Social Services Department, 1965–72

Department Job Category	Dollar Change	Percent of Departmental Total	Percent Due to Employment Change	Percent Due to Price-Level Change	Percent Due to Real Wage Change
Health Services Administration					
Executive	1,550,679	6.3	49.4	39.2	11.4
Delivery-medical	5,183,878	21.0	15.8	74.0	10.2
Delivery-nonmedical	1,440,689	5.8	56.4	52.6	- 9.0
Laborer	2,131,302	8.6	26.5	50.8	22.7
Clerical	3,782,966	15.3	24.6	69.2	6.2
Other	10,603,160	42.9	14.9	47.7	37.5
Departmental total	24,692,674	—	21.5	56.3	22.2
Social Services Department					
Executive	841,394	0.4	43.2	37.2	19.6
Delivery-supervisor	33,553,413	16.4	36.6	30.5	32.9
Delivery-investigator	48,821,984	23.8	29.8	40.3	29.9
Laborer	7,966,669	3.9	57.5	36.7	5.8
Clerical	71,738,679	35.0	56.8	36.8	6.4
Other	42,017,179	20.5	42.4	29.9	27.7
Departmental total	204,939,318	—	43.6	34.9	21.5

Source: New York City Executive Budget and Supporting Schedules, 1965–66 and 1972–73 (New York: Office of the Mayor, March 1965 and March 1972).

TABLE 3.A.19

Components of New York City Direct Labor Cost Change for
Delivery and Nondelivery Personnel in HSA and
Social Services Department, 1965-72

Department Job Category	Dollar Change	Percent of Departmental Total	Percent Due to Employment Change	Percent Due to Price-Level Change	Percent Due to Real Wage Change
Health Services Administration					
Delivery	6,624,567	26.8	22.4	68.4	9.3
Nondelivery	18,068,107	73.2	21.2	51.8	26.9
Departmental total	24,692,674	—	21.5	56.3	22.2
Social Services Department					
Delivery	82,375,397	40.2	31.3	35.7	33.1
Nondelivery	122,563,921	59.8	51.8	34.4	13.7
Departmental total	204,939,318	—	43.6	34.9	21.5

Source: New York City Executive Budget and Supporting Schedules, 1965-66 and 1972-73 (New
York: Office of the Mayor, March 1965 and March 1972).

270

TABLE 3.A.20

Laspeyres Price Index for New York City Nonlabor Expenditures, 1965 to 1970

Object Class	1965a	1966	1967	1968	1969	1970	1971
Total	100.0	101.9 (1.9)b	105.0 (3.0)	108.2 (3.1)	112.0 (3.5)	117.2 (4.6)	121.5 (3.7)
Supplies	100.0	101.3 (1.3)	104.3 (3.0)	105.5 (1.1)	106.6 (1.1)	109.5 (2.7)	108.5 (-0.9)
Materials	100.0	101.4 (1.4)	103.7 (2.3)	104.1 (0.4)	109.1 (4.8)	113.6 (4.1)	116.7 (2.7)
Equipment	100.0	104.6 (4.6)	107.4 (2.6)	109.3 (1.8)	113.6 (3.9)	116.9 (2.9)	121.0 (3.6)
Contractual services	100.0	102.0 (2.0)	105.2 (3.1)	110.0 (4.6)	115.3 (4.8)	122.1 (5.9)	129.8 (6.3)

Note: Years used are fiscal years.

aBase year: 1965 = 100.
bFigures in parentheses are annual percentage changes.

Source: David Greytak and Robert Dinkelmeyer, "The Components of Change in New York City's Non-Labor Costs—Fiscal Years 1965-1970: Supplies, Materials, Equipment and Contractural Services," Working Paper no. 13, Maxwell Research Project on the Public Finances of New York, 1972.

NOTES

1. This comparative analysis is carried out in considerably greater detail in Richard D. Gustely, "A Comparison of Changes in City Government Labor Costs Among the Ten Largest U.S. Cities: 1966-1971" (Internal Working Paper No. 11, Maxwell Research Project on the Public Finances of New York City, Syracuse University, Syracuse, N.Y., November 1972).

2. U.S. Department of Commerce, Bureau of the Census, City Government Finances (Washington, D.C.: U.S. Government Printing Office).

3. Comptroller of the City of New York, Annual Report (New York: Office of the Comptroller).

4. This correction is reported in more detail in Gustely, op. cit.

5. The theory of analysis of nonlabor expenditure increases is treated in some detail in David Greytak and Robert Dinkelmeyer, "The Components of Change in New York City's Non-labor Costs—Fiscal Years 1965-1970: Supplies, Materials, Equipment, and Contractual Services" (Internal Working Paper No. 13, Maxwell Research Project on the Public Finances of New York City, Syracuse University, Syracuse, N.Y., December 1972).

6. New York City Executive Budget and Supporting Schedules (New York: Office of the Mayor).

7. The material presented here draws heavily from a detailed analysis of direct labor costs for the Police, Fire, and Environmental Protection Departments, which is presented in Richard D. Gustely, "The Components of Changes in New York City Government Labor Costs—1965-1972: Police, Fire and Environmental Protection" (Internal Working Paper No. 4, Maxwell Research Project on the Public Finances of New York City, Syracuse University, Syracuse, New York, August 1972).

8. A list of representative occupations in each job category for all departments is included in Appendix to this chapter.

9. In terms of the model formulated in the preceding section,

$$\text{if} \quad L = E \cdot P \cdot W'$$

$$\text{then} \quad \Delta L = Z_1 \Delta E + Z_2 \Delta P + Z_3 \Delta W'$$

where ΔL, ΔE, ΔP, $\Delta W'$ are respectively the increase in direct labor cost, the increase in employment, the increase in price level, and the increase in real wages. The coefficients Z_1, Z_2, Z_3 are respectively $\frac{\hat{\Delta} L}{\Delta E}$, $\frac{\hat{\Delta} L}{\Delta P}$, $\frac{\hat{\Delta} L}{\Delta W'}$ and may be interpreted, for example, as showing the effect on direct labor costs of a one-unit change in employment, given that real wages and the price level have been held constant. The $\frac{\Delta L}{\Delta E}$ notation is used to denote estimated values (See preceeding section).

10. The material here draws heavily from two papers by Bernard Jump, "The Cost of Providing Retirement and Social Security Benefits in New York City: Trends, Causes, and Prospects, 1961-1972" and "The Cost of Providing Retirement and Social Security Benefits to New York City: Projections to 1980" (Internal Working Papers Nos. 9 and 10, Maxwell Research Project on the Public Finances of New York City, Syracuse University, Syracuse, N.Y., October 1972).

11. New York City Administrative Code, Sections B18-41.0 and B18-45.0

12. See Martin E. Segal and Company, Inc., The Retirement Systems of the City of New York (7 vols.; New York: Martin E. Segal, 1962-64), Part One, p. 151.

13. If $R = E \cdot P \cdot W' \cdot C$, then $\Delta R = r_1 \Delta E + r_2 \Delta P + r_3 \Delta W' + r_4 \Delta C$, where the r_1 show the marginal responsiveness of retirement costs to a unit change in the appropriate explanatory factor, for example, $r_1 = \frac{\Delta R}{\Delta E}$. It should be noted that r_2 and r_3 are derived from an estimate of the marginal responsiveness of total retirement costs to changes in money wage rates—that is, first the effects of increased wage rates are determined, and then the effect of inflation on wage rate levels is used to impute the effects of inflation (and therefore of real wage levels) on retirement cost increases. The exact methods used to estimate the coefficients are described above (See pp. 180).

14. These elasticities are defined analogously to those of equation (24)—that is, $^\eta E = \frac{r_1 E}{R}$, $^\eta P = \frac{r_2 P}{R}$, $^\eta W = \frac{r_3 W'}{R}$, and $^\eta C = \frac{r_4 C}{R}$. All other elasticities used in this model will be defined analogously to these.

15. The material used here draws heavily on Greytak and Dinkelmeyer, op. cit.

16. Specifically, $\Delta Q = g_1 \Delta E$, where ΔQ is the change in real deflated nonlabor expenditures. The coefficient (g), which measures change in the average real dollar worth of materials, equipment, supplies, and contractual services per employee, is estimated to be $716.

17. New York City Administrative Code, Sections B18-41.0 and B18-45.0.

18. See equation (25).

273

19. This equation is obtained from the estimation of the coefficients of equation (13a). For the Fire Department, which yields $\Delta N = 1\Delta Q + \$2,393,010\Delta P'$, the relationship between labor and nonlabor costs is assumed to be of the form $\Delta Q = g_1\Delta E$. Having estimated the value of g_1 as $\$1,285$, substitution for ΔQ in the above equation yields equation (35).

20. Each plan pays death and disability benefits as well as the basic retirement benefits. For further details of the NYCERS plans, see New York City Administrative Code, Sections B3-36.6, B3-38.0, B3-42.0, B3-36.2, B3-36.5, and B3-36.3.

21. This equation has been derived from equation (13a) and the substitution of $\Delta Q = g_1\Delta E$, where, in this case, g_1 was calculated to be $\$8,354$.

22. Board of Education Retirement System of the City of New York, Rules and Regulations: As amended to July 15, 1969, Sections 11-14.

23. The model as expressed in equation (53) was obtained after the substitution of $g_1\Delta E$ for ΔQ; g_1 has, in this case, been estimated to have the value $\$796$.

24. This estimate is based on records of the New York City Board of Higher Education.

25. Due to the unavailability of pension membership figures for higher education employees, the estimates of the coefficients given in equation (59) are based upon the assumption that all teachers in higher education are members of TRS and, therefore, the employment and average wage figures used for direct labor costs are applicable.

26. As in the other departments, implementation of the model required an estimate of g_1 in order to allow substitution of $\Delta Q = g_1\Delta E$ in equation (13). The estimated value of g_1 in this case is $\$3,074$.

27. The estimation of this model, as in the abovementioned nonlabor expenditure model, requires the estimation of g_1 in the equation $\Delta Q = g_1\Delta E$, and its substitution into the basic equation (13a). In this case, the estimated value of g_1 is $\$32,198$.

28. In disaggregated form, the appropriate equations are as follows:

$$\Delta L = Z_1\Delta E + Z_2\Delta P + Z_3\Delta W'$$

$$\Delta R = r_1\Delta E + r_2\Delta P + r_3\Delta W' + r_4\Delta C$$

$$\Delta N = n_1 g_1\Delta E + n_2\Delta P'$$

$$\Delta T = \Delta T$$

29. The tax-saving figures are based on the assumption that 20.4 percent of welfare expenditures and 59 percent of school expenditures are financed from local sources. The assumption for welfare was derived from average figures for New York State; the assumption for school expenditures was based on data derived from the State Comptroller's Annual Report.

4

EMPLOYMENT, REAL WAGE,
AND WORK LOAD INCREASES

The explanation of New York City's expenditure patterns in the preceding chapter is based on a partitioning of expenditure changes into an employment, a real wage, a price, and a pension contribution rate component. Since changes in these factors "drive" the model presented here, it is essential to understand the determinants of such changes. The subject of this chapter, therefore, is the real wage and the employment components of expenditure increases, with the focus being on workload changes as a major determinant. There are clearly other such determinants to be studied—for example, price-level changes, which are mostly determined by exogenous factors, and the collective bargaining process, which surely plays a role in determining the real wage, pension contribution, and price effects (since cost-of-living wage increases are included in the price effect)—but these are beyond the scope of this research.

It should be emphasized at the outset that the subject here is public employee workload, and not public employee productivity. While the latter subject is clearly of more interest, the measurement of productivity in the public sector has long defied scholars and practitioners alike. The current state of the art is simply put—in the case of most public functions, output cannot be measured. This analysis will not attempt even marginally to extend this literature.[1]

The research question here is cast in terms of inputs. Specifically, the question is whether the increase in employee workload is somehow commensurate with the increase in the level of employment and real labor cost. In the absence of output measures, this information still does not allow statements about whether labor cost increments are somehow economically efficient. It does, however, provide some objective information on the increase in work activity over a given period and in that respect, gives some crude basis for the judgment about whether labor and employment increases were warranted. Moreover, a study of historical workload changes may give some hint as to the pattern of demands of workers for wage rate increases and the numbers of new employees needed to maintain constant workloads. In fact, the analytical framework below is cast in exactly these terms.

The specific purpose of this chapter is to link changes in city government employment and changes in the average real wages of New York City government employees to changes in employee workload. Regrettably, the linkage is not made in precise terms—there is no systematic model such as that developed in the preceding chapter. The relationship established here is simply a comparison of relative increases in workload as opposed to total payments or number of employees. It should be emphasized again that no attempt is made to define or measure output, and therefore no direct evidence on employee productivity will be presented. Inferences based on this work should be tempered accordingly.

It is important to emphasize the nature of the measure of labor cost employed in this study—that is, in order to compare labor cost with measures of workload and employment, it is necessary to use a per-employee labor cost measure. In a statistical sense, average labor costs represent the wages of an average employee. As an average, its level and behavior over time are influenced by a number of factors. The effects of one factor affecting all monetary variables in the system—inflation—has been estimated by the use of real rather than nominal average wage costs. The effects of other factors influencing the level and behavior of average real wage rates remain. In particular, no attempt has been made to correct for the effects that shifts in the mix of employees between high and lower grade or wage levels may have had on departmental average wage costs. Thus, it is possible for average wage rates in any department to have increased slowly (rapidly), even though the wage rate received by all employees increased rapidly (slowly), if there has been a relatively rapid increase in the number of employees at the lower (higher) grade and wage levels. While, from the point of view of wage policy, the levels and changes in in-grade wage rates are of great importance, for the purpose at hand, labor cost and average wages are the measures of principal interest.

In the remainder of this chapter, each city government function will be discussed in this context. First, the types of activities that are performed within each department and the various methods of, and problems associated with, measuring these activities will be discussed. Second, the workload indexes selected for comparison will be examined in time series to determine the trend of workload over the period. These trends will be further compared with trends in the composition of city population in the hope of identifying—in broad terms—the reasons behind such workload increases. Finally, the composition and growth in average real wages and employment will be reviewed and compared to the trends in workload per employee.

Before proceeding, additional cautions are in order about what these data show and the limitations inherent in the analysis. The contention that workload changes may be interpreted as being related to real wage and employment changes is based upon two assumptions: the existence of an equilibrium position in the base period of the comparison and the absence of any disturbances (on employment and real wages) other than changes in workload. The first condition above might not be met, if previous workload increases had not been compensated for at the beginning of the initial period—that is to say, the catch-up problem. The second might not be met, if, over the period in question, there were changes in the production function that affected the quantitative workload comparisons. An example of the latter would be extensive substitution of capital for labor, which would make work measures per employee appear to be increasing. While both these assumptions do cast doubt on the success and usefulness of a strict comparison of workload changes with changes in real wages and employment, they are not so serious that such a comparison cannot still provide general insight into one of the factors that influence wage and employment determination. Nevertheless, the material below in no way analyzes the productivity-wage rate problem of the city, and, consequently, the focus is on presenting empirical results derived and not on interpretation or analysis.

NEW YORK CITY POLICE DEPARTMENT

Workload Measurement Problems[2]

The New York City Police Department (hereafter referred to as the NYPD) presents one of the more difficult problems in measuring the activities of the city government. Its activities cover a wide range, including crime prevention, investigation, and solution, and a variety of other public safety functions. However, of the measures available, some would seem more representative of these day-to-day activities than others. For example, the assumption that net crime cases represent investigated cases allows an approximation of what is undoubtedly a major daily activity of the NYPD. On the other hand, the number of arrests made or cases cleared (those considered "solved" by the NYPD without regard to court disposition of the case) are representative of a less frequent, though equally important, activity. Several such measures will be considered here in the aggregate (whenever possible, over the 1960-70 decade) as representative of major measurable NYPD activities.

One set of measures used to represent work activities is related to the major crime categories used by the NYPD. The major class of crime is felonies, which are defined to include most crimes against the person, such as murder, rape, and assault, as well as drug selling, robbery, and burglary. Misdemeanors and violations include less serious crimes, such as prostitution, liquor law offenses, disorderly conduct, possession of dangerous drugs, and lesser degrees of some felonies. A third category, offenses not required in the (New York State) report (which will be referred to here as offenses), includes unlicensed peddling, loitering, and administrative code violations, such as unnecessary noise, uncovered rifles, and street obstruction at building sites.

All criminal cases are investigated to some degree; police are dispatched to the scene of crimes called in, and reports are filed for all cases. Therefore, the number of net cases (as opposed to reported cases, which may include incorrect or false reports) is used here as an indicator of investigative activity. Arrests and summonses and "cleared cases" for the three crime categories will also be considered as further measures of work performed in crime-related functions.

Before presenting the empirical data on changes in the amount of crimes in New York City, it should be noted that the crime reporting system was modified in a manner that precludes accurate comparison of crime statistics before and after 1966, except for the category of offenses. The revision in the reporting system was a requirement that all crimes be reported and that all reports be listed under the proper crime category. Before 1966, it was alleged to be customary for precincts to omit reports of some crimes or to downgrade the seriousness of some crimes in their reports to Police Headquarters.[3] This revision caused a huge increase in the number of felonies reported in 1966 over 1965 and a (smaller) increase in the number of misdemeanors and violations reported, while offenses decreased somewhat. Thus, a comparable 10-year trend in crimes reported and investigated cannot be constructed.

Aggregate Workload Measures

While all of these problems should cause hesitance in directly inferring policy from these results, it still would seem useful to examine available workload trends. The trends examined here include

TABLE 4.1

NYPD Workload Measures: Net Crime Cases, 1960-70

Year	Felonies	Misdemeanors and Violations	Offenses
1970	489,137	535,354	239,037
1969	434,066	535,507	99,324
1968	416,771	527,603	65,378
1967	371,672	426,941	50,838
1966	304,156	382,455	53,185
Percent change	61	39	349
1965	166,075	338,693	57,474
1964	150,690	319,761	55,394
1963	133,793	299,709	62,376
1962	122,141	281,636	69,662
1961	113,340	257,416	59,738
1960	108,491	248,746	53,591
Percent change	53	36	7

Source: City of New York Police Department, Annual Reports, 1960-70 (New York: City of New York Police Department).

the categories of crime cases, crime cases cleared, arrests and summonses, patrol duty, and emergency services.

Table 4.1 shows the growth in net cases between 1960 and 1970 for felonies, misdemeanors and violations, and offenses. The data show that net felony cases increased by 53 percent between 1960 and 1965 and by 61 percent between 1966 and 1970. Misdemeanors and violations more than doubled over the decade, and the pattern of arrests for offenses is erratic, though there were sharp increases in the late 1960s.

From these data, it seems clear that the volume of NYPD activity has increased substantially over the 10-year period. The reasons for such an increase are many, and those that are known are difficult to quantify. Still, it is possible to standardize (or at least compare) increased crime rates, for example, for changes in the city population. Table 4.2 presents the abovementioned workload measures corrected for population change. As indicated there, all measures of police work activity increased more rapidly than population.

TABLE 4.2

Selected NYPD Workload Indicators
per 10,000 Population, 1966 and 1970*

	1966	1970	Percent Change
Net felony cases	386	620	60
Net misdemeanor and violation cases	486	678	40
Net offense cases	68	303	346
Emergencies	35	59	69
Personal injury vehicle accidents	48	61	27

*Estimates of population of the trend between 1960 and 1970

Source: City of New York Police Department, Annual Reports, 1966 and 1970 (New York: City of New York Police Department).

Cases cleared, as noted earlier, are those that have been changed from an "unsolved" to a "solved" basis, usually by arrest or summons. Since one of the major functions of a police department employee is to clear cases, these might be considered another measure of workload. Table 4.3, therefore, presents measures of cases cleared for each of the crime categories for the city as a whole. The pattern is one of acceleration in work activity during the decade—whether this is due to changes in the amount of work performed or changes in the reporting system cannot be determined from these data.

The third crime-related workload measure examined here is numbers of arrests and summonses. Though it is connected to the cases-cleared measure because an arrest or summons often leads to a clearance, there is not a one-to-one relationship. One arrest might cause several cases to be cleared because of multiple offenses on the part of one individual; on the other hand, several arrests might only clear one case in instances of group crime. Table 4.4 presents data on arrests and summonses in each of the crime categories for the 1960-70 period, and, again, a pattern of increase is evident. (Although there is no arrest category comparable to the offense category, there is a category of arrests and summonses for violations, offenses, and traffic infractions, including parking violations, and in this group, arrests and summonses rose by only 30 percent and 4 percent, respectively.)

TABLE 4.3

NYPD Workload Measures:
Crime Cases Cleared, 1960-70

Year	Felonies	Misdemeanors and Violations	Offenses
1970	115,348	272,998	140,348
1969	105,943	264,732	95,991
1968	91,910	232,091	63,141
1967	71,900	184,946	50,733
1966	54,308	166,942	53,032
Percent change	112	64	165
1965	57,221	180,005	57,448
1964	51,151	171,481	55,373
1963	46,719	162,221	62,365
1962	43,339	153,482	69,610
1961	40,065	138,203	59,704
1960	37,469	134,239	53,523
Percent change	53	34	7

Source: City of New York Police Department, Annual Reports, 1960-70 (New York: City of New York Police Department).

Another crime-related measure representative of NYPD workload would be prevention, or crimes not committed. Unfortunately, there is no way of measuring, or even approximating, this activity. However, it might be assumed that one major deterrent of crime is patrol duty, and, therefore, changes in patrol exposure hours may be somewhat representative of changes in workload related to crime prevention. The number of man-hours of patrol exposure (the number of men on patrol multiplied by the number of patrol hours) has increased by 26 percent over the 1964-70 period. (See Table 4.5.) Still, it cannot be argued that crime prevention has necessarily increased by a like amount, since some of this increase can be attributed to a switch to two-man patrol cars.

Noncrime functions also constitute part of police employee workload. A wide range of services are performed, including licensing (for example, of taxicabs, taxi drivers, firearms), marine and aviation unit services, identification of missing persons, emergency

TABLE 4.4

NYPD Workload Measures:
Arrests and Summonses, 1960-70

Year	Felonies	Misdemeanors and Violations	Violations Offenses and Traffic Infractions
1970	94,024	259,654	3,187,227
1969	75,044	237,897	3,162,037
1968	63,566	189,568	2,785,420
1967	62,289	143,387	3,095,132
1966	58,026	131,891	3,053,541
Percent change	62	96	4
1965	54,868	139,790	2,897,282
1964	52,526	132,940	2,659,874
1963	45,837	122,336	2,556,146
1962	41,950	111,406	2,528,002
1961	38,211	99,738	2,313,575
1960	35,629	99,772	2,226,810
Percent change	53	40	30

Source: City of New York Police Department, Annual Reports, 1960-70 (New York: City of New York Police Department).

services, and traffic safety services. Of these, emergency services rendered and motor vehicle accidents involving personal injury are examined below as representative of noncrime police functions.

Emergency services cover a wide range of occurrences, including asphyxia cases, accidents (other than motor vehicle), removal of persons locked in vaults and buildings, suicide attempts, dangerous physical conditions, and services rendered to the Fire Department and other departments. As indicated in Table 4.6, the number of cases of emergency service rendered increased 73 percent between 1960 and 1970.

Personal injury vehicle accidents might be considered as representative of the traffic-related functions of the NYPD. In reality they probably only constitute a small portion when traffic control functions,

TABLE 4.5

NYPD Workload Measures: Patrol Duty, 1964-70

Year	Man-hours of Exposure
1970	73,941,613
1969	73,447,054*
1968	70,196,177
1967	63,761,881
1966	61,510,285
1965	61,245,877
1964	58,636,901
Percent change	26

*This figure does not include overtime.

Source: City of New York Police Department, Annual Reports, 1964-70 (New York: City of New York Police Department).

TABLE 4.6

NYPD Noncrime Workload Measures, 1960-70

Year	Emergency Services	Motor Vehicle Accidents Involving Personal Injury or Death
1970	46,417	48,254
1969	35,443	49,409
1968	39,884	49,519
1967	42,563	46,237
1966	38,137	45,307
1965	34,122	42,302
1964	26,976	42,239
1963	28,220	39,721
1962	29,499	38,569
1961	26,636	35,487
1960	26,869	37,472
Percent change	73	29

Source: City of New York Police Department, Annual Reports, 1960-70 (New York: City of New York Police Department).

accidents involving property damage,* and the enforcement of traffic and parking laws are taken into consideration. As shown in Table 4.6, accidents involving personal injury increased 29 percent between 1960 and 1970, from 37,472 to 48,254.

No systematic attempt is made in this study to explain these aggregate workload changes. One possible cause—an increase in population size—must be ruled out because of the approximate constancy of the city population from 1960 to 1970. (See also Table 4.2.) The causal factors, therefore, must lie within the changed composition of the city's population.

It seems obvious from the numerous activity measures discussed above that aggregate workload has increased for the entire NYPD over the 1960-70 period. It is not clear from this discussion, however, that aggregate workload increased at a faster rate than the employment of the department. To investigate the relationship between workload and employment increase, these activity measures are examined on a per-employee basis for the years 1965 and 1971. Before beginning this examination, a few points should be made regarding what these per-employee ratios actually represent. The first is whether the denominator of the per-employee ratio should be total employment or some component—for example, uniformed employment. While it is obvious that supportive personnel (clerical, labor, and administrative) are not directly engaged in such activities as making arrests and providing emergency services, their presence clearly affects the level of work performed by those members directly engaged in a given activity. Even if finer breakdowns of employees were used in calculating workload figures, the information would not be truly reflective of actual activities. All patrolmen, for example, do not perform equal amounts of work. Crime levels and emergencies are determined to some extent by areas of the city; patrolmen in high-crime areas undoubtedly do more work than those in low-crime areas. In addition to this inequality, it must be recognized that the same categories of incidents are not necessarily similar in the amount or quality of work involved—that is to say, an arrest of a murder suspect may be quite different from the arrest of a shoplifter, for example, on the basis of hazard, if nothing else. Again, the amount of time spent investigating and clearing serious crimes may be much greater than that for lesser crimes.

The workload-per-employee figures do not allow even a guess at how the types of workload are distributed or whether, in fact,

---

*Police are far more likely to be called to the scene of an accident involving personal injury than one involving property damage.

people with equal workloads are performing equal amounts of work. Nor can it be assumed that the average figure derived here is really representative of the amount of work done by those actually in a position to perform the specific tasks. Still, due to the lack of adequate disaggregate data, total NYPD employment is used as a basis for determining per-employee workload.

NYPD employment data for the 1965-71 period are used in estimating workloads per employee.* However, crime statistics are not available on a comparable basis for this period, and so approximations were required. (As noted above, changes in crime reporting systems made in 1966 make crime data before and after that date incomparable.) For those categories not affected by the changed reporting system, the growth between 1960 and 1970 was used to calculate 1971 figures, and actual 1965 data were used. For the remaining categories, the procedure used was to calculate annual growth rates on the basis of 1966-70 data and to extrapolate these rates to estimate the 1965 and 1971 statistics.

The data in Table 4.7 show that all classes of work activity per employee (except those directly related to motor vehicles) rose over the six-year period. In general, except in the offenses category, the increases seem heaviest in the serious crime categories. The three crime categories combined (that is, total crimes) showed a 61 percent increase in investigative workload per employee, from 23.79 percent in 1965 to 36.18 percent in 1971. (Note again that a major portion of the increase for net offenses can be attributed to 1970, when offenses increased 141 percent over 1969.)

Although these data provide only fragmentary evidence, the conclusion to be drawn is that total police work activity increased faster than Police Department employment. Attention is now turned to a comparison of the per-employee workload (or activity) increases and average real wage increases.

Workload, Employment, and Real Wage Growth

It was argued above that employee workload is related to potential city government discretionary actions with respect to labor costs in two ways. First, if average workload is growing, it may be desirable to increase total employment in order to slow this

---

*Budgeted NYPD positions have been used for 1965 and 1971. Actual positions might be lower than these figures and, to the extent this is true, the workload per man used in this report may be somewhat understated.

TABLE 4.7

Selected NYPD Workload Indicators per Employee, 1965 and 1971

Year	Net Felonies	Net Misdemeanors and Violations	Net Offenses	Serious Crimes	Total Crimes
1971	14.11	14.91	7.16	29.02	36.18
1965	9.63	12.54	1.62	22.17	23.79
Percent change	47	19	342	31	52

Year	Summonses: Serious Crimes	Arrests and Summonses: Violations, Offenses, Traffic Infractions	Cases Cleared: Serious Crimes	Emergency Services	Personal Injury Motor Vehicle Accidents
1971	9.98	84.61	11.45	1.33	1.27
1965	6.94	103.24	6.85	1.26	1.51
Percent change	44	-18	67	6	-16

Source: City of New York Police Department, Annual Reports, 1965 and 1971 (New York: City of New York Police Department).

287

growth. Alternatively, if average workload declines, an argument might be made to reduce total employment. Second, if average workload is growing, it may result in the granting of compensating increases in real wage rates (that is, wages corrected for inflation). On the other hand, decreases in average workload might cause employers to demand cuts in real wages. Obviously, these arguments are based upon the assumptions that average workload is measurable and that it was initially at some "proper" level.

(It is necessary to note here that the direction of causation in the relationships described above is from workload to employment and/or real wages. There is a possibility of a reverse relationship. Specifically, workload increases may result from an agreement between labor and management for higher wages. Similarly, workload increases might result from conscious efforts on the part of management to reduce the amount of employment. Because of these possibilities, the comparisons that follow should only be viewed as indicating a general trend rather than a strict relationship.)

In order to compare growth in aggregate employment as well as department-wide average real wages with workload,* it is necessary to use measures of workload that apply to the NYPD as a whole. In this instance, measures of net crimes, net serious crimes, arrests and summonses on serious crimes, and cases of serious crimes cleared per employee were used. This emphasis on serious crimes (felonies, misdemeanors, and violations) reflects a belief that these offenses require more time for investigation and solution than, for example, traffic violations and, therefore, are a better indication of departmental workload than other less serious crimes.

Table 4.8 presents the average annual growth in the per-employee workload measures, in employment and in real wages. Although we must recognize the limitations in the data, these results still point to two general conclusions. First, when employment growth is adjusted for average workload increases, it is clear that the average workload of the NYPD is increasing at a rate in excess of the increase in employment. Stated differently, the real employment growth of the NYPD (employment growth corrected for increases in workload) has been greater than 3.1 percent. Secondly, the growth in workload has been greater than growth in real wages—that is, on the average, NYPD employee workloads have increased more rapidly than have NYPD labor costs—that is, average real wages.

---

*Appendix Tables 4.A.1-4.A.3 show the structure and growth of real wages and employment between 1965 and 1972 for the NYPD.

TABLE 4.8

NYPD: Average Annual Growth Rates
in Selected Workload Measures, Employment,
and Real Wages
(as percent)

	Workload	Employment	Real Wage
Net crimes per employee*	8.3	—	—
Net serious crimes per employee	4.6	—	—
Arrests and summonses on serious crimes per employee	6.3	—	—
Cases cleared on serious crimes per employee	8.9	—	—
Total employment	—	3.1	
Average real wages	—	—	2.1

*Includes felonies, misdemeanors, and violations.

Sources: City of New York Police Department, Annual Reports, 1960-70 (New York: City of New York Police Department); and New York City Executive Budget and Supporting Schedules, 1965-66 and 1972-73 (New York: Office of the Mayor, March 1965 and March 1972).

FIRE DEPARTMENT

Workload Measurement Problems

The Fire Department is engaged in a variety of activities, foremost among which, of course, is fighting fires. In addition to actual fires, the department responds to a significant number of false alarms, and, although this cannot be considered as an intended function of the department, it cannot be disregarded when considering activities of employees. The Fire Department also responds to emergency situations where there are potential dangers of fire or explosion and to other emergencies that it has the expertise to handle, such as smoke and odor conditions, water leaks and floods, collapses and cave-ins, and first-aid needs. In addition, the department is engaged in fire prevention activities, such as the inspection of public buildings and places where hazardous materials are stored, as well as the issuing of permits for the handling, storage, or sale of hazardous materials. A final function involves crime combating, in so far as the Fire Department investigates fires of suspicious origin and in some cases makes arrests.

Though it is obvious that there is considerable diversity among the activities of the New York Fire Department, quantification of these activities seems relatively straightforward. Three measures will be used here as indicators of changing workloads in the Fire Department, both in the aggregate and on a per-employee basis. These are (1) the number of actual fires, (2) the number of false alarms, and (3) the number of emergencies responded to. These measures have been selected because they appear to represent the basic activities that would generally be carried out on a daily basis by Fire Department personnel.

Aggregate Workload Measures

Table 4.9 presents the historical trend of workload, measured in terms of these three activities, and shows a trend of marked increase. The same pattern is shown in Table 4.10, where these figures are corrected for changes in population size. The same data, computed on a per-employee basis (See Table 4.11), also depict a rapid workload increase. Again, it should be noted that the workloads discussed are averages and that the number of employees includes nonuniformed personnel who are never actually involved in fighting fires—though these employees no doubt contributed to the effectiveness of uniformed personnel. Therefore, these may be understatements of the true workload of those employees in a position to perform the services described. The averages may also misrepresent individual workloads because some areas of the city may have a higher incidence of fires or emergencies than others. Likewise, the dangers involved in the firefighting occupation are not reflected in these measures.

Workload, Employment, and Real Wage Growth

The comparison of aggregate employment growth, as well as average real wage growth, with growth in employee workload requires

TABLE 4.9

Fire Department: Measures of Total Workload, 1960-71

Year	Fires	False Alarms	Emergencies
1971	124,876	104,958	49,536
1970	127,249	88,407	45,999
1969	126,204	72,060	41,054
1968	127,826	60,945	39,249
1967	91,161	48,106	33,231
1966	90,290	37,414	27,084
1965	85,592	32,814	24,305
1964	79,477	26,759	22,173
1963	74,680	21,961	20,836
1962	69,991	20,279	18,719
1961	61,644	18,530	17,509
1960	60,941	N.A.[a]	16,868
Percent change	105	466[b]	194

[a]N.A.: not available.
[b]1961-71.

Source: City of New York Fire Department, Annual Reports, 1960-71 (New York: City of New York Fire Department).

TABLE 4.10

Selected Fire Department Workload Indicators
per 10,000 Population, 1960 and 1970

Year*	Fires	Emergencies
1970	158	63
1960	78	22
Percent change	103	186

*Estimates of population for noncensus years are based on an extrapolation of the trend between 1960 and 1970.

Source: City of New York Fire Department, Annual Reports, 1960 and 1970 (New York: City of New York Fire Department).

TABLE 4.11

Fire Department: Measures of Workload per Employee,
1965 and 1971

Year	Fires	False Alarms	Emergencies
1971	791	665	314
1965	612	235	174
Percent change	29	183	81

Source: City of New York Fire Department, Annual Reports, 1965 and 1971 (New York: City of New York Fire Department).

TABLE 4.12

Fire Department: Average Annual Growth Rates
in Selected Workload Measures, Employment,
and Real Wages
(as percent)

	Workload	Employment	Real Wage
Total alarm responses per employee	9.7	—	—
Total fire responses per employee	4.4	—	—
Total emergency responses per employee	10.3	—	—
Total false alarm responses per employee	19.0	—	—
Total employment	—	0.7	—
Average real wages	—	—	3.7

Source: City of New York Fire Department, Annual Reports,
1960-71 (New York: City of New York Fire Department); New York
City Executive Budget and Supporting Schedules, 1965-66 and 1972-73
(New York: Office of the Mayor, March 1965 and March 1972).

measures that reflect the activities of the entire department.* Therefore, the indexes shown in Table 4.12 relate to most Fire Department
activities, with the notable exception of inspections. These indexes
include total fire responses, total emergency responses, total false
alarm responses, and total alarm (fires plus emergencies plus false
alarms) responses. The data presented in this table allow a comparison of real wage, employment, and workload growth.

In sum, the results reinforce the findings for the NYPD, indicating two important conclusions. First, real employment (adjusted
for workload changes) increased substantially more than the increase
in aggregate employment. Secondly, average real wages increased

_____

*Appendix Tables 4.A.1-4.A.3 show the structure and growth
of real wages and employment between 1965 and 1972 for the Fire
Department.

less rapidly than workload, although only slightly less rapidly than the average annual growth in reported fires in the city.

ENVIRONMENTAL PROTECTION ADMINISTRATION

Workload Measurement Problems[4]

No single measure of activity is representative of all the varying types of sanitation* services performed, which include refuse collection and disposal, street cleaning, removal of abandoned vehicles, and snow removal. To make workload measurement even more difficult, some of these activities are performed in more than one way—for example, street cleaning is done manually, by sweeper trucks, and by flusher trucks. Other measurement difficulties arise because more than one kind of measure may be applied to a particular sanitation-work activity. Refuse collection, for example, can be measured in terms of truckloads or truck shifts or in terms of tons of refuse collected. The trends in workloads related to winter activities pose a different set of problems—that is, the level of snow-removal, plowing, and salt-spreading activity is at least partly dependent on the weather conditions of a given year.

For the purposes here, some general measures of workload are needed to represent the trend in departmental activity over the past decade. Both truck shifts and tons collected will be used as measures of refuse collection and disposal activities; flusher shifts and (power) broom shifts and miles swept will be used as indicators of street-cleaning activities; and equipment shifts (of combined trucks and salt spreaders) as well as tons of salt spread and miles of street salted will be used as snow and ice removal activity measures.

Aggregate Workload Measures

Workload measures for EPA are shown in Table 4.13. As indicated, there were increases in all categories of EPA work activity. The same pattern is found when changes in workload of the department are related to city population changes. (See Table 4.14.) It is interesting to note that the 30 percent increase in tons of refuse

---

*The changing activities of the Environmental Protection Agency (EPA) will be discussed here with sole reference to Department of Sanitation activities.

TABLE 4.13

EPA: Measures of Total Workload, 1960-61/1969-70

Year	Refuse Collection Truck Shifts	Street Cleaning Flusher Shifts	Street Cleaning Broom Shifts	Snow and Ice Removal: Equipment Shifts
1969-70	448,198	6,736	63,312	8,408
1968-69	427,294	5,893	64,256	6,947
1967-68	428,839	11,783	69,450	3,923
1966-67	414,735	15,398	65,075	6,458
1965-66	410,156	14,118	72,060	3,575
1964-65	404,962	19,107	70,620	4,419
1963-64	401,584	20,812	69,906	5,109
1962-63	390,444	26,836	68,776	4,423
1961-62	390,739	28,737	65,402	4,208
1960-61	376,738	29,666	57,573	5,269
Percent change	19	-77	10	60

Source: New York City Department of Sanitation, Annual Progress Report and Statistical Review, 1960-71 (New York: N.Y.C. Department of Sanitation).

TABLE 4.14

Selected EPA Workload Indicators per 10,000 Population, 1960-61 and 1969-70

Year	Tons of Refuse	Tons of Salt Spread
1969-70	4,621	188
1960-61	3,544	93
Percent change	30	102

Source: New York City Department of Sanitation, Annual Progress Report and Statistical Review, 1960-71 (New York: N.Y.C. Department of Sanitation).

TABLE 4.15

EPA: Average Annual Growth Rates
in Selected Workload Measures, Employment,
and Real Wages
(as percent)

	Workload	Employment	Real Wage
Tons of refuse collected per employee	1.6	—	—
Miles of street swept per employee	1.5	—	—
Miles of street salted per employee	0.5	—	—
Tons of refuse incinerated per employee	0.9	—	—
Total employment	—	1.3	—
Average real wages	—	—	2.6

Sources: New York City Department of Sanitation, Annual Progress Report and Statistical Review, 1960-71 (New York: Department of Sanitation); and New York City Executive Budget and Supporting Schedules 1965-66 and 1972-73 (New York: Office of the Mayor, March 1965 and March 1972).

collected per 10,000 population was accompanied by an increase of only 18 percent in truck shifts for refuse collection. Similarly, tons of salt spread per 10,000 population showed a 102 percent increase over 1960-61, although snow and ice removal equipment shifts only increased by 60 percent.

Workload, Employment, and Real Wage Growth

A comparison of real wage and employment growth* with the measures of workload for the EPA are shown in Table 4.15. The

---

*Appendix Tables 4.A.1-4.A.3 show the structure and growth of real wages and employment between 1965 and 1972 for the EPA.

measures used include tons of refuse collected, miles of street swept, miles of street salted, and tons of refuse incinerated. In terms of scope, the most labor-intensive activity of these is refuse collection. As a result, this index would appear to reflect a larger amount of departmental activity than the other measures.

Although we must recognize their limitations, the data in Table 4.15 still suggest two important conclusions. First, growth in real employment (after adjustment for changes in workload) was greater than the 1.3 percent yearly average increase in aggregate employment. Second, real wages increased slightly more rapidly than any of the measures of average workload investigated. These conclusions can be contrasted to those for police and fire, where workload increased more rapidly than either employment or real wages.

BOARD OF HIGHER EDUCATION

Workload Measurement Problems

Measuring workloads for higher education is perhaps even more difficult than for police, fire, or sanitation because of the particular intricacies involved in defining the "outputs." The following discussion will explore the problems involved and discuss workloads in the aggregate and on a per-employee basis.

The difficulty in defining workloads for higher education is that most measures that can be generalized oversimplify the actual work performed. In higher education, teaching staffs are allocated to subject areas. An overall workload figure implies that teaching one subject is the same as teaching any other subject, which is probably not true as far as effort on the part of the instructor is concerned. Using the average number of students per instructor as an indicator presents a problem in that it probably overstates the number of pupils some instructors teach and understates the number for others. While this is true for any average, it is particularly applicable here because enrollment in higher education classes can vary tremendously. There may be large numbers of students in required classes and only a handful in advanced courses in some subjects.

Another problem in measuring workload is in deciding how to define what it is. Is it the number of students in a class, or what the students are taught? It is obviously difficult to try to measure what was taught by measuring what was learned (in terms of test scores, for example) because of the many other factors that influence the learning process (such as parents' influence and pressure from peers). In addition to teaching, many instructors engage in activities that are not readily quantifiable in terms of workload (for example, academic adviser, committee member).

Notwithstanding these problems, general measures of workload will be used here as crude indicators of workload trends in higher education from 1964 to 1971. In addition, per-employee workloads will be calculated on the basis of all employees, as in earlier sections of this chapter. The measures to be used will be total enrollment, pupils per employee, total graduates, and graduates per employee. Enrollment figures are felt to be representative of amounts of workload as measured by pupil contact, while the number of graduates measures amounts of workload in teaching—that is, graduation implies the successful teaching of a particular program of study.

Aggregate Workload Measures

The workload measures discussed above are presented in Table 4.16. As shown there, the number of enrolled students rose by 70 percent between 1964 and 1971, while, over the same time period, the number of graduates increased 99 percent. Even after correcting for population changes, the number of students enrolled per 10,000 population increased 70 percent between 1964 and 1971, and the number of graduates per 10,000 population increased 100 percent over the same period. (See Table 4.17.)

The growth in workload, however, did not keep pace with the growth in departmental employment. The number of students per

TABLE 4.16

Higher Education Workload Measures, 1964 and 1971

Year	Number of Students Enrolled	Number of Graduates	Year	Number of Students per Employee	Number of Graduates per Employee
1971	207,631	24,933	1971	12.13	1.46
1964	121,857	12,556	1965	20.04	2.11
Percent change	70	99		-39	-31

Source: Unpublished data from the New York State Department of Education.

297

TABLE 4.17

Selected Higher Education
Workload Indicators per 10,000 Population,
1964 and 1971

Year	Number of Students Enrolled per 10,000 Population	Number of Graduates per 10,000 Population
1971	263	32
1964	155	16
Percent change	70	100

Source: Unpublished data from the New York State Department of Education.

TABLE 4.18

Higher Education: Average Annual Growth Rates
in Selected Workload Measures, Employment,
and Real Wages
(as percent)

	Workload	Employment	Real Wage
Total enrollment per employee	-6.9	—	—
Total graduation per employee	-4.4	—	—
Total employment	—	14.7	—
Average real wages	—	—	2.0

Sources: Unpublished data from the New York State Department of Education; New York City Executive Budget and Supporting Schedules, 1965-66 and 1972-73 (New York: Office of the Mayor, March 1965 and March 1972).

employee fell by 39 percent between 1964 and 1971, while, over the same period, the number of graduates per employee fell by 31 percent. (See Table 4.16.)

Workload, Employment, and Real Wage Growth

A comparison of growth in workload with that of employment and real wages* is shown in Table 4.18. Even though we take into account the limitations inherent in the data, these results still indicate that, while workload decreased over the period, both employment and real wages increased. Specifically, while average workload decreased by 4.4 percent to 6.9 percent, employment increased in excess of 14 percent and real wages by 2 percent.

PUBLIC SCHOOLS

Workload Measurement Problems

Many of the problems encountered in measuring public school workloads are similar to those that have already been discussed in the section of higher education. Due to data unavailability, student enrollment is used as the basic unit of workload measurement for public schools. However, there is probably a more even distribution of pupils among teachers in public schools than is the case for higher education because there are fewer specialized subjects. Therefore, average workload figures based on enrollments are probably more representative in the case of public schools. Finally, high school graduates will also be used as a measure of teaching workload performed, though the above limitations also apply.

Aggregate Workload Measures

As indicated in Table 4.19, total enrollment increased by 15 percent between 1960 and 1971; however, between 1964-65 and 1970-71, diplomas granted fell by 14 percent. Roughly the same trend was registered in education workload per 10,000 population. (See Table 4.20.)

---

*Appendix Tables 4.A.1-4.A.3 show the structure and growth of real wages and employment between 1965 and 1972 for higher education.

TABLE 4.19

Public Schools Workload Measures, 1960-71

Fall	Total Enrollment	Year	Diplomas Granted
1971	1,138,442	1970-71	44,219
1970	1,132,071	1969-70	43,641
1969	1,141,873	1968-69	46,951
1968	1,109,877	1967-68	46,699
1967	1,095,957	1966-67	46,246
1966	1,077,845	1965-66	42,647
1965	1,060,054	1964-65	51,610
1964	1,054,201	—	—
1963	1,045,468	—	—
1962	1,027,380	—	—
1961	1,004,229	—	—
1960	986,697	—	—
Percent change	15	—	-14

Sources: Data on enrollment are derived from unpublished tables of the Bureau of Educational Data Systems, New York State Department of Education; data on diplomas are derived from New York City Board of Education, Report on Graduates, June 1965 through June 1971 (New York: N.Y.C. Board of Education).

TABLE 4.20

Public Schools Workload Indicators per 10,000 Population, 1960 and 1970

Year	School Enrollment per 10,000 Population	Year	Diplomas Granted per 10,000 Population
1970	1,434	1970-71	56
1960	1,268	1964-65	66
Percent change	13		-15

Note: Estimates of population for noncensus years are based on an extrapolation of the trend between 1960 and 1970.

Sources: Data on enrollment are derived from unpublished tables of the Bureau of Educational Data Systems, New York State Education Department; data on diplomas are derived from New York City Board of Education, Report on Graduates, June 1965 through June 1971 (New York: N.Y.C. Board of Education).

TABLE 4.21

Public Schools: Measures of Workload per Employee, 1965 and 1971

Year	Enrollment per Employee	Graduates per Employee
1971	14.30	0.56
1965	17.90	0.65
Percent change	-20	-14

Sources: Data on enrollment are derived from unpublished tables of the Bureau of Educational Data Systems, New York State Education Department; data on diplomas are derived from New York City Board of Education, Report on Graduates, June 1965 through June 1971 (New York: N.Y.C. Board of Education).

TABLE 4.22

Public Schools: Average Annual Growth Rates
in Selected Workload Measures, Employment,
and Real Wages
(as percent)

	Workload	Employment	Real Wage
Total enrollment per employee	-3.7	—	—
High school graduates per employee	-7.0	—	—
Total employment	—	4.6	—
Average real wages	—	—	1.2

Sources: Unpublished tables of the Bureau of Educational Data Systems, New York State Department of Education; New York City Board of Education, Report on Graduates, June 1965 through June 1971 (New York: N.Y.C. Board of Education); and New York City Executive Budget and Supporting Schedules, 1965-66 and 1972-73 (New York: Office of the Mayor, March 1965 and March 1972).

Per-employee workload measures are shown in Table 4.21. As indicated there, total enrollment per education employee fell by 20 percent between 1965 and 1971, while high school graduates per employee fell by 14 percent.

Workload, Employment, and Real Wage Growth

The measures that make possible a comparison of workload with employment-compensation* changes are included in Table 4.22. The comparison of these measures yields some interesting results. First, real employment (adjusted for the change in enrollment per employee) in public schools increased only slightly—the decrease in enrollment per employee being offset by a slightly larger increase in aggregate employment. However, when workload is measured

---

*Appendix Tables 4.A.1-4.A.3 show the structure and growth of real wages and employment between 1965 and 1972 for public schools.

301

by high school graduates, real employment as defined above actually declined. Second, a positive rate of growth in real wages (1.2 percent per year) still occured in spite of the actual decline in both workload measures.

SOCIAL SERVICES DEPARTMENT

Workload Measurement Problems

Defining the function of the Social Services Department itself is problematic, since it performs many different activities. The main one is obviously the dispensing of assistance (or "welfare"), generally in monetary form. There is also the function of guidance, counseling, or referrals to help the public assistance recipient with general problems or for the purpose of finding employment. In addition, there is a screening function, both in accepting new cases and in continuing cases already accepted. There is an implified function of making clients self-sufficient enough not to need public assistance. This listing of functions is not exhaustive of services performed by the department.

It is clear that these functions are difficult to measure, especially given the limitations of the data. It is even more difficult to generalize the workload measures to a per-employee basis. No two cases are alike; some may require large amounts of time and effort, others may require very little. Certain types of cases may need much more attention than others—aid to families with dependent children might need more specialized services, for more people, than aid to the elderly. There is no way to determine how the types of cases are divided among department employees.

Recognizing these difficulties, an attempt will still be made to discover general trends in workloads in the Social Services Department. The measures to be used, both in the aggregate and on a per-employee basis (where data permit), will be the monthly average number of cases (of all types), persons receiving public assistance in New York City from 1960 to 1971, and number of applications received and cases cleared from 1967 to 1971. The latter category is included because it may be assumed that extra work is involved in either screening new cases or closing current cases.

Aggregate Workload Measures

As indicated in Table 4.23, the average monthly number of cases (of all types) increased by 247 percent between 1960 and 1971, while

TABLE 4.23

Social Services Workload Measures, 1960-71

Year	Average Monthly Number of Cases	Average Monthly Number of Persons Receiving Assistance	Total Applications Received	Total Cases Cleared
1971	474,599	1,206,508	155,602	114,068
1970	418,842	1,095,031	140,950	113,835
1969	379,715	1,016,405	155,663	105,843
1968	326,083	889,261	127,838	77,573
1967	255,710	707,539	102,758	64,751
1966	205,574	568,115	—	—
1965	192,084	510,493	—	—
1964	173,684	454,168	—	—
1963	156,067	399,621	—	—
1962	147,697	363,542	—	—
1961	142,553	347,801	—	—
1960	136,902	325,771	—	—
Percent change	247	270	51	76

Source: For average monthly data, City of New York Department of Social Services, Monthly Statistical Report (New York: Department of Social Services, 1967-71; mimeographed); for other data, Statistical Supplement to Annual Report for 1970 (Albany, N.Y.: N.Y.S. Department of Social Services; mimeographed).

303

the average monthly number of clients increased by 270 percent. Further, there was a 51 percent increase in applications received between 1967 and 1971, and over the same time period, cases cleared increased by 76 percent. As presented in Table 4.24, both the average monthly number of cases per 10,000 population and the average monthly number of persons receiving assistance per 10,000 population increased by more than 200 percent.

Per-employee workload is presented in Table 4.25. Total department employees are used in calculating these figures because the supportive services of clerical, administrative, and other personnel affect the workload of delivery personnel (such as caseworkers and supervisors). (Employment data are available for 1965 and 1971 only.) As shown in Table 4.25, the average monthly number of cases per employee rose slightly between 1965 and 1971, while the average monthly number of clients per employee remained almost constant.

Workload, Employment, and Real Wage Growth

Table 4.26 presents the data relating to growth in workload, employment, and real wages for social services.* The measures of workload employed here were total cases served per employee and total persons served per employee. The results indicate that both employment and real wages increased more rapidly than workload.

At this point, it is helpful to note that a basic reason for the slow growth in workload in social services can be traced to the large growth in nondelivery employees (clerks and typists, especially). When workload is measured using social workers as a base, caseloads have increased substantially (as much as 40 percent).

HEALTH SERVICES ADMINISTRATION[5]

Workload Measurement Problems

There are many difficulties in analyzing the activities involved in public-sector provision of health and hospital care. Unfortunately, no data are available to enable the measurement of activities of the

---

*Appendix Tables 4.A.1-4.A.3 show the structure and growth of real wages and employment between 1965 and 1972 for social services.

TABLE 4.24

Selected Social Services Workload
Indicators per 10,000 Population, 1960 and 1970

Year	Average Monthly Number of Cases	Average Monthly Number of Persons Receiving Assistance
1970	531	1,387
1960	176	419
Percent change	202	231

Note: Estimates of population for non-census years are based on an extrapolation of the trend between 1960 and 1970.

Source: Derived from Statistical Supplement to Annual Report for 1970 (Albany, N.Y.: N.Y.S. Department of Social Services; mimeographed).

TABLE 4.25

Social Services: Measures of Workload per Employee, 1965 and 1971

Year	Average Monthly Number of Cases	Average Monthly Number of Persons Receiving Assistance
1971	13.85	35.22
1965	13.23	35.15
Percent change	5	0.2

Source: Derived from Statistical Supplement to Annual Report for 1970 (Albany, N.Y.: N.Y.S. Department of Social Services; mimeographed).

TABLE 4.26

Social Services: Average Annual Growth Rates
in Selected Workload Measures, Employment,
and Real Wages
(as percent)

	Workload	Employment	Real Wage
Total cases served per employee	0.8	—	—
Total persons served per employee	*	—	—
Total employment	—	11.5	—
Average real wages	—	—	1.8

*Less than 0.05 percent

Sources: Statistical Supplement to Annual Report for 1970 (Albany, N.Y.: N.Y.S. Department of Social Services; mimeographed); New York City Executive Budget and Supporting Schedules 1965-66 and 1972-73 (New York: Office of the Mayor, March 1965 and March 1972).

Health Services Administration, other than those directly related to hospitals.

Hospitals provide a variety of services in caring for their patients, including room and board services, laboratory tests, medication, surgery, rehabilitation, diagnoses, and therapy. Therefore, a single workload measure is not representative of the varied activities performed. In addition, all patients do not receive the same kinds and amounts of the different services. For these reasons, general measures will be used here to analyze the change in aggregate workload of the Health Services Administration. (Workload per employee cannot be calculated, as data pertaining to hospital employees only are not available.)

The measures to be considered as indicators of overall workload are the number of patient-days of care rendered, the number of outpatient and emergency room visits, and the number of laboratory tests performed (both inpatient and outpatient). Data for these measures are not available for the same years, but general trends may be assumed from the time periods available.

Aggregate Workload Measures

Table 4.27 presents workload measures for hospital employees. Patient days of care rendered for general hospital services (including medical-surgical, pediatrics, and maternity services) decreased 3 percent between 1966 and 1970, while emergency room and outpatient department visits increased 23 percent over the 10-year period from 1960-70. Laboratory tests administered, which relate to workloads performed by both the laboratory technicians and members of the medical staff, increased 57 percent between 1966 and 1970. As shown in Table 4.28, patient days of care per 10,000 population decreased between 1966 and 1970, while outpatient and emergency room visits per 10,000 population increased by 21 percent between 1960 and 1970.

In sum, workloads have increased in outpatient services but decreased in inpatient services as indicated by measures used here. Further, laboratory tests increased considerably for combined inpatients and outpatients between 1966 and 1970.

Workload, Employment, and Real Wage Growth

Because of data unavailability, the workload figures used in Table 4.29 are based upon the trend in outpatient visits and outpatient laboratory tests, while the employment and real wage figures pertain to the Health Services Administration. The assumption involved

306

TABLE 4.27

Health and Hospitals Corporation
Workload Measures, 1960-70

Year	Patient Days of Care	Outpatient and Emergency Room Visits	Laboratory Tests (Inpatient and Outpatient)
1970	2,544,973	4,555,000	20,083,177
1969	2,493,081	4,239,000	16,845,039
1968	2,552,902	4,273,000	15,629,512
1967	2,568,643	4,575,000	14,493,079
1966	2,624,605	4,900,000	12,803,416
1965	—	3,871,000	—
1964	—	4,573,000	—
1963	—	4,304,000	—
1962	—	4,005,000	—
1961	—	3,903,000	—
1960	—	3,715,000	—
Percent change	-3	23	57

Sources: For general care and laboratory test data, Hospital Statistics Service, "Statistical Profile, 1966-70" (New York: Health and Hospitals Corporation, no date; mimeographed); for outpatient and emergency room data, Hospital Statistics Service, "Hospital Statistical Data" (New York: Health and Hospitals Corporation, no date; mimeographed).

TABLE 4.28

Selected Health and Hospitals Corporation
Workload Indicators Per 10,000 Population,
1960, 1966, and 1970

Year	Patient Days of Care	Year	Outpatient and Emergency Room Visits
1970	3,224	1970	5,770
1966	3,332	1960	4,774
Percent change	-3		21

Note: Estimates of population for non-census years are based on an extrapolation of the trend between 1960 and 1970.

Sources: For care data, Hospital Statistics Service, "Statistical Profile, 1966-1970" (New York: Health and Hospitals Corporation, no date; mimeographed); for outpatient and emergency room data, Hospital Statistics Service, "Hospital Statistical Data" (New York: Health and Hospitals Corporation, no date; mimeographed).

307

TABLE 4.29

Health Services: Average Annual Growth Rates
in Selected Workload Measures, Employment,
and Real Wages
(as percent)

	Workload	Employment	Real Wage
Total outpatient visits per employee	−5.1	—	—
Total outpatient laboratory tests per employee	9.7	—	—
Total employment	—	2.3	—
Average real wages	—	—	1.7

Sources: Hospital Statistics Service, "Statistical Profile, 1966-1970" (New York: Health and Hospitals Corporation, no date; mimeographed); Hospital Statistics Service, Hospital Statistical Data (New York: Health and Hospitals Corporation, no date; mimeographed); New York City Executive Budget and Supporting Schedules, 1965-66 and 1972-73 (New York: Office of the Mayor, March 1965 and March 1972).

here is that the trend in outpatient visits to the Hospitals Corporation closely resembles the trend in visits to Health Services Administration clinics. Because of the nature of this assumption, these workload figures should be regarded as only rough approximations.

These data comparing growth in real wages and employment* with workload growth are shown in Table 4.29. Because of the disparity in the workload measures employed here, it is not possible to conclude with any degree of certainty whether real departmental employment rose or fell, or whether real wage increases represented compensation because or in spite of workload trends.

---

*Appendix Tables 4.A.1-4.A.3 show the structure and growth of real wages and employment between 1965 and 1972 for health services (excluding hospitals).

SUMMARY AND CONCLUSIONS

The purpose of this chapter has been to link (in a rough way) changes in employee workload to changes in aggregate employment and labor costs—that is, real wages.

Growth in workload was reported to vary widely among departments. The greatest growth in per-employee workload occurred in police and fire (measured by total arrests and total fires, respectively) and the slowest growth (an actual decline) was registered in higher education and in public schools (measured by total enrollment).

Relative growth in workload, employment, and real wages was also reported to vary widely among departments. For both the Police and Fire Departments, workload per employee grew faster than either aggregate employment or average labor costs. On the other hand, for higher education and public schools, per-employee workload decreased, while both average real wages and aggregate employment increased. Between these two extremes, average workload in the EPA increased more slowly than real wages, but faster than employment, while workload in social services increased slightly more slowly than employment or real wages. Because of the nature of the data, no conclusion could be drawn for health services.

Finally, the limitations of this type of analysis for policy guidance should again be underscored. The problems of workload measurement as described above are numerous. Although some aspects are readily quantifiable (for example, number of fires, tons of refuse), others (such as crime prevention and fire prevention) present seemingly insurmountable problems. Because of these shortcomings, it would be incorrect here to conclude a strict relationship between changes in workloads per employee and changes in average real wages and employment. Rather, this intent here is merely to lay out an approximate relationship in an aggregate departmental sense.

TABLE 4.A.1

Total Employment in Seven New York City Departments,
1965 and 1972

Department	1965		1972		Percent Change
Police					
Uniformed	26,734		31,895		19.3
Nonuniformed	1,329		2,790		109.9
Total		28,063		34,685	23.6
Fire					
Uniformed	13,199		13,592		2.3
Nonuniformed	797		1,108		39.0
Total		13,996		14,700	5.0
EPA					
Uniformed	11,405		12,124		6.3
Nonuniformed	7,413		8,468		14.2
Total		18,818		20,592	9.4
Public schools					
Delivery	51,372		67,476		31.3
Nondelivery	7,860		13,721		74.6
Total		59,232		81,197	37.1
Higher education					
Delivery	3,730		9,519		155.2
Nondelivery	2,830		7,601		168.6
Total		6,560		17,120	161.0
Social services					
Delivery	6,834		10,709		56.7
Nondelivery	7,690		20,463		166.1
Total		14,524		31,172	114.6
Health					
Delivery	1,435		1,659		15.6
Nondelivery	3,235		3,829		18.4
Total		4,670		5,488	17.5

Source: New York City Executive Budget and Supporting Schedules, 1955-66 and 1972-73 (New York: Office of the Mayor, March 1965 and March 1972).

TABLE 4.A.2

Average Real Wages in Seven New York City Departments,
1965 and 1972
(in dollars)

Department	1965		1972		Percent Change	
Police						
Uniformed	8,685		10,254		18.1	
Nonuniformed	5,727		5,767		0.7	
Total		8,554		9,893		15.7
Fire						
Uniformed	8,603		11,299		31.3	
Nonuniformed	6,919		7,141		3.2	
Total		8,507		10,986		29.1
EPA						
Uniformed	7,421		8,972		20.9	
Nonuniformed	7,189		8,484		18.0	
Total		7,330		8,771		19.7
Public schools						
Delivery	8,669		9,783		12.9	
Nondelivery	7,018		6,902		-1.3	
Total		8,540		9,295		8.8
Higher education						
Delivery	11,138		12,690		13.9	
Nondelivery	5,885		7,075		20.2	
Total		8,870		10,197		15.0
Social services						
Delivery	6,650		8,454		27.1	
Nondelivery	5.036		5,575		10.7	
Total		5,796		6,564		13.3
Health						
Delivery	6,611		6,873		4.0	
Nondelivery	5,824		6,822		17.1	
Total		6,065		6,837		12.7

Source: New York City Executive Budget and Supporting Schedules, 1965-66
and 1972-73 (New York: Office of the Mayor, March 1965 and March 1972).

TABLE 4.A.3

Average Annual Growth Rate in Employment and
Real Wages for Personnel
in Seven New York City Departments, 1965 and 1972
(percent)

Department	Employees		Real Wages	
Police				
Uniformed	2.6		2.4	
Nonuniformed	11.2		0.1	
Total		3.1		2.1
Fire				
Uniformed	0.3		4.0	
Nonuniformed	4.8		0.5	
Total		0.7		3.7
EPA				
Uniformed	0.9		2.7	
Nonuniformed	1.9		2.4	
Total		1.3		2.6
Public schools				
Delivery	4.0		1.7	
Nondelivery	8.3		-0.2	
Total		4.6		1.2
Higher education				
Delivery	14.3		1.9	
Nondelivery	15.2		2.7	
Total		14.7		2.0
Social services				
Delivery	6.6		3.5	
Nondelivery	15.0		1.5	
Total		11.5		1.8
Health				
Delivery	2.1		0.6	
Nondelivery	2.4		2.3	
Total		2.3		1.7

Source: New York City Executive Budget and Supporting Schedules, 1965-66 and 1972-73 (New York: Office of the Mayor, March 1965
and March 1972).

NOTES

1. Recent work in this general area is to be found in Jesse Burkhead, "The Evaluation of Changes in Local Government Expenditure: Cost, Workload, Quality, and Productivity," in Local Government Finances in New York State, 1959-1969, Report to the Temporary Commission on the Powers of Local Government (Syracuse, N.Y.: Metropolitan Studies Program, The Maxwell School, Syracuse University, August 1971); Harry P. Hatry and Donald M. Fisk, "Improving Productivity and Productivity Measurement in Local Governments" (paper prepared for the National Commission on Productivity, June 1971); and Robert D. Reischauer, "The State and Local Fiscal Crisis in Perspective" (Washington, D.C.: The Brookings Institution, 1971; mimeographed).

2. For an extended discussion, see Elaine Morley, "The Measurement of Public Sector Activity in New York City with reference to the New York City Police Department" (Internal Working Paper No. 14, Maxwell Research Project on the Public Finances of New York City, Syracuse University, Syracuse, N.Y., December 1972).

3. New York Times, April 5, 1966.

4. For an extended discussion, see Donald Phares, with Elaine Morley, "The Measurement of Public Sector Output in New York City with Reference to Sanitation" (Internal Working Paper No. 5, Maxwell Research Project on the Public Finances of New York City, Syracuse University, Syracuse, N.Y., August 1972).

5. For an extended discussion, see Donald Phares and Elaine Morley, "The Measurement of Public Sector Activity with Reference to Health and Hospitals Services" (Internal Working Paper No. 12, Maxwell Research Project on the Public Finances of New York City, Syracuse University, Syracuse, N.Y., September 1972).

CHAPTER

5

**THE FISCAL AND
INCOME DISTRIBUTION
EFFECTS OF STATE ASSUMPTION**

The longer-term projections of revenues and expenditures of
the New York City government clearly indicate a growing fiscal imbalance. One alternative for redressing this fiscal imbalance would
call for the shifting of financial responsibility for burdensome municipal services to a broader jurisdiction—a regional or a state level of
government. This kind of centralization alters only the scale of the
governmental unit to which fiscal authority over a service or set of
services is assigned. Actual functional and policy authority over the
level and mix of services can be retained by the smaller jurisdiction,
while financial decisions are moved to the broader base.

Such structural reform has been given serious consideration
in New York, where the principal candidates for financial centralization are welfare and education. Not only do these services account
for 20.5 percent of the current municipal budget but they have also
evidenced rapid growth. In these terms, both services may be considered a burden or strain on the public fisc of the city. In many
states, the welfare function is already financed and, to a large extent,
administered by the state government. Education, however, remains
partly locally financed in all states except Hawaii. In many instances,
however, the education function has independent taxing power rather
than being dependent on the general taxing power of the city, as is
the case in New York.

The material in this chapter describes and assesses the fiscal
consequences of shifting financial responsibility for welfare and
education to the State of New York. Two aspects of such a shift are
of particular importance. The first is the budget relief that the city
would realize through fiscal centralization of these functions; this
is considered immediately below. The second is the change that would
occur in the tax burden of New York City residents. Therefore, a
methodology that permits measurement of the impact of centralization

on the distribution of interpersonal tax burden is described. The results of this procedure are then reported, first for education, and then for welfare. Finally, the broader implications of the findings are discussed.

EFFECTS ON THE CITY BUDGET

If financing for either or both functions were shifted to the state government, then the relief to the city budget would equal the amount of current expenditures for those functions that are now financed from the city's own resources. Whether the response to such relief would be a reduction in taxes or a reallocation of the freed resources to other services is not the question here. Rather, the purpose is to identify the amount of the financial change in the event of functional shifts.

As may be seen from the data presented in Table 5.1, per capita locally raised current revenues of the New York City government had reached $563 by 1971. If locally raised funds for welfare were no longer required, $75.97 per capita would be freed for other purposes; if locally raised funds for education were no longer required, $127.34 per capita would be freed for other purposes; and, if both functions were removed from the responsibility of the city government, a total of $203.31 per capita would be available either for spending elsewhere or for tax reduction. These computations give a clear indication of the magnitude of the governmental fiscal relief involved.

TABLE 5.1

Per Capita Locally Raised Revenues for
Education and Welfare in New York City, 1967-71

Current Locally Raised Revenues	1967	1971	Average Annual Percent Increase
Total	$348.82	$563.10	15.36
For education	$80.68	$127.34	14.46
Percent of total	23.12	22.61	
For welfare	$26.26	$75.97	47.33
Percent of total	7.52	13.49	

Source: Comptroller of the City of New York, Annual Report (New York: Office of the Comptroller, 1967 and 1971).

315

The harder question, however, is the magnitude of the individual fiscal relief that may be involved and the variation in this relief across income classes.

EFFECTS ON INDIVIDUAL TAX BURDEN

The individual tax burden effects derived from shifting education and/or welfare financing to the state government are not necessarily as favorable as the city government budget relief—that is, since state government taxes must rise, the residents of the city may not experience a reduction in overall tax burden. To measure such effects, the empirical questions raised here are of two sorts: The first concerns the effect on the overall tax burden of city residents, and the second concerns differential effects across income levels. These two questions are examined simultaneously in the analysis below. However, before proceeding with the analysis, two steps are necessary. First, an appropriate income distribution series for New York City residents must be estimated, and, second, the tax burdens by income class must be computed on the basis of a set of assumptions about tax shifting. Then, the effects of the shift in financing responsibility on the tax bills of city residents can be delineated.

Income Distribution

The first step in the computation of tax burden by income class requires the determination of the number of family units in each class. The requisite data would seem to be available in the Census of Population for 1970, but serious shortcomings in those data require that they be modified. The most severe limitations in the Census data are the exclusion of capital gains income and income underreporting, particularly for income other than wages and salaries. Both shortcomings result in an understating of income, especially for the higher-income brackets.

The adjustment of the Census income distribution requires a rather complicated procedure. For this purpose, information from the Census, U.S. Department of Commerce, and Internal Revenue Service are utilized.[1] The adjustment procedure may be summarized in five steps. First, total capital gains income in the New York standard metropolitan statistical area (SMSA) is derived from the Internal Revenue Service data.[2] That income is allocated across income classes in New York according to the national distribution of capital gains among income groups. Second, data obtained from the U.S. Department of Commerce[3] permit the estimation of that percent of income underreported in Census data: (1) wages and salaries,

(2) property income, (3) proprietors' income, and (4) transfer payments. Captured in these data are such items as imputed rents and interests, and food stamps.4 Next, those two adjustments are applied to the reported Census income data. The result is a new distribution, termed here "economic" income. (For example, a family having an income of $12,000 according to the Census would have an economic income that included the $12,000-plus income from capital gains and the other sources itemized above.) The fourth step is an adjustment of the number of families in any given income class. In the case above, for example, the family with an income of $12,000 may actually have an economic income that would move it out of the $10,000-$14,999 income class as reported in the Census. Finally, the economic income distribution is cross-classified by family size, and the New York City distribution is separated from the New York SMSA distribution.

The data presented in Table 5.2 show a comparison of the original Census income distribution and the economic income distribution. The same information is depicted graphically in the Lorenz curve in Figure 5.1. The diagonal line through the origin in Figure 5.1 defines perfect equality—for example, 20 percent of the people would earn 20 percent of the income, 50 percent of the people would earn 50 percent of the income, and so on. The dotted curve shows the Census distribution of income, and the solid curve represents the distribution of economic income. Since the area between either curve and the main diagonal measures the extent of inequality, the graphic representation permits evaluation of the relative equality of the two distributions.

As might be expected, these data show a reduction in the number of families in the lower-income classes and an especially large increase in the highest-income class. However, in general, the overall character of the income distribution is not markedly changed.*

It is possible to allocate various state and local taxes to income brackets if only a set of assumptions is made about who finally pays these taxes. The kinds of taxes considered here are (1) the local property tax, (2) a state property tax, (3) the state income tax, and (4) the state sales tax. Once the burden of each tax among income classes is computed, the next step is to discern the tax burden effects of changing the method of financing welfare and education (public schools) costs.

---

*The Gini coefficient, a measure of the equality of a distribution, is 0.43680 for the Census income distribution and 0.43227 for the economic income distribution derived here. (See also Figure 5.1.)

TABLE 5.2

Distribution of Families Among Income Classes in New York City by Census and Economic Income, 1969

Income Class (dollars)	Number of Family Units*	
	Census Income	Economic Income
0 - 999	216,413	210,726
1,000 - 1,999	212,959	18,665
2,000 - 2,999	196,094	100,356
3,000 - 3,999	186,497	129,917
4,000 - 4,999	182,258	109,590
5,000 - 5,999	201,524	135,539
6,000 - 6,999	197,098	139,539
7,000 - 7,999	192,168	191,764
8,000 - 8,999	181,310	221,582
9,000 - 9,999	157,912	181,525
10,000 - 11,999	292,764	316,149
12,000 - 14,999	294,428	431,840
15,000 - 24,999	393,809	482,880
25,000 and over	139,775	376,558

*Family units include both families and unrelated individuals.

Source: Roy W. Bahl and Walter Vogt, "State Assumption of Welfare and Education Financing: Income Distribution Consequences" (Internal Working Paper No. 17, Maxwell Research Project on the Public Finances of New York City, Syracuse University, Syracuse, N.Y., May 1973).

THE SHIFTING METHODOLOGY

Before the actual allocation of taxes is made, the shifting assumptions must be postulated. In particular, the local property tax in New York City must be adjusted to reflect the possibility of its burden being exported from the area. This is the subject treated immediately below. The discussions following deal with the assumptions used in allocating the other taxes. However, little if any attention is paid to describing the structures of the New York State sales and income taxes, since their features are well known. A state property tax is considered here because of its prominence in the Fleischmann Report[5] on education finance in New York State, and its

FIGURE 5.1

Lorenz Curves for New York City

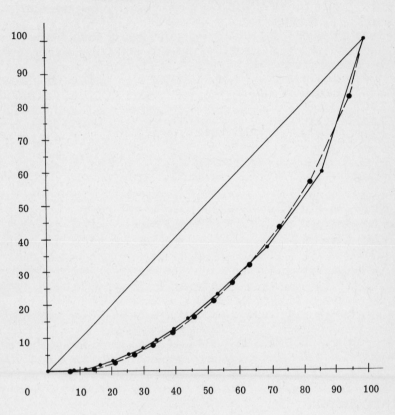

Source: Roy W. Bahl and Walter Vogt, "State Assumption of Welfare and Education Financing: Income Distribution Consequences," Working Paper no. 17, Maxwell Research Project on the Public Finances of New York City, May 18, 1973.

specifics, where required in the analysis, will use the policies suggested in that report.

This analysis deals with three possible alternatives for shifting the financing of education or welfare to the state level. Although there are numerous other combinations or alternative methods for such shifting, it was reasoned that, if New York City were to experience some expenditure relief (increase) by the shifting of a function, then the easiest tax to adjust (raise or lower) would be the property tax. For this reason, the local property tax was selected for this analysis. On the other hand, the taxes that the state would seem most likely to increase, if it incurred new expenditure responsibility, were thought to be the state personal income tax, a combination of the state income and sales taxes, and a new state property tax. The results presented in this analysis rely on the assumption that these are the taxes under consideration. Different results would, of course, be obtained if some other combination of taxes were considered—for example, a shift from a city sales tax to a state corporate income tax.

The Local Property Tax

There are three components of the local property tax base: (1) residential, (2) utilities and special franchises, and (3) other non-residential. (See Table 5.3.) In the calculation of the tax burden imposed by the local property tax, several assumptions are made with respect to each of these components. First, the residential

TABLE 5.3

Proportion of New York City Property Taxes
Paid by New York City Residents, 1969

	Amount of Property Taxes Raised (dollars)	Percent of Total Equalized Value
Property associated directly with residential use	404,677,466	56.96
Property associated with residential business activity	72,951,000	10.24
Utility property associated with residential use	40,709,280	5.73
Total equalized value associated with residential use	518,337,746	72.93

Source: David Bjornstad, "The New York City Property Tax Base: Definition, Composition and Measurement" (Internal Working Paper No. 7, Maxwell Research Project on the Public Finances of New York City, Syracuse University, Syracuse, N.Y., October 1972).

portion of the property tax is assumed to be fully shifted to the user of the property. The tax is then allocated according to estimates of housing expenditure for each individual income class. (Housing expenditures were derived for each income class by capitalizing estimated monthly rents at 8.5 percent over a 10-year period.6 Hence, a total housing value may be imputed to each income class.) The equalization rate and the tax rate are then applied to obtain a total property tax payment for each class. Second, property taxation on special franchises is assumed to be fully shifted forward and exported from New York State.* One-half of the property taxes on utilities is also assumed to be fully shifted forward to the consumer in the form of higher prices.7 Since data are not available on the consumption of utilities,8 these taxes are allocated according to total taxable consumption in each income class.

The third assumption concerns the commercial and industrial components of the property tax. In this instance, tax burdens are computed on the basis of full forward shifting—that is, a tax burden is assigned to each income class on the basis of total taxable consumption. A necessary prerequisite for this calculation is to estimate the amount of property taxes exported from the state and then deduct that from the total. Business property taxes exported from New York State are crudely derived as follows: taxes on properties classified as factories, hotels, theaters, lofts, and office buildings are assumed to be exported; taxes on properties classified as warehouses, garages, store buildings, miscellaneous, and vacant lots are assumed to be borne by local residents.

The tax burden effects of the federal income tax offset, or of rent supplements, are not considered in this analysis.

State Income Tax

The allocation of the state income tax burden among income classes involves a less arbitrary set of assumptions. New York State taxable income is estimated for any given bracket as follows: From economic income, an amount equal to one-half of the sum of capital gains, transfer payments, estimated nonreported income, and estimated deductions and exemptions is subtracted. Capital gains, transfer payments, and estimated nonreported income are identifiable components in the original definition of economic income; the last item is obtained from the data collected by the New York State Income Tax Department.9

---

*Special franchise is composed largely of railroad property, and for this reason, it was decided to shift this entire category out of New York City.

The next step is to estimate a tax liability for each income class. If the resulting estimate of total New York State income tax liability for New York City residents does not equal state reported actual payments by city residents, the estimate is raised or reduced in each class by an appropriate multiplier. The result then adds up to the reported state total.

State Sales Tax

The state sales tax is assumed to be fully shifted forward—that is, the tax would be borne by consumers in the form of higher prices. Calculation of the sales tax burden for any given income class is based on the amounts of sales tax deduction allowable for federal income tax purposes. The total amount of sales tax revenues apportioned among New York City residents is 85 percent of the amount collected in New York City.[10]

Tax Burden Distribution

The procedure just discussed allows the burden, by income class, to be measured for each tax. The results are presented in Table 5.4. In the property tax column, only the percent of school property taxes is noted, since the initial focus is on the education function. It should be reiterated that the total amount of each tax allocated pertains only to New York City residents. Thus, of revenues from these three tax sources collected from New York City residents, the over-$25,000 income group pays about 47 percent.

The corresponding effective rates—taxes per $1 of income—are shown in Table 5.5. These data show the regressivity of the property tax.[11] The burden of the tax per $1 of economic income falls more heavily on the low-income groups—that is, those in the $1,000-$1,999 bracket—where 4.38 cents of every $1 of income go to the property tax. The effect is comparatively mild in the high-income groups—that is, those in the $15,000-$24,999 bracket, where 1.12 cents per $1 of income are paid in property taxes. By contrast, the state income tax is progressive. It ranges from an effective rate of zero in the first three income classes to 3.36 cents per $1 of economic income in the $25,000-and-over class. The state sales tax shows a somewhat regressive tendency. It ranges from 1.81 cents per $1 of income in the $1,000-$1,999 class to 1.08 cents per $1 of income in the $25,000-and-over class.

Column (4) of Table 5.5 summarizes the total effective rate per $1 of income for all three taxes. Together, the three taxes depict

TABLE 5.4

Distribution of Tax Payments in New York City by
Income Class, 1969
(as percent)

Income Class (dollars)	Local School Property Tax	State Income Tax	State Sales Tax	Total
1,000 - 1,999	0.26	—	0.14	0.10
2,000 - 2,999	1.78	—	0.85	0.69
3,000 - 3,999	2.59	0.03	1.13	1.01
4,000 - 4,999	2.35	0.13	1.25	1.01
5,000 - 5,999	3.13	0.43	1.87	1.52
6,000 - 6,999	3.24	0.53	2.02	1.63
7,000 - 7,999	3.38	0.52	2.46	1.76
8,000 - 8,999	2.63	1.08	3.27	2.56
9,000 - 9,999	4.01	1.30	3.14	2.48
10,000 - 11,999	9.03	4.22	7.08	6.23
12,000 - 14,999	15.73	10.98	12.48	12.12
15,000 - 24,999	20.81	21.58	18.66	20.44
25,000 and over	27.45	59.20	44.69	47.43
Total	99.00	100.00	99.05	99.99

*Totals may not add to 100 percent due to rounding.

Source: Roy W. Bahl and Walter Vogt, "State Assumption of Welfare and Education Financing: Income Distribution Consequences" (Internal Working Paper No. 17, Maxwell Research Project on the Public Finances of New York City, Syracuse University, Syracuse, N.Y., May 1973).

a structure of tax burden that is mildly U-shaped. The effective rate first falls as income rises, reaches a low at about the $7,000-$7,999 income class, and then rises consistently. Therefore, it might be characterized as regressive up to an economic income class of about $7,000-$7,999 and mildly progressive thereafter.

SHIFTING THE EDUCATION FUNCTION

The assessment of tax-burden effects on New York City residents if education (public schools) financing is moved completely to the state government requires a number of specific computational steps. Those steps, along with the necessary assumptions, are as follows:

1. The tax relief to the New York City taxpayer effected by the city government is the amount of local property tax devoted to education.

2. The total increase in cost to the state government equals the total amount of local resources raised for education by all local governments in New York State.*

TABLE 5.5

Distribution of Tax Payments in New York City by
Income Class, 1969
(in cents)

Income Class (dollars)	Local School Property Tax	State Income Tax	State Sales Tax	Total*
1,000 - 1,999	4.38	—	1.81	6.20
2,000 - 2,999	3.64	—	1.30	4.94
3,000 - 3,999	2.93	0.06	0.95	3.95
4,000 - 4,999	2.52	0.24	1.00	3.77
5,000 - 5,999	2.23	0.53	0.99	3.76
6,000 - 6,999	2.03	0.58	0.94	3.57
7,000 - 7,999	1.87	0.50	1.02	3.39
8,000 - 8,999	1.89	0.77	1.01	3.68
9,000 - 9,999	1.72	0.95	1.00	3.68
10,000 - 11,999	1.58	1.27	0.93	3.79
12,000 - 14,999	1.46	1.57	0.86	3.89
15,000 - 24,999	1.12	2.11	0.79	4.03
25,000 and over	0.89	3.36	1.08	5.33

*Rows may not add to totals because of rounding.

Source: Roy W. Bahl and Walter Vogt, "State Assumption of Welfare and Education Financing: Income Distribution Consequences" (Internal Working Paper No. 17, Maxwell Research Project on the Public Finances of New York City, Syracuse University Syracuse, N.Y., May 1973).

---

*This is a necessary assumption because it must be assumed that New York City's shifting of education finance to the state will be

3. The actual share of the incremental cost to the state as borne by New York City residents varies with (a) the particular tax used by the state to finance the increment and (b) the share of the particular tax base accounted for by the city.

Considered here are three options for the state in raising the appropriate revenues to support the added cost of education: first, the state property tax; second, the state income tax; and third, a combination of the state sales and income taxes. The impact of each is reported for New York City taxpayers.

Shifting to a State Property Tax

The first alternative entails financing the increased education cost with a state property tax, as suggested in the Fleischmann report. If the fiscal year 1969 is used for purposes of analysis, the total increase in education cost to the state is estimated to be $1.88 billion.[12] This is computed by estimating education expenditures by local governments, financed from local property taxes, and assuming that state assumption would involve "picking-up" this amount.

Since New York City's share of total New York State equalized value is 46.7 percent, then $875.64 million of the cost increase would be borne by the New York City tax base. When compared to real property taxes raised in New York City in 1969 for education ($710.6 million), the effect of shifting to a state property tax would include a net increase of $165 million for New York City taxpayers. However, it is estimated here that New York City residents pay only 72.9 percent of local property taxes and that the balance is exported from the area. Therefore, the total amount of state property tax paid by local residents under such a shift would be $638.61 million. After adjustments for tax exporting, city residents contributed (in 1969) $518.14 million to education property taxes. Hence, the shift would mean a net property tax increase of $120.47 million for city residents—that is, a 16.9 percent increase, or a $15.38 per capita increase. This increment, when translated into an increase in property tax payments per dollar of equalized value, amounts to 2.2 cents.

The increased burden that would be derived from the shift can be disaggregated among income classes, when the additional property tax cost of $120.47 million is allocated on the basis of estimated housing expenditures as described above. The results of this procedure

---

part of a similar action for all local districts in New York State. A first step will be to estimate how much of the total increase in the New York State tax would be paid by New York City residents.

TABLE 5.6

Changes in Distribution of Tax Payments in New York
City by Income Class as Result of Shifting Education
Finance from Local to State Property Tax
(in cents)

Income Class (dollars)	Net Change in Property Taxes Paid per Dollar of Economic Income
1,000 - 1,999	1.06
2,000 - 2,999	0.86
3,000 - 3,999	0.68
4,000 - 4,999	0.59
5,000 - 5,999	0.52
6,000 - 6,999	0.47
7,000 - 7,999	0.43
8,000 - 8,999	0.41
9,000 - 9,999	0.40
10,000 - 11,999	0.37
12,000 - 14,999	0.34
15,000 - 24,999	0.26
25,000 and over	0.20

Source: Roy W. Bahl and Walter Vogt, "State Assumption of
Welfare and Education Financing: Income Distribution Consequences"
(Internal Working Paper No. 17, Maxwell Research Project on the
Public Finances of New York City, Syracuse University, Syracuse,
N.Y., May 1973).

are shown in Column (1) of Table 5.6 as the estimated change in property tax payments per $1 of income.*

The conclusion implicit in Table 5.6 is that when education
financing is moved from the city property tax to a state property tax,
there is an increase in property taxes across all income classes.
Because property taxation is regressive, the largest increment in

---

*These net tax changes are calculated as averages for different
family sizes within a given income class. Because of this, and because of rounding, the (algebraic) product of these net changes and
mean class (economic) incomes may not sum to the net changes in
total financing. This caveat applies equally to the remaining estimates.

tax per $1 of income would occur in the lower-income classes. For example, families in the $1,000-$1,999 income class would experience a 1.06 cent increase in property tax payments per $1 of economic income. By contrast, families in the highest-income class would realize an increase of only a 0.20 cents per $1 of economic income. Because the distribution of effective property tax rates is regressive before this shift, the result is to accentuate the disparity in effective rates as between successively higher income tax rates.

Shifting to a State Income Tax

A second option is to shift education financing from the local property tax to the state income tax. (It is assumed that the present income tax structure is increased by the same proportion in each income class in order to generate new revenues.) Since New York City accounts for 43.7 percent of total state individual income taxes, the city would bear 43.7 percent ($819.50 million) of the increased state government costs for education. The shift in financing would initially reduce property tax payments in the city by $710.46 million, of which $518.14 million would be paid by local taxpayers because of exporting. Thus, if the state adopted the income tax to finance added educational expenditures, the net "cost" to city residents would be an estimated $301.36 million, or $38.77 per capita. However, while the overall city burden would rise, the distribution of the burden as among income classes would change because of the shift from a regressive to a progressive financing source. The reduction in property tax burden across income classes is easily seen from Table 5.7. The increase in income tax payments is obtained by allocating the $819.5 million to be raised according to the existing distribution of income tax burden. (See Table 5.4.) The data in Table 5.7 show that all income classes save the two highest would experience tax reductions.

On average, tax burden reduction for a family in the $1,000-$1,999 income class would be 4.57 cents per $1 of income. A family in the middle-income bracket ($10,000-$11,999 income class) would receive a tax reduction of only 0.49 cents per $1 of income. On the other hand, families in the $25,000-and-over bracket would experience an average tax increase of 2.16 cents per $1 of economic income.

The data in Table 5.7 may be further refined to show a different burden effect for different family sizes. The data in Table 5.8 show the tax burden effects of shifting from a local property tax to a state income tax, cross-classified by income class and family size. A shift to a state income tax would tend to reduce the tax burden more for larger family sizes, an effect that is caused by the structure of

327

TABLE 5.7

Changes in Distribution of Tax Payments in New York
City by Income Class as Result of Shifting
Education Finance from Local Property to State Income Tax
(in cents)

Income Class (dollars)	Net Change in Taxes Paid per Dollar of Economic Income
1,000 - 1,999	- 4.57
2,000 - 2,999	- 3.74
3,000 - 3,999	- 2.92
4,000 - 4,999	- 2.49
5,000 - 5,999	- 2.05
6,000 - 6,999	- 1.73
7,000 - 7,999	- 1.43
8,000 - 8,999	- 1.16
9,000 - 9,999	- 0.87
10,000 - 11,999	- 0.49
12,000 - 14,999	- 0.11
15,000 - 24,999	+ 0.75
25,000 and over	+ 2.16

Source: Roy W. Bahl and Walter Vogt, "State Assumption of Welfare and Education Financing: Income Distribution Consequences" (Internal Working Paper No. 17, Maxwell Research Project on the Public Finances of New York City, Syracuse University, Syracuse, N.Y., May 1973).

the state income tax. For example, in the low-income group ($1,000-$1,999), the burden reduction would range from 4.48 cents for a family of two to 4.72 cents for a family of six or more. On the other hand, in the high-income group ($25,000 and over), the tax-burden increases per $1 of income would range from 2.3 cents for a family of two to 1.79 cents for a family of six or more.

In summary, it can be concluded that a shift from a local property tax to a state income tax for the financing of education would have the following effects:

1. It would increase the aggregate net cost to New York City residents by $301.36 million, or by $38.77 per capita.

2. It would reduce the tax burden on all income classes below $15,000 and increase the tax burdens on residents with incomes over $15,000.

TABLE 5.8

Changes in Distribution of Tax Payments in New York City by Income Class and Family Size as Result of Shifting Education Finance from Local Property to State Income Tax (in cents)

Income Class	Net Change in Taxes Paid per Dollar of Economic Income — Family Size					
	1	2	3	4	5	6 or more
$1,000 - $1,999	- 4.35	- 4.48	- 4.55	- 4.73	- 4.64	- 4.72
2,000 - 2,999	- 3.63	- 3.64	- 3.72	- 3.80	- 3.83	- 3.83
3,000 - 3,999	- 2.85	- 2.86	- 2.91	- 2.97	- 2.99	- 2.99
4,000 - 4,999	- 2.08	- 2.50	- 2.55	- 2.60	- 2.62	- 2.62
5,000 - 5,999	- 1.25	- 1.96	- 2.24	- 2.28	- 2.31	- 2.31
6,000 - 6,999	- 0.98	- 1.46	- 1.74	- 2.01	- 2.11	- 2.11
7,000 - 7,999	- 0.64	- 1.13	- 1.40	- 1.65	- 1.86	- 1.92
8,000 - 8,999	- 0.32	- 1.16	- 0.99	- 1.25	- 1.46	- 1.82
9,000 - 9,999	- 0.19	- 0.50	- 0.75	- 0.99	- 1.23	- 1.57
10,000 - 11,999	+ 0.26	- 0.12	- 0.39	- 0.63	- 0.83	- 1.22
12,000 - 14,999	+ 0.48	+ 0.25	- 0.00	- 0.21	- 0.43	- 0.79
15,000 - 24,999	+ 1.14	+ 1.15	+ 0.93	+ 0.73	+ 0.52	+ 0.05
25,000 and over	+ 2.49	+ 2.30	+ 2.29	+ 2.26	+ 1.83	+ 1.79

Source: Roy W. Bahl and Walter Vogt, "State Assumption of Welfare and Education Financing: Income Distribution Consequences" (Internal Working Paper No. 17, Maxwell Research Project on the Public Finances of New York City, Syracuse University, Syracuse, N.Y., May 1973).

3. Within any one income class, more tax relief per $1 of income would be granted for large families than for small families.

Shifting to a Combination of the State Income and Sales Taxes

The final alternative considered is to shift the financing of education from a local property tax to a combination of the state income tax and a 3 percent increase in the state sales tax. As above, the incremental cost to the state of assuming responsibility for education would be $1.88 billion.

A 3 percent addition to the state sales tax is estimated to yield $1.02 billion. The difference between these two figures ($854.19 million) is assumed to be financed by an increase in the state income tax. Of the $1.02 billion in new state sales taxes, 44.6 percent ($455.57 million) would be raised in New York City, on a basis of estimated state sales tax collections in the city. Of this amount, it is assumed that 85 percent ($387.24 million) would be borne by New York City residents. Of the $854.19 million in new state income taxes, 43.7 percent ($372.28 million) would be paid by New York City residents. In total, New York City residents would incur increased state income and sales taxes of $759.52 million. As noted above, the amount of local property taxes removed would be $518.14 million. It is estimated that, in aggregate, New York City residents would increase their tax payments by $241.38 million, or by $31.06 per capita. The tax burden effects of this increase in taxes among income classes are shown in Table 5.9.

The distribution of tax burden among income classes shown in Table 5.9 indicates that families in all except the three highest income classes would receive reductions in their tax burdens. In general, the amount of tax relief decreases as income increases. For example, families in the $1,000-$1,999 income group would experience a reduction of 2.28 cents per $1 of income. Families in the $10,000-$11,999 income class would receive tax relief of only 0.14 cents per $1 of income. On the other hand, families in the $12,000-$14,999 brackets and the $25,000-and-over bracket would experience tax increases per $1 of income of 0.04 and 1.59 cents respectively. This result would occur because of a shift from a regressive property tax to a progressive income tax.

From Table 5.10, it can be seen that the amount of tax burden decrease or increase depends on the level of income under consideration and on the size of the family. For instance, in the low-income group ($1,000-$1,999), the size of the tax decrease varies inversely with family size (as the family size increases, the tax relief decreases).

TABLE 5.9

Changes in Distribution of Tax Payments in New York
City by Income Class as Result of Shifting Education
Finance from Local Property Tax to Combination of
State Income and Sales Taxes
(in cents)

Income Class (dollars)	Net Change in Taxes Paid per Dollar of Economic Income
1,000 - 1,999	- 2.28
2,000 - 2,999	- 2.15
3,000 - 3,999	- 1.81
4,000 - 4,999	- 1.39
5,000 - 5,999	- 1.06
6,000 - 6,999	- 0.86
7,000 - 7,999	- 0.64
8,000 - 8,999	- 0.51
9,000 - 9,999	- 0.31
10,000 - 11,999	- 0.14
12,000 - 14,999	+ 0.04
15,000 - 24,999	+ 0.52
25,000 and over	+ 1.59

Source: Roy W. Bahl and Walter Vogt, "State Assumption of
Welfare and Education Financing: Income Distribution Consequences"
(Internal Working Paper No. 17, Maxwell Research Project on the
Public Finances of New York City, Syracuse University, Syracuse,
N.Y., May 1973).

On the other hand, in the middle-income group ($10,000-$11,999), the
size of the tax decrease varies directly with family size. In the high-
income group, the size of the tax increase decreases as family size
increases.

In general, it can be concluded that the results of shifting the
financing of education from a local property tax to a combination of
the state income and sales taxes would be as follows:

1. In aggregate, New York City residents would pay $214.38
million more in taxes.

2. The distribution among income classes is, however, progressive, and, therefore, all but the highest-income classes would
experience tax relief.

TABLE 5.10

Changes in Tax Payments in New York City by Income Class and Family Size as Result of Shifting Education Finance from Local Property Tax to Combination of State Income and Sales Taxes

(in cents)

Income Class (dollars)	Net Change in Taxes Paid per Dollar of Economic Income Family Size					
	1	2	3	4	5	6 or more
1,000 - 1,999	- 2.60	- 2.66	- 2.39	- 2.14	- 1.92	- 1.99
2,000 - 2,999	- 2.38	- 2.39	- 2.22	- 2.01	- 1.95	- 1.95
3,000 - 3,999	- 1.99	- 1.98	- 1.85	- 1.71	- 1.66	- 1.66
4,000 - 4,999	- 1.39	- 1.58	- 1.48	- 1.35	- 1.29	- 1.29
5,000 - 5,999	- 0.87	- 1.19	- 1.19	- 1.10	- 1.03	- 1.03
6,000 - 6,999	- 0.77	- 0.88	- 0.88	- 0.91	- 0.88	- 0.88
7,000 - 7,999	- 0.51	- 0.63	- 0.63	- 0.67	- 0.69	- 0.72
8,000 - 8,999	- 0.29	- 0.84	- 0.40	- 0.45	- 0.48	- 0.64
9,000 - 9,999	- 0.11	- 0.27	- 0.29	- 0.33	- 0.37	- 0.52
10,000 - 11,999	+ 0.09	- 0.08	- 0.11	- 0.17	- 0.22	- 0.36
12,000 - 14,999	+ 0.14	+ 0.12	+ 0.10	+ 0.03	+ 0.00	- 0.14
15,000 - 24,999	+ 0.60	+ 0.64	+ 0.60	+ 0.52	+ 0.49	+ 0.32
25,000 and over	+ 2.02	+ 1.56	+ 1.59	+ 1.58	+ 1.42	+ 1.43

Source: Roy W. Bahl and Walter Vogt, "State Assumption of Welfare and Education Financing: Income Distribution Consequences" (Internal Working Paper No. 17, Maxwell Research Project on the Public Finances of New York City, Syracuse University, Syracuse, N.Y., May 1973).

3. The tax relief associated with this functional shift is proportional to family size but depends on the income class under consideration.

SHIFTING THE WELFARE FUNCTION

Before analyzing the tax burden effects on New York City residents of shifting welfare financing completely to the state government, a number of computational steps and assumptions must be outlined.

1. The city government tax relief to the New York City taxpayer is estimated as 20.5 percent of total city expenditures on welfare.[13]

2. It is assumed that the removal of welfare costs from the New York City government would result in the city government's reducing its property tax levy by the extent of the cost savings.

3. The increased cost to the state government is estimated as 20.5 percent of all New York State local government expenditures for welfare.

Based on these assumptions, the three alternatives considered were a shift to a state property tax, to a state income tax, and to a combination of the state sales and income taxes.

This 20.5 percent estimate of net local expenditure on welfare is a statewide average. This proportion is probably low for both New York City and for certain other welfare districts outside New York City. The lower 20.5 percent estimate was used in lieu of a higher proportion for two reasons: (a) it was not possible to identify accurately (from local sources) the proportion of local welfare expenditures for all welfare districts in New York State, and (b) the higher proportion in New York City may be due in part to a broader scope of welfare services offered. In any case, it is clear that the implication for this study of using a higher percentage local contribution for New York City, and assuming that this amount would be financed by the state, would be a greater amount of tax relief for New York City residents.

Shifting to a State Property Tax

If the financing of the welfare function were shifted from a local property tax to a state property tax, the estimated increase in welfare costs to the state would be $494.4 million. Since New York City's share of total New York State equalized value is 47.3 percent, the amount that would be borne by New York City is $233.85 million. The burden of New York City residents is estimated to be 72.9 percent of this figure ($170.55 million). On the other hand, the city would reduce its budget by 20.5 percent of $1.67 billion (or $341.65 million), of which 72.9 percent ($249.17 million) would be borne by the residents of New York City. The effect of this shift, therefore, would be to reduce the city property taxes paid by residents by $249.17 million and increase state taxes in the city (a property tax) by $170.55 million. In aggregate, then, the city residents would reduce their burden by $78.61 million. The amount of taxes raised from New York City residents for welfare is thus estimated to decrease by 31.5 percent, or $10.11 per capita.

The burden of this shift among income classes is calculated by allocating the tax savings of $78.61 million on the basis of estimated housing expenditures. The estimated tax savings per income class derived from this procedure are shown in Table 5.11. The figures

TABLE 5.11

Changes in Distribution of Tax Payments in New York
City by Income Class as Result of Shifting Welfare
Finance from Local to State Property Tax
(in cents)

Income Class (dollars)	Net Change in Taxes Paid per Dollar of Economic Income
1,000 - 1,999	- 0.69
2,000 - 2,999	- 0.56
3,000 - 3,999	- 0.44
4,000 - 4,999	- 0.38
5,000 - 5,999	- 0.34
6,000 - 6,999	- 0.31
7,000 - 7,999	- 0.28
8,000 - 8,999	- 0.28
9,000 - 9,999	- 0.26
10,000 - 11,999	- 0.24
12,000 - 14,999	- 0.22
15,000 - 24,999	- 0.17
25,000 and over	- 0.13

Source: Roy W. Bahl and Walter Vogt, "State Assumption of Welfare and Education Financing : Income Distribution Consequences" (Internal Working Paper No. 17, Maxwell Research Project on the Public Finances of New York City, Syracuse University, Syracuse, N.Y., May 1973).

indicate that the tax burden changes per $1 of economic income would be greater, the lower the income class considered. For example, the reduction in the low-income group ($1,000-$1,999) would be, on the average, 0.69 cents per $1 of income. On the other hand, the reduction for the high-income group ($25,000 and over) would be much less, 0.13 cents per $1 of income. Although the effects of such a shift would be to reduce the burden by a greater amount on low incomes than high incomes, it should be kept in mind that such a shift would do nothing to alter the regressive nature of the property tax shown in Column (1) of Table 5.5.

Shifting to a State Income Tax

The second alternative is to shift financing from a local property tax to a state income tax. In this case, since New York City residents pay 43.7 percent of total state individual income taxes, they would bear 43.7 percent of the increased cost to New York State ($494.40 million), or $216.05 million. City resident property tax payments would be reduced by $249.17 million, but the amount of state income taxes paid by city residents would increase by $216.05 million. On balance, aggregate city resident taxes would be reduced by $33.12 million. This is a reduction of 13.2 percent, or $4.26 per capita. The net effect of the reduced property tax burden and the increased income tax burden across income classes is presented in Table 5.12. The data there show that a shift from a local property tax to a state income tax would reduce the tax burden on the low-income group ($1,000-$1,999) by 2.2 cents per $1 of income, whereas the reduction for a family in the middle-income group ($10,000-$11,999) would be 0.47 cents per $1 of economic income. On the other hand, families in the high-income group would experience tax increases of 0.37 cents per $1 of economic income.

The distribution of these average tax burden changes across family size is shown in Table 5.13. From this table, it can be seen that a family of two in the low-income class would receive a tax reduction of 2.15 cents, whereas a family of six or more in that class would receive a tax reduction of 2.27 cents. Similarly, families of two and six or more in the middle-income group ($10,000-$11,999) would experience tax burden reductions of 0.37 cents and 0.68 cents, respectively. Families of the same sizes in the high-income group would experience tax increases of 0.41 and 0.27 cents respectively.

In summary, it can be concluded that a shift from a local property tax to a state income tax for the financing of welfare would
1. reduce the aggregate net cost to New York City residents;

TABLE 5.12

Changes in Distribution of Tax Payments in New York
City by Income Class as Result of Shifting Welfare
Finance from Local Property Tax to State Income Tax
(in cents)

Income Class (dollars)	Net Change in Taxes Paid per Dollar of Economic Income
1,000 - 1,999	- 2.20
2,000 - 2,999	- 1.79
3,000 - 3,999	- 1.41
4,000 - 4,999	- 1.21
5,000 - 5,999	- 1.03
6,000 - 6,999	- 0.90
7,000 - 7,999	- 0.78
8,000 - 8,999	- 0.70
9,000 - 9,999	- 0.60
10,000 - 11,999	- 0.47
12,000 - 14,999	- 0.34
15,000 - 24,999	- 0.04
25,000 and over	+ 0.37

Source: Roy W. Bahl and Walter Vogt, "State Assumption of Welfare and Education Financing: Income Distribution Consequences" (Internal Working Paper No. 17, Maxwell Research Project on the Public Finances of New York City, Syracuse University, Syracuse, N.Y., May 1973).

2. grant a greater amount of tax relief per $1 of economic income to low-income families than to high-income families;

3. grant more tax relief per $1 of income to larger families than smaller families.

Shifting to a Combination of the State Income and Sales Taxes

The final alternative is to shift the financing of welfare from a local property tax to a combination of the state income tax and a new state sales tax of 1 percent. Using this alternative, the new cost to the state of assuming welfare financing would be $494.4 million.

TABLE 5.13

Changes in Distribution of Tax Payments in New York City by Income Class and Family Size as Result of Shifting Welfare Finance from Local Property Tax to State Income Tax (in cents)

Income Class (dollars)	Net Change in Taxes Paid per Dollar of Economic Income Family Size					
	1	2	3	4	5	6 or more
1,000 – 1,999	– 2.09	– 2.15	– 2.19	– 2.27	– 2.23	– 2.27
2,000 – 2,999	– 1.74	– 1.75	– 1.79	– 1.83	– 1.84	– 1.84
3,000 – 3,999	– 1.39	– 1.37	– 1.40	– 1.43	– 1.44	– 1.44
4,000 – 4,999	– 1.09	– 1.20	– 1.23	– 1.25	– 1.26	– 1.26
5,000 – 5,999	– 0.81	– 0.99	– 1.08	– 1.10	– 1.11	– 1.11
6,000 – 6,999	– 0.69	– 0.82	– 0.90	– 0.98	– 1.02	– 1.02
7,000 – 7,999	– 0.57	– 0.70	– 0.77	– 0.85	– 0.91	– 0.92
8,000 – 8,999	– 0.45	– 0.78	– 0.64	– 0.72	– 0.78	– 0.87
9,000 – 9,999	– 0.42	– 0.50	– 0.57	– 0.64	– 0.71	– 0.80
10,000 – 11,999	– 0.26	– 0.37	– 0.45	– 0.52	– 0.57	– 0.68
12,000 – 14,999	– 0.18	– 0.25	– 0.32	– 0.37	– 0.44	– 0.53
15,000 – 24,999	+ 0.06	+ 0.06	+ 0.00	– 0.05	– 0.11	– 0.24
25,000 and over	+ 0.47	+ 0.41	+ 0.41	+ 0.40	+ 0.28	+ 0.27

Source: Roy W. Bahl and Walter Vogt, "State Assumption of Welfare and Education Financing: Income Distribution Consequences" (Internal Working Paper No. 17, Maxwell Research Project on the Public Finances of New York City, Syracuse University, Syracuse, N.Y., May 1973).

337

A 1 percent addition to the state sales tax is estimated to generate $340.35 million in new revenues. The difference between these two figures ($154.05 million) is assumed to be financed by an increased state income tax. Of the $340.35 million in new state sales taxes, 44.6 percent (or $151.80 million) would be raised in New York City, and, of this amount, it is assumed that 85 percent ($129.03 million) would be borne by New York City residents. Of the $154.05 million in new state income taxes, 43.7 percent ($67.32 million) would be paid by New York City residents. In total, then, New York City residents would incur new state taxes of $67.32 million plus $129.03 million, or $196.35 million. As noted in the two alternatives discussed above, the amount of local property taxes removed would be $249.17

TABLE 5.14

Changes in Distribution of Tax Payments in New York
City by Income Class as Result of Shifting Welfare
Finance from Local Property Tax to Combination of
State Income and Sales Taxes
(in cents)

Income Class (dollars)	Net Change in Taxes Paid per Dollar of Economic Income
1,000 - 1,999	- 1.43
2,000 - 2,999	- 1.26
3,000 - 3,999	- 1.03
4,000 - 4,999	- 0.84
5,000 - 5,999	- 0.70
6,000 - 6,999	- 0.61
7,000 - 7,999	- 0.52
8,000 - 8,999	- 0.49
9,000 - 9,999	- 0.41
10,000 - 11,999	- 0.35
12,000 - 14,999	- 0.29
15,000 - 24,999	- 0.12
25,000 and over	+ 0.18

Source: Roy W. Bahl and Walter Vogt, "State Assumption of Welfare and Education Financing: Income Distribution Consequences" (Internal Working Paper No. 17, Maxwell Research Project on the Public Finances of New York City, Syracuse University, Syracuse, N.Y., May 1973).

TABLE 5.15

Changes in Distribution of Tax Payments in New York City by Income Class and
Family Size as Result of Shifting Welfare Finance from Local Property Tax to
Combination of State Income and Sales Taxes
(in cents)

Net Change in Taxes Paid per
Dollar of Economic Income

Income Class (dollars)	Family Size					
	1	2	3	4	5	6 or more
1,000 - 1,999	- 1.51	- 1.55	- 1.47	- 1.41	- 1.33	- 1.36
2,000 - 2,999	- 1.33	- 1.33	- 1.29	- 1.23	- 1.22	- 1.21
3,000 - 3,999	- 1.10	- 1.08	- 1.05	- 1.01	- 1.00	- 1.00
4,000 - 4,999	- 0.86	- 0.90	- 0.86	- 0.83	- 0.82	- 0.82
5,000 - 5,999	- 0.68	- 0.74	- 0.73	- 0.70	- 0.69	- 0.68
6,000 - 6,999	- 0.62	- 0.63	- 0.62	- 0.62	- 0.61	- 0.60
7,000 - 7,999	- 0.53	- 0.53	- 0.52	- 0.52	- 0.52	- 0.52
8,000 - 8,999	- 0.44	- 0.67	- 0.45	- 0.45	- 0.45	- 0.48
9,000 - 9,999	- 0.39	- 0.42	- 0.41	- 0.42	- 0.42	- 0.45
10,000 - 11,999	- 0.31	- 0.36	- 0.36	- 0.36	- 0.37	- 0.39
12,000 - 14,999	- 0.29	- 0.29	- 0.29	- 0.30	- 0.29	- 0.32
15,000 - 24,999	- 0.12	- 0.11	- 0.11	- 0.12	- 0.12	- 0.15
25,000 and over	+ 0.31	+ 0.17	+ 0.18	+ 0.17	+ 0.15	+ 0.15

Source: Roy W. Bahl and Walter Vogt, "State Assumption of Welfare and Education Financing: Income Distribution Consequences" (Internal Working Paper No. 17, Maxwell Research Project on the Public Finances of New York City, Syracuse University, Syracuse, N.Y., May 1973).

million. This means that, in aggregate, city resident tax payments would be reduced by $52.82 million (21.1 percent), or $6.79 per capita. The change in tax burden by income class caused by reducing aggregate taxes by $52.82 million is shown in Table 5.14. Table 5.15 shows the same information cross-classified by family size.

The data in Table 5.14 reveal that all but the highest-income group ($25,000 and over) would experience reductions in tax burden from the shift under consideration. The low-income group ($1,000-$1,999) would benefit from the greatest tax relief of 1.43 cents per $1 of income. The middle-income group ($10,000 -$11,999), would experience tax relief of 0.35 cents per $1 of income, and the high-income group would incur tax increases of 0.18 cents per $1 of income.

The tax burden changes across family size vary according to the level of income considered. For instance, from Table 5.15, it can be seen that, in the low-income group ($1,000-$1,999), the tax burden decrease would vary inversely with family size—that is, a family of two would receive a greater tax burden decrease than a family of six or more. The effect on the middle-income group ($10,000-$11,999) is just the opposite; here a family of two would receive a smaller tax burden decrease than a family of six or more. In the high-income group, no general statement as to the relationship between family size and tax burden increases can be made from Table 5.15.

In summary, the effects on New York City residents of shifting welfare financing to a combination of the states sales and income taxes would be

1. to reduce the aggregate amount of New York City resident taxes by $52.82 million, or $6.79 per capita, and

2. to grant tax relief between income classes such that, the lower the family income, the greater the tax relief.

SUMMARY AND CONCLUSIONS

The results of the analysis undertaken here make it clear that the effect on New York City residents of shifting the financing of welfare or education to the state may not be as favorable as one might expect. In fact, because New York City taxpayers also pay New York State taxes, their tax burdens may increase. For example, though shifting the financing of education to New York State would reduce city budget expenditures by $710.6 million, the aggregate effect on the city taxpayer would be to increase taxes paid by $120.47 million, if costs were shifted to a property tax; by $361.36 million, if costs were shifted to the income tax; and by $214.38 million, if costs were shifted to a combination of the state sales and income taxes. On the other hand, shifting the welfare function to the state would not only reduce city budget expenditures by $341.64 million but would also reduce the aggregate burden on New York City taxpayers. If the shift were to a property tax, the reduction in aggregate burden would be $78.61 million; if it were to the income tax, it would be $33.12 million; and, if it were to a combination of the sales and income taxes, it would be $52.82 million.

The question, then, is the difference between the two tax systems and the degree to which New York City expenditures would be supported by taxpayers who live outside the city. If current expenditure patterns continue, after responsibility for education financing is shifted to the state, then it may be assumed that New York City taxpayers would bear some of the burden of supporting education outside the city. On the other hand, part of the burden of the local share of supporting welfare would be shifted from New York City taxpayers to people who live outside the city.

NOTES

1. Most of the basic work in developing this procedure was done by Professor William Oakland of Johns Hopkins University. It is described in considerable detail in Roy W. Bahl and Walter Vogt, "State Assumption of Welfare and Education Financing: Income Distribution Consequences" (Internal Working Paper No. 17, Maxwell Research Project on the Public Finances of New York City, Syracuse University, Syracuse, N.Y., 1973).

2. The Internal Revenue Service data used are for fiscal 1969.

3. U.S. Department of Commerce, Bureau of Economic Analysis, Survey of Current Business (Washington, D.C.: U.S. Government Printing Office, May 1971), p. 21.

4. The exact inclusions are outlined in Bahl and Vogt, op. cit., Appendix A.

5. Report to the New York State Commission on the Quality, Cost and Financing of Elementary and Secondary Education, Vol. I (Albany, N.Y.: New York State Commission on the Quality, Cost and Financing of Elementary and Secondary Education, 1971), Chapter 2.

6. The estimates of monthly rent were obtained from Survey Research Center, A Panel Study of Income Dynamics, Vol. I: Study Design, Procedures, Available Data; Vol. II: Tape Codes and Indexes (Ann Arbor: Institute for Social Research, University of Michigan, 1972).

7. For a detailed explanation of this assumption, see Bahl and Vogt, op. cit.

8. Expenditures for public utilities are available in the Bureau of Labor Statistics (BLS) 1961 studies of consumer expenditures. However, because these figures are so dated, and because of the difference in the BLS income and the income definition here, the BLS estimates were not used.

9. The average deductions used per income class were estimated for single versus married joint filers of New York State income tax returns for 1969 from data in New York State Department of Taxation and Finance, Office of Tax Research, Bureau of Tax Statistics, Personal Income (Albany, N.Y.: Department of Taxation and Finance, 1969).

10. The amount of sales tax collected in New York City is reported in New York State Division of the Budget, Office of Statistical Coordination, New York State Statistical Yearbook: 1971 (Albany, N.Y.: Division of the Budget, 1971).

11. For reasons indicated in Vogt, op. cit., Appendix A, the estimates for the $0-$999 income class are inaccurate. The major reason for this, as indicated in the working paper, is the inclusion of losses in the averages of the $0-$999 income classes. Further, it is reasoned that there are many older citizens in this income class who may have little or no income but are able to consume from past savings. In order to get correct estimates of burden for this class, a method of establishing the amount of losses included in it or for including consumption from savings would be needed. However, this would then make the first class different (in methodological terms) from the remaining classes, and, therefore, comparisons between the first and all other classes would be invalid. For this reason, it was decided to omit the estimates of tax burden for the $0-$999 income class.

12. Comptroller of the State of New York, Special Report on Municipal Affairs (Albany, N.Y.: Office of the Comptroller, 1970), p. 19.

13. The 20.5 percent figure is an estimate of welfare expenditures from local sources in New York State and is found in Advisory Commission on Intergovernmental Relations, State and Local Finances: Significant Features 1967 to 1970 (Washington, D.C.: U.S. Government Printing Office, 1969).

MAXWELL RESEARCH PROJECT ON THE PUBLIC
FINANCES OF NEW YORK CITY

WORKING PAPERS

Number	Title	Author
1	"The Fiscal Setting for Reform-ing Government Structure in New York City"	Alan K. Campbell
2	"The Structure and Perfor-mance of the New York City Tax System"	David J. Bjornstad
3	"The Expenditure Implica-tions of Political Decentral-ization"	Astrid E. Merget
4	"The Components of Changes in New York City Government Labor Costs--1965-1972: Po-lice Fire and Environmental Protection"	Richard D. Gustely
5	"The Measurement of Public Sector Output In New York City with Reference to Sani-tation"	Donald L. Phares assisted by Elaine Morley
6	"The Components of Changes in New York City Government Labor Costs--1965-1972: Social Services, Health Services, Pub-lic Services, Higher Education"	Richard D. Gustely
7	"The New York City Property Tax Base: Definition, Compo-sition and Measurement"	David J. Bjornstad
8	"Fiscal Dimensions of Govern-ment Reform in Greater London"	Astrid E. Merget
9	"The Cost of Providing Retire-ment and Social Security	

Number	Title	Author
	Benefits to Employees: Trends, Causes, and Prospects, 1961-1972"	Bernard Jump
10	"The cost of Providing Retirement and Social Security Benefits to New York City: Projections to 1980"	Bernard Jump
11	"A Comparison of Changes in City Government Labor Costs Among the Ten Largest U.S. Cities: 1966-1971"	Richard D. Gustely
12	"The Measurement of Public Sector Activity in New York City with Reference to Health and Hospitals Services"	Donald Phares Elaine Morley
13	"The Components of Change in New York City Non-Labor Costs—Fiscal Year 1965-1970: Supplies, Materials, Equipment and Contractual Services"	David Greytak Robert Dinkelmeyer
14	"The Measurement of Public Sector Activity in New York City with Reference to Police Services"	Elaine Morley
15	"Measuring the Costs of Governmental Decentralization: The New York City Police Department"	Robert J. Wolfson
16	"The Components of Expenditure Change: An Analysis of the Technique and An Application to Changes in City Government Labor Costs"	Richard D. Gustely
17	"State Assumption of Welfare and Education Financing: Income Distribution Consequences"	Roy W. Bahl Walter Vogt

in, 4-6; relation to wages and
workloads, 276-313 (Board of
Higher Education, 299; Environmental Protection Administration, 295-296; Fire Department,
290-293; Health Services Administration, 306-308; Police Department, 286-289; Public
Schools, 301-302; Social Sciences
Department, 304; summary of,
312)
Environmental Protection Administration, workload measurements
in, 293-295 (relation to wages
and employment, 295-296)
Environmental Protection Administration expenditures, historical
analysis of, 204-211 (direct labor
costs, 205-206; nonlabor costs,
208-209; retirement system
costs, 206-208; total costs, 210-
211)
Expenditures (see Government expenditures; names of specific
types, e. g. Nonlabor expenditures)

Fire Department, workload measurements in, 289-290 (relation
to wages and employment, 290-
293)
Fire Department expenditures,
historical analysis of, 196-204
(direct labor costs, 197-198;
nonlabor costs, 201-203; retirement system costs, 198-201;
total costs, 203-204)

Government employment (see Employment [government])
Government expenditures, 157-275
(see also names of specific types,
e. g. Public School expenditures)
all departments, 232-235; comparison with other cities, 163-

174 (functions of expenditures,
169-173; objects of expenditures,
164-169; summary of, 173-174)
forecasts for 1979, 235-248 (by
function, 238-244; by object, 244-
248; summary, 248) historical
growth of, 158-163 (functions of
expenditures, 161; objects of expenditures, 158-161; summary
of, 161, 163) historical trends in,
analysis of with model, 183-235;
model to simulate growth of, complete model, 180-182 (direct labor
expenditures, 175-177; limitations
and assumptions of, 182-183) nonlabor expenditures, 179-180; retirement system expenditures,
177-179; use of, 183-235

Headquarters firms, location of,
17
Health Services Administration,
workload measurements in, 304-
306; relation to wages and employment, 306-308
Health Services Administration expenditures, historical analysis
of, 225-228 (direct labor costs, 225;
nonlabor costs, 226-227; retirement system costs, 226; total
costs, 227-228
Housing characteristics of population, 37-43

Income, average, and type of industry, 130-134; changes in, 21-
26 (City versus SMSA, 21-23)
distribution of, 316; of residents,
effect of changes in on income tax
revenues, 118-130; sources of,
23-26
Income taxes (city), 115-136; bases
of, 115-136 (effect on of employment changes, 130-134; effect on
of residence changes, 134-136)

347

effect on of increased state responsibility, 315-316; historical growth of, 67-74; from income taxes, 115-136 (effect on of employment changes, 130-134; effect on of residence changes, 134-136) intercity comparisons of, 74-77; from property taxes, 79-103; from public utility taxes, 103-114 (effect on of employment changes, 112-114) relation to changes in economic structure, 78-153 (summary of, 143-153) from sales taxes, 136-141 (effect on of employment changes, 141; industrial variation in, 139-141)

Taxable property, compositional, changes of, 45-61 (market value [total], 45-48)

Taxes, analyses of yield and rate structure of, relation to economic structure changes, 78-141; distribution of in city, effect on of increased state responsibility, 322-323; effect on city of increased state responsibility, 316-341 (local property tax, 320-321; state income tax, 321-322, 327-333, 335-340; state property tax, 325-327, 333-335; state sales tax, 322, 330-333, 336-340; summary of, 340-341)

Teachers Insurance and Annuity Association—College Retirement Equities Fund, 220-221

Teachers Retirement System, 212, 220

TIAA (see Teachers Insurance and Annuity Association)

Transfer expenditures, Social Services Department, 231-232

Transit Authority, retirement plan, 207

Wages (government), relation to workloads and employment, 276-313 (Board of Higher Education, 299; Environmental Protection Administration, 295-296; Fire Department, 290-293; Health Services Administration, 306-308; Police Department, 286-289; Public Schools, 301-302; Social Services Department, 304; summary of, 312)

Welfare, state responsibility for, 333-340 (state income tax, 335-336; state property tax, 333-335; state sales and income tax, 336-340; summary of, 340-341) [see also Social Services Department]

Workloads, measurements of, Board of Higher Education, 296-299 (Environmental Protection Administration, 293-295; Fire Department, 289-290; Health Services Administration, 304-306; Police Department, 278-286; Public Schools, 299-301; Social Services Department, 302-304; summary of, 312) relation to wages and employment, 276-313 (Board of Higher Education, 299; Environmental Protection Administration, 295-296; Fire Department, 290-293; Health Services Administration, 306-308; Police Department, 286-289; Public Schools, 301-302; Social Services Department, 304; summary of, 312)

ROY W. BAHL is a Professor of Economics and Director of the Metropolitan Studies Program in the Maxwell School of Citizenship and Public Affairs at Syracuse University. Previously, he held positions on the Economics faculty at West Virginia University and as a fiscal economist for the International Monetary Fund in Washington, D.C.

Dr. Bahl has published widely in the areas of state and local finance and urban economics. He is the author of numerous books and monographs, and his articles have appeared in such journals as the National Tax Journal, Journal of Regional Science, Journal of Finance, and the Public Administration Review. He has consulted widely in the area of urban public finance for federal, state, and local agencies as well as for the private sector and has had extensive experience as a fiscal adviser to national and local governments in the Far East, India, Africa, and South America.

Dr. Bahl holds a B.A. degree from Greenville College in Greenville and an M.A. and Ph.D. in Economics from the University of Kentucky.

DAVID GREYTAK is Associate Professor of Economics in the Maxwell School of Citizenship and Public Affairs at Syracuse University. He was a codirector of the Maxwell Project on the Public Finance of New York City and currently serves as the Director of the Urban Transportation Institute and Associate Director of the Metropolitan Studies Program at Syracuse University.

Dr. Greytak has published in the areas of urban and regional economics and public finance in the Journal of Regional Science, National Tax Journal, Traffic Quarterly, Public Administration Review, Regional and Urban Economics, Annuals of Regional Science, and Regional Studies.

Dr. Greytak holds a B.A. from St. Edward's University in Austin, Texas, M.A. and Ph.D. degrees from Washington University in St. Louis and was a Postdoctoral Fellow in the Institute for Applied Urban Economics at Indiana University.

ALAN K. CAMPBELL is Professor of Political Science and Dean of the Maxwell School of Citizenship and Public Affairs at Syracuse University. He is also on the Research Advisory Board of the Committee for Economic Development, a member and Trustee of the National Academy of Public Administration, and a member of the

Overseas Visitors Committee of the John F. Kennedy School of Government at Harvard University. In the past he has served as Deputy Comptroller of the State of New York and was Chairman of the Local Government Committee at the 1967 New York State Constitutional Convention.

Dr. Campbell has published widely in the areas of public administration, urban governance and finance, and intergovernmental relations. In addition to books and monographs he has published articles in Public Administration Review, National Vivic Review, The Political Science Quarterly, The Annals, Urbans Studies Quarterly, National Tax Journal, City, and Compact.

Dr. Campbell holds a B.A. from Whitman College, an M.P.A. from Wayne State University, and a Ph.D. in Political Economy and Government from Harvard University.

URBAN INCENTIVE TAX CREDITS: A
Self-Correcting Strategy to Rebuild Central
Cities
>   Edward M. Meyers
>   and John J. Musial

A PLANNING, PROGRAMMING AND BUDGETING
MANUAL: Resource Allocation in Public Sector
Economics
>   James Cutt

REVENUE SHARING: Legal and Policy Analysis
>   Otto G. Stoltz

FISCAL PRESSURES ON THE CENTRAL CITY:
The Impact of Commuters, Nonwhites, and
Overlapping Governments
>   Werner Z. Hirsch, Phillip E. Vincent,
>   Henry S. Terrell, Donald C. Shoup,
>   and Arthur Rosett

LOCAL GOVERNMENT PROGRAM BUDGETING:
THEORY AND PRACTICE With Special Reference
to Los Angeles
>   Werner Z. Hirsch, Sidney Sonenblum,
>   and Ronald K. Teeples

WHERE HAVE ALL THE DOLLARS GONE?
Public Expenditures for Human Resource Development
in New York City 1961-1971
>   Charles Brecher